P9-ARD-991

STABILIZING AN
UNSTABLE ECONOMY

STABILIZING AN UNSTABLE ECONOMY

Hyman P. Minsky

New York   Chicago   San Francisco   Lisbon   London
Madrid   Mexico City   Milan   New Delhi
San Juan   Seoul   Singapore
Sydney   Toronto

The *McGraw·Hill* Companies

Copyright © 2008 by Hyman Minsky. All rights reserved. Printed in the United States of America. Except as permitted under the United States Copyright Act of 1976, no part of this publication may be reproduced or distributed in any form or by any means, or stored in a data base or retrieval system, without the prior written permission of the publisher.

6 7 8 9 0 WFR/WFR 0

ISBN 978-0-07-159299-4
MHID 0-07-159299-7

First edition published in 1986 by Yale University Press.

Printed and bound by Worldcolor/Fairfield

McGraw-Hill books are available at special quantity discounts to use as premiums and sales promotions, or for use in corporate training programs. To contact a representative, please visit the Contact Us pages at www.mhprofessional.com.

This book is printed on acid-free paper.

CONTENTS

FOREWORD

When Hyman Minsky's book originally was published more than two decades ago, it was ahead of its time. This is often the case with economic thinkers. Joseph Schumpeter enjoys greater influence today than he did in his own time, and the seminal ideas of John Maynard Keynes gained broad influence well after they were published. So too with the indefatigable Minsky. Although he was a force to be reckoned with during the 1970s and 1980s, his ideas never have been more salient than today. If Minsky were alive today, he could justly claim "I told you so" to those who have paid close attention to economics and finance in the last few decades. There is no better moment to reissue this Minsky classic.

Like Keynes (about whom Minsky published a biography in 1975) and Schumpeter, Minsky was centrally concerned with business cycles. The Keynesianism that became dominant following World War II focused chiefly on the politically popular aspects of Keynes' writings. Too few recalled that Keynes recommended monetary action before fiscal activism and budget surpluses during periods of growth. For too many policymakers, Keynesianism meant deficit spending as an all-too-easy and automatic fix. There was a growing sense that Keynesianism had conquered the business cycle, as reflected in terminology like "soft landing" and "mid-course correction."

Hyman Minsky forged a different and important connection with Keynes. He emphasized the volatility of investments, pointing out that the underlying uncertainty of the cash flow from investments has powerful repercussions on the balance sheets of business. It was an important insight that deserved much greater attention.

After monetarism eclipsed Keynesianism in the late 1970s and 1980s, Minsky's insights again were not given their due. Even at its zenith in the early 1980s, monetarism failed to cope effectively with the changing structure of the financial system, which Minsky so eloquently dealt with in his broad analytical approach. Meanwhile, econometrics had become almost a religion among economists and financial analysts. But Hyman Minsky did not allow his analysis to be constrained by statistical models. He sagely understood that mathematical equations cannot properly account for significant crucial structural changes or shifts in behavioral patterns in economics and finance.

I was attracted to the work of Hyman Minsky early on in my career in the financial markets. In my own work, I became increasingly concerned by how debt continued to grow more rapidly than nominal gross national product. I attribute this unwholesome development to the rapid securitization of financial assets, the globalization of financial markets, and vast improvements in information technology that facilitated, among other things, the quantification of risk taking. The risks inherent in exploding debt have been heightened by the failure of official policymakers to put into place safeguards that encourage financial institutions to balance their entrepreneurial drive with their fiduciary responsibilities.

Hyman Minsky's insights help us understand the key financial developments of recent decades. Few understood as well as Minsky the self-reinforcing dynamic of speculative corporate finance, decreasing debt quality, and economic volatility that has come to characterize our times. He called corporate borrowing for the purpose of repaying debt "speculative finance," which in turn drives up investment and asset prices. He explained how the bullish rise in employment, investment, and profits tends to confirm, in the minds of business leaders and bankers, the soundness of an approach that ultimately fosters volatility and unacceptable risk. In a colorful phrase that could be the watchword for the Age of Enron, Minsky cautioned against "balance-sheet adventuring."

What followed the original publication of this book, therefore, hardly would have surprised its author—from the savings and loan and banking crises in the late 1980s and early 1990s; to the Mexican and Korean debt travails, the Russian debt default, and the near hemorrhaging of the markets caused by the excessive leveraging of Long-Term Capital Management in the 1990s; to the bursting of the high-tech bubble in 2000.

And now we confront the subprime mortgage crisis. Some have dubbed this a "Minsky moment," but the observation belittles the range and depth of Minsky's work. Now is the time to take seriously the insights of Hyman Minsky and build upon his groundbreaking work in order to find ways of putting our financial system on a more solid footing.

Henry Kaufman

PREFACE AND
ACKNOWLEDGMENTS
TO THE FIRST EDITION

It is now clear that output, employment, and prices in advanced capitalist economies with complicated and evolving financial structures are liable to fluctuate. It is also clear that the instability natural to our type of economy has been stabilized since World War II. In particular, even though there have been enormous stresses and strains in the economic and financial system, a collapse of asset values, an uncontrolled epidemic of bankruptcies, and a deep and long-lasting depression have been avoided.

The instability so evident since the late 1960s was not as marked in the first two decades after World War II. This leads to the question, "What is there about our type of economy that causes its overall behavior to change so radically?"

The answer to this question requires an understanding of how profit-seeking businessmen and bankers transform an initially robust financial system (one not hospitable to financial crises) into a fragile financial system (one that is hospitable to financial crises). The market system of determining financial relations and valuing assets gives signals that lead to the development of relations conducive to instability and to the realization of instability. Periods of stability (or of tranquility) of a modem capitalist economy are transitory.

Stabilizing an Unstable Economy tries to explain why our economy is so liable to fluctuations and how the obvious instability has been contained. Even though the worse that could have happened—a great depression—has been avoided, it nevertheless is true that the performance of the economy has been substantially poorer in recent years than in the two decades immediately after World War II. Furthermore, the success in stabilizing the instability since the late 1960s has been inadvertent, for the theories underlying policy ignored the critical variables that make it possible to "stabilize" our inherently unstable system. Policy, while broadly successful, has not addressed the deteriorating performance of the economy. Thus an agenda for reform follows the historical, theoretical, and institutional material.

Stabilizing an Unstable Economy is in the post-Keynesian tradition, which I take to mean that Keynes provides us with the shoulders of a giant upon which we can stand in order to see far and deep into the essential character of advanced capitalist economies. However, being post-Keynesian does not mean being slavishly dependent on the works of the "Great Man." I hope I do not make points by citing Keynes; if I do, I apologize now.

My intellectual debts are many: from my education I owe a great debt to Oscar Lange, Henry Simons, and Josef Schumpeter. From recent years I owe a great deal to my colleagues in Trieste—the faculty and students at the Centro di Studi Economici Avanzati, in particular the post-Keynesian contingent of Jan Kregel, Paul Davidson, and the late Sidney Weintraub.

Once again, I am grateful to Maurice Townsend for his encouragement and the insights he so freely shares.

A special debt is owed to Joan Robinson, who was often wrong in especially incisive ways.

At the Twentieth Century Fund I want to thank Carol Barker, Waiter Klein, and Gary Nickerson—especially Gary who kept the faith when I was weary and discouraged. Ted Young whipped a manuscript that was far too long into shape, eliminating pearls of wisdom that distracted from the clarity of the message. Beverly Goldberg took over the final preparation of the work.

The book could not have been completed without the help and understanding of the secretarial staff at the Economics Department at Washington University under the supervision of Bess Erlich and Susan Hilton. Special thanks are due Karen Rensing and Anne Schroeder. When I needed access to data from the monster, Washington University's computer, Chris Varvares came to the rescue.

Hyman P. Minsky

MINSKY'S *STABILIZING AN UNSTABLE ECONOMY*: TWO DECADES LATER

Dimitri B. Papadimitriou
and L. Randall Wray

As we prepared this new edition of Hyman P. Minsky's most comprehensive work—first published in 1986—the U.S. financial system faced its worst crisis since the 1930s. The remarkable explanatory power of this book demonstrates that Minsky has been relevant not only for financial crises during his lifetime but for the dot.com implosion of the U.S. stock market and the subprime housing meltdown we are witnessing now. Minsky was always ahead of his time. Remember, Minsky first wrote about financial instability in the late 1950s, and accurately predicted the transformation of the economy that would not become apparent for nearly a generation. While we have read this book many times, our careful re-reading to write this introduction impressed upon us Minsky's depth of analysis and his theoretical contributions for understanding the operation of the modern and complex capitalist economy. There is, quite simply, no equal to it.

There has been a steady demand for the book since it went out of print. Used copies offered on the Internet command prices upward of a thousand dollars. In 2007, interest in Minsky's work suddenly exploded as the financial press recognized the relevance of his analysis to the rapidly unfolding mortgage-backed securities market meltdown. Indeed, in this book Minsky examined a number of financial crises in detail, several of which involved similar financial instruments, such as commercial paper, municipal bonds, and Real Estate and Investment Trusts (REITs) (pp. 46, 96 below). More important, he explained why the economy tends to evolve in such a way that these crises become more likely. Further, if the crises are successfully contained—as they have been so far—then risky practices are "validated." This sets the stage for subsequent crises that probably will be allowed for the possibility of explosive growth (Minsky 1957b). In some of his earliest work, he added institutional ceilings and floors to produce a variety of possible outcomes, including steady growth, cycles, booms, and long depressions. He ultimately came back to these models in some of his last papers written at the Levy Economics Institute (Minsky and Ferri 1991). It is clear, however, that the results of these analyses played a role in his argument that the New Deal and post-war institutional arrangements constrained the inherent instability of modern capitalism, producing the semblance of stability.

At the same time, he examined financial innovation, arguing that normal profit seeking by financial institutions continually subverted attempts by the authorities to constrain money supply growth (Minsky 1957a). This is one of the main reasons he rejected the LM curve's presumption of a fixed money supply. Indeed, central bank restraint would induce innovations to ensure that policy could never follow a growth rate rule, such as that propagated for decades by Milton Friedman. These innovations would also stretch liquidity in ways that would make the system more vulnerable to disruption. If the central bank intervened as lender of last resort, it would validate the innovation, ensuring persistence of new practices. Minsky (1957a) examined the creation of the federal-funds market, showing how it allowed the banking system to economize on reserves in a way that would internally determine the money supply. The first serious tests of financial innovations came in 1966 in the municipal bond market and the second in 1970 with a run on commercial paper—but each of these was resolved through prompt central bank action. Thus, while the early post-war period was a good example of a "conditionally coherent" financial system, with little private debt and a huge inherited stock of federal debt (from World War II's deficits), profit-seeking innovations would gradually render the institutional constraints less binding. Financial crises would become more frequent and more severe, testing the ability of the authorities to prevent "it" from happening again. The apparent stability would promote instability.

EXTENSIONS OF THE EARLY WORK

With his *John Maynard Keynes (JMK)*, Minsky provided an alternative analysis of Keynes's theory. (See p. 133 below for his summary of the intentions of that book.) This book provides his most detailed presentation of the "financial theory of investment and investment theory of the cycle." The two key building blocks are the "two price system" that he borrows from Keynes and the "lender's and borrower's risk" often attributed to Michael Kalecki but actually also derived from Keynes. Minsky distinguishes between a price system for current output and one for asset prices. Current output prices can be taken as determined by "cost plus a mark-up," set at a level that will generate profits. This price system covers consumer goods and services, investment goods, and even goods and services purchased by government. In the case of investment goods, the current output price is effectively a supply price of capital—the price just sufficient to induce a supplier to provide new capital assets. However, this simplified analysis can be applied only to purchases of capital that can be financed out of internal funds. If external (borrowed) funds are involved, then the supply price of capital also includes explicit finance costs—most importantly the interest rate but also all other fees and costs—that is, supply price increases due to "lender's risk."

There is a second price system for assets that can be held through time. Except for money, the most liquid asset, these assets are expected to generate a stream of income and possibly capital gains. Here, Minsky follows Keynes's treatment in Chapter 17, the most important chapter of the *General Theory*, according to Minsky. The important point is that the prospective income stream cannot be known with certainty and thus depends on subjective expectations. We obtain a demand price for capital assets from this asset price system: how much would one pay for the asset, given expectations concerning the future net revenues that it can generate? This calculus is, however, too simplistic, because it ignores the financing arrangements. Minsky argued that the price someone is willing to pay depends on the amount of external finance required—greater borrowing exposes the buyer to higher risk of insolvency. This is why "borrower's risk" must also be incorporated into demand prices.

Investment can proceed only if the demand price exceeds the supply price of capital assets. Because these prices include margins of safety, defined as sufficient collateral, they are affected by expectations concerning unknowable outcomes. In a recovery from a severe downturn, margins are large as expectations are muted; over time, if an expansion exceeds pessimistic projections, these margins prove to be larger than necessary. Thus, margins will be reduced to the degree that projects are generally successful. Here we recall Minsky's famous taxonomy of financing profiles: hedge finance, where prospective income flows cover interest and principal; speculative finance, where near-term income flows will cover only interest; and Ponzi finance, where near-term receipts are insufficient to cover interest payments, so that debt increases. Over the course of an expansion, these financial stances evolve from largely hedge profiles to include ever-rising proportions of speculative and even Ponzi positions.

From his early work, Minsky recognized that financiers' desire to raise leverage and move to more speculative positions could be frustrated. If results are more favorable than expected, an investor attempting to engage in speculative finance could remain hedged because his income is greater than he anticipated. Thus, while Minsky did not incorporate the now well-known Kalecki relation in *JMK*, he did recognize that an investment boom could raise aggregate demand and spending through the multiplier and generate more sales than projected. Later, he explicitly incorporated the Kaleckian result, where aggregate profits equal investment plus the government's deficit in the truncated model. Thus, in an investment boom, profits would be increasing along with investment, helping to validate expectations and encouraging even more investment. This added credence to his proposition that the fundamental instability in the capitalist economy increases until it reaches a speculative frenzy.

In addition, in the early 1960s, he had argued that impacts on private sector balance sheets would depend on the stance of the government's balance sheet (Minsky 1963). A government-spending-led expansion would allow the private sector to expand without creating fragile balance sheets—government deficits would add safe treasury debt to private portfolios (one of the effects of deficit spending discussed in Chapter 2 below). A robust expansion, however, would tend to cause tax revenues to grow faster than private sector income so that the government budget would "improve" (move toward surplus) and the private sector balance would deteriorate (move toward deficit). Once he added the Kalecki equation to his exposition (as he does in this volume, pp. 17, 162), he could explain how this countercyclical movement of the budget would automatically stabilize profits—limiting both the upside in a boom and the downside in a slump.

With the Kalecki view of profits incorporated in his investment theory of the cycle, Minsky argued that investment is forthcoming today only if investment is expected in the future—since investment in the future will determine profits in the future (in the skeletal model) (p. 163). Furthermore, because investment today validates the decisions undertaken "yesterday," expectations about "tomorrow" affect ability to meet commitments that were made when financing the existing capital assets. There is thus a complex temporal relation involved in Minsky's approach to investment that could be easily disturbed (pp. 213–218). Once this is linked to the "two price" approach, it becomes apparent that anything that lowers expected future profitability can push the demand price of capital below the supply price. This reduces investment and today's profits below the level necessary to validate the past expectations that demand prices were based on when previous capital projects were begun. The margins of safety that had been included in borrower's and lender's risk can prove to be inadequate, leading to revisions of desired margins of safety going forward.

Minsky continually developed his financial instability hypothesis to incorporate the extensions made to his investment theory over the course of the 1960s, 1970s, and 1980s. He added the Kalecki equation; incorporated the two price system; and included a more complex treatment of sectoral balances. Over the years, he improved his approach to banks, recognizing the futility of Federal Reserve attempts to control the money supply. He also expanded the analysis to treat all entities like banks. He argued that anyone could create money; the problem is to get it accepted (p. 79)—since anyone could acquire assets by issuing liabilities. He argued that while the Fed had been created to act as lender of last resort, by making business debt liquid, the Fed no longer discounted paper (p. 54). Indeed, most reserves supplied by the Fed come through open market operations, which greatly restricts the Fed's ability to ensure safety and soundness of the system by deciding which collateral to accept and by taking a close look at balance sheets of borrowers. Instead, the Fed had come to rely on Friedman's simplistic monetarist view that the primary role of the Fed is to "control" the money supply and thereby the economy as a whole—which it cannot do, as attempts to constrain reserves only induce innovative bank practices and encourage expansion of "non-bank" sources of finance, ultimately requiring lender-of-last-resort interventions and even bailouts that validate riskier practices (p. 106). Together with countercyclical deficits to maintain demand, such a policy not only prevents deep recession but also creates a chronic inflation bias.

CAN IT HAPPEN AGAIN?

Minsky frequently argued that the Great Depression represented a failure of capitalism that was resolved only by the creation of the Big Government and Big Bank, a phrase he frequently used to denote the size of government, the level of public expenditure, and the central bank, and by the various New Deal reforms (p. 221; Minsky 1993). While the economy that emerged from World War II was fundamentally different and appeared to be robust, Minsky always questioned whether "IT" (the Great Depression) might happen again. His answer was a contingent "no": the ceilings and floors put in place made a debt deflation impossible in the first few decades after the war. However, the evolution of the economy in the context of the apparently robust financial structure *could* open the door to a snowball of defaults that would overwhelm such constraints. This would become more likely if the institutional constraints failed to adapt to changing circumstances—or, worse, if the lessons of the Great Depression were forgotten so that dangerous "free market" ideology came to dominate policy. Of course, both of these events came to pass.

Minsky formulated what he termed his Anti-Laissez-Faire Theme: "in a world where the internal dynamics imply instability, a semblance of stability can be achieved or sustained by introducing conventions, constraints and interventions into the environment" (Minsky and Ferri 1991). He insisted the problem is that orthodox, neoclassical theory–based economics cannot provide any insight into our economy. This is because instability as well as the mere existence of depression could not be explained by standard theory except through internal shocks and stubborn workers who refused to allow wages to respond—indeed, unemployment must be seen by orthodoxy as retribution for obstinacy (p. 154). The mainstream canon dictates more laissez-faire as the solution to "disequilibrium." By contrast, incoherent market results are "natural," according to Minsky, requiring intervention to prevent the invisible hand from operating: "To contain the evils that market systems can inflict, capitalist economies developed sets of institutions and authorities, which can be characterized as the equivalent of circuit breakers. These institutions in effect stop the economic processes that breed the incoherence and restart the economy with new initial conditions ..." (Minsky et al., 1994). Furthermore, "The aptness of institutions and interventions will largely determine the extent to which the path of the economy through time is tranquil or turbulent: progressive, stagnant, or deteriorating" (ibid).

Postwar growth was biased toward investment spending, especially after 1970. While the federal government grew quickly relative to GDP in the cold war build-up, and while state and local government increased their shares through the early 1970s, government spending remained relatively constant thereafter. Much of the "Keynesian" policy in the postwar period sought to encourage investment to raise aggregate demand while increasing transfer payments for the elderly and those left behind by the "rising tide" that *did not* lift all boats. Minsky critiqued this policy stance from the early 1960s on arguing that it would generate financial instability and inflation, even as it worsened inequality (Minsky 1965, 1968, 1972, 1973). This is because investment-led growth would transform the financial system from a robust structure into an increasingly fragile one. Further, both investment and transfer payments would impart an inflationary bias—only made worse by the institutional floors that prevent serious recessions and that validate riskier behaviors.

Minsky's best treatment of this inflation bias is presented in Chapter 11 of this volume, using a markup approach to the aggregate price level. We will not provide a detailed exposition here, but the basic idea is that prices of the consumption goods part of the current output price system are set as a markup over costs—mostly wage costs in that sector. The markup in turn is determined by spending on consumption goods in excess of the consumption by the workers that produced them—that is, by workers in the investment sector and the government sector, by foreigners, and by transfer recipients (retirees, those on AFDC and unemployment compensation, etc.). This was a theme in Minsky's earliest work and one of the main reasons he vehemently opposed the Kennedy/Johnson War on Poverty (Minsky 1965, 1968). He insisted that a "rising tide" boosted by investment spending would never "trickle down" to the poor, and indeed would tend to increase inequality by favoring the workers with the highest skills working in industries with the greatest pricing power. Further, paying people not to work would raise demand for consumer goods without increasing supply. Thus, he disapproved of welfare not only on the grounds that it simply "institutionalized unemployment," forcing dependency, but also because it would be inflationary. As we will see below, Minsky favored instead direct job creation and a high-consumption strategy. The policy mix actually adopted—inducements to invest, welfare, and bailouts—increased financial fragility and inequality even as it lent a stagflationary bias to the economy.

EVIDENCE

As discussed, Minsky argued that the apparent stability achieved since World War II is not due to normal market processes but rather attributable to the existence of Big Government and Big Bank. In Part 2 of this book, Minsky examines the empirical evidence, arguing that each time the economy seemed to be poised for a crash, a combination of budget deficits plus lender-of-last-resort intervention maintained aggregate demand, income flows, and, especially, asset prices and profit flows. We will briefly summarize the cases he examined, and add several more from the period after this book was originally published.

First, we believe it is useful to update Tables 13.3 and 13.5, presented in Chapter 13, which present two measures of the size of government, looking accounting necessity—as Minsky had recognized in the early 1960s, and as Wynne Godley's sectoral approach demonstrated (Minsky 1963; Godley 1999). If the private sector retrenched, simply returning to a more normal small surplus, aggregate demand would fall by half a dozen percentage points.

In retrospect we now know that the Clinton surpluses were short-lived, because they drove the economy into a recession as the private sector *did* retrench. The stock market crashed but eventually began to recover (except for the NASDAQ—which was never able to attain previous highs). This was in part due to the growing budget deficit that restored business balance sheets and, again, helped jumpstart another anemic "jobless" recovery. Remarkably, financial market participants quickly regained confidence and looked for other speculative endeavors, while U.S. households quickly returned to deficit spending. Financial markets entered a wave of innovation arguably unmatched in history. Real estate markets boomed as mortgage availability spread to households previously excluded; real estate prices grew faster than ever before; and homeowners "cashed out" equity as they borrowed against capital gains in order to finance consumption. All of this was helped by the low interest rate policy maintained by the Fed by the belief that better monetary policy (guided by the "New Consensus Macroeconomics") would constrain inflation, and by an implicit Greenspan promise that the Fed would never let anything bad happen again.

THE POLICY PROBLEM

Keynes's General Theory identified two fundamental flaws of the capitalist system: chronic unemployment and excessive inequality. Minsky added a third: instability is a normal result of modern *financial* capitalism (p. 112, 315). Further, persistent stability cannot be achieved—even with apt policy—because it changes behavior in ways that make "*IT*" likely. For this reason, Minsky rejected any notion of "fine-tuning"—even if policy did manage to achieve transitory stability that would set off processes to reintroduce instability. Hence, "[t]he policy problem is to devise institutional structures and measures that attenuate the thrust to inflation, unemployment, and slower improvements in the standard of living without increasing the likelihood of a deep depression" (p. 328). However, success could never be permanent; policy would have to continually adjust to adapt to changing circumstances.

After *Stabilizing* was published, Minsky argued that the relative stability of the post-war period had led to development of Money Manager

Capitalism—a much more unstable version of the "57 Varieties of Capitalism." In a very prescient piece (Minsky 1987), Minsky predicted the explosion of home mortgage securitization that eventually led to the subprime meltdown in 2007. Indeed, he was one of the few commentators who understood the true potential of securitization. In principle, all mortgages could be packaged into a variety of risk classes, with differential pricing to cover risk. Investors could choose the desired risk–return tradeoff. Thrifts and other regulated financial institutions would earn fee income for loan origination, for assessing risk, and for servicing the mortgages. Financial engineering would place the collateralized debt obligations (CDOs), slicing and dicing to suit the needs of investors. Two decades later, Minsky's predictions were validated with a vengeance.

Minsky (1987) argued that securitization reflected two developments. First, it was part and parcel of the globalization of finance, as securitization creates financial paper that is freed from national boundaries. German investors with no direct access to America's homeowners could buy mortgage-backed securities originating in U.S. real estate markets. As Minsky was fond of pointing out, the unparalleled post World War II depression-free expansion in the developed world (and even in much of the developing world) has created a global glut of managed money seeking returns. Packaged securities with risk weightings assigned by respected rating agencies were appealing for global investors trying to achieve the desired proportion of dollar-denominated assets. It would be no surprise to Minsky to find that the value of securitized American mortgages came to exceed the value of the market for federal government debt, nor that the subprime problems quickly spread around the world.

The second development assessed by Minsky (1987) is the relative decline of the importance of banks (narrowly defined as financial institutions that accept deposits and make loans) in favor of "markets." (The bank share of all financial assets fell from around 50% in the 1950s to around 25% in the 1990s.) This development itself was encouraged by the experiment in monetarism (1979–82; it decimated the regulated portion of the sector in favor of the relatively unregulated "markets"), but it was also spurred by continual erosion of the portion of the financial sphere that had been ceded by rules, regulations, and tradition to banks. The growth of competition on both sides of the banking business—checkable deposits at non-bank financial institutions that could pay market interest rates, and the rise of the commercial-paper market that allowed firms to bypass commercial banks—squeezed the profitability of banking. Minsky (1987) observed that banks appear to require a spread of about 450 basis points between interest rates earned on assets and those paid on liabilities. This covers the normal rate of return on capital, plus the required reserve "tax" imposed on banks (reserves are non-earning assets) and the costs of servicing customers.

By contrast, financial markets can operate with much lower spreads precisely because they are exempt from required reserve ratios, regulated capital requirements, and much of the costs of relationship banking. At the same time, the financial markets were freer from New Deal regulations that had made financial markets safer. This meant not only that an ever larger portion of the financial sector was free of most regulations but that competition from "markets" forced policy-makers to relax regulations on banks. By the time of the real estate boom that eventually led to the current subprime mortgage crisis, there was no longer any essential difference between a "commercial bank" and an "investment bank." The whole housing sector, which had been made very safe by the New Deal reforms, had been transformed into a huge global casino. Minsky argued (p. 51) that the New Deal reforms related to home finance had been spurred by a common belief that short-term mortgages, typically with large balloon payments, had contributed to the Great Depression; ironically, the "innovations" in home mortgage finance leading up to the speculative boom largely recreated those conditions.

As we write, the U.S. financial sector is in a crisis that is spreading around the world. It will take some time to sort out the causes and to realize all of the consequences. Many commentators have referred to the crisis as a *Minsky moment*, questioning whether we have become a *Ponzi nation*. At this point, we can surmise that the financial innovations of the past decade greatly expanded the availability of credit, which then pushed up asset prices. That, in turn, not only encouraged further innovation to take advantage of profit opportunities but also fueled a debt frenzy and greater leveraging. Four things tipped the balance of sentiments from fear toward greed: the Greenspan "put," namely the belief that the Fed would not allow bad things to happen, with evidence drawn from the arranged Long-Term Capital Management rescue, as well as the quick reduction of interest rates in the aftermath of the dot.com bust, plus the new operating procedures adopted by the Fed called the New Monetary Consensus, which include gradualism, transparency, and expectations management, meaning no surprises. The Clinton boom and the shallow 2001 recession led to a revised view of growth, according to which expansions could be more robust without inflation and recessions would be brief and relatively painless. All of this increased the appetite for risk, reduced risk premia, and encouraged ever more leverage. In addition, securitization, hedging, and various kinds of insurance such as credit default swaps appeared to move risk to those best able to bear it. If Minsky had been able to observe the past half-decade, he would have labeled it a period with a radical suspension of disbelief.

We do not know whether "IT" will happen this time around, but there is already a growing movement for reregulation. In the final sections we concentrate on the direction that policy might take.

AGENDA FOR REFORM

In this book, Minsky offered an agenda for reform that focused on four main areas:

- Big Government (size, spending, taxation)
- Employment strategy (employer of last resort)
- Financial reform
- Market power

He argued that all kinds of capitalism are flawed but that we can develop one in which the flaws are less evident (p. 328). As discussed above, he favored a capitalism with lower investment and higher consumption, one that maintains full employment, and one that fosters smaller organizations. He wanted to shift the focus of policy away from transfers and toward employment (p. 326). He was skeptical that anything close to full employment could be attained without direct job creation by government—a position he had held since the early 1960s. Thus, he pointed to various New Deal employment programs, such as the Civilian Conservation Corps and National Youth Administration, as examples to guide creation of a comprehensive employer-of-last-resort (ELR) program—arguing that only government can offer an infinitely elastic demand for labor, which is necessary for full employment (p. 343). He estimated a comprehensive program's costs at about 1.25% of national output—which is in line with more recent estimates of others promoting such programs (Harvey 1989, Wray 1998) and with current real-world experience in Argentina and India. In addition, Minsky would offer a universal child allowance, equal to about 1.33% of GDP (p. 334). Together, these programs would replace most welfare and unemployment compensation spending, providing more opportunity and dignity for participants than current programs do. Moreover, his programs would be less inflationary. Unlike welfare, which pays people not to work and thereby increases demand for output without increased supply, a jobs program would be geared to produce useful output. He also anticipated the objection that full employment must be inflationary by proposing a relatively fixed and uniform program wage that would actually help to stabilize wages by providing an anchor (p. 348). (Over the recent past, these arguments have been explored in considerable detail by advocates of employer-of-last-resort policies—with conclusions similar to Minsky's.) Finally, he would reduce barriers to labor force participation by eliminating the payroll tax and by allowing retirees to work without losing Social Security benefits.

Minsky also preferred policies that would encourage equity finance rather than debt finance, such as elimination of corporate taxes that impute earnings to equity owners. Because he believed that bank size is related to the size of firms with which banks do business, he favored a policy that supports small- to medium-size banks (p. 355). He would have loosened some of the New Deal constraints for these banks, so that they could provide more of the services required by their smaller customers. Instead, U.S. policy has moved in the opposite direction, exempting the largest banks from Glass-Steagall regulations before ultimately gutting the New Deal reforms. Hence, banking has become much more concentrated than it was when Minsky made these proposals; at the same time, as mentioned before, policy and innovations have favored "markets" over "banks," which has also promoted even further consolidation. Minsky was a strong advocate of increasing the Fed's oversight of banks by shifting to the use of the discount window rather than open-market operations in reserves provisioning (p. 361). Indeed, one can see in Minsky's proposals an argument for the sort of system later adopted in Canada, with zero reserve requirements from lowering the "reserve tax" and interest paid on positive reserve balances or charged on overdrafts. Chairman Bernanke has hinted that the Fed might begin paying interest on reserves in a few years, and in response to the subprime mess he has proposed policy that would encourage greater use of the discount window. Perhaps this is one area in which real-world policy might move closer to Minsky's proposal—albeit in reaction to a major financial crisis. For the most part, however, policy has moved ever further away from Minsky's proposals as New Deal restraints were lifted, "freeing" the financial system—with predictable results.

Later, while at the Levy Economics Institute, Minsky continued his policy work advocating institutions for modern capitalism. He argued that capitalism is dynamic and comes in many forms, and that the 1930s reforms are no longer appropriate for the money-manager form of capitalism (Minsky 1996). It is not a coincidence that this stage of capitalism has seen the rise of neoconservative ideology that wants to dismantle what is left of

New Deal and "Keynesian-era" policies. Outside the U.S., this is called neoliberalism. Everything from financial institution regulation to public provision of retirement income has been under attack by privatizers (Wray 2005). However, Minsky argued that free-market ideology is dangerous, particularly at this money-manager stage. Ironically, the "invisible hand" could not do too much damage in the early postwar period given the low level of private debt, with private portfolios full of government debt, and with memories of the Great Crash generating conservative behavior. However, now, with private debt ratios much higher and after a decade of leveraging in an environment that promoted greed over fear, the invisible hand promoted increasingly risky behavior.

Thus, Minsky's alternative policy proposals in the 1990s were designed to reduce insecurity, promote stability, and encourage democracy. He continued to support job creation, greater equality of wages, and child allowances. With other Levy Institute scholars, he pushed President Clinton to create a system of community development banks (Minsky et al., 1993). His proposal went much further than the program that was actually adopted—to increase the range of financial services provided to underserved neighborhoods. He supported a proposal by Levy Institute scholar Ronnie Phillips to create a system of narrow banks that would offer deposits while holding only the safest assets (Treasury securities) (Minsky 1994). In other words, he offered a range of policy proposals for the financial sector that went in almost the opposite direction from the policy actually adopted.

CURRENT CHALLENGES

We will end this introduction by briefly mentioning four challenges facing the U.S. economy today and into the foreseeable future:

1. Chronic trade deficits

2. Growing inequality

3. Continuing budget shift toward transfers

4. Fallout from the subprime crisis

Minsky's work sheds light on the policy implications in all of these areas. Given U.S. import propensities, any time the economy grows at a reasonable pace, so does the trade deficit. While most commentators worry about U.S. ability to "finance" the trade deficit, that is not the real concern, because the trade deficit exists only to the extent that the rest of the world desires U.S. dollar-denominated assets. Still, there are two worries raised by persistent deficits. First, there are effects on U.S. employment and wages. The correct response to a trade deficit is to create jobs for those who are displaced by imports. Minsky's employer-of-last-resort program is a first step, although many of the lost jobs are higher-paying, so there must also be retraining and other programs to help individual job-losers. While a highly developed country like the U.S. should bias policy toward open markets, it need not allow unfair competition from nations that use unfair labor practices such as child labor, prison labor, and wages below subsistence-level; hence, "fair trade" rather than "free trade" should guide policy-making.

Second, given the necessity of balance between internal (private and government) and external sectors, a current account deficit means that either the U.S. government or the U.S. private sector, or a combination of the two, must run a deficit equal to the foreign balance. Since 1996, the U.S. private sector has run an almost continual deficit that we believe to be an unsustainable stance for the medium term. However, in current conditions it appears that a full-employment economy would probably generate a current account deficit of at least 4% of GDP. If the private sector were to run a surplus of about 3% which is approximately the long-run average in the postwar period, the government sector's deficit would need to be about 7% of GDP. That appears to be politically infeasible, and it probably is not economically desirable, either. Recall that Minsky saw deficits as generating a higher markup because they create a claim on output in excess of the wage bill in the consumption sector. This is offset to some extent by net imports—which allow consumers to purchase output that U.S. workers did not produce. However, to the extent that a dollar devaluation does improve the trade balance because the price elasticity of import demand is not sufficiently high, a condition opposite to the Marshall-Lerner principle, named for economists Alfred Marshall and Abba Lerner, inflation of imported commodities can be passed through to U.S. consumers. During 2007, a big problem has been the third "energy crisis" since 1970. This has led to rapidly rising oil prices that have fed through to U.S. consumer prices, compounded by a falling dollar. As we write, the Fed has chosen to maintain financial stability rather than aggressively fight inflation, which in our view is the correct response. It is not clear, however, how long policymakers will choose to ignore inflation. A repeat of the Paul Volcker years—tight policy even with rising unemployment—is possible. Minsky probably would advocate some set of policies to lower trade and budget deficits.

By various measures, the degree of inequality today is as high as it was on the eve of the Great Depression. Indeed, the income *gains* achieved by the top 1% of income earners during 2003–05, $525 billion, was greater than the *total* income, $380 billion in 2005, going to the bottom 20% of the population. Redistributing just half of those gains to the lowest quintile would have increased income at the bottom by 70%. Further, real income for most wage-earning males has not increased since the early 1970s. As noted above, Minsky was always skeptical of the use of transfers to redistribute income, preferring to do it through job creation and by biasing wage increases toward lower-income workers. Indeed, in the mid 1960s he provided calculations to demonstrate that provision of jobs would go a long way toward elimination of poverty. Kelton and Wray (2004) updated Minsky's analysis, showing that families with at least one worker holding a full-time, year-round job have a very low probability of falling below the poverty line. Hence, Minsky's employer-of-last-resort program paying a basic wage, preferably a living wage, complemented with a child allowance would eliminate most poverty. The extra GDP created by lowering measured unemployment on the order of two percentage points is several times greater than necessary to satisfy the extra consumption that would be enjoyed if all families could be brought above the poverty line. Hence, it is really not necessary to implement "Robin Hood" take-from-the-rich-to-give-to-the-poor schemes in order to eliminate poverty. Minsky rightly argued, however, that extremes of income and wealth are not compatible with democracy. Thus, the case for limiting income and wealth at the top has more to do with creating a more just society than with redistributing income to eliminate poverty.

Minsky also advocated constraints on growth of wages for skilled workers to reduce the inequality of wage income (Minsky 1965, 1968, 1972). He argued that to the extent that at least part of inflation is caused by wage cost-push, it is due mostly to wages of skilled and, in the past, unionized workers; hence, their wage growth should be held somewhat below productivity growth, while low-wage workers should receive wage gains above productivity gains. In this way, the spread between skilled wages and unskilled wages would be reduced even as inflation pressures could be reduced. It has been a long time since the U.S. has faced serious upward pressures on wages and prices, but as of 2007 it looks as if the deflationary pressures that have kept inflation largely at bay, low-wage competition in China and India, might have run their course. As mentioned above, it is not impossible that the current policy mix could induce a return of stagflation.

President Clinton ended "welfare as we know it," eliminating Aid to Families with Dependent Children in favor of Temporary Assistance for Needy Families, with restrictive time limits. However, because he did not provide jobs for adults pushed off welfare, or child allowances, his "reforms" have only increased insecurity without providing any real solutions. In any case, "welfare" was always a small program, with most transfers going to aged persons and most social spending occurring in Old Age, Survivors, and Disability Insurance and in Medicaid. In recent years, there has been a major push by neoconservatives to scare the population with tales of tens of trillions of dollars of future revenue "shortfalls" in the Social Security and Medicare programs. These analyses are almost entirely incorrect, as many Levy Institute publications have documented over the years (Papadimitriou and Wray 1999). They mostly focus on projections of a divergence of program revenues and costs, and then conclude that we should raise taxes or cut spending *today* in order to build up a trust fund surplus to be used *later* to finance the deficits.

We will not repeat arguments that we have made elsewhere, but we will make two points consistent with Minsky's analysis. First, as the number of senior citizens grows relative to the population of normal working age, this will tend to increase the markup of consumption goods prices, for the reasons we discussed earlier. The solution cannot be *financial*—regardless of the method used to put income into the hands of retirees of the future, their spending on consumer goods will be inflationary so long as their total share of consumption rises *unless they participate in production of those consumer goods*. This is why Minsky continually argued that the solution to growing numbers of retiring baby-boomers is to remove barriers to working beyond age 65 (p. 344). In addition, raising the employment rates of the unemployed and those out of the labor force will increase the supply of output, as increasing employment of women, high school dropouts, minorities, and immigrants can help to satisfy the demands of growing numbers of retirees.

Second, most of the "unfunded liabilities" of the federal government are in the Medicare program. The problem is not funding but two characteristics of health care more generally: prices rise faster than the general price level, so that a rising share of nominal GDP is devoted to health care; and with medical advances and rising expectations of a wealthy society, a growing share of real resources is devoted to health care. Thus, the problem is by no means restricted to Medicare and Medicaid, as private health insurance also faces rising costs—and reacts by pushing patients off private funding and onto the government's purse. To some extent, the rising share of GDP going to health care is neither unexpected nor undesirable: this is a heavily labor-intensive sector with little growth in productivity over time, a condition known as "Baumol's cost disease," and it should be expected that health becomes a bigger focus of economic activity in a rich—and aging—society that can easily meet most other material human needs.

On the other hand, health care reform is a recognized policy issue that cannot be ignored; nor can solutions be found in simplistic slogans like "privatization" or "single-payer." Society will have to decide what portion of resources it wants to devote to health care, how much of that should be devoted to the final few weeks of life of aged people, and the best way to organize delivery and payment for services rendered. Complaining about "unfunded mandates" simply obfuscates the issues. Including the costs of health care in the production costs of consumer goods is almost certainly the worst way to "pay for" health care services in a global economy when the competition does not bear these costs. Moreover, even if the U.S. producers did not face external competitors, the days of what Minsky called "Paternalistic Capitalism" are over. Neither firms nor unions have sufficient power to ensure that employee compensation includes adequate health care covered by prices of final output.

The final issue we address here is the likely fallout from the subprime crisis, which demonstrates serious problems with the "New Financial Architecture" created by the money managers over the past two decades. As relatively unregulated markets took market share away from banks, regulators reduced regulation and oversight of banks to allow them to compete. In addition, banks were allowed to engage in balance-sheet adventuring by moving activities off their balance sheets to economize on reserves and capital, and to avoid scrutiny. Relationship banking was replaced by "originate and distribute" brokerage business, in which all kinds of loans were packaged into securities that were sliced and diced into ever riskier tranches. Credit risk was assigned to pools of borrowers based on proprietary models with statistical data based on a few years of historical experience. Securities purchases were heavily leveraged with short-term credit such as commercial paper, often with complex contingent backup facilities provided by banks. Hence, the risks were not really moved off of bank balance sheets but rather would come back to banks at the worst possible time—when markets experienced difficulty and asset prices fell.

We now know that these models did not account for systemic risk, and that the individual borrower risk was never assessed—on the belief that it was sufficient to hold a diversified pool with "known" risks of classes of borrowers. Almost all of the incentive was placed on throughput, or quantity of loans originated, and almost none on ability to pay. Minsky always argued that a skeptical loan officer is required to assess the character of each individual borrower. A relationship should be developed so that the borrower's performance today is understood to have an impact on tomorrow's access to credit. Unfortunately, financial markets were transformed into spot markets based only on price, with quantity of credit essentially unconstrained. As Minsky's good friend Albert Wojnilower insists, at some points in the business cycle, the demand for credit can be virtually infinite at any price, hence quantity constraints are necessary to prevent a runaway speculative boom. Or, as Minsky had often said, the fundamental instability in a capitalist economy is upward, and policy must constrain this thrust.

Restoration of relationship banking should be a priority. Minsky's proposal to favor small and medium-size banks would be a step in the right direction, even if it were difficult to achieve. Banking is far more concentrated today than it was two decades ago, and the U.S. has lost about half of its banking institutions. Because there is an explicit public guarantee of bank liabilities, bank equity is at risk of loss only when banks make bad loans. Return on equity can be increased by raising leverage as well as by purchasing riskier assets—both of which increase the potential that public funds will be required to protect depositors. For this reason, restrictions on types of assets permitted as well as on required capital ratios must be part of bank regulation and supervision. While Basle requirements provide some guidance, the problem is that risk classifications are too broad, and larger banks are allowed to use internal models to assess risk—exactly what contributed to the subprime market mess. Furthermore, off-balance-sheet operations, such as recourse, are allowed and mostly unsupervised. Basle agreement permit individual countries to increase supervision as needed, but there are always pressures to competitively relax restraints. For this reason, more international cooperation will be required to restore the necessary degree of oversight. And, as many commentators have remarked during the subprime crisis, a proper balance between "fear" and "greed" must be restored. This means that interventions must be designed so that equity holders can lose while depositors are rescued. That, in turn, is facilitated by maintaining separation between "banks" and "markets," with oversight of banks restored.

CONCLUSION

Minsky provided the twentieth century's most astute analysis of *financial capitalism*, and his insights remain highly relevant. We hope that our introduction provides some context and guidance to this book, which provides Minsky's most comprehensive treatment. As the original Foreword by the

Director of the Century Fund and Minsky's own Preface indicate, the book required a long gestation period. We have corrected numerous typographical errors in the figures and mathematical expositions, as well as a few obvious errors in the text, but have left the exposition alone—even where it appeared somewhat cryptic—on the assumption that it is probably exactly the way Minsky wanted it. Minsky's style can be difficult, but it offers rewards with subsequent readings. This new edition will make it possible for new generations to own a copy of an economics and finance masterpiece.

We would like to thank Yeva Nersisyan (University of Missouri–Kansas City) and Deborah Treadway (Levy Economics Institute) for their editorial assistance in producing this new edition. We would also like to thank Leah Spiro of McGraw-Hill for her timely suggestion to republish Minsky's work. Minsky dedicated the first edition to Esther Minsky, and we would like to thank her for her support and friendship over the years. Special thanks are due to Alan and Diana Minsky for their support for this project. Of course, our greatest debt is to our friend and mentor, Hyman Minsky.

REFERENCES

Harvey, Phillip, *Securing the Right to Employment*, Princeton: Princeton University Press, 1989.

Kelton, Stephanie and L. Randall Wray, "The War on Poverty after 40 Years: A Minskyan Assessment," The Levy Economics Institute of Bard College, Public Policy Brief No. 78, 2004.

Minsky, Hyman P., "Central Banking and Money Market Changes," *Quarterly Journal of Economics*, 71, 1957a, 171–187.

Minsky, Hyman P., "Monetary Systems and Accelerator Models," *American Economic Review*, 47, 6 (December), 860–883.

Minsky, Hyman P., "A Linear Model of Cyclical Growth," *The Review of Economics and Statistics*, 41, 2, Part 1 (May), 133–145.

Minsky, Hyman P., "Discussion," *American Economic Review*, 53, 2 (May), 401–412.

Minsky, Hyman P., "Longer Waves in Financial Relations: Financial Factors in the More Severe Depressions," *American Economic Association Papers and Proceedings*, 54, 324–332.

Minsky, Hyman P., "The Role of Employment Policy," in Margaret S. Gordon, ed., *Poverty in America*, San Francisco: Chandler Publishing Company, 1965.

Minsky, Hyman P., "Effects of Shifts of Aggregate Demand upon Income Distribution," *American Journal of Agricultural Economics*, 50, 2 (May), 328–339.

Minsky, Hyman P., "Economic Issues in 1972: A Perspective," notes from a presentation to a symposium on The Economics of the Candidates sponsored by the Department of Economics at Washington University, St. Louis, Missouri, October 6, 1972.

Minsky, Hyman P., "The Strategy of Economic Policy and Income Distribution," *The Annals of the American Academy of Political and Social Science*, 409 (September), 92–101.

Minsky, Hyman P., memo on securitization, Minsky Archives, The Levy Economics Institute of Bard College, 1987.

Minsky, Hyman P., "Profits, Deficits and Instability: A Policy Discussion," in D. B. Papadimitriou, ed., *Profits, Deficits and Instability*, London: Macmillan, 1992.

Minsky, Hyman P., "Finance and Stability: The Limits of Capitalism," The Levy Economics Institute of Bard College, Working Paper No. 93, 1993.

Minsky, Hyman P., "Financial Instability and the Decline (?) of Banking: Public Policy Implications," The Levy Economics Institute of Bard College, Working Paper No. 127, 1994.

Minsky, Hyman P., "Uncertainty and the Institutional Structure of Capitalist Economies," The Levy Economics Institute of Bard College, Working Paper No. 155, 1996.

Minsky, Hyman P. and P. Ferri, "Market Processes and Thwarting Systems," The Levy Economics Institute of Bard College, Working Paper No. 64, 1991.

Minsky, Hyman P. and C. Whalen, "Economic Insecurity and the Institutional Prerequisites for Successful Capitalism," The Levy Economics Institute of Bard College, Working Paper No. 165, 1996.

Minsky, Hyman P., D. Delli Gatti and M. Gallegati, "Financial Institutions, Economic Policy, and the Dynamic Behavior of the Economy," The Levy Economics Institute of Bard College, Working Paper No. 126, 1994.

Minsky, Hyman P., D. B. Papadimitriou, R. J. Phillips, and L.R. Wray, "Community Development Banking: A Proposal to Establish a Nationwide System of Community Development Banks," The Levy Economics Institute of Bard College, Public Policy Brief No. 3, 1993.

Papadimitriou, Dimitri and L. R. Wray, "How Can We Provide for the Baby Boomers in Their Old Age?," The Levy Economics Institute of Bard College, Policy Note No. 5, 1999.

Wray, L. Randall, *Understanding Modern Money: The Key to Full Employment and Price Stability*, Northampton: Edward Elgar, 1998.

Wray, L. Randall, "A Keynesian Presentation of the Relations among Government Deficits, Investment, Saving, and Growth," *Journal of Economic Issues*, 23, 4, 977–1002.

Wray, L. Randall, "The Political Economy of the Current U.S. Financial Crisis," *International Papers in Political Economy*, 1, 3, 1994, 1–51.

Wray, L. Randall, "Can a Rising Tide Raise All Boats? Evidence from the Kennedy-Johnson and Clinton-era expansions," in Jonathan M. Harris and Neva R. Goodwin, eds., *New Thinking in Macroeconomics: Social, Institutional and Environmental Perspectives*, Northampton: Edward Elgar, 150–181.

Wray, L. Randall, "The Ownership Society," The Levy Economics Institute of Bard College, Public Policy Brief No. 82, 2005.

ECONOMIC PROCESSES, BEHAVIOR, AND POLICY

As we approach the last decade of the twentieth century, our economic world is in apparent disarray. After two secure decades of tranquil progress following World War II, in the late 1960s the order of the day became turbulence—both domestic and international. Bursts of accelerating inflation, higher chronic and higher cyclical unemployment, bankruptcies, crunching interest rates, and crises in energy, transportation, food supply, welfare, the cities, and banking were mixed with periods of troubled expansions. The economic and social policy synthesis that served us so well after World War II broke down in the mid-1960s. What is needed now is a new approach, a policy synthesis fundamentally different from the mix that results when today's accepted theory is applied to today's economic system.

Although vital problems like personal safety, honesty, and integrity transcend pure economic concerns, my focus is upon stabilizing the economy. Perhaps naively, a premise in what follows is that if the economy provides basic security and a sense of personal worth for all—because work is available for all—many social problems will recede to manageable proportions.

In an era when performance failures demonstrate the need for economic reform, any successful program of change must be rooted in an understanding of how economic processes function within the existing institutions. That understanding is what economic theory is supposed to provide. Even as institutions and usages are not ordained by nature, neither is economic theory. Economic theory is the product of creative imagination; its concepts and constructs are the result of human thought. There is no such thing, per se, as national income, aside from a theory of how to combine elements in the economy into this special number; demand curves do not confront sellers—customers do; the way in which money and finance affect the behavior of the system can be perceived only within a theory that allows money and finance to affect what happens.

Unfortunately, the economic theory that is taught in colleges and graduate schools—the equipment of students and practitioners of economics over the past thirty years and the intellectual basis of economic policy in capitalist democracies—is seriously flawed. The conclusions based on the models derived from standard theoretical economics cannot be applied to the formulation of policy for our type of economy. Established economic theory, especially the highly mathematical theory largely developed after World War II, can demonstrate that an abstractly defined exchange mechanism will lead to a coherent, if not an optimum, result.[1] However, this mathematical result is proven for models that abstract from corporate boardrooms and Wall Street. The model does not deal with time, money, uncertainty, financing of ownership of capital assets, and investment. If, on the other hand, the factors from which theory abstracts are important and relevant, if financial relations and organizations significantly influence the course of events, then the established economic theory does not furnish an underpinning for the proposition that coherence results from the type of decentralized market economies that exist. In fact, the Wall Streets of the world are important; they generate destabilizing forces, and from time to time the financial processes of our economy lead to serious threats of financial and economic instability, that is, the behavior of the economy becomes incoherent.[2]

In the mid-1960s, after behaving well for some twenty years, the economy began to behave in a manner that cast serious doubts on the validity of the standard theory. Beginning with the credit crunch in 1966, we experienced a sequence of financial near crises (the others occurred in 1970,

---

1. A serious statement of this mathematical theory that recognizes its limitations is Kenneth J. Arrow and Frank H. Hahn, *General Competitive Equilibrium* (San Francisco: Holden-Day, 1971).
2. Among modern economists the post-Keynesians most clearly articulate this view. See Paul Davidson, *Money and the Real World* (New York: Wiley, 1972); Jan Kregel, *The Reconstruction of Political Economy: An Introduction to Post-Keynesian Economics* (London: Macmillan, 1973); Hyman P. Minsky, *John Maynard Keynes* (New York: Columbia University Press, 1975); Hyman P. Minsky, *Can "IT" Happen Again? Essays on Instability & Finance* (Armonk, N.Y.: M. E. Sharpe & Co., 1982); Sidney Weintraub, *Keynes, Keynesians, and Monetarists* (Philadelphia: University of Pennsylvania Press, 1978).

1974–75, 1979–80, and 1982–83), each one growing progressively more severe. Officials and pundits alike responded to these cycles by calling for a rejection of the macroeconomic theory derived from the work of John Maynard Keynes and a return to the presumably tried and true analysis of classical microeconomic theory. In truth, however, the economy is now behaving in the way that Keynes's theory holds that a capitalist economy with a fragile financial structure and a big government is expected to behave. The error is in current economic theory, which grossly misinterprets Keynes's work.[3]

A theory that denies what is happening can happen, sees unfavorable events as the work of evil outside forces (such as the oil crisis) rather than as the result of characteristics of the economic mechanism, may satisfy the politicians' need for a villain or scapegoat, but such a theory offers no useful guide to a solution of the problem. The existing standard body of economic theory—the so-called neoclassical synthesis, which takes on both a monetarist and an establishment Keynesian garb—may be an elegant logical structure, but it fails to explain how a financial crisis can emerge out of the normal functioning of the economy and why the economy of one period may be susceptible to crisis while that of another is not.[4]

The economic instability so evident since the late 1960s is the result of the fragile financial system that emerged from cumulative changes in financial relations and institutions over the years following World War II. The unintended and often unnoticed changes in financial relations, and the speculative finance induced by the successful functioning of the economy,

3. John Maynard Keynes, *The General Theory of Employment Interest and Money* (New York: Harcourt Brace, 1936), is the key work for understanding how a capitalist economy with sophisticated, complex, and evolving financial institutions behaves.

4. For the purposes of this book, Don Patinkin, *Money, Interest and Prices*, 2d ed. (New York: Harper and Row, 1965), will be considered the model of the neoclassical synthesis. This neoclassical synthesis is also the underpinning of Milton Friedman, "A Theoretical Framework for Monetary Analysis," *Journal of Political Economy* 78 (March–April 1970), pp. 193–238; Robert A. Gordon, *Friedman's Monetary Framework: A Debate with His Critics* (Chicago: University of Chicago Press, 1974); and James Tobin, *Asset Accumulation and Economic Activity* (Chicago: University of Chicago Press, 1980). The neoclassical synthesis presumably integrates the price theory inherited from Walras with insights derived from Keynes.

have made the rules for monetary and fiscal policy based on the experience of the 1950s and the early 1960s invalid. No set of monetary and fiscal manipulations by themselves can reestablish and sustain the relative tranquility of the 1950s and early 1960s. Fundamental institutional changes similar in scope to the basic reforms of the first six years of the Roosevelt presidency are necessary if we are to recapture such relative tranquility. If reform is to be successful it needs to be enlightened by a theoretical vision that enables us to understand the causes of the instability that is now so evident.

For a new era of serious reform to enjoy more than transitory success it should be based on the understanding of why a decentralized market mechanism—the free market of the conservatives—is an efficient way of handling the many details of economic life, and how the financial institutions of capitalism, especially in the context of production processes that use capital intensive techniques, are inherently disruptive. Thus, while admiring the properties of free markets we must accept that the domain of effective and desirable free markets is restricted. We must develop economic institutions that constrain and control liability structures, particularly of financial institutions and of production processes that require massive capital investments. Paradoxically, capitalism is flawed precisely because it cannot readily assimilate production processes that use large-scale capital assets.

It may also be maintained that capitalist societies are inequitable and inefficient. But the flaws of poverty, corruption, uneven distribution of amenities and private power, and monopoly-induced inefficiency (which can be summarized in the assertion that capitalism is unfair) are not inconsistent with the survival of a capitalist economic system. Distasteful as inequality and inefficiency may be, there is no scientific law or historical evidence that says that, to survive, an economic order must meet some standard of equity and efficiency (fairness). A capitalist economy cannot be maintained, however, if it oscillates between threats of an imminent collapse of asset values and employment and threats of accelerating inflation and rampant speculation, especially if the threats are sometimes realized. If the market mechanism is to function well, we must arrange to constrain the uncertainty due to business cycles so that the expectations that guide investment can reflect a vision of tranquil progress.

The Reagan administration and its program, largely enacted in 1981, may have been a response to a vision that something was seriously wrong with the economy, but it was based on a misdiagnosis of what was wrong and on a theory of how the economy functioned that is inconsistent with the basic institutions of capitalism. The financial fragility that led to the instability so evident since the 1960s was ignored. The deregulation drive and the successful effort to bring the inflation rate down by large-scale and protracted monetary constraint and unemployment exacerbated the financial instability that was so evident in 1967, 1970, 1974–75, and 1979–80. Lender-of-last-resort interventions, which had papered over the problems of the fragile financial structure in the intermittent crises of the late 1960s and 1970s, became virtually everyday events in the 1980s. The crisis of mid-year 1982—which saw the Penn Square Bank of Oklahoma City fail and the collapse of the Mexican peso—seems to have ushered in a regime of permanent financial turbulence. In 1984–85 we witnessed lender-of-last-resort interventions to manage the reorganization of the Continental Illinois Bank of Chicago, the refinancing of Argentina, the collapse of state-insured thrift institutions in Ohio and Maryland, and a virtual epidemic of bank failures in the farm states. Containing instability is a major task of economic policy in the 1980s; this is far different from the tasks of economic policy in the 1950s and 1960s.

The protracted unemployment and bankruptcies and near bankruptcies of firms and banks radically transformed the labor force from being income-oriented to being job-security oriented. Job security is no longer being guaranteed by government macroeconomic policy; the only guarantee that labor now enjoys seems to be the right to make concessionary wage settlements. These concessions by workers mean that the cost push part of the business cycle is attenuated—but it also means that consumer demand due to increasing wage income will be less buoyant during an expansion. If anything, the Reagan reforms made prospects for instability worse—but like many things in the economy and politics the full effect of the reforms will not be felt for some time. Even as a deficit-aided strong recovery leads to an apparent success for Reaganomics, the foundations for another round of inflation, crises, and serious recession are being laid.

Economic systems are not natural systems. An economy is a social organization created either through legislation or by an evolutionary process of invention and innovation. Policy can change both the details and the overall character of the economy, and the shaping of economic policy involves both a definition of goals and an awareness that actual economic processes depend on economic and social institutions.

Thus, economic policy must be concerned with the design of institutions as well as operations within a set of institutions. Institutions are both legislated and the result of evolutionary processes. Once legislated, institutions take on a life of their own and evolve in response to market processes. We cannot, in a dynamic world, expect to resolve the problems

largest concentrations of private power should, in the interest of efficiency as well as stability, be reduced to more manageable dimensions.

Social justice rests on individual dignity and independence from both private and political power centers. Dignity and independence are best served by an economic order in which income is received either by right or through a fair exchange. Compensation for work performed should be the major source of income for all. Permanent dependence on expanding systems of transfer payments that have not been earned is demeaning to the recipient and destructive of the social fabric. Social justice and individual liberty demand interventions to create an economy of opportunity in which everyone, except the severely handicapped, earns his or her way through the exchange of income for work. Full employment is a social as well as an economic good.

It would be naive to assume that all stated social and economic goals are mutually consistent. Emphasis on one objective may decrease the ability to achieve other goals, so priorities must be set. I tend to favor personal freedom and democratic rights; the safeguarding of so-called property rights—even if property rights lead to the narrow economic efficiency of orthodox theory—is not to my mind equal to the extension of individual liberty and the promotion of social justice. These beliefs affect my policy positions.

Although this book is mainly concerned with economic theory and some interpretive economic history, its aim is to draw up an agenda for the reform of our malfunctioning economy. Effective reforms must be consistent with the processes of the economy and not violate the character of the people. Without an understanding of the economic process, and without a passionate, even irrational commitment to democratic ideals, an agenda for change, in response to a perceived need for change, can become the instrument of demagogues who play on fears and frustrations and offer panaceas and empty slogans.[7]

The proposals for reform to be advanced will necessarily be painted with a broad brush. Details will have to be refined by Congress, by an

---

7. Henry C. Simons, *A Positive Program for Laissez Faire* (Chicago: University of Chicago Press, 1934), reprinted in Henry C. Simons, *Economic Policy for a Free Society* (Chicago: University of Chicago Press, 1948), puts forth a serious conservative program of institutional reform and policy operation that remains a model of political economy. In spite of the passage of fifty years, the substance of Simons's proposals are still worth considering.

administration, and, let us hope, by the debate of an enlightened public willing to think hard about the direction the economy is to take.[8]

The major flaw of our type of economy is that it is unstable. This instability is not due to external shocks or to the incompetence or ignorance of policy makers. Instability is due to the internal processes of our type of economy. The dynamics of a capitalist economy which has complex, sophisticated, and evolving financial structures leads to the development of conditions conducive to incoherence—to runaway inflations or deep depressions. But incoherence need not be fully realized because institutions and policy can contain the thrust to instability. We can, so to speak, stabilize instability.[9]

---

8. In his 1926 pamphlet "The End of Laissez-Faire," vol. 9, Collected Works, *Essays in Persuasion*, op. cit., pp. 272–94, Keynes cited Burke as identifying "one of the finest problems in legislation, namely, to determine what the State ought to take upon itself to direct by the public wisdom, and what it ought to leave, with as little interference as possible, to individual exertion." (Keynes's citation is McCulloch in his *Principles of Political Economy*.) Burke's statement of the policy problem is as valid today as it was in his day.

9. There is now ample evidence to indicate that almost all systems which are multidimensional, nonlinear, and time dependent are endogenously unstable. See Richard L. Day, "Irregular Growth Cycles," *American Economic Review* 72, no. 3 (June 1982), and "The Emergence of Chaos From Classical Economic Growth," *Quarterly Journal of Economics*; Alessandro Vercelli, "Fluctuations and Growth: Keynes, Schumpeter, Marx and the Structural Instability of Capitalism," in R. Goodwin, M. Kurger, and A. Vercelli, *Nonlinear Models of Fluctuating Growth* (New York: Springer, 1984); Peter S. Albin, *Microeconomic Foundations of Cyclical Irregularities and Chaos*, Center for the Study of System Structure and Industrial Complexity, John Jay College, City University of New York, May 1985. It is also known that if unstable systems are constrained by ceilings and floors, then an econometric analysis of the resulting time series will indicate that this system is stable. See John M. Blatt, "On the Econometric Approach to Business-Cycle Analysis," *Oxford Economic Papers* (N.S.), vol. 30 (July 1978). For an early analysis of constrained explosive series, see Hyman P. Minsky, "A Linear Model of Cyclical Growth," *Review of Economics and Statistics* XLI, no. 2, Part 1 (May 1959), and "Monetary Systems and Acceleration Models," *American Economic Review* 47 (Dec. 1957).

PART 2

ECONOMIC
EXPERIENCE

A DEEP RECESSION BUT NOT A DEPRESSION IN 1975: THE IMPACT OF BIG GOVERNMENT

In the first quarter of 1975 (and again in midyear 1982), it seemed as if the American and the world economy was rushing toward a depression that might approach the severity of the Great Depression of the 1930s. Not only was income declining rapidly and the unemployment rate exploding, but virtually each day saw another bank, financial organization, municipality, business corporation, or country admit to financial difficulties. For example, in October 1974 the multi-billion-dollar Franklin National Bank of New York failed (at the time it was the largest American bank ever to fail), and in early 1975 the billion-dollar Security National Bank of New York was merged to prevent overt failure. During 1974–75 more banks failed, and more assets were affected than in any period since World War II. Moreover, the Real Estate Investment Trust (REIT) industry, with some $20 billion in assets, experienced a severe run that led to many bankruptcies and work-outs. In 1982, a virtual epidemic of savings banks failed, and in midyear a spectacular bank failure—that of Penn Square in Oklahoma City—led to large losses at some of the citadels of American banking: Chase Manhattan, Continental Illinois, and Seafirst. Then, in mid-1982 the Mexican peso collapsed, and default on multi-billion-dollar debts by a spate of Latin American countries seemed imminent.[1]

In addition, 1975 was marked by New York City's financial crisis, the failure of W. T. Grant and Company, the need for Consolidated Edison to sell assets to New York state in order to meet payment commitments,

---

1. The crisis of 1981–82 had an echo in 1984 when the overt failure of Continental Illinois was prevented by a massive infusion of funds from the Federal Reserve, the FDIC, and a consortium of giant banks, and a further crisis of Latin debts threatened the solvency of many of the largest banks.

and the walking bankruptcy of Pan Am. In 1982, fiscal insolvencies by municipalities were averted, but everyday names like International Harvester and Braniff were covert or overt bankrupts. In both episodes financial disarray seemed to be contagious, and there were fears that all asset values would soon be affected. A financial crisis seemed to be in the making. But in May 1975 and in November 1982 the downward movement was abruptly halted and a strong business cycle expansion began.

The episodes of instability so evident in 1974–75 and 1982 were not isolated events. Since 1966, the American economy has intermittently exhibited pervasive instability. Serious threats of financial disarray loomed in 1966, 1970, and 1979, but these financial crises were not of the scope and magnitude of 1974–75 and 1982. Even though the financial difficulties in 1974–75 and 1981–82 were more serious than in the other episodes, and even though money-market participants and the regulating authorities began to behave as if a full-fledged financial crisis reminiscent of what happened in 1929–33 was imminent, no full-fledged crisis took place.

The difficulties in 1966 were followed by a pause in the growth of income and a slight rise in unemployment; the combination was called a growth recession. The next four episodes of financial trauma, in 1970, 1974–75, 1979, and 1981–82, led to recessions; those of 1974–75 and 1981–82 were serious. The depth of the decline in 1974–75 and the limping nature of the recovery that followed, due largely to the persistence of financial difficulties, make what happened in 1974–75 either a mildly serious depression or a deep recession. The recession of 1981–82 can be characterized in the same way.

The financial trauma and recession after 1966 are not the only evidence of increased instability in the U.S. economy. The years since 1966 have been characterized by the worst inflation the country has experienced in times of peace. Furthermore, in the expansions that followed each financial crisis, the rate of inflation reached higher levels than after the prior expansion. Although unemployment rates have mostly been at high levels and capacity utilization rates at low levels since 1975, the annual rise in the basic inflation rate (the consumer price index [CPI]) never fell substantially below 6 percent until after the severe recession of 1981–82.

In order to design economic policy for the United States, it is necessary to understand why our economy is significantly more unstable now than earlier in the postwar period and why this instability did not lead to a deep and persistent depression. The performance of the American economy in the past decade may be nothing to be proud of, but at least the disaster of a Great Depression was avoided.

What, then, prevented a deep depression in 1975 and 1982? The answer centers on two aspects of the economy. The first is that Big Government stabilizes not only employment and income but also business cash flows (profits) and as a result asset value.[2] The second aspect is that the Federal Reserve System, in cooperation with other government agencies and private financial institutions, acts as a lender of last resort. It will be argued that the combined behavior of the government and of the central bank, in the face of financial disarray and declining income, not only prevents deep depressions but also sets the stage for a serious and accelerating inflation to follow. The institutions and usages that currently rule have not prevented disequilibrating forces from operating. What has happened is that the shape of the business cycle has been changed; inflation has replaced the deep and wide trough of depressions.

CHRONOLOGY OF THE 1973-75 RECESSION

The recession of 1973-75 covered six quarters, from October (or November) 1973 to April (or May) 1975, making it the longest recession since World War II. However, these six quarters fall into two phases: a mild dip that ran four quarters, from October 1973 to October 1974, and a precipitous drop that lasted two quarters, from October 1974 to April 1975. Although the first phase can be attributed to the oil shock repercussions of the Arab-Israeli War in 1973, the second phase resulted from the workings of the economy.

During the third quarter of 1974 and the first quarter of 1975, the sky seemed ready to fall. In September 1974, the index of industrial production stood at 125.6 (1967 = 100); six months later, this index was down sharply to 110.0, a drop at a 24.8 percent annual rate. Similarly, price-deflated gross national product (GNP) in 1972 dollars stood at $1,210.2 billion in the third quarter of 1974 and at $1,158.6 billion in the

---

2. This is a proposition derived from the work of Kalecki. See Michael Kalecki, *Selected Essays on the Dynamics of the Capitalist Economy (1933–1970)* (Cambridge: Cambridge University Press, 1971), Chapter 7, "The Determinants of Profits." See also Hyman P. Minsky, *Can "IT" Happen Again? Essays on Instability & Finance* (Armonk, N.Y.: M. E. Sharpe, Inc., 1982), Chapter 2, "Finance and Profits: The Changing Nature of American Business Cycles," pp. 14–58.

first quarter of 1975, an annual rate of decline of 8.5 percent (see Table 2.1). Between September 1974 and March 1975 civilian employment fell at a 6.7 percent annual rate.

If the rate of decline over the six-month period (the last quarter of 1974 to the first quarter of 1975) had continued for another six months, then a very deep depression would have been under way. But instead of continuing to decline, the economy's fall was checked sharply in the second quarter of 1975, and a slight upturn began. Payroll employment increased in April 1975 over March 1975. The index of industrial production, which was falling at a 23 percent annual rate in the first quarter, turned around and was increasing at a 10.6 percent rate in the three months ending September 1975. Price-deflated GNP shifted from a 9.2 percent annual rate of decline in the first quarter of 1975 to a 3.3 percent annual rate of increase in the second quarter of 1975, and a larger 11.9 percent rise in the third quarter.

Two sharp reversals in the path of the economy thus took place within approximately six months. First, a modest recession was transformed into a precipitous drop, and then, some six months later, there was a sharp braking of the decline and an almost immediate turnaround to a rapid expansion. These sudden reversals are indicative of instability. They are evidence that the economy was more unstable in 1974–75 than it was earlier in the post-war era.

Instability increases uncertainty. It is more difficult to make decisions in an economy that changes sharply than in an economy that changes gradually. Increased uncertainty, in and of itself, is a damper on economic activity, especially long-lived investment. But a more important point, particularly under capitalism, is that the instability tends to be amplified. Decision makers begin to seek early warning signals and become too sensitive to short-term indicators of change in the economy. One result is that investors begin to prefer the large immediate financial gains that can be made by being right on the swings over the more lasting and secure— though smaller—gains that can be made by investments that facilitate longer-run economic growth and development. In terminology that echoes Keynes, in an unstable economy speculation dominates enterprise.

What Happened during 1974–75

Over the last quarter of 1974 and the first quarter of 1975, it looked as if the U.S. economy was heading toward a generalized financial crisis, and, if history was any guide, a deep depression would follow. Income decreased

Table 2.1:   Developments in 1973–75 (Quarterly)

	GNP		GNP Growth Rates (Annual Rates)		Price Deflators GNP		Unemployment Rates
	Current Dollars	Deflated 1972 Dollars	Current Dollars	Price Deflated	Index (1972 = 100)	% Change (Annual Rate)	%
1973 (1)	1,265.0	1,227.7	15.8	8.8	103.04	6.5	5.0
(2)	1,287.8	1,228.4	7.4	.2	104.84	7.2	4.9
(3)	1,319.7	1,236.5	10.3	2.7	106.73	7.4	4.8
(4)	1,352.7	1,240.9	10.4	1.4	109.01	8.8	4.8
1974 (1)	1,370.9	1,228.7	5.5	–3.9	111.58	9.8	5.0
(2)	1,391.0	1,217.2	6.0	–3.7	114.28	10.0	5.1
(3)	1,424.4	1,210.2	9.9	–2.3	117.70	12.5	5.6
(4)	1,441.3	1,186.8	4.8	–7.5	121.45	13.4	6.7
1975 (1)	1,433.6	1,158.6	–2.1	–9.2	123.74	7.8	8.1
(2)	1,460.6	1,168.1	7.7	3.3	125.04	4.3	8.7
(3)	1,526.5	1,201.5	19.9	11.9	127.21	7.1	8.6
(4)	1,573.2	1,217.4	12.2	5.4	129.22	6.5	8.5

SOURCE: *Economic Report of the President,* January 1976. U.S. Government Printing Office, Washington, 1976.

IMPACTS OF BIG GOVERNMENT

Although the U.S. government owns very little of the means of production and provides few services directly, it is big. Unlike governments in many countries, it does not own and operate railroads, electric utilities, and telephone systems, nor does it run or pay for comprehensive medical services. Aside from the Tennessee Valley Authority, some nuclear installations, and the remnants of a postal system, it is difficult to think of any means of production owned by the federal government. In spite of a long and glorious history, the naval yards and army arsenals have been abandoned; military procurement now takes the form of contracts to ostensibly private firms.

To understand how our government is big, government spending must be divided into four parts: (1) government employment and spending on government production (e.g., the armories of history, the postal service, and the personnel portion of military spending); (2) government contracts (e.g., for airplanes and missiles from Lockheed, paper from think tanks such as the Rand Corporation, or highways built by the friendly neighborhood contractor); (3) transfer payments (e.g., Social Security, Medicare, unemployment insurance, and Aid to Families with Dependent Children [AFDC]); and (4) interest on the government debt.

In recent years neither government employment nor government contracts, aside from the military, have made government bigger in terms of its aggregate demand, financial flows, and portfolio effects. The government is bigger now mainly because military spending, transfer-payment schemes, and the costs of servicing the national debt have grown. Transfer-payment schemes in particular have become so large a part of government since World War II that the cyclical impact of government spending is now largely determined by their impact.

A transfer payment is a one-sided transaction, in contrast to an exchange, which is two-sided. In a transfer payment, a unit receives cash or goods and services in kind without being required to offer anything in exchange. A transfer-payment recipient conforms exactly to the economic status of a dependent child. A unit receiving a transfer payment does not provide inputs into the production process. Because the recipient produces no outputs, transfer-payment receipts are not part of the GNP, although they are part of a consumer's disposable (after-tax) income.

If one receives income as the result of a contribution, however meager, to the production of something "useful," then, roughly speaking, he is putting something into the output pot even as the income constitutes a right to take something out. In a market economy, the market value of what a production unit finances for its workers and owners to take out cannot be greater than the excess of the unit's sales proceeds over purchased inputs for any considerable period of time without the production unit running into financial difficulties. The excess of sales proceeds over the costs of purchased nonlabor inputs normally finances the entitlements a production unit's workers and investors can take out of the economy's output. If GNP is considered to be a pot, then the value of what the participants in production can take out is related to the value of what they put in. A transfer payment as part of disposable income finances taking out without requiring any offsetting contribution to the pot. The cliche "fair exchange is no robbery" applies to income received from work, but it does not necessarily apply to income received as a transfer payment. Today, a good part of the rights to taking out are based on legislated, moral, or customary usages, not on explicit current or past contributions.

A worker on unemployment insurance receives funds without making a current contribution to output. If the same worker received the same income on a work relief or Work Projects Administration (WPA)-type program, then he can be presumed to have made a contribution to GNP equal to his income. If the WPA output is useful and is *sold*, WPA-type relief for the unemployed is less inflationary than unemployment insurance. If the WPA output is useful even if it is not sold in a market, then it makes a contribution to the well-being of those who find the output useful, and, presumably, a tax or user's fee offset to all or part of the WPA spending could be collected. The military payroll as well as the income derived from defense contracts are income receipts that make no contribution to current useful output, and are at least as inflationary as transfer payments.

Because of the greater weight of transfer payments in government-spending schemes over the past years, the direct impact of much of government spending is on disposable income without any initial effect on employment and measured GNP. Measurements and problems of definition are involved, of course, in these distinctions. If the federal government spent as much on employing doctors and nurses, for example, as it now spends on Medicare and Medicaid, then such health care spending would not be considered a transfer payment, but instead a government purchase of goods and services.

Big Government was one cause of the halt in the sharp decline of the economy from the second quarter of 1974 to the first quarter of 1975 and the reversal toward the strong expansion that occurred in the spring and summer of 1975. With Big Government, a fall in national income automatically leads to a massive government deficit.

To understand how Big Government stopped the economy's free fall, it is necessary to delve into the different impacts of government deficits on our economy: the *income* and *employment effect*, which operates through government demand for goods, services, and labor; the *budget effect*, which operates through generating sectoral surpluses and deficits; and the *portfolio effect*, which exists because the financial instruments put out to finance a deficit must appear in some portfolio. The first effect is familiar and is dealt with in models that set out how GNP is determined. The second and third impacts of government are often ignored; they are important, however, because the economy is both an income-producing and -distributing system and a complicated, interdependent, and sophisticated financial system.[3]

Once these various facets are recognized, the effect of Big Government on the economy is much more powerful and pervasive than is allowed by the standard view, which neglects the financial-flow and portfolio implications of a government deficit. The standard view focuses solely on the direct and secondary effects of government spending, including transfer payments and taxes on aggregate demand. The expanded view allows both for the cash flows that other sectors need in order to fulfill commitments and for the need for secure assets in portfolios in the aftermath of a financial disturbance.

The reversal, during the winter of 1975, of the steep decline in income took place because the federal government's automatic reflex was to throw money at the problem, without considering longer-term benefits and costs. Thus, the truth of the essential Keynesian proposition—that increased government spending and tax cuts, if carried far enough, will halt a precipitous decline of the economy—was conclusively demonstrated in the recession of 1974–75. As a result of the 1975 experience, the issues in economic theory and policy that we should have to face are not about the ability of

---

3. The first effect is examined in the text book analysis of the multiplier. See any elementary text book, for example, Paul A. Samuelson, *Economics*, 9th ed. (New York: McGraw-Hill Book CO., 1973), pp. 220–33. The second effect is mainly emphasized in the Kaleckian analysis, in Michael Kalecki, op. cit. The third effect shows up in Warren McClam, "Financial fragility and instability: monetary authorities as borrowers and lenders of last resort," Chapter 11, in C. P. Kindleberger and J. P. Laffargue, *Financial Crises Theory, History and Policy* (Cambridge: Cambridge University Press, 1982); and W. C. Brained, and J. Tobin, "Pitfalls in Financial Model Building," *American Economic Review* LVIII (May 1968), pp. 99–122.

prodigious government deficit spending to halt even a very sharp recession but about the relative efficiency of specific measures and the side and after effects associated with particular policy strategies. Given the proven power of the deficits of Big Government, the overriding policy issue really should be the determination of the structural effects and objectives of government action. Once government is big, it must be concerned not only with aggregates but with for whom to produce, how to produce, and what kind of output to produce.

The Reagan effort to reduce government—which has failed so far because of the impact of defense spending, entitlements, and interest payments—would, if successful and if carried too far, make our economy more susceptible to downside instability. The Big Government impact was clearly evident in the recession of 1981–82 and the recovery of 1983–84. The power of Big Government and enormous deficits to contain downside instability was demonstrated.

Income and Employment Effects

In the conventional theory of income determination, government either creates employment (e.g., hiring people or buying goods or services), supplies income (e.g., Social Security), or spends on services for people (e.g., Medicare and Medicaid). Government also takes income from people by taxes and fees. When the government hires someone, a useful service is presumably provided. Similarly, when the government purchases something (from, say, a defense contractor) something useful is presumably produced. On the other hand, when the government transfers income to people, there is no direct effect on employment and output. Nothing that is presumably useful is exchanged for the income, and the economic impact comes only as the recipient spends the funds that are transferred.

In the standard view of how government affects the economy, government spending on goods and services is considered a component of aggregate demand, along with consumption and investment, but government transfer payments are not. The rules governing consumption spending are expressed as a function of disposable income, various measures of wealth or net worth, and the payoff from using income to acquire financial assets (i.e., interest rates). Transfer payments, as well as Social Security taxes and personal income taxes, enter into the analysis indirectly by way of disposable income and its effect on consumer spending.

Because of the way matters are measured, the impact on GNP of a dollar spent to hire leaf rakers in the public parks is greater than a dollar given in welfare or unemployment benefits. In 1975 the government distributed some $80 billion in Social Security payments. If 50 percent of the amount paid on Social Security had been spent on wages for the aged in a variety of work programs, then GNP would have been higher by some $40 billion. It is clearly a normative economic and sociological question whether it is better for a country to provide income for the aged through jobs, either in private industry or in make-work projects, or to provide income through transfer payments. It should also be noted that military spending constitutes part of GNP.

The distinction between transfer payments, taxes, and government spending on goods and services in the calculation of GNP is valid if and, in truth, only if we divorce the measure of GNP from any welfare connotation and treat it purely as an output measure that is transformed into a current period demand for labor (i.e., into employment). Government purchases of goods (such as a bomb or paper clips) and of services (whether of a general, a private soldier, a senator, or an engineer) are related to employment directly, as workers are hired and goods or services are produced. They are also related to employment indirectly through consumers' disposable income, as the employed workers, business managers, and profit receivers spend on consumption and investment goods. Transfer payments also affect employment indirectly, as they provide additional disposable income for households and additional gross profits for business. Thus, the simple straightforward way in which government affects employment is an important part of the picture.

Government spending, especially in excess of taxes, is a determinant of income. In terms of spending, the big increase over the postwar era has been in transfer payments to persons and grants-in-aid to state and local governments, as shown in Table 2.2. In 1950, early in the post–World War II era, total federal government spending was $40.8 billion (some 14 percent of GNP); $10.8 billion (about 25 percent of government spending) was transfer payments to persons. In sharp contrast, in 1975 total federal government spending was $356.9 billion (some 24 percent of GNP); transfer payments were $146.1 billion (40 percent of the total government spending). The other government programs that have grown rapidly are the grants-in-aid to state and local governments. These grew from $2.3 billion in 1950 to $54.2 billion in 1975 (from 5 to 15 percent of government spending).

There are differences between the ways various major components of government spending developed over the longer haul of 1950–69 and the seven years of ostensibly conservative government under Presidents Richard Nixon and Gerald Ford. Between 1950 and 1969, total government

Table 2.2: Federal Government Expenditures, 1950 and 1969–75 (Billions of Dollars)

| Year | Total Expenditures | Purchase of Goods & Services | | | Transfer Payments to Persons | Grants in Aid to State & Local Gov. | GNP |
		Total	National Defense	Other			
1950	40.8	18.7	14.0	4.7	10.8	2.3	286.2
1969	188.4	97.5	76.3	21.2	50.6	20.3	935.5
70	204.2	95.6	73.5	22.1	61.3	24.4	982.4
71	220.6	96.2	70.2	26.0	72.7	29.0	1063.4
72	244.7	102.1	73.5	28.6	80.5	37.5	1171.1
73	264.8	102.0	73.4	28.6	93.2	40.6	1306.3
74	300.1	111.7	77.4	34.3	114.5	43.9	1406.9
75	356.9	123.1	84.0	39.2	146.1	54.2	1499.0
As % of GNP							
1950	14.3	6.5	4.9	1.6	3.8	0.8	
1969	20.1	10.4	8.2	2.3	5.4	2.2	
70	20.8	9.7	7.5	2.2	6.2	2.5	
71	20.7	9.0	6.6	2.4	6.8	2.7	
72	20.9	8.7	6.3	2.4	6.9	3.2	
73	19.4	7.8	5.6	2.2	7.1	3.1	
74	21.3	7.9	5.5	2.4	8.1	3.1	
75	23.8	8.2	5.6	2.6	9.8	3.6	

SOURCE: *Economic Report of the President*, January 1976. U.S. Government Printing Office, Washington, D.C., 1976.

purchases of goods and services increased by a factor of 5, the national defense component rose by a factor of 5.45, and the civilian government function rose by a factor of 4.51. Over this same period, transfer payments to individuals also increased by a factor of almost 5. Thus, in the period when relatively liberal administrations dominated Washington, government purchases of goods and services and transfer payments to persons increased at about the same rate.

In contrast, between 1969 and 1975 federal government purchases of goods and services rose 26 percent, with national defense spending increasing 10 percent and the other civilian functions rising 85 percent—but transfer payments to persons scored nearly 200 percent! In 1975, they were almost 20 percent greater than government purchases of goods and services, compared with 1950 and 1969, when they were very much less.

Transfer payments consist of a large array of entitlement programs; as such they tend to increase automatically whenever the economy enters a recession. In addition, because they are programs already in existence, it is relatively easy for Congress and any administration to increase their "generosity" as the economy enters a recession.

Although unemployment rates went to 8.9 percent in May 1975, in no quarter during 1973–75 did disposable personal income decline (see Table 2.3). One reason was the way transfer payments by government exploded. Between the first quarter of 1973 and the fourth quarter of 1975, disposable personal income increased by $247.8 billion, and government transfer payments increased by $65.2 billion; 26.3 percent of the rise in disposable personal income was accounted for by transfer payments. As a percentage of disposable personal income, they stood at 12.69 percent in the first quarter of 1973, peaked at 15.96 percent in the third quarter of 1975, and retreated to 15.72 percent in the last quarter of 1975.

As a result of the explosive growth of transfer payments, in 1975 almost *one out of every six dollars* that households had to spend or had spent for them on consumption was a result of a federal or a state program that granted this income or service independently of current work performed (i.e., output created). As a case in point, unemployment insurance, which was at a $5.3 billion annual rate in the second quarter of 1974, rose to a $19.4 billion annual rate during the second quarter of 1975. Such a dramatic rise in unemployment insurance payments helps to explain why the sharp downturn was reversed so quickly.

I will ignore questions that must be raised about the efficiency and equity of an economy in which one-sixth of total disposable income

**Table 2.3:   Transfer Payments and Disposable Personal Income,
1973–75 (Quarterly)***

	Disposable Personal Income	Government Transfer Payments to Individuals[†]	Government Transfer Payment ÷ Disposable Personal Income %
1973 (1)	866.6	110.0	12.69
(2)	891.7	111.9	12.55
(3)	914.1	114.5	12.53
(4)	939.9	117.5	12.50
1974 (1)	953.8	123.5	12.95
(2)	968.2	130.7	13.50
(3)	996.1	138.4	13.89
(4)	1015.9	145.5	14.43
1975 (1)	1024.0	157.7	15.40
(2)	1081.7	169.4	15.66
(3)	1087.1	172.4	15.96
(4)	1114.4	175.2	15.72

SOURCE: *Economic Report of the President*, January 1976. U.S. Government Printing Office,
Washington, D.C., 1976.
*All data are expressed in annual rates, seasonally adjusted.
[†]Total government: Federal as well as state and local governments.

is the result of entitlement programs. The existence of a large, increasing
proportion of disposable income that is independent of employment or of
the profitability of business is beneficial, for it sustains demand and thus prevents a very deep and sustained fall of the economy during a recession. On
the other hand, the existence of such programs, combined with a tendency
to expand their scope when the economy is in recession, is harmful, for they
impart an inflationary bias to the economy. The increase in disposable
income, even as output and employment decreased in 1973–75, is one reason prices kept on rising throughout the recession.

Transfer payments, which provide income without work, set floors to
money wage rates. Each improvement in transfer-payment schemes has the
effect of raising the price at which some people will enter the labor market.
The effective productive capacity of the economy is eroded by decreasing
labor force participation when price-deflated transfer-payment schemes are
improved, especially if, as is our practice, eligibility depends on being either
unemployed or out of the labor force.

CASH-FLOW EFFECTS OF BIG GOVERNMENT

A fundamental proposition in economics is that the sum of realized financial surpluses (+) and deficits (−) over all units must equal zero. This follows from the simple point that every time some unit pays money for the purchase of current output, some other unit receives money. Because the different sectors of the economy (e.g., households, business firms, government, and financial institutions) are consolidations of elementary units, this proposition also holds for the various aggregations. If the federal government spends $73.4 billion more than it collects in taxes, as it did in 1975, then the sum of the surpluses and deficits over all other sectors equals $73.4 billion surplus. As is shown in Table 2.4 for annual data and Table 2.5 for quarterly data in 1973–75, the sum of the surpluses and deficits of the various behavioral and accounting sectors was zero (within small margins due to data imperfections).

The household surplus or deficit is the difference between disposable personal income and personal outlays. Almost always, except in deep depressions (and then only in an economy with a small government), households generate a surplus. But this surplus as a percentage of household disposable income varies quite markedly. Table 2.4 shows that household saving ran from 6.08 percent of disposable income in 1972 to 8.05 percent in 1973, 7.52 percent in 1974, and 8.9 percent in 1975. In both 1973 and 1975, the household saving ratio increased sharply. Each jump in the household saving ratio is associated with a jump in the deficit of some other subdivision of the economy. In 1973, the jumping deficit was that of business; in 1975, it was the government's deficit that jumped.

Private investment is undertaken by the business sector. The business sector deficit is the excess of plant and equipment, inventory, and corporate housing investment over business internal funds (retained earnings plus capital consumption allowances). This deficit was $47.9 billion in 1972, jumped to $79.0 billion in 1973, remained high at $67.8 billion in 1974, and fell sharply to $21.5 billion in 1975. The business deficit, as a percentage of gross private investment, rose from 26.7 percent in 1972 to 35.8 percent and 32.4 percent in 1973 and 1974, respectively, and then fell to 10.95 percent in 1975.

The path of the deficit in total government (federal, state, and local) showed a $10 billion swing in both 1973 and 1974—a decrease in 1973 but an increase in 1974—and a $60 billion increase in 1975. The $60 billion increase in 1975 must show up either as a decrease in the deficits or as an increase in the surpluses of other sectors. Part of it appeared in a $15.6 billion

Table 2.4: Sectoral Surpluses and Deficits, 1972–75
(Billions of Dollars)

	1972	1973	1974	1975
Households				
Disposable personal income	801.3	903.1	983.6	1,076.8
Personal outlays	−751.9	−830.4	−909.5	−987.2
Personal saving (surplus)	+49.4	+72.7	+74.0	+89.6
Business				
Gross internal funds	131.3	141.2	141.7	174.8
Gross private investment	−179.2	−220.2	−209.5	−196.3
Deficit or surplus	−47.9	−79.0	−67.8	−21.5
Government				
Federal gov. deficit or surplus	−17.3	−6.9	−11.7	−73.4
State gov. deficit or surplus	13.7	12.9	8.1	10.0
Total gov. deficit or surplus	−3.6	+6.0	−3.6	−63.4
Total surpluses	49.4	78.7	74.0	89.6
Total deficits	−51.5	−79.0	−71.4	−84.9
Discrepancy	−2.1	−.3	+3.6	+4.7
Household savings as % of disposable personal income	6.08	8.05	7.52	8.92
Business deficit as % of gross private investment	26.73	35.88	32.4	10.95

SOURCE: *Economic Report of the President*, January 1976. U.S. Government Printing Office, Washington, D.C., 1976. 1976.

increase in household saving, which led to the household saving ratio being 8.92 percent of personal disposable income. Another part showed up in the huge increase of $33.1 billion in business gross internal funds, a rise of some 23.4 percent. (In 1975, the year of a major increase in unemployment and a sharp decrease in price-deflated GNP, gross business profits increased by 23.4 percent.) Another component that offset the rise in the government deficit was a fall of some $13.2 billion in investment, mainly the result of inventory liquidation. The $60 billion rise in the total government deficit was thus offset by a $15.6 billion rise in personal saving and a $46.3 billion decrease in the business sector deficit. In 1975 the government deficit, therefore, was mainly offset by a rise in corporate cash flows. Business profits, correctly defined, were sustained and increased even as the country was in a severe recession!

The data for the first quarter of 1973 to the third quarter of 1975 serve to emphasize how a major increase in the government deficit is

Table 2.5: Sectoral Surpluses and Deficits, 1973–1975 (Quarterly)

	1973				1974				1975		
	(1)	(2)	(3)	(4)	(1)	(2)	(3)	(4)	(1)	(2)	(3)
Households											
Disposable personal income	866.8	891.7	914.1	939.9	953.8	968.2	996.3	1015.9	1024.0	1081.7	1087.1
Personal outlays	806.1	821.8	840.3	853.4	872.6	901.4	931.7	932.4	950.4	974.2	1001.3
Personal savings surplus	60.7	69.9	73.8	86.5	81.2	66.8	64.6	83.5	73.6	107.5	85.9
Business											
Gross internal funds	138.6	138.7	141.3	145.9	147.1	142.0	134.2	143.1	154.7	171.8	185.6
Gross private investment	207.2	213.7	223.8	236.1	218.1	207.5	202.2	210.0	177.1	177.0	202.7
Deficit or surplus	−68.6	−75.0	−82.5	−90.2	−71.0	−65.5	−68.0	−66.9	−22.4	−5.2	−25.1
Government											
Federal government Deficit or surplus	−10.9	−7.4	−4.8	−4.6	−5.3	−7.9	−8.0	−25.5	−53.7	−102.2	−70.5
State & local Deficit or surplus	+15.9	+13.2	+12.4	+10.1	+9.4	+8.2	+9.1	+5.9	+5.7	+8.8	+12.9
Deficit or surplus	+5.0	+5.8	+7.7	+5.5	+4.1	+.3	+1.1	−19.6	−48.0	−93.4	−57.6
Total surpluses	65.4	75.8	81.5	92.0	85.2	67.1	65.6	83.6	73.6	107.5	85.9
Total deficits	−68.4	−75.0	−82.5	−90.2	−71.0	−65.6	−68.0	−86.5	−70.4	−98.6	−82.7
Discrepancy	−3.0	+.8	−1.0	+1.8	+14.2	+1.6	−2.4	+2.9	+3.2	+6.9	+3.2

SOURCE: *Economic Report of the President*, January 1976. U.S. Government Printing Office, Washington, D.C., 1976.

associated with a movement toward surplus by other sectors of the economy. Gross internal funds of the business sector ranged in the narrow band of $134.2 to $147.1 billion in the eight quarters of 1973–74. No discernible trend was evident during this time. However, in the first three quarters of 1975, gross internal funds of business measured $154.7, $171.8, and $185.6 billion. (The data are in annual rates and seasonally adjusted.) Between the third quarter of 1974 and the third quarter of 1975, business gross internal funds rose by 36.8 percent in spite of the fall in national income and employment.

The federal government deficit was at an annual rate of $102.2 billion in the second quarter of 1975. This deficit was $94.3 billion greater than the deficit in the second quarter of 1974, so there had to be a $94.3 billion swing in other sectors' surpluses or deficits in order to offset this massive change. This swing was broken down as follows: household personal saving rose by $40.7 billion, business's gross internal funds increased by $28.2 billion, and investment fell by $30.5 billion. Of the total swing, some $40 billion was reflected in personal saving, and some $60 billion was reflected in an increase in business internal funds or in a decrease in business investment. Both the annual and quarterly data show that even as the economy plunged into a deep recession the gross internal funds accruing to business increased.

In the American economy, business is carried on within a system of borrowing and lending based on margins of safety. Two measures of the margin of safety are the ratio of the cash flows due on debt to the cash flow debtors receive and the ratio of the present value of expected cash flows discounted over the future to the face value of outstanding debts. The boom of the 1970s and the longer-run evolution of the economy over the postwar era were associated with a large increase in short-term debt issues by business and a proliferation of financial institutions that finance such debt by issuing their own, usually short-term, obligations. The major determinant of the quantity of such short-term debt that business can carry is the internal funds that are generated by operations.

In the absence of Big Government and the huge deficit that automatic and discretionary policy combined to generate in 1975, a plunge of the economy, as it occurred in 1974–75, would have been associated with a plunge in corporate cash flows. Business debt-carrying capacity and the margins of safety in the system of borrowing and lending would have decreased. Even in the absence of actual bankruptcies, such decreases in business cash flows would have forced efforts by business to contract commitments. In fact, business gross profitability increased in 1975, so that a forced or induced curtailment of commitments did not take place.

In 1975, the impact of Big Government by way of the massive deficit it generated was critical in braking the decline and quickly reversing the recession into an expansion. The full import of government as a preventer of cumulative declines and as a sustainer of economic activity cannot be appreciated without recognizing the significance of the proposition that the sum of the surpluses and deficits over all sectors must equal zero. The efficiency of Big Government can be questioned, but its efficacy in preventing the sky from falling cannot be doubted.

The above examination is based on accounting identities, which do not incorporate any behavioral relations. A mere presentation of accounting identities is not a theory and does not lead to any causal inferences. In order to understand what happened, we must look at how the end result is achieved (i.e., how the sectoral surpluses and deficits, when summed over all sectors, equal zero). We must therefore formulate ideas about what are the *determining* and what are the *determined* items in the accounting tables (i.e., introduce assumptions on how the economy actually works so that the end result is always achieved).

To a considerable extent, household personal outlays are responsive to changes in income. This passive household saving and consumption behavior is attenuated by the existence of both household wealth and consumer debt. Some forty years ago, when John Maynard Keynes first formulated his theory in terms of passive consumption behavior, household wealth and consumer installment credit were a much smaller part of the total economic picture than in the 1970s.

The large household saving ratios of 1974 and 1975, which were referred to earlier, were in good part a reflection of the collapse of automobile sales. Part of the increase in household saving in 1974–75 took the form of a reduction in household borrowing to finance automobile and other purchases. If a pause takes place in the rate at which consumer credit is extended, even as disposable income is sustained or increased, then the saving ratio will be high, as in 1975, and an improvement in the liquidity position of households will take place. With a lag, this accumulation of household liquidity will lead to a jump in consumer spending. Those households that have not been strongly and directly affected by unemployment during a recession tend to increase the ratio of spending to disposable income once an accumulation of liquid assets and a decrease of debt relative to income take place. As a result of this impatience to spend, a recession with a high saving ratio, such as that of 1975, is followed by a recovery in which the saving ratio is low. When the ratio of saving out of disposable income falls, the consumer becomes a "hero" in leading the economy out of a recession. The heroism of the consumer, however, is a lagged response to the high saving ratio of the recession.

The observed variability in the ratio of saving to disposable income is evidence that consumer behavior is not fully passive. Nevertheless the relation between consumer spending and present and past developments in the economy is fairly well known and relatively stable. We know that personal outlays will almost always lie between 95 and 91 percent of personal disposable income. Furthermore, if the saving ratio is high (i.e., toward the 8–9 percent range for a time), then it will soon be followed by a burst of spending that lowers it toward 6 percent.

The household saving entry in Tables 2.4 and 2.5 is therefore largely determined by how the system is operating and how it has operated in the recent past, as is the entry for *government revenue*. Congress, the state legislatures, and various local authorities pass laws that set tax schedules. As a result, the amount collected in taxes, given any set of tax laws, depends on the behavior of the economy.

On the other hand, the two items in the tables that vary quite independently of how the economy is currently functioning, and hence are the *determining* or causal factors in what happens, are *business investment* and *government spending*. Business investment is largely, if not completely, determined by today's views on the future. Of course, the past and present behavior of the economy, which will help set current views about tomorrow, affects both the scale of the facilities that will be built and the way in which these facilities will be financed. What bankers and businessmen think today about revenues and out-of-pocket costs over the next twenty-five years and more basically determines whether and at what terms financing for long-life projects will be forthcoming. Investment, rather than being currently or historically determined, is based upon views about the future.

The other item in Table 2.5 that is largely independent of the current operation of the economy is government spending, which is submerged in the government deficit or surplus side of the table. Spending programs that largely consist of the purchase of goods and services are set in the budget and are, within minor limitations, determined by congressional action. Another component of government spending, which is covered by the rubric of transfer payments, is similar to taxes in that legislation, together with administrative regulations, sets up formulas for entitlement. The actual expenditures depend on the behavior and economic position of various households.

As a consequence of these dependent and independent relations, a fall in income due to a decline in investment spending or a rise in the consumer saving ratio will lead to a rise in takings from entitlement programs and a fall in government tax receipts. Combined with the program of discretionary government spending and tax changes, this will lead to a large increase in the government deficit. This deficit must be offset by an equal move toward surplus by the business and household sectors. As the move toward surplus on the part of the business sector leads to an increase in business gross profits after taxes, an increase in the debt-carrying capacity of the business sector takes place even as the economy moves into a recession. Furthermore, a large household saving ratio will be induced by the government deficit; this implies that, with a lag, there will be an autonomous rise in consumer spending. This autonomous rise will take place after the downward movement of the economy has been halted and after the high saving ratio has led to both a decrease in household debt relative to income and a rise in household holdings of liquid assets.

In the absence of a large government sector in 1975, two downward processes would have been started. Fist, private investment would have fallen even more than it did because of further inventory liquidation and a decrease in, if not abandonment of, investment programs already in process. Second, disposable personal income would have fallen faster, even faster than personal outlays, so that the household sector saving ratio would have been smaller. That is, in the absence of Big Government, an initial retrenchment of investment would have triggered downward movements: Decreases in business inventory investment and household disposable income would have been part of a cumulative process. Both consumption expenditures and investment expenditures decrease in an effort "by the economy" to eliminate a "virtual" excess of saving (surplus) over investment (deficits). However, the fall in household spending and business investment decreases the flow of business internal funds—which tends to increase the business deficit for any level of investment. A cumulative interactive decline in household income, household spending, business investment, and business cash flows is likely to occur. This, of course, is the interactive process that leads to deep depressions.

Big Government, with its potential for automatic massive deficits, puts a high floor under an economy's potential downward spiral. Although this high floor is important in itself, it is particularly important in a world with business and household debt because corporate gross profits and household savings are essential to validate such debt.

Without the emergence of a huge government deficit in 1975, the debt-carrying capacity of business and households would have been severely compromised. Such compromising, due to an iterative, downward spiral of income and profits, led to the debt deflations and deep depressions of the past. The sectoral budget impact of Big Government that sustains business profits is precisely what makes such a cumulative interactive decline impossible.[4]

Balance-Sheet Implications

Financial instruments are absorbed or created whenever Big Government runs a surplus or a deficit. In particular, whenever Big Government generates a huge deficit during a recession, other sectors, including financial organizations such as banks, savings banks, and insurance companies, acquire the government debt issued to finance the deficit.

We live in an economy with a complex financial system. In this system the surplus sectors—in 1975 it was households—are not required to acquire directly the liabilities of deficit units. Instead, they can finance these deficits indirectly by acquiring the liabilities of financial institutions. In our economy, banks, savings institutions, insurance companies, and pension funds, among other institutions, are likely to be the immediate owners of the debts of business, government, and households. Households acquire the liabilities of financial institutions such as pension rights, insurance-policy cash-surrender values, demand deposits, and various types of savings or time deposits. Consequently, much of the direct impact of swings in deficits and surpluses among sectors will be on the assets acquired and sold by financial institutions.

Wide swings in the placement of government debt between several financial and nonfinancial sectors took place during recent years. Table 2.6 shows the total acquisition of government debt, Treasury and agency issues combined, by private domestic sectors between 1972 and 1975. The acquisition of government debt by government bodies (such as the Federal Reserve System, government agencies, and government-sponsored agencies) and by foreigners has been subtracted from the total issued to derive private domestic acquisition.

---

4. Irving Fisher, "The Debt Deflation Theory of Great Depressions," in *Econometrica* 1 (Oct. 1983), and *Booms and Depressions* (New York: Adelphi, 1932) are still fine statements of the interactions that lead to a great depression. See also Hyman P. Minsky, "Debt-Deflation Processes in Today's Institutional Environment," *Banco Nazionale de Lavoro Quarterly Review* 143 (Dec. 1982).

Table 2.6:   Total Private Domestic Acquisition of U.S. Government Securities, 1972–75 (Billions of Dollars)

	1972	1973	1974	1975
Households	.6	20.4	14.5	−.9
Nonfinancial corporations	−2.4	−1.8	3.5	16.1
State & local governments	−3.4	−.2	−.1	−5.8
Total nonfinancial sectors	1.6	18.8	18.1	21.1
Commercial banking	6.5	−1.3	1.0	30.3
Savings and loan assoc.	4.3	*	3.3	11.1
Mutual savings banks	1.4	−.5	.1	3.6
Credit unions	.8	.2	.2	1.9
Life insurance	.3	.1	*	1.3
Private pension funds	1.0	.6	1.1	5.4
State & local gov. ret. funds	−.6	.1	.6	1.7
Other investment co.	−.4	−.1	−.3	−1.0
Total financial sectors	13.6	−.4	6.7	57.1
Total all domestic sectors	15.2	18.4	24.9	78.1

SOURCE: Flow of Funds Data, Board of Governors of the Federal Reserve System.

In 1972, 1973, and 1974, the total acquisition of government debt by private sectors showed only modest changes, although the totals rose a bit each year. In 1972 the major purchasing sectors were financial institutions: commercial banks, savings and loan associations, and mutual savings banks acquired $12.2 billion of government debt. In 1973 and 1974, however, the major acquiring units were in the nonfinancial sector—in particular, households: In 1973 households acquired $20.4 billion of government debt, so that all the other private domestic sectors combined decreased their holdings by some $2.0 billion. In 1974 households acquired $14.5 billion, and nonfinancial business acquired $3.5 billion. In 1974 there was a net acquisition of government debt by the financial sector, largely by the mortgage-related savings and loan associations. This acquisition by savings and loan associations reflected the emerging decline in housing.

In 1975 the pattern of net acquisition of government debt changed markedly from that of previous years. In this year the nonfinancial sectors acquired some $20 billion of government debt, as in 1973 and 1974, but, in sharp contrast, the holdings of households decreased, while those of nonfinancial corporations increased by $16.1 billion. Also, state and local government holdings rose sharply. However, the big change that occurred was in the amount acquired by the financial sectors. These sectors obtained some $57.1 billion of government debt in 1975, $50.4 billion more than in 1974. Of the $50.4 billion increase, $30.3 billion was acquired by commercial banks and $11.1 billion by savings and loan associations. The huge acquisition of government debt by commercial banks and other financial organizations thus financed the government deficit, and in the process, the balance sheets of the acquiring organizations were markedly changed.

Government debt is free of default risk; whatever the government debt contract says will be forthcoming will, in fact, be forthcoming. This contract is in nominal terms; price level changes can and do affect the purchasing power of government debt. Furthermore, government debt is marketable, and its marketability is ultimately guaranteed by the Federal Reserve System, a guarantee that does not necessarily extend to other debt. Thus, the owners of government securities are assured of the ability to modify their portfolio as their needs or preferences change. In a sense, by acquiring government debt in 1975, banks, savings and loan associations, life insurance companies, and pension funds were able to store financing power; they were able to shift it from the time of slack private demand to some future period when private financing demand is strong. The inflationary potential of a massive deficit such as the one that occurred in 1975 is *not* felt fully during the time of the deficit; rather it occurs largely in the subsequent boom when the assets acquired during the recession are undone.

Table 2.7 exhibits the net acquisition of various financial assets by the commercial banking sector for the years 1972–75. A striking change is evident in the amounts acquired over these years. In 1972 the commercial banking sector obtained $78.3 billion of financial assets. Although in 1973 acquisitions increased to in excess of $100 billion, during 1974 they tapered off to $84 billion, and in 1975 they were a relatively modest $32.9 billion. The commercial banking sector was a driving, determining factor in the economy during 1972–73, but a passive, acquiescing one in 1975.

Another striking change across the period 1972–75 was the composition of the assets acquired by banks. In 1973 some $52.1 billion, or more than 50 percent of the net assets, were bank loans not elsewhere classified (NEC) (i.e., bank loans to business). Commercial banks also acquired $19.8 billion of mortgage and $10.6 billion of consumer credit in 1973. It is evident that the banking sector was deploying its financial resources toward the private sectors. The sharp recession year of 1975, however, stands in stark contrast to what happened in 1973. Not only did commercial banking acquire only $32.9 billion of financial assets in 1975, but $30.3 billion of the assets acquired were U.S. government debt. Bank loans NEC decreased

Table 2.7:   Commercial Banking: Net Aquisition of Financial Assets, 1972–75 (Billions of Dollars)

	1972	1973	1974	1975
Net acqs. of financial assets	78.3	100.2	83.9	32.9
Demand deposits + currency	.2	.3	−.2	*
Total bank credit	75.4	83.3	62.2	27.8
Credit-market instruments	70.5	86.6	64.6	26.6
U.S. govt. securities	6.5	−1.3	1.0	30.3
Direct	2.4	−8.8	−2.6	29.1
Agency issues	4.1	7.6	3.6	1.2
Other securities + mortgages	25.7	25.9	19.1	6.4
S & L obligations	7.2	5.7	5.5	1.3
Corporate bonds	1.7	.5	1.1	2.1
Home mortgages	9.0	11.0	6.5	1.9
Other mortgages	7.8	8.8	6.1	1.2
Other cr. excl. security	38.4	62.0	44.5	−10.1
Consumer credit	10.1	10.6	2.8	−.6
Bank loans NEC	28.5	52.1	39.5	−12.9
Open-market paper	−.2	−.8	2.2	3.4
Corporate equities	.1	.1	—	—
Security credit	4.8	−3.4	−2.4	1.2
Vault cash + member bank reserves	− 1.0	3.5	−3	1.0
Other interbank claims	1.4	6.0	7.1	−5.4
Miscellaneous assets	2.3	7.2	15.0	9.5

SOURCE: Flow of Funds Data, Board of Governors of the Federal Reserve System.

by $12.9 billion and consumer credit went down, fractionally, by $.6 billion. Also, mortgage acquisition fell to $3.1 billion. All in all, in 1975 bank resources were being deployed away from business and toward government.

One implication of the large increase in government debt and deficits that occurred during the recession year of 1975 is that various businesses and financial institutions were able to acquire safe and secure assets, which improved the liquidity of portfolios, even as aggregate income and employment fell. A reduction in private business indebtedness could take place while banks increase their total assets and total liabilities. When government had been small and the outstanding debt not large, a sizable increase in government debt held in various private portfolios, including the portfolios of banks, could not take place during a recession. In these circumstances, a decrease in private business debt necessarily meant a decrease in demand and time deposits. A cumulative interactive decline in business debt and the public's holding of demand and time deposits did not occur in 1975 because there was the large and increasing volume of public debt outstanding that could enter the portfolios of banks and business.

In 1975, because of Big Government and the large increase in government debt, the default risk of business and bank portfolios decreased. As businesses liquidated inventories, they decreased their indebtedness to banks and acquired government debt. Banks and other financial institutions acquired liquidity by buying government debt rather than by decreasing their assets and liabilities. The public, both households and business, not only acquired safe assets in the form of bank deposits and savings deposits, but were able to decrease their indebtedness relative to income. The existence of a large and increasing government debt thus acted as a significant stabilizer of portfolios during the threatening period of 1975.

A DEEP RECESSION BUT NOT A DEPRESSION IN 1975: THE IMPACT OF LENDER-OF-LAST-RESORT INTERVENTION

In 1974–75 (and in 1969–70 and in 1981–82), as we have seen, a cumulative decline in the economy, involving interactions among financial market variables and the income that flows from the production of output, started, gained momentum, and quite suddenly stopped, averting a full-fledged debt deflation. One reason why the interactive process did not fully develop was the existence of Big Government, whose huge deficits maintained final demand and sustained business profits even as income declined. The other reason was prompt and effective lender-of-last-resort interventions by the Federal Reserve System, the FDIC, and cooperating private institutions.

Whereas Big Government stabilizes output, employment, and profits by its deficits, the lender of last resort stabilizes asset values and financial markets; for example, the Federal Reserve buys, stands ready to buy, or accepts as collateral financial assets that otherwise are not marketable; it thereby substitutes, or stands ready to substitute, its own riskless liabilities for assets at risk in various portfolios. Whereas Big Government operates on aggregate demand, sectoral surpluses, and increments of government liabilities in portfolios, the lender of last resort works on the value of the inherited structure of assets and the refinancing available for various portfolios. Both sets of stabilizing efforts are necessary to contain and reverse an income decline associated with financial trauma such as took place in 1974–75 (and in 1969–70 and 1981–82).

The lender of last resort must intervene promptly and assure the availability of refinancing to prevent financial difficulties from turning into an interactive cumulative decline that could lead to a great depression. To do this, it must make it unnecessary for the units being protected to have to sell out positions in assets at a loss in order to meet financial commitments. Once banks, financial units, and ordinary firms, as well as state and municipal governments, are forced to try to refinance their positions through extraordinary channels, the lender of last resort must either provide accommodations or chance the development of a debt deflation.

The need for lender-of-last-resort operations will often occur before income falls steeply and before the well nigh automatic income and financial stabilizing effects of Big Government come into play. If the institutions responsible for the lender-of-last-resort function stand aside and allow market forces to operate, then the decline in asset values relative to current output prices will be larger than with intervention; investment and debt-financed consumption will fall by larger amounts; and the decline in income, employment, and profits will be greater. If allowed to gain momentum, the financial crisis and the subsequent debt deflation may, for a time, overwhelm the income and financial stabilizing capacity of Big Government. Even in the absence of effective lender-of-last-resort action, Big Government will eventually produce a recovery, but, in the interval, a high price will be paid in the form of lost income and collapsing asset values.

Even though the lender-of-last-resort function of the Federal Reserve was of vital importance in stabilizing the economy in 1966, 1969–70, 1974–75, and 1981–82, this function and the operations it entails are poorly understood. A lender of last resort is necessary because our economy has inherent and inescapable flaws that lead to intermittent financial instability. Conventional theory is not hospitable to the thought that market capitalism left to its own devices will, from time to time, experience financial crises that can lead to bone-crunching depressions.

If economic policies that affect the structure and operations of financial markets and institutions are to have a chance at being successful, then those aspects of our economy that make a lender of last resort necessary must be understood. By regulating the structure of financial institutions and by controlling the type of financial practices allowed, policy that is based on understanding can hope to decrease the likelihood of financial instability.

The creation of a lender-of-last-resort function was a major objective of the legislation establishing the Federal Reserve System in 1913, but that original objective has been subverted by a view that the primary and dominant function of the Federal Reserve System is controlling the money supply. This later view ignores the likelihood that the normal functioning of our economy will lead to the development of fragile, and thus unstable, financial relations. Any prescription for the behavior of the Federal Reserve must be tempered by the recognition of its obligation—implied in its role as lender of last resort—to ensure that the financial system as a ·whole functions in a normal, or a nondisruptive, way. If the financial system does become disruptive, then the Federal Reserve, or other central banking organizations, must be prepared to intervene and correct the situation by furnishing liquidity or absorbing potential losses. However, this refinancing and socialization of potential losses imposes costs as well as benefits on the economy, for it affects the behavior of the economy after the lender-of-last-resort operations have been carried out. Because the Federal Reserve has the responsibility, so to speak, to pick up the pieces when things go wrong, it must be concerned with and guide the growth and evolution of financial practices in periods of tranquility as well as when circumstance forces it to intervene.

Historically, episodes of severe financial instability have led to controversy about the structure of financial institutions and have often triggered institutional changes. The Federal Reserve System was created as a reaction to the panic of 1907, and the FDIC was a reaction to the bank failures of the Great Depression. As yet, the financial traumas of the past two decades have not led to any serious legislated institutional changes aimed at correcting the perceived causes of financial instability, mainly, I suspect, because the financial instability during these episodes has not led to deep depressions of the type that followed earlier episodes. However, the absence of deep depressions does not mean an absence of adverse consequences; the lender-of-last-resort actions that were undertaken have, in effect, set the stage for subsequent inflationary bursts. The special instability of recent years, in which the economy oscillates between prospective runaway inflation and incipient debt deflation, is a side effect of the methods used to avoid a debt deflation and deep depression.

THE SUBSTANCE OF LENDER-OF-LAST-RESORT OPERATIONS

The Franklin National Bank was declared insolvent on October 8, 1974. At that date it had $3.6 billion in assets, sharply lower than the $5.0 billion it reported at year end 1973. The troubles of the Franklin National Bank became public early in May 1974, and from that time to the end of July

1974, total assets fell by $.9 billion. Over this same period, liabilities to depositors and to banks fell by $1.6 billion, money-market liabilities dropped by $.8 billion, and deposits in foreign branches slipped by $.5 billion. The $2.9 billion drain of deposits was offset by the reduction in assets and $1.4 billion of borrowing at the Federal Reserve.[1]

After Franklin National's difficulties became public it was not able to buy federal funds or to sell jumbo (over $100,000 and uninsured) certificates of deposit; such an inability to buy funds or to retain deposits is called a run. In order to enable the Franklin National to meet its payment commitments as deposits fled, the Federal Reserve System lent it $1.4 billion. The Franklin National's position was thus refinanced by the Federal Reserve System, and this refinancing of a position or, alternatively phrased, enabling a bank or a financial market to withstand a run, is the essential lender-of-last-resort function.

After the Franklin National Bank was declared insolvent, the FDIC stepped in and arranged for the offices and deposit liabilities of the Franklin National to be taken over by another bank, the newly organized European-American Bank and Trust Company. The FDIC took the questionable assets of the failed Franklin National Bank and fully protected all depositors, even those with deposits that exceeded the statutory insurance limit. The FDIC took the questionable assets into its portfolio and gave the successor cash or bankable assets from those the Federal Reserve Bank had accepted as collateral for Franklin National Bank's borrowings. When the FDIC took questionable assets into its portfolios and gave cash, or acceptable assets, to the European-American Bank, it assured that all the liabilities of the Franklin National, except equity, would be honored. It was performing a lender-of-last-resort action.

At the end of 1973, the REITS had outstanding $4.0 billion of open-market paper; at the end of 1974, this industry had $.7 billion of such paper outstanding. A run on REITs occurred when the difficulties they were facing over construction loans became public knowledge. As a result, about $3.3 billion of open-market paper was run off and replaced by loans from commercial banks. When commercial banks refinanced the distressed REITs, they were also performing a lender-of-last-resort act.

---

1. In the following I rely to a good extent on Andrew Brimmer, *International Finance and the Management of Bank Failures* (Washington, D.C.: Brimmer, 1976). The Federal Reserve's lender of last resort intervention in 1984 in the "avoided" bankruptcy of the Continental Illinois Bank of Chicago was much greater than in the Franklin National case.

In each of the above cases, as in many other cases (such as the bailing out of New York City, Pan Am, and Consolidated Edison), a key element in the development of a crisis is a run. The normal functioning of a unit with short-term debt outstanding requires the issurance, or sale, of new short-term debt in order to fulfill commitments. A run occurs when potential lenders, or buyers of liabilities, believe that there is a significant chance that payments on the issuer's debt will not be made on schedule. At such times, the borrowing firm cannot induce loans or the purchase of its liabilities by offering higher interest rates.

An institution that performs a lender-of-last-resort function guarantees that the terms of some contracts will be fulfilled, regardless of market conditions or the business situation of the particular debtor. Thus, a lender of last resort diminishes the risk of default of the assets it guarantees. Assets with low default risk are readily marketable—they are liquid. When the Federal Reserve extends the domain of instruments that it protects against default, it is increasing the effective quantity of liquid assets and thus of assets that have the properties of money in the community. The assets protected by the Federal Reserve as a lender of last resort are liabilities of some bank or similar institution, which in turn are used to finance activity or to finance positions in assets. Any extension of Federal Reserve lender-of-last-resort protection to new institutions or to new financial instruments increases the overall financing capacity of the economy, and when this increased capacity is utilized, asset prices and lending activity increase. Even as the use of lender-of-last-resort powers effectively aborts an incipient financial crisis, the additional financing ability introduced by the extension of liquid asset status to new institutions or to new credit instruments, creates the possibility of a future inflationary expansion.

SPECIFICATION OF FINANCIAL RELATIONS

A fundamental attribute of our economy is that the ownership of assets is typically financed by debts, and debts imply payment commitments. Over the near term—for most financial institutions and many ordinary business organizations—payment commitments on debts often exceed the cash that the unit expects to receive from its basic operations. These units expect to borrow to obtain the funds needed to repay debt. Even if a unit expects to receive enough cash by selling output or assets, the purchasers of these outputs or assets often have to borrow. Borrowing, selling assets, and selling output in markets whose normal functioning depends on financial arrangements working well are attributes of our economy. The smooth functioning of a complex interdependent financial system is necessary for the normal functioning of the U.S. economy; anything that disrupts financial markets has an adverse effect on output, employment, and asset values.

Financing arrangements in which borrowing is necessary to repay debt is speculative finance. Over a run of years in which serious depressions are avoided and in which banks and other financial institutions prosper, the weight in our economy of units that depend on speculative finance increases. In an economy characterized by privately owned capital assets, uncertainty, and profit-maximizing behavior by business, good times induce balancesheet adventuring. The process by which speculative finance increases, as a proportion of the total financing of business, leads to higher asset prices and to increased investment. This leads to an improvement in employment, output, and business profits, which in turn proves to businessmen and bankers that experimenting with speculative finance was correct. Such deviation-amplifying reactions are characteristic of unstable systems—and thus of our economy.

The multi-billion-dollar corporations, which dominate our economy, borrow in a wide array of financial markets and from many different institutions in order to carry out their operations and fulfill their financial contracts. In such a complex network of debt, the day-to-day financial operations of any unit with short-term debt can be characterized as the financing and refinancing of positions, namely, they "do what banks do." In our economy, nonfinancial corporations have many of the liability management attributes of banks.

Any prudent unit engaging in speculative finance will have alternative financing facilities available, including some backup financing in case some primary channel either becomes too expensive or is no longer available. These backup channels function as their proximate lenders of last resort. However, these special lenders of last resort have to be able to withstand a surge of demand for financing. In order to be able to do this, they in turn need some fallback source that will finance an increase in their assets.

The Federal Reserve System is the ultimate fallback source of financing in the U.S. economy, even though the proximate fallback source may be some special government agency like the FDIC or a private consortium of typically giant, commercial banks. The Federal Reserve makes it unnecessary for firms and financial institutions that cannot refinance their positions to try to raise cash by selling assets or borrowing at highly penal rates. Federal Reserve lender-of-last-resort actions, directly or indirectly, set floors under the prices of assets or ceilings on financing terms, thus socializing some of the risks involved in speculative finance. But such socialization of risks in financial markets encourages risk-taking in financing positions in capital assets, which, in turn increases the potential for instability when carried out for an extended period.

THE LENDER-OF-LAST-RESORT FUNCTION

The Federal Reserve was given the responsibility of assuring a flexible currency so that it could carry out its original mandate to act as lender of last resort. Federal Reserve currency is therefore readily available to substitute for bank deposits in the portfolios of households and businesses whenever a 'run on banks occurs. In substituting Federal Reserve deposits or notes for customers' deposits, Federal Reserve banks acquire assets that banks had acquired in financing commerce and production, thus refinancing qualified institutions and markets.

By such refinancing, the lender of last resort short-circuits the need of the institution in difficulty to acquire funds by selling out its position in financial and real assets, which can lead to sharp declines in asset values. Such declines can lead to insolvency, not only for the institutions initially affected, but also for other institutions holding such assets. Lender-of-last-resort interventions prevent the value of assets owned by financial institutions from falling so far that general loss of liquidity or a widespread inability to sustain the face value of deposits and other debts occurs. These interventions ensure that the losses incurred by a bank or other institution when its assets fall in market value will not be passed through to the depositors at the bank. In this way, lender-of-last-resort operations, undertaken to prevent the amplification of particular losses by setting floors under the value of assets, socialize some of the private risks that exist in an economy in which borrowing and lending are important.

Unless the economy is such that depression-inducing financial instability would occur from time to time in the absence of Federal Reserve intervention, the Federal Reserve System is largely superfluous. The Federal Reserve was set up in the years just before World War I because it was felt that the malfunctioning that had frequently taken place in the economy before and after the turn of the century had been caused by the instability of the financial system, as exhibited in a series of panics and crises culminating in the Knickerbocker Trust Crisis of 1907. The absence of a well-reasoned economic theory accounting for the origin of financial panics and crises was no barrier to the creation of the Federal Reserve, because the existence of financial instability was there for all to see.

Only one serious full-blown financial crisis—in 1929–33—has occurred since the Federal Reserve System was organized. At that time, the malfunctioning of the economy was attributed in part to imperfections of the financial system. One response to the crisis was the reform of the banking structure and the Federal Reserve System. Another response was the introduction of new institutions such as the FDIC and the Securities and Exchange Commission (SEC) to regulate banks and financial practices.

From the 1930s to the early 1960s, no serious financial disturbances took place. Because of the financial assets and liquidity inherited from World War II, the significantly larger size of the federal government (the result of the cold war and various transfer payment schemes), and some positive uses of fiscal policy to run deficits when needed, the United States, Japan, and the industrialized countries of Western Europe achieved a significantly closer approximation to full employment over a sustained period of time (twenty years) than they had ever achieved before. Occasional mild recessions took place, inflation at modest rates persisted, and sectoral problems such as increasing youth unemployment (especially black) in the United States emerged. But on the whole the economies seemed to be working well. Indeed, their success led to the resurrection of economic doctrines that held that a capitalist economy would tend, by its own workings, to establish full employment. This view was buttressed by the flowering of mathematical economics that "proved" in a rigorous way that, albeit under heroic assumptions, a decentralized market mechanism would lead to a coherent result. The heroic assumptions ruled out the existence of money, time, uncertainty, and expensive capital assets (i.e., the "economy" of economic theory differs in essential ways from that of our economy).[2]

There were mild deviations from full employment during the transitory era of stability that ruled from 1946 to 1966, but they were imputed either to errors of fine-tuning by those who held that fiscal intervention was needed (the conventional Keynesians) or to errors of money-supply control by those who held that fiscal intervention was not needed (the emerging

---

2. See Paul Davidson, *Money and the Real World*. For the length that neoclassical theorists have to go, in the sense of artificial assumptions, when they try to deal with these problems, see Frank H. Hahn, *Money and Inflation* (Cambridge: MIT Press, 1983).

monetarists). Neither of these two competing schools of analysis and policy advice accepted that there were economic processes at work within a capitalist economy with a sophisticated financial system that tend to generate first an inflationary expansion and then conditions conducive to financial instability.

The economic theory of the 1950s and 1960s—and the lack of a financial crisis during those years—so constrained the thinking of mainstream economists that the possible development of financial instability, and thus the need for the Federal Reserve to function as lender of last resort, was ignored. As a result, the standard economic theory of the late 1960s and the early 1970s offered no guidelines to the Federal Reserve and the fiscal authorities as to how and when lender-of-last-resort functions should be carried out to abort the development of a serious crisis and as to how the inflationary side effects of such intervention should be minimized.

One facet of lender-of-last-resort responsibilities deals with the emergency action taken when a crisis is a clear and present danger. This involves operations that replace private liabilities with Federal Reserve liabilities and the absorption of private losses by the Federal Reserve or other agencies. The need for this type of action is intermittent—six such interventions have taken place since 1965. The second facet of the Federal Reserve's lender-of-last-resort action follows from the right of an insurer to require reasonable and prudent behavior of the insuree. If a lender of last resort agrees to pick up the pieces in case of a problem, it has a right and a responsibility to control and prevent business practices that tend either to create or to worsen financial crises.

The Federal Reserve control over stock market margin requirements and the fully amortized fixed-term mortgage were introduced in the aftermath of the Great Depression because the thinking of the day imputed the developments of 1929–33 to excessive stock market speculation and the short-term nature of the standard mortgage.[3] In recent years, we have seen many institutional changes in banking and finance. These changes have been permitted even though the authorities have no theory enabling them to determine whether the changes taking place in financial practices tend to increase or to decrease the overall stability of the financial system.[4]

---

3. See *Debts and Recovery, 1929–1937* (New York: The Twentieth Century Fund, 1938).

4. Paul Meek, *U.S. Monetary Policy and Financial Markets* (New York: Federal Reserve Bank, 1982). See also Thomas J. Cahiil and Gillian G. Garcia, *Financial Deregulation and Monetary Control* (Stanford: Hoover Institution Press, 1982).

In the absence of such a theory, the authorities ignored the evolution of bank position making from asset management to liability management and saw no significance in the explosive growth of financial institutions with speculative liability structures with which banks were seriously involved, such as REITs. Today's fashionable economic theory argues that markets are stable and efficient. This puts the Federal Reserve under pressure to allow financial practices to evolve in response to "market forces." A permissive attitude toward banking and financial market structure is now dominant.[5]

Central banking in the United States includes not only the Federal Reserve System but also assorted regulatory agencies such as the FDIC, the SEC, and the Comptroller of the Currency, as well as consortia of private banks. If this complex of organizations is to prevent and control financial instability, its actions must be guided by an economic theory that allows financial instability to be a result of the functioning of financial markets in a capitalist economy. Unless a theory can define the conditions in which a phenomenon occurs, it offers no guide to the control or elimination of the phenomenon.

BANKING USAGES

The ways in which commercial banks finance business, households, and government units determine the composition of bank assets, which—along with the liabilities banks use to finance their activity—determine both how lender-of-last-resort operations can be carried out and the economic effect of such operations. One important change since the 1920s in the way funds are supplied to banks is the reversal in the relative importance of Federal Reserve discount and open-market operations. When commercial banks relied on the discount window for a sizable proportion of their reserve position, the Federal Reserve was involved in regular, everyday banking relations with member banks. But once the Federal Reserve's main reserve-supplying activity consisted of buying and selling securities on the open market, it stopped having intimate and continuing business relations with member banks.

If the Federal Reserve acts as a normal-functioning supplier of funds to banks through the discount window, then as long as banks value this source of funds they will conform to business and balance-sheet standards

---

5. The bankruptcy and subsequent covert nationalization of Continental Illinois in 1984 led to a temporary muting of the call for greater permissiveness and less regulation in banking.

set down by the Reserve banks. On the other hand, if Federal Reserve credit is supplied to banks by means of open-market operations in government securities, then the customer relationship between a member bank and the Federal Reserve loses its power to affect member-bank behavior. The power of the Federal Reserve to affect member-bank behavior through normal banking relations was much diminished after World War II. This diminution of Federal Reserve clout, to use a concept drawn from Chicago politics, was not offset by an increased sophistication of Federal Reserve examination and regulation of banks.

To elaborate this point, the 1913 Federal Reserve Act envisaged that both the lender-of-last-resort function and some of the normal-functioning supply of reserves would be carried out through the discount window at the district Federal Reserve banks. In the gold-standard world, for which the act was written, a primary source of bank reserves was specie. In addition, bank reserves were also created as the Federal Reserve banks acquired assets by discounting loans submitted by member banks. As a result, the Federal Reserve banks were part of a hierarchical system in which commercial banks lent to the public (business, government, and households), and the Federal Reserve lent to commercial banks. If, as in the 1920s, bank borrowing from the Federal Reserve through the discount window is an important source of total bank reserves, then the interest rate set by the Federal Reserve for its lending operations is an important determinant of the financing terms that commercial banks offer. The control of borrowing terms by Federal Reserve banks affects the terms on which banks can profitably lend to their customers.[6]

The instrument used in central bank operations through the discount window (the eligible paper) resulted from commercial bank lending to business customers. Typically such business debt, even if secured, as the 1913 theory required, has a poor, if not nonexisting, secondary or resale market, and could not, prior to the creation of the Federal Reserve System, be readily negotiated if a bank required funds. By making an entire set of business paper owned by banks at least a conditionally liquid asset, the Federal Reserve System increased the liquidity of the financial system. This in turn changed the acceptable asset and liability structures of banks. One result was the boom of the 1920s, and because of the financial practices that developed during the boom, the series of crises that ran from 1929 through the winter of 1933.

---

6. W. Randolph Burgess, *The Reserve Banks and the Money Market* (New York: Harper, 1927).

The Great Depression and the postwar era saw a substitution of government debt for business loans owned by banks as the instrument used in Federal Reserve day-to-day operations. After the debacle of the 1930s, discounting at the Federal Reserve no longer provided the mass of bank reserves that did not reflect specie owned by the Federal Reserve. In the later period, the mass of non-specie-based bank reserves was due to the ownership of government securities. Instead of Federal Reserve normal operations taking the form of setting the terms on which it would rediscount for a member bank, normal operations now mainly center on the purchase and sale of government debt on an open market. This means that Federal Reserve operations undertaken to affect bank reserves no longer use the same markets and instruments as lender-of-last-resort operations. In the 1913 model, lender-of-last-resort operations and the control of bank lending were both operated through the discount window. In the years since the Great Depression, the control of bank lending has been operated by means of open-market operations, and, until 1966, there was no need for active intervention by the Federal Reserve System to prevent serious financial instability. Since 1966, however, in the episodes of financial instability, the discount window was again used when the Federal Reserve had lender-of-last-resort responsibilities thrust upon it.

The evolution of banking practices and the shift from discounting to open-market operations have eliminated the normal-functioning banking-asset basis of relations between the Federal Reserve and member banks. The Federal Reserve is thus not acting on the basis of the intimate knowledge of banking practices that would result if banks were normally borrowing from the Federal Reserve. The Federal Reserve has an implicit obligation to protect bank depositors from losses, but it has little power to prevent bank practices that may force it to acquire assets from banks in order to protect deposits. It also has an explicit obligation to assure the availability of adequate financing to business.

LENDER-OF-LAST-RESORT CONCEPTS

In recent years monetarism has impinged on the consciousness and guided the actions of politicians, pundits, the public, and the personnel of the Federal Reserve itself. As a result, the view has grown that the sole function of the Federal Reserve is to control the performance of the economy by controlling the money supply, however defined. In this view, the Federal

Reserve is held to be virtually all-powerful in determining, albeit indirectly, income, employment, and price levels; it seems that a state of perpetual economic bliss would result if the Federal Reserve would only get its open-market operations right. In fact, the Federal Reserve is not that powerful in determining the money supply, and the money supply does not control income. In the short run, market behavior dominates Federal Reserve actions in determining the effect of finance on income, while in the longer run the introduction of new financial usages and the evolution of both new and old financial practices rule the roost.

While the Federal Reserve is not able to determine the short-run path of money, income, employment, and prices, it is always able to substitute claims on itself for other claims in the money market, in bank portfolios, and in the hands of the public. Claims on the Federal Reserve are always introduced into portfolios of banks, businesses, and households in an exchange for some claim owned or created by a government, bank, business, or household unit. The terms on which the Federal Reserve is willing and able to make such exchanges set a floor on the price of the items the Federal Reserve might acquire. If there is a significant excess supply of some instrument in a market, be it a government bond, private commercial paper, bank loan, bank deposit, or capital asset, then the price of the instrument can fall markedly. In a world in which refinancing of positions is important, namely where there exists a significant volume of short-term debt, the ability of a borrower to meet financial commitments is thrown into question when the price of its instruments in the market falls markedly. If the Federal Reserve is willing and able to introduce claims on itself into the economy by purchasing such instruments and thus refinancing such borrowers, then a limit or floor price to such instruments is set.

The fixing of a minimum price of some financial instrument or real asset is an essential lender-of-last-resort action. The Federal Reserve is capable of being a lender of last resort as long as the basic money of the economy is a Federal Reserve liability, such as Federal Reserve notes or deposits at the Federal Reserve. The Federal Reserve is able to set a minimum price to some set of assets unless an actual or expected inflation leads to the loss of monetary power by the government. The value of Federal Reserve liabilities is based on the existence of substantial taxes, which must be paid in Federal Reserve liabilities to the government's account at the Federal Reserve. As long as the federal government is an effective taxing authority, as long as a major part of government expenditures are financed by taxes, and as long as the government "banks" at the Federal Reserve, conditions cannot arise in which Federal Reserve liabilities no longer function as money.[7] In these circumstances the Federal Reserve can be an effective lender of last resort.

Lender-of-last-resort powers provide the Federal Reserve with powerful medicine, but like most powerful medicines, they can have serious side effects. One is the lagged inflationary impact of increases in liquidity due to lender-of-last-resort operations. Every time the Federal Reserve and the institutions that act as specialized lenders of last resort extend their protection to a new set of institutions and a new set of instruments, the inflationary potential of the financial system is increased.

During the great contraction of 1929–33, the Federal Reserve failed to live up to the expectation that it would be an effective lender of last resort; as a result the FDIC was created. Over the postwar era, and most particularly after the commercial-paper fiasco of 1970, a quite formalized two-tier lender-of-last-resort structure emerged for the commercial-paper market. In this two-tier structure, the Federal Reserve System is the lender of last resort to member banks (particularly to giant member banks), and giant member banks are the lenders of last resort to the institutions and organizations that use the commercial-paper market. This two-tier market is formalized in the practice requiring units that sell commercial paper to have open lines of credit at commercial banks at least as large as their outstanding commercial paper.

When the FDIC arranges for a failed bank to be merged into another institution (e.g., the acquisition of Seafirst of Seattle by Bank of America), or when commercial banks refinance REITs, we see lender-of-last-resort operations in their contemporary dress. From a somewhat broader point of view, the lender-of-last-resort function is an extension of normal business refinancing arrangements. In Britain, lender-of-last-resort operations grew out of the normal banking process by which money market institutions financed part of their position at the Bank of England. Whereas in America a particular bank is the borrower, in Britain borrowing at the Bank of England takes place when a market has run into difficulties. In both cases, however, it is market phenomena that cause the need for the operation.

---

7. In truth the government fiscal posture must be in surplus from time to time or if appropriate situation arise for Federal Reserve money to be valuable, as long as Federal Reserve assets are mainly government debt. If Federal Reserve assets are mainly private business debt, Federal Reserve and bank money will be valuable as long as business earns sufficient profits to fulfill its obligations to banks. Note that in the bank/business relation there is a built in acceptable rate of non-fulfillment by business: the profit adequacy relates to business as a whole, not to each and every business.

The operations of the central bank as a lender of last resort are presumably not guided by the profitability of the transaction, but rather by the needs of financial markets and the economy. If the lender-of-last-resort function is decentralized so that commercial banks and the FDIC do part of the job, then it may be necessary for these organizations to act in a way that violates canons of good business practice. Commercial banks may be required to acquire paper that they really would rather not buy, banks may be required to make loans at concessionary terms, and the FDIC may be required to choose an expensive, or other than the least costly, way of liquidating a failed bank.

THE NEED FOR INSTITUTIONAL REFORM

The weakness of the banking and financial system was so evident in the fall of 1974 that Arthur Burns, then chairman of the Federal Reserve System, informed the American Bankers Association in October of his concern with "maintaining the soundness of our banking system." After noting that "questions have been raised about the strength of our nation's, and indeed the world's, banking system," Burns pinpointed five causes for his concern:

> first, the attenuation of the banking systems' base of equity capital; second, greater reliance on funds of a potentially volatile character; third, heavy loan commitments in relation to resources; fourth, some deterioration in the quality of assets; and, fifth, increased exposure to the larger banks to risks entailed in foreign exchange transactions and other foreign operations.

Burns concluded his talk by noting that "our regulatory system failed to keep pace with the need," and that "a substantial reorganization [of the regulatory machinery] will be required to overcome the problems inherent in the existing structural arrangement."[8]

---

8. A. E. Burns, talk to American Bankers Association, Oct. 1974. Released by Board of Governors, Federal Reserve System, Washington, D.C., Oct. 1974. Each of the weaknesses pinpointed by Burns in his 1974 talk was evident, perhaps in a more extreme form, in 1980–82.

The weaknesses that Burns pinpointed in the banking system were an out-growth of the way the banks and the financial system evolved over the entire postwar era. The critical weakness in Burns's analysis is that he imputes the difficulties he sees to either a laxness of regulatory zeal or, perhaps, some rather trivial mistake in how the regulatory bodies were organized, rather than to a fundamental behavioral characteristic of our economy.

But the 1974–75 weakness was the third since 1966 that required intervention, and it has been followed by three more such episodes. Because the problems of these incipient crises resemble the financial instability that regularly plagued the economy before World War II, the Federal Reserve needs to recognize that instability is a fundamental characteristic of an economy with financial institutions such as those of the United States. That is, the theory that guides Federal Reserve behavior must admit the possibility that financial crises are the result of factors that are internal to the working of our economy.

In the following sections, to illustrate how the hierarchical organization of the lender-of-last-resort function worked in 1974–75, we will first look at what happened to banks, with particular emphasis on developments in the Franklin National Bank, and then at developments at a peculiar set of financial institutions—REITs. The examination of REITs is worthwhile because they are creatures of the explosively speculative 1970s. Furthemore, the way in which the crisis of the REITs was faced illustrates the problems inherent in the current hierarchical organization of the lender-of-last-resort function, for, in the current organization, what is done to effect a temporary resolution of one crisis-prone situation tends to breed another crisis-prone situation. Some of the problems of the commercial banks in 1975 and 1976 were the result of having acted as the residual, or backup, lender of REITs in 1974, when a massive run on REIT commercial paper took place.

An examination of the REITs episode shows how actions beyond the narrowly defined lender-of-last-resort functions are necessary to make weakened or infected institutions healthy again. The need to act as a lender of last resort and to protect other institutions that do part of the job ties the hands of the Federal Reserve with respect to operations supposedly aimed at the control of income, employment, and prices. Successful lender-of-last-resort operations can result in subsequent inflation, possibly at an accelerating rate, because the debts that caused the trouble are now in another private portfolio, and if these private portfolios are to he made healthy, then the underlying cash flows have to increase. And one way to increase these cash flows is to finance an inflationary expansion. Inasmuch as the successful execution of lender-of-last-resort functions extends the domain of Federal

Reserve guarantees to new markets and to new instruments, there is an inherent inflationary bias to these operations; by validating the past use of an instrument, an implicit guarantee of its future value is extended. Unless the regulatory apparatus is extended to control, constrain, and perhaps even forbid the financing practices that caused the need for lender-of-last-resort activity, the success enjoyed by these interventions in preventing a deep depression will be transitory; with a lag, another situation requiring intervention will occur.

The need for lender-of-last-resort intervention follows from an explosive growth of speculative finance and the way in which speculative finance leads to a crisis-prone situation. To avoid this, institutional reforms that constrain corporate external finance and the capabilities of banks and other financial institutions to support explosive situations may be needed.

THE BANK FAILURES OF 1973–75: THE MECHANISM OF "CENTRAL BANKING" AS THE LENDER OF LAST RESORT

The recession of 1973–75 was accompanied by the largest burst of bank failures since the Great Depression of the 1930s. Dollar figures, however, do not mean what they used to, especially in banking. Not only have economic growth and inflation infected the dollar figures, but there has been a significant move toward giant and branch banking since World War II. Nevertheless, the fact that four of the banks that required special intervention in 1973–75 had more than $1 billion in assets and that the Franklin National Bank was, by a factor of two or three, the largest bank that had failed up to then are impressive indicators of the magnitude of the problem. The four billion-dollar-problem banks of 1974–75 were the United States National Bank of San Diego, which was declared insolvent on October 18, 1973; the Franklin National Bank of New York, which was closed on October 8, 1974; the Security National Bank of New York, which was merged in early 1975 to abort a failure; and the billion-dollar Commonwealth Bank of Detroit, which was sustained by extraordinary loans from the Federal Reserve. In addition to the size of the banks, it is worth noting that the Franklin National was at least a peripheral Wall Street (money-market) bank.

During this period, failed and nearly failed banks were merged into another institution; they were not closed and liquidated. The FDIC either accepted a liability by guaranteeing some assets or infused cash in exchange for assets that the successor institution rejected. Although the legal liability of the FDIC for deposits is given by a ceiling set in legislation, the merging of failed banks into solvent institutions means that all of the deposits in the failed banks are honored.

The Franklin National Bank and the Security National Bank were both based in Long Island, and the failure of the Franklin National Bank induced some of the difficulties experienced by the Security National Bank. The difficulties of the Franklin National affected business and asset values on Long Island and thus further weakened the already poor position of the Security National.

In addition to the failure of billion-dollar banks, there was a spate of other bank failures and banks "in difficult circumstances" in the years after 1974. In 1975 thirteen banks failed, and in the first ten months of 1976 fourteen banks failed. None of these banks was in the billion-dollar class, but their assets ranged from $100 to $475 million. By way of contrast, in 1969—a previous period of financial disturbances—the largest of the nine banks that either folded or had their deposits assumed by another bank had only $11.4 million in deposits. The situation in 1974–76 was substantially different from that which ruled in earlier years.

From the beginning of deposit insurance in 1934 up through 1974, some 506 banks with deposits totaling $3.6 billion failed. In the years 1934–72, 496 banks folded with deposits of $1.1 billion. During the two years (1973 and 1974) in which the National Bank of San Diego and the Franklin National Bank failed, the total deposits of all FDIC-assisted bank closures were more than twice as large as the deposits in failed banks in the agencies' first thirty-eight years.[9]

In bank examination, loans are classified according to whether or not the examining body sees any problems with them. The relation between the dollar amount of problem loans and the total of bank capital funds determines whether a bank is classified as a problem bank; such banks are more closely supervised by the regulatory authorities than banks not considered to be problems. Toward the end of 1975 and early in 1976, the formal lists

---

9. Note that the data on failed banks exclude cases such as the Security National Bank, which was "merged," or the Continental Illinois, which was refinanced and normalized. Furthermore, a bank such as the Franklin National enters the data with the assets on the date of failure rather than with the assets before a partial liquidation takes place while the Federal Reserve is sustaining the walking bankrupt.

of problem banks kept by the authorities became public. A number of the leading banks, including such giants as Chase Manhattan of New York, the third-largest in the country, were revealed to be on the list.

Neither the bank failures nor the publicity about the problems that identified banks were having set off a cumulative debt-deflation process. The way in which the Franklin National Bank situation was handled by the Federal Reserve, as well as the way in which the difficulties of smaller banks were taken care of, meant that situations that would have triggered runs on financial institutions in earlier epochs failed to do so in 1975–76. The various failures were accordingly interpreted by historians and analysts as isolated incidents rather than as symptoms of systemic collapse.

THE TECHNIQUE USED

The effective way in which lender-of-last-resort powers were used successfully prevented a cumulative reaction in 1974–75. Losses on assets by banks, financial institutions, and corporations were either absorbed by government agencies such as the Federal Reserve and the FDIC or covered up by keeping institutions liquid even though the fair market valuation of their assets implied a negative net worth.[10] For example, the values of assets on the books of insolvent institutions were kept at their historic costs, rather than at their lower current market values, so that their books would show a positive net worth, enabling them to continue to accept deposits and sell liabilities (i.e., positions could be refinanced). The technique used by the Federal Reserve and the FDIC in aiding failed and failing banks, which validated all of the banks' liabilities, made the refinancing of problem institutions possible.

A significant number of bank debtors, especially the REITs, whose debts were acquired by banks when they were unable to sell commercial paper, were unable to pay even the contractual interest rates on their debts, let alone to repay the principal amounts due in 1974, 1975, and 1976. Although these organizations were in default, formal bankruptcy was avoided, instead, plans were adopted to "work out" the debt. This meant that banks acquired real estate and development land in exchange for bank debts, and

---

10. In the case of the Financial Corporation of America in 1984–85 it was recognized by the institutions and the authorities that all that was necessary was to keep an organization liquid. See *Wall Street Journals*, March 9, 1985.

also that interest rates and terms to maturity on REIT debts were set so as to be consistent with their low expected cash receipts. The difference between market interest rates and the interest paid accrued as debt of the REIT.

Such work-out schemes usually involved the creditors keeping the debtor under tight control; the creditors have a Frequent opportunity to pull out of the restructuring deal and force bankruptcy. In some ways the restructuring approach to insolvent and illiquid debtors can be interpreted as a means by which the banks and other creditors can control the time when they elect to recognize losses and include them in their income statements and balance sheets. This approach meant that the various financial difficulties that appeared in 1973–75 were handled in different ways, depending on the special institutions involved.

In each case, the Federal Reserve, because it has the ultimate weapon for validating a debt structure—namely the ability to create Federal Reserve liabilities—had to play an overt or covert role, often substituting its liabilities for those of private banks or other private borrowers. But the Federal Reserve's power to create money need not be used in every instance; a lender-of-last-resort problem can be handled indirectly by letting it be known that Federal Reserve credit would be available if necessary. It is important to emphasize that, because the Federal Reserve System is directly or indirectly the lender of last resort to the financial system as it exists, any constraint placed on Federal Reserve flexibility (e.g., by mandating mechanical rules of behavior) attenuates its power to act. Rules cannot substitute for lender-of-last-resort discretion.

On the other hand, the FDIC is by law responsible for the insured deposits at a failed bank. This amount is now $100,000 per account, but it was $20,000 at the time of the failures under discussion. In the giant bank failures of 1973–75, however, the FDIC found a presumably sound bank that would assume the nonequity liabilities of the failed institution and acquire those assets of the impaired institution that it deemed "good." This deposit-assumption technique requires that the FDIC acquire the "bad" assets of the failed institution and give the successor institution cash for the deficient assets, which validates all nonequity liabilities in the impaired institution. The technique used by the FDIC in 1973–75 effectively insured *all* deposits, including deposits at *overseas* branches, rather than the amount set by legislation.

The journey of a bank to failure takes time, unless the failure occurs as a result of discovered fraud. The San Diego National Bank, which failed in October 1973, was a serious problem bank at least one year before its closing. The Franklin National Bank was closed on October 8, 1974, but its extreme difficulties were public knowledge in May 1974. Given the public nature of much bank data and the knowledge that banks necessarily have of one another's position (because of interbank loans and the market in Certificates of Deposits), a run will quickly take place on a bank known or believed to be in difficulty.

In a modern banking environment, bank runs are much more polite affairs than in earlier times, when clamoring crowds would gather outside a bank in distress to exchange deposits for currency. In modern banking, with deposit insurance, the individual retail deposit is fully insured by the FDIC, which means that an individual depositor with a fully insured account in a failed bank only risks a possible day or so delay in obtaining his funds. As a result, retail depositors do not clamor for cash at a bank in difficulty.[11]

Other depositors in a bank that fails will be carrying compensating deposits for credit lines or credit used. If the credit line has been drawn on, then the depositor has an offsetting debt to the bank. In this case, the failure of the bank will cause at most temporary inconvenience and perhaps embarrassment as the borrower seeks new credit sources. Business organizations (i.e., those who have the option) always try to have alternative sources of financing. Once a bank's difficulties surface, its business borrowers will expand their existing capacity to borrow funds from alternative sources and open new financing channels. Even if the bank survives the public crisis it will lose customers.

The large debts of banks (corporate deposits, $100,000 and over negotiable certificates of deposit [CDs], repurchase agreements, and borrowings on the federal funds markets [interbank overnight loans]) are presumably at risk if a bank's liabilities exceed its assets. Once a bank's difficulties become apparent, it cannot place any more of these market-oriented liabilities, and federal-fund borrowings will run off (unless some "Central Bank" guarantee exists). As the outstanding liabilities fall due, the weakened bank cannot sell or place substitutes; it cannot roll over its debts, so it cannot refinance its position through the market. The only place where funds can be obtained to meet clearing losses and refinancing failures is at the discount window of its Federal Reserve Bank.

The first step on the road to failure is thus market awareness of the difficulties facing a bank, which leads to a run in the form of the nonrenewal

---

11. In 1985 old fashioned runs, with clamoring crowds at the doors, look place on thrift institutions in Ohio and Maryland that were insured by private and state funds. Such runs occurred because a lack of confidence in the solvency of the state insurance fund developed.

of CDs, inability to sell federal funds, and problems in executing repurchase agreements that can be offset only by borrowing at the Federal Reserve. Quite quickly, then, a substantial part of the total liabilities of a large bank in distress becomes debts to its regional Federal Reserve Bank. Only later, when the bank failure becomes overt, will the FDIC enter the picture.

It should be pointed out that the debts to the Federal Reserve System almost always carry a lower interest rate than money-market obligations. The nonpenal character of the Federal Reserve's discount rate thus represents a subsidy to a failing bank. During a run, the Federal Reserve acquires "clean" assets of the bank under pressure, while "suspect" assets remain in the bank's portfolio. Once a bank is acknowledged as insolvent, the FDIC steps in to validate all or some of the deposits, depending on whether the FDIC acts via the merger or the liquidation route. In any event, the handling of a bank failure, unless it is a small bank and a simple case of fraud uncovered by the examination procedure, requires the cooperation and coordination of the Federal Reserve System and the FDIC.

While there are political, organizational, competence, and historical reasons for separating the Federal Reserve System and the FDIC, there is clearly no economic rationale for the separation. Before a large bank fails, it is likely that market awareness would have forced the foundering institution into the arms of the Federal Reserve, but if a Federal Reserve Bank refuses to accomodate a failing bank, then the FDIC will have to rush in and make good by infusing resources into the bank. The FDIC might very well require loans or accommodating open-market operations by the Federal Reserve System if it is to do this: the FDIC never has a billion dollars of cash on hand. No matter what route is taken when a major bank fails, the Federal Reserve must play an important role as the various lender-of-last-resort steps are taken.

Given the primacy of the Federal Reserve in making lender-of-last-resort operations possible, the FDIC should be more clearly integrated with the Federal Reserve than it currently is. It should, perhaps, be a semi-autonomous subsidiary. Certainly the bank-examination aspects of the FDIC and the Federal Reserve should be integrated, especially if inputs from bank examinations are to become part of an early warning system for problem banks.[12]

---

12. Hyman P. Minsky, "Suggestions for a Cash Flow Oriented Bank Examination," *Proceedings of a Conference on Bank Structure and Competition*, Federal Reserve Bank of Chicago, 1975.

THE FAILURE OF THE FRANKLIN NATIONAL BANK

At the end of 1973, the Franklin National Bank was the twentieth-largest bank in the United States, with assets of approximately $5 billion. On October 8, 1974, it was declared insolvent, and its deposits were assumed by the European American Bank. On that date its total assets were $3.6 billion, of which some $1.7 billion was financed by borrowings at the Federal Reserve Bank of New York.

As the Franklin National's bankruptcy did not cause a panic, although the deep drop of the economy in 1974–75 and the subsequent incomplete recovery may, in part, be due to its failure, the lender-of-last-resort intervention by the Federal Reserve can be viewed as having been carried out in good fashion. In executing this operation, the Federal Reserve enabled the Franklin National to meet its obligations to depositors in its overseas branches. It extended to deposits at overseas branches the protection that the Federal Reserve and the FDIC offer to domestic deposits.

The Franklin National Bank was in fact three banks under one corporate umbrella:[13] a retail bank on Long Island; a wholesale bank in New York City; and an overseas branch in London, opened in 1969. The funds of the London bank were bought, often at a premium, in the London market and were used to make loans in the Eurodollar market. These loans were often made at narrow interest-rate spreads above the cost of money. By the end of 1973, Franklin National had about $1 billion in deposits at its London branch, another $1.4 billion in its New York wholesale branch, and some $2.6 billion of assets in its retail (mainly) Long Island operation.

The problems of the Franklin National did not suddenly come about in 1974. As early as December 1972 examiners had classified $193 million out of a loan portfolio of $1,821 million as substandard. Classified loans thus represented 10.6 percent of the total. In June 1974, as the run on the Franklin National was under way, classified loans rose slightly to 12.7 percent of the total. The weak performance of the bank's domestic loan portfolio was of great significance in leading the bank to bankruptcy.

The Franklin National's weak position is underlined by its earnings record. Even before its problem surfaced, the Franklin National's earnings as a percentage of total assets were low. In 1970, this ratio was 0.66 percent, at a time when other large banks were earning 0.98 percent on assets.

---

13. See Brimmer, *International Finance and the Management of Bank Failures*, op. cit.

By 1972 the Franklin National was earning but 0.30 percent on assets, whereas the other large New York banks were earning 0.78 percent. A 0.30 percent return per dollar of assets does not leave much room for error or profit erosion. As the economy entered a regime of double-digit inflation and double-digit interest rates, the asset values, cash flows, and liquidity of the Franklin National were adversely affected. In these circumstances, by early 1974 the Franklin National's earnings evaporated.

In 1972 controlling interest in the Franklin National was acquired by a Luxembourg corporation controlled by Michele Sindona, an Italian banker. The purchase price was some $40 million for 21 percent of the Franklin National Bank. For $40 million, Sindona gained control of some $5 billion of assets, $125 of assets for every dollar of investment. In a bank in which the management and the board of directors own but a small percentage of the stock, as was true in the Franklin National's case, the ratio of the management's financial involvement to the total assets managed can become minute. In these circumstances, unless the integrity of management is beyond reproach, the possibility that bank assets can be conveyed to the managers should be a major concern of the authorities.

The developments that led to the Franklin National Bank's precarious position can be traced. On May 3, 1974, just prior to the public announcement of the passing of a dividend, the Franklin National had $4.7 billion in assets. Of its total liabilities, some $.9 billion were borrowed overseas, and some $1.3 billion were owed to the New York money market. At this date, it had zero borrowing from the Federal Reserve, and the foreign branch was actually furnishing a trivial amount ($7 million) to the home office.

On May 17, 1974, soon after the bank's difficulties became public, total assets were down some $400 million. Money-market liabilities were $600 million, a drop of some $700 million in two weeks, and deposits at the foreign branch were down $160 million. The foreign branch now owed the head office some $100 million. To offset these run-offs and the erosion of other deposits, the Franklin National borrowed $960 million from the Federal Reserve.

The banking community's lack of confidence in the Franklin National is evident from the behavior of both its federal-funds and its due-to-banks accounts. On May 3 the Franklin National showed a $500 million federal funds liability and a $300 million due-to-banks liability. On May 17 federal-funds borrowings were zero, and the due-to-banks account was down to $13 million. There was also some run-off of domestic time deposits in these first two weeks of crisis.

From May 17 until its closing, the Franklin National Bank became increasingly dependent on the Federal Reserve Bank. By the end of July, the Franklin National was borrowing some $1.4 billion at the Federal Reserve, and some $350 million of liabilities of the foreign branch were owed to the home office. Domestic demand and time deposits had shrunk to $1.2 billion from the $1.8 billion of May 3, 1974. As a result of the obvious protection being given the institution by the Federal Reserve, it was able to raise some funds through the federal-funds market.

When the Franklin National Bank was finally declared insolvent on October 8, its total assets were down to $3.6 billion, a drop of almost 25 percent from the $4.7 billion of five months earlier, when its troubles became public. Of its total liabilities at closing, $1.7 billion was to the Federal Reserve discount window. The combination of a $1.1 billion drop in total assets and a rise of $1.7 billion in debt due to the Federal Reserve meant that an enormous run-off of private liabilities of the Franklin National was affected.

As a purely technical operation, the refinancing of the Franklin National by the Federal Reserve Bank of New York was beautifully carried out. There was no visible general panic and flight from either the Eurodollar market or from bank CDs. This relative calm existed in spite of the nearly simultaneous failure of a large German bank in June 1974.[14] The near simultaneity of two international bank failures would have caused panic in international financial markets except for the fact that the Federal Reserve was, in effect, validating the deposits in the London office of the Franklin National Bank, thus preventing a serious run from developing on the European offices of other American banks whose exposure to both domestic and overseas losses was considered high. A run on the overseas deposits of one of these larger banks would have generated an overall market panic, which, if it had gone unchecked, would have brought about conditions conducive to a deep depression.

It may have been correct for the Federal Reserve to protect the depositors in the Franklin National's overseas operations. What was amiss in the developments of 1974, however, was that, after protecting the economy against the worst possible consequences of the run on the Franklin National, the Federal Reserve did not propose significant reforms of the overseas operations of American banks.

---

14. Ibid.

THE REITS AND THE GIANT COMMERCIAL BANKS AS LENDERS OF LAST RESORT

REITs were the boom financial industry of the early 1970s. These organizations are a creature of the tax laws—if they pay 90 percent of their earnings in dividends, they do not have to pay a corporate income tax. Although REITs could and did own property, own mortgages, or finance construction, the major difficulties in 1974 centered on the REITs that financed construction.[15]

As recently as 1968, the total assets of REITs were about $1 billion. They grew to about $14 billion in 1972, a compound annual growth rate of 93 percent over the four years. In 1973 total assets continued to rise strongly to $20.2 billion, a 45 percent increase over 1972, but at the end of 1974 their growth slowed. In that year the assets of REITs stood at $21.2 billion, an increase of only 5 percent, and at the end of 1975 they dropped to $19.5 billion.

Although a REIT could wholly own and operate real estate, that was a rarity; the REITs that financed construction were heavily indebted. Since these REITs, like other financial businesses, work with other people's money, their profits depend on the difference between the return on assets and the costs due to liabilities. As the REIT business exploded in the early 1970s, the industry depended ever more heavily on short-term financing; this made profits and the market value of REIT equity shares vulnerable to run ups in interest rates.

Table 3.1 gives the balance sheets of REITS over the 1972–75 period. The changes in these balance sheets indicate some of the dimensions of the crisis that REITs faced. In 1972 some 36.6 percent of the $13.9 billion of assets was financed by equity, whereas in 1973 the figure dropped to only 28.7 percent of the then $20 billion of assets (25 percent in 1974). Thus, the boom, which peaked in 1974, was accompanied by increasing leverage.

At the same time, the debt structure of REITs underwent marked changes. In 1972 bank loans were 21.6 percent and open-market paper was

---

15. The factual information used here comes from Joseph F. Sinkey, Jr., *A Look at the REIT Industry and Its Relationships with Commercial Banks*, Federal Deposit Insurance Corporation, Banking and Economic Research Section, Division of Research, Washington, D.C., 1976. The interpretation is mine.

Table 3.1:   REITs, 1972–75 (Billions of Dollars)

	1972	1973	1974	1975
Physical assets	2.5	3.2	4.3	6.9
Multi-family structures	.8	1.1	1.4	2.3
Nonresidential structures	1.7	2.2	2.9	4.7
Total financial assets	11.4	17.0	16.9	12.6
Home mortgages	2.8	4.1	4.4	3.5
Multi-family mortgages	2.9	3.7	3.9	3.3
Commercial mortgages	4.9	7.4	7.7	6.6
Miscellaneous assets	.8	1.9	.9	-1.2
Total assets	13.9	20.2	21.2	19.5
Credit-market instruments	8.8	14.4	16.0	15.7
Mortgages	1.2	1.5	1.6	1.9
Multi-family residential	.4	.5	.5	.6
Commercial	.8	1.0	1.1	1.3
Corporate bonds	1.4	1.9	2.1	2.2
Bank loans NEC	3.0	7.0	11.5	10.7
Open-marker paper	3.2	4.0	.7	.8
Equity (estimated)	5.1	5.8	5.2	3.8

SOURCE: Flow of Funds Data, Board of Governors of the Federal Reserve System.

23.0 percent of total assets; in 1973, however, bank loans increased to 34.7 percent, and open-market paper slid to 19.8 percent. Consequently, of the $6.3 billion increment in total assets that took place in 1973, some $4.0 billion was financed by bank loans and some $.8 billion was financed by open-market paper. It seems that the incremental financing during 1973 was much more speculative than the inherited liability structure; by the end of 1973 REITs were much more dependent on short-term financing than in 1972 or earlier. Furthermore, by 1973 the weight of construction financing in total REIT business had increased.

A decision to invest, and a decision to finance an investment program, is a decision to make payments as the work progresses. REITs were heavily involved in financing the construction of multifamily housing, condominium complexes, and commercial properties, which require short-term financing while the completion of the property or of units for sale is awaited. REITs borrowed short-term to obtain the funds for their construction loans.

Because of the nature of the output being financed, the borrowers have nothing of real value from the time a project is started until the time it is finished. A half-tiled swimming pool or two stories of a six-story apartment building are not worth very much. A decision to embark on such a construction project is equivalent to a commitment to a series of short-term loans by both the borrower and the lender; the money for the next step in the project has to be forthcoming on schedule. A REIT that is financing such projects has to acquire funds as they are needed and has to pay the going market rate at the time funds are acquired.

REITs make profits by charging more than they pay for money; such making on the carry, as it is called, is a characteristic of financial institutions. But the borrower constructing a condominium or apartment complex in Florida, California, or Colorado has no cash receipts until the units are sold or the apartment complex is finished and rented at some target occupancy rate, when take-out or permanent financing by, say, an insurance company will deliver funds that can then be used to pay off construction debts. During the construction period the borrower has no cash flow, but interest is falling due each period on the borrower's short-term debts. To handle this, projects are often financed by discounted notes that accrue interest income to the lender over their life.

Accrued income poses a dilemma for REITs. Income is accruing; they need to pay 90 percent of earnings in dividends to retain their tax advantage, but there is no cash flow. In these circumstances, the REITs have to borrow in order to pay dividends. The income of the contractor, and the payment of the discounted note to the REITs, is realized only as the permanent financing takes over when the construction project is sold or rented. Any increase in interest rates during the construction period and any delay in finishing the project or in selling or renting units raises the cost. Any increase in the long-term interest rates as the project is under way decreases the size of the mortgage that the expected rents, or the expected income of any potential buyer, can carry. This tends to lower the market price of the construction project as a finished capital asset. If both delays and an increase in short- and long-term interest rates take place, the possibility arises that the costs of the project may exceed its present market value: A present value reversal takes place in which construction costs exceed the value of the asset produced.

Borrowing in order to pay dividends is one form that Ponzi finance (which is described in detail in chapter 9) takes. The run-up of interest rates, construction delays, and excess supply of finished apartments that developed in 1974 so compromised the capital of the REITs that they found it difficult to sell commercial paper. REIT commercial paper fell from $4 billion in 1973 to less than $1 billion in 1974.

The only available source of funds to REITs in 1974 was the commercial banks, which in that year increased lending to REITs to $11.5 billion from the $7.0 billion at the end of 1973. Banks were accepting paper from institutions that could no longer sell their paper on the open market. Obviously, at some stage in this process even the bankers must have known that they were making loans to organizations whose creditworthiness was suspect. Making loans because of other than profit-making considerations is characteristic of lender-of-last-resort operations. When the commercial banks refinanced the REITs as the open market closed, they were acting as surrogate lenders of last resort.

Commercial bankers act as lenders of last resort either in their own longterm interest or under pressure from the central bank. Whether the Federal Reserve pressured banks to refinance REITs is not known. However, in 1970, when the Chrysler Corporation's financing arm was under money-market pressure, the Federal Reserve did let it be known that it looked favorably on the organization of a consortium to refinance the Chrysler unit.

On the other hand, such pressure may not have been necessary. The loans to big REITs were mostly from syndicates, and the giant banks involved in these syndicates had a mutual interest in not taking enforced losses at one fell swoop as the REITs proved unable to meet their obligations. Furthermore, they were concerned with the impact that REIT default would have on the value of other construction-related assets in their portfolios. Bankers may thus have viewed refinancing the REITs as the best thing to do; it would enable them to phase any losses they saw fit into the income statement to offset later income. Alternatively, the bankers could hope that a recovery in asset values, perhaps through inflation, would make loans to the REIT—or the property they acquired in restructuring the liabilities of REITs—worth at least as much as their book value.

The REIT episode is a classic speculative bubble. But the big crash that usually results did not take place, because institutional lenders refinanced the REITs and because the examining bodies went along with this business judgment. No matter how much the bank or the banking authorities may speak of the restructuring of loans, the true present value of the assets acquired by the refinancing banks may be substantially less than the value on the books. As a result of the REIT episode, commercial banks had weakened balance sheets and therefore increased vulnerability to disturbance after future speculative periods. The financial system was weaker than if the REIT bubble had not occurred. But in the short run, the economy was stronger than if the consequences had been damned and the REIT industry had been swept aside altogether.

1974–75 AS A CLASSIC EXERCISE

In many ways, 1974–75 can be considered as a classic example of the exercise of lender-of-last-resort responsibilities by the Federal Reserve System. In spite of public failures and widespread knowledge of possible further difficulties among important financial organizations, there was no crisis and no panic. There were plenty of sticky moments, units did go bankrupt, stock market prices did fall markedly, and a serious recession did take place. This recession was moderated and turned around by the income and financial repercussions of Big Government (discussed in chapter 2).

But the success of 1974–75 (and 1981–82) should not breed complacency. The events of these years show that, by its normal functioning, our economy breeds conditions conducive to financial crises and that the apt resolution of these crises depends on prompt and effective intervention by central bank organizations. If in such circumstances, effective action is not forthcoming, more serious financial and economic crises than those experienced in 1974–75 would occur.

The success achieved by the authorities in preventing a financial crisis from fully developing is not a free good. The way in which the Federal Reserve carried out its lender-of-last-resort function in the Franklin National Bank situation meant that Federal Reserve protection was explicitly extended to all overseas deposits at US.-chartered member banks. This extension of protection meant that after 1974 the international financial markets were given a green light for expansion. In particular, the massive growth of deposits in the foreign offices of giant U.S. banks after 1974 was facilitated by this protection. Thus, the success of 1974–75 planted the seeds for future difficulties, which came home with the chronic third world debt crisis of the 1980s. Similarly, the run on the commercial paper of REITs in 1974 was met by bank credit replacing open-market credit. In this process, the integrity of the commercial-paper market was sustained even as the commercial banks engaged in concessionary finance. Once again an institution and a usage were protected, but at the price of weakened bank portfolios.

The 1974–75 success in aborting the threat of a financial crisis and in containing the contraction in income and employment meant that the difficulties were not the signal for a wave of institutional reform. The end result of the 1974–75 experience was an extension in Federal Reserve protection, even as its power to prevent the emergence of crisis-prone situations was not enhanced. In effect, the responsibilities of the Federal Reserve were increased, but its power was not. Nothing in what happened in 1974–75, and in what has been done subsequently, diminished the likelihood that there will be another threat of a serious recession or even a mild depression down the road. As we now know, 1981–82 witnessed a more serious set of financial episodes that, as they dragged on through the 1980s, required more extensive lender-of-last-resort intervention than even 1974–75.

THE SKY HAS NOT FALLEN YET

The sharp drop in output and the explosive rise in unemployment in the third quarter of 1974 and the first quarter of 1975 were accompanied by the failure of Franklin National Bank, the troubles of the REITs, and a spate of business bankruptcies. It looked as if the economy was on the verge of a great depression; as if the sky were about to fall. But the disaster failed to occur. The combination of a massive government deficit (augmented by a tax rebate) and the lender-of-last-resort interventions contained the decline and quickly reversed the course of the economy.

In 1969–70, when the Penn-Central railroad collapsed and there was a run on the commercial-paper market, a combination of increased government deficits and lender-of-last-resort intervention contained the recession and sustained a recovery.

Two more episodes of threatened financial collapses that were contained by a combination of massive government deficits and lender-of-last-resort interventions have occurred since 1974–75—in 1979–80 and then in 1981–82. Following the 1974–75 intervention, a sustained recovery into a sharp inflation, which triggered a flight from the dollar—both internationally and domestically. In 1978–79 it seemed as if the dollar-centered international monetary systems were about to break down, as the dollar fell sharply against the other currencies. In the United States the flight took the form of a burst of investments in collectibles, a flurry of speculation in metals, and a rapid rise in household debts.

The Federal Reserve reacted by shifting policy so that the money supply rather than interest rates would be the proximate target of policy. This practical monetarism quickly led to a sharp rise in interest rates. As far as the international flight from the dollar was concerned, the Fed's actions conformed to the rules developed over the nineteenth century for the behavior of the Bank of England as the manager of a thin gold-reserve gold standard.[16]

---

16. R. S. Sayers, *Bank of England Operations (1890–1914)* (London: P. S. King & Sons, 1936).

The domestic flight from the dollar was broken by the high interest rates, which greatly increased the carrying costs of sterile assets like gold and silver, as well as the pay-off from holding short-term assets. A price for this policy shift—aside from a short six-month recession in 1980—was the threatened collapse of the Hunt fortune and Bache and Company,[17] the virtual bankruptcy of a major Pennsylvania bank, and the need for concessionary loans to Chrysler. These led to lender-of-last-resort interventions by the Federal Reserve, although the easing of interest rates was transitory.

Aside from the details of who failed and the nature of the organizations involved, the 1981–82 recession conforms quite remarkably to that of 1974–75. Once again there was a sharp decline in income and output and a dramatic rise in unemployment; once again there was a massive increase in deficits (the extreme Keynesian side of Reaganomics), once again there were both quiet trauma and spectacular declines, and once again there was a spate of lender-of-last-resort interventions by the Federal Reserve. Once again, as the unemployment and bankruptcies situations were getting worse, some six months after a major lender-of-last-resort intervention there was a sharp turnaround in income and employment. Once again the sky did not fall.

The 1981–82 recession and Federal Reserve intervention as well as the aftermath in 1983 and 1984 differed from the 1974–75 in the extent of the international involvement. The climactic events that led to Federal Reserve intervention as a lender of last resort were the collapse of a promotional bank (Penn Square) in Oklahoma and a run to the dollar, especially the collapse of the Mexican peso. It might well be argued that the shift to practical monetarism in 1979 was triggered by a run from the dollar and the abandonment of practical monetarism, for greater discretion, was triggered by a run to the dollar.

Even though the sky did not fall in 1982 and the recovery through early 1984 was almost spectacular, the sky is not wholly secure. Continuing problems of weakened financial institutions, including the spectacular tribulations of Continental Illinois Bank of Chicago, show that the economy is far from reattaining the largely tranquil progress of the first years after World War II. An evident endogenous coherence of the 1950s and early 1960s has been replaced by an apparent endogenous incoherence that has been contained by lender-of-last-resort interventions and the profit-sustaining repercussions of Big Government. As a result of the interventions a breakdown has not occurred.

---

17. Stephan Fey, *Beyond Greed* (New York: Penguin, 1983).

The lender-of-last-resort interventions and the massive government deficits that have succeeded in preventing the sky from falling are strong medicine. Strong medicine often has side effects. Furthermore, we know that the system can evolve so that medicine that was effective in one regime or one set of structures may not be effective in another. In order to examine these issues we need a theory of why our system is susceptible to threats of the sky falling and how particular policy interventions may be successful at one time and ineffective at others.

THE EMERGENCE
OF FINANCIAL
INSTABILITY IN
THE POSTWAR ERA

The debate about the proper organization of the monetary and financial system, which has been a continuing issue in U.S. history, was muted during the two decades of economic tranquility and progress after World War II. The economy's more than adequate performance and the unusual stability of the domestic and international banking and financial system were taken to mean that we had finally gotten things right after nearly two hundred years of experimentation. Although there was little political controversy about money and even less significant new legislation, the monetary and financial system was undergoing meaningful evolutionary changes.[1]

The dynamics of the financial system that lead to institutional change result from profit-seeking activities by businesses, financial institutions, and households as they manage their affairs. In this process innovation occurs, so that new financial instruments and institutions emerge and old

---

1. The monetary history of the United States includes: (1) the assumption of state debts in Washington's term; (2) the First, and more significantly, the Second United States Bank: (3) the wildcat banking era; (4) the National Banking Act; (5) greenbacks and the resumption of specie; (6) "thou shalt not crucify mankind on a Cross of Gold"; (7) the Federal Reserve Act; and (8) the reforms of the Roosevelt era.

Unfortunately, the leading history of the American monetary experience, Milton Friedman and Anna Schwartz, *A Monetary History of the United States, 1867–1960* (Princeton: Princeton University Press, 1963), is marked by the authors' strongly held theoretical priors. Friedman and Schwartz is akin to a lawyer's brief for monetarism.

instruments and institutions are used in new ways. These changes, along with legislated and administrative changes that reflected the aura of success of this period, transformed the financial and economic system from one in which a financial crisis was unlikely into one that was vulnerable to crises. Financial instability surfaced again in the credit crunch of 1966. Since then the evolution of the financial system has continued in an environment where responses to instability and the interventions that contain the instability condition institutional and structural changes.

AN ASIDE: SOME ORGANIZING PRINCIPLES

Before we look at the developments that caused turbulence to replace tranquility, some organizing principles need to be introduced. Our economy is capitalist, using complex, elaborate, and expensive capital equipment, and has a sophisticated, complex, convoluted, and evolving financial system that makes the indirect ownership of wealth possible. Because it is capitalist, our economy depends upon the pursuit of private incomes and wealth for the creation and maintenance of capital assets as well as for current production.

As debts are used to finance control over capital assets, one view of our economy is of a complex system of money in/money out transactions. Every financial instrument—be it short-term note, bond, deposit, insurance policy, or share of stock—is a commitment to pay cash at some time, or if some event occurs. The time may he precise (specified in the contract) or open (on demand or conditional upon events). Deposits at banks and savings institutions (where payment will be at the demand or order of the depositor) and contingent-payment contracts (such as pension or life insurance agreements) are open contracts. Common or equity shares are peculiar contingent commitments: the firm must make profits and declare dividends for the owner of equity to receive cash.

Cash is needed to fulfill these commitments. The cash can be obtained from funds on hand (which only moves the problem back one step), from payments for contributions to the production of income (wages and profits), from the moneys generated by owned financial contracts, from the sale of physical or financial assets, or from borrowing. The above list exhausts the possibilities, except for the creation of cash—which is open only to the government and—in a special way—to banks (although in principle every unit can "create" money—the only problem for the creator being to get it "accepted").[2]

A firm's balance sheet, which lists physical and financial assets on one side and liabilities on the other, and its income statement can be interpreted as indicating the sources and uses of cash. The difference between sales revenues and out-of-pocket costs are the grossest of profits. This gross profit is a cash flow; it is earned, so to speak, because of the nature of the firm's markets, capital assets, and organization. Another type of cash flow to a unit is from financial instruments that it owns; these cash flows represent contract fulfillment by others. In addition to the cash flows originating in gross profits and contract fulfillments, a unit can acquire cash by selling physical or financial assets or pledging assets or future income.

Liabilities, the other side of a firm's balance sheet, are commitments to make payments; the payments are dedicated to both repaying and servicing debt. Cash to meet these payment commitments can be obtained either from the gross profit cash flow, cash on hand, the sale of assets, or borrowing. A unit that expects its cash receipts to exceed its cash payments in each time period is engaged in what we will call hedge finance. On the other hand, an organization from which the contractual cash flow *out* over a time period exceeds its expected cash flow *in* is engaged in either speculative or Ponzi finance. A unit in a speculative or Ponzi financing posture obtains the cash to satisfy its debtors by selling some assets, rolling over maturing debt, or new borrowing; such units are dependent upon financial market conditions in a more serious way than units whose liability structures can be characterized as hedge financing.

Banks, deposit institutions like savings and loan organizations, and other users (business, households, and government) of short-term debt are faced with the possibility that cash outflows will exceed cash receipts over some period. Units particularly vulnerable to cash drains will tend to hold cash or readily marketable assets, or will have some type of guaranteed refinancing available. Those assets that cannot be used readily to generate cash, such as the physical plant of operating firms and loans in portfolios of banks, can be called the *position* of the unit; they are the stock in trade of the organization and are often specialized to the firm or an industry. If there is a sudden cash drain from the unit, then the needed cash can be generated

---

2. The introduction and explosive growth of money market funds and various broker cash-management accounts in the 1980s show that liabilities that function like money can be created by institutions that are not banks.

only by dealing in other than these key assets or by borrowing. The act of acquiring cash to finance the assets essential to a unit's business is called, following banking terminology, *making position*, and the instrument used for such purposes is the position-making asset or debt. An asset or debt is a good position-making instrument if it has a broad and active market. Furthermore, the market for a position-making asset should be resilient in that there will be a flood of orders to buy this asset if the price falls a bit; its price, then, will not change much under normal sales pressure.

Perhaps this position-making problem can be better understood by referring to the operations of banks and other financial institutions that usually separate the asset-acquisition and cash-management functions. Commercial bank lending largely takes the form of lines of credit that borrowers draw down as business requires. As a result, a loan will appear on a bank's books at the same time the borrower draws on the proceeds of the loan: the lending bank loses its cash (bank reserves) simultaneously with the activation of a loan. For a member bank, this means a debit will appear in the bank's deposit at its Federal Reserve bank simultaneously with a loan.

In each bank there is an executive (or an office in today's giant banks) who is responsible for assuring that a bank's cash position—for member banks the deposit at the Federal Reserve—is kept at the required level. This official needs to be able to generate cash flows in favor of the bank. According to the textbook versions, a bank with a deficiency in its reserves will restrict lending. In fact, in modern commercial banking, each day's loans are the result of prior commitments. The loan portfolio and a bank's loan strategy are not subject to rapid change in order to bring reserves into line with reserve requirements.

A unit's commitments to pay cash will be widely acceptable as a liquid or monetary asset if it seems certain that the unit can, by its own actions, force a net cash flow in its favor. As long as wealth owners are confident that a bank can force a net flow of cash in its favor, then its liabilities will be held as liquid assets. Once this confidence evaporates, wealth owners will no longer willingly hold the unit's liabilities. This sets off a cash drain, which tests the unit's ability to force a cash flow in its favor.[3]

Ultimately, the acceptance of a bank's liabilities rests upon its ability to cut off or slow down its lending to achieve a flow of cash in its favor. But

---

3. This is the meaning of R. S. Sayers's dictum that "A bank and most especially a Central Bank has a duty to be rich." R. S. Sayers, *Bank of England Operations (1890–1914)* (London: P. S. King & Sons, 1936).

cutting off lending is a drastic step; it is in effect a liquidation of the going business of the bank. Furthermore, it adversely affects the prospects of those businesses that normally borrow from the bank. A bank therefore needs some way of forcing a cash flow in its favor without affecting its basic lending posture. The instruments used for this are the position-making instruments. A well-functioning bank arranges its asset structure so that it always has assets that can be used to force cash to flow toward it without forcing a halt to its basic line of business, the short-term financing of commerce and industry.

At the end of World War II the commercial banks were replete with government securities. The government-security market was the primary position-making market, and the Treasury bill was the primary position-making instrument. Banks that had excess cash would buy Treasury bills, and banks that had cash (reserve deposit) deficiencies would sell Treasury bills. These sales and purchases would go through either independent dealers or dealer departments in large banks.

The government-security market is a dealer market, unlike the stock market, which is a brokers' market. In a dealers' market, bonds are actually bought by the marketing organization and then sold out of its position; the dealer owns that in which he trades, if only for a brief interval. In a brokers' market, marketing organizations bring buyers and sellers together, but brokers never own the instruments being traded. Thus, dealers have inventories that need financing. In the Treasury-bill market, a dealer might buy and sell a very large amount during a business day, and may be left with a sizable inventory to carry over to the next day. The dealer's need to finance its position leads it to borrow from banks and nonbank organizations with excess cash. Dealers who buy and sell instruments used in position-making are required for the smooth functioning of the banking system; they tend to dampen fluctuations in the price of the security as the supply on the market varies.

Banks are profit-seeking organizations that strive to make the largest profit consistent with the risks they wish or are allowed to bear. Bankers make money by selling their services in making payments over distance and time, by arranging financing, and by making on the carry on a fund they manage; making on the carry requires that the interest rate on assets be greater than the interest rate on liabilities.

Profits made by bankers increase as bankers discover ways of increasing the return on their assets or decreasing the cost of their liabilities. To do this, banks innovate by introducing new ways of financing business and raising funds: new instruments, new types of contracts, and new institutions regularly emerge in a financial system made up of profit-seeking units.

THE EVOLUTION OF BANK POSITION-MAKING INSTRUMENTS

The instruments used by commercial banks in position-making evolved over the postwar period. In the beginning the primary position-making instrument was the Treasury bill; banks sold the asset (Treasury debt) in order to increase cash holdings and bought bills when they had excess cash. When Treasury bills are used in position-making, banks substitute one asset (business loans) for another (Treasury securities) or vice versa.

The buying or selling of Treasury debt by banks and large-scale holders of cash requires that a set of dealers exist who buy and sell the instruments for cash. Whenever dealers increase their holdings of Treasury debt they need cash, which they acquire by borrowing. On the other hand, whenever the inventory of Treasury bills in dealers hands decrease, they repay debts. Dealers thus increase or decrease their liabilities as their inventory increases or decreases: they make position by operating upon their liabilities. Although commercial banks are a basic source of money to government-bond houses, corporations and others with short-term excess cash also lend to dealers. From time to time, however, dealers may have government debt in position that they cannot finance by borrowing from their normal bank or nonbank sources. In such cases, dealers must have standby sources of funds for a dealers' market to function smoothly. One option would be to allow bond dealers to borrow at the Federal Reserve banks, but this option has not been adopted. Instead, in the 1950s and 1960s one of the very large New York banks—Manufacturers Hanover Trust—refrained from lending to dealers as a *normal* part of its business. But if all other sources of financing were closed to the dealers, they borrowed from Manufacturers Hanover. It was understood that if Manufacturers Hanover ran a reserve deficiency because it financed bond dealers, Manufacturers Hanover would have access to the discount window of the Federal Reserve.[4]

This indirect access to the Federal Reserve was an adequate solution to the problem of standby position-making in an environment characterized by large holdings of government debts by banks. It obviously would not be effective if banks did not use Treasury debt to make position.

---

4. Hyman P. Minsky, "Central Banking and Money Market Changes," *Quarterly Journal of Economics* LXXI (May 1957); reprinted in Hyman P. Minsky, *Can "IT" Happen Again? Essays on Instability & Finance* (Armonk N. Y.: M. E. Sharpe & Co., 1982).

Changes in the proportion of loans and U.S. government securities in the portfolio of commercial banks from 1946 to 1984 are traced in Table 4.1. After a wartime high of $76.5 billion in 1946, the dollar amount of government securities in bank portfolios remained essentially constant through the mid-1960s, at which time the amount began to increase. However, as is evident from Table 4.1, the increases in government debt held through 1974 were largely in Agency issues that, while fully guaranteed by the U.S. government, are not really available for position-making, because their markets tend to be thin. Moreover, as the size of position-making activity is related to the total financial assets, the decline in the percentage of government securities to total assets (shown in Table 4.1) from the end of World War II until the mid-1970s indicates that government-security holdings were becoming less capable of handling the position-making activity of the banks.

If an organization cannot make position by selling or buying an asset such as a Treasury debt, then it can make position by increasing or decreasing its borrowings. In the postwar era an alternative to the Treasury security market as a position-making market for commercial banks appeared with the development of the federal-funds market. Federal funds are deposits at the Federal Reserve banks; by the middle of the 1950s it became common for the very largest banks and for a set of smaller banks that were well located for such transactions to use them as a position-making instrument. Federal funds remain a major position-making instrument, and the federal-funds market rate—the interbank lending rate on such deposits—is now a key interest rate in the economy.

Bank assets have grown relative to bank holdings of deposits at the Federal Reserve and vault cash. Table 4.2 exhibits the percentage of vault cash and reserves at the Federal Reserve to total bank financial assets; this ratio fell from 13.6 percent in 1946 to 4.6 percent in 1975 and 2.0 percent in 1984. Since the total volume of position-making activity is related to the volume of financial assets, banks need to develop a wide array of position-making instruments—and markets—in order to be able to function with such lower ratios of cash and reserves to total assets. For total assets to have increased relative to the reserve deposits and vault cash, the commercial banks had to develop reserve-economizing types of liabilities. Banks have been innovative in creating instruments that can be used to generate a flow of reserves toward a particular bank if the need arises, even as they free reserves in the banking system.

One such reserve-economizing deposit was the large-denomination certificate of deposit (CD), which is, at least in principle, negotiable.

Table 4.1:   Commercial Banking: Total Financial Assets, Government Securities, and Loans at Year End

Year End	Total Financial Assets (Billions of Dollars)	Total U.S. Government Securities	Loans	Government/ Financial Assets %	Loans/ Financial Assets %	U.S. Government Agency	% Agency of U.S. Government Securities
1946	134.2	76.5	24.0	57.0	17.9	1.0	1.3
1950	149.5	64.5	25.9	43.1	28.8	1.9	2.9
1955	187.4	65.2	83.4	34.8	44.5	2.9	4.4
1960	228.3	63.9	120.0	28.0	52.5	2.3	3.6
1965	340.7	66.0	203.8	19.4	59.8	5.8	8.8
1970	504.9	76.4	310.8	15.1	61.6	13.9	18.2
1973	728.8	88.8	478.1	12.2	65.6	29.6	33.3
1974	800.1	89.5	535.7	11.2	67.0	33.2	37.1
1975	834.6	119.5	533.6	14.3	63.9	34.6	28.9
1976	906.0	139.6	577.5	15.4	63.7	36.0	25.8
1977	1000.4	138.5	659.5	13.8	65.7	36.8	26.5
1978	1147.2	139.0	773.8	12.1	67.4	43.8	31.5
1979	1276.8	146.5	877.2	11.5	68.7	51.2	34.9
1980	1389.5	172.1	938.7	12.4	67.5	60.9	35.4
1981	1522.6	183.9	1029.5	12.1	67.6	70.7	38.4
1982	1611.2	211.8	1074.4	13.1	66.7	78.2	36.9
1983	1757.4	258.1	1158.8	14.7	65.9	79.0	30.6
1984	2012.9	261.5	1328.4	13.0	65.8	78.5	30.0

SOURCE: Flow of Funds Accounts, 1952–1984, Board of Governors of the Federal Reserve System, Washington, D.C., April 1985. Data from 1946 and 1950 from ibid., 1946–1975, December 1976.

Table 4.2:   Commercial Banking: Vault Cash and Reserves for Selected Years, 1946–84

Year	Bank Financial Assets	Vault Cash	Member Bank Reserves	Total Cash & Reserves	% of Cash & Reserves to Financial Assets
1946	134.2	2.0	16.1	18.2	13.6
1950	149.5	2.2	17.7	19.9	13.2
1955	187.4	2.7	19.0	21.7	11.6
1960	228.3	3.3	17.1	20.4	8.9
1965	340.7	4.9	18.4	23.3	6.8
1970	504.9	7.0	24.2	31.2	6.2
1975	834.6	12.3	26.1	38.4	4.6
1980	1389.5	19.8	27.5	47.3	3.4
1984	2012.9	18.6	21.8	40.4	2.0

SOURCE: Flow of Funds Accounts, 1952–1984, Board of Governors of the Federal Reserve System, Washington, D.C., April 1985. Data from 1946 and 1950 from ibid., 1946–1975, December 1976.

Introduced in the banking system in the early 1960s, it soon became a favorite vehicle for the investing of large-scale holdings of short-term funds. The growth of CDs in the early 1960s enabled bank credit to expand substantially faster than the reserve base. In the period leading up to the credit crunch of 1966, when the reserves of member banks grew at an annual rate of 2.6 percent, time deposits (which include such negotiable CDs) grew much more rapidly—at a 10.7 percent clip, while total bank credit grew at 8.0 percent. Consequently, the growth of time deposits enabled banks to get around the constraint on the growth of bank credit that reserves would have imposed.

Another technique used by government bond dealers and commercial banks to make position is the repurchase agreement—a contract for the simultaneous sale of an asset (say, a packet of government debt) and its repurchase at a fixed date (e.g., tomorrow, a week from today). The price of the sale and subsequent purchase of the asset is fixed in the contract; as the prices are set by negotiation, the return to the purchaser is really an interest rate on the amount involved. A repurchase agreement with a bank in effect removes a deposit from the base used to determine required reserves. They can also be used to evade ceilings on interest rates.

Banks also borrow from foreign banks to make position. The dollars borrowed abroad (Eurodollars) are another example of a type of liability that does not absorb reserves. When an American bank's branch in London borrows Eurodollars and transfers the funds to the home office, the borrowed funds amount to a reserve deposit for the U.S. bank that does not lead to a liability that absorbs reserves.

If the Eurodollar borrowing leads to the sale of, say, German marks for dollars, the result may be an increase in reserve deposits at the Federal Reserve System, depending upon whether the central banks are concerned about the exchange rate. In the credit stringency of 1970, banks that had foreign branches were able to evade restrictive Federal Reserve policies by raising funds and placing credits in these branches. After the 1970 liquidity squeeze, many banks opened overseas branches in order to position themselves to better withstand future periods of reserve constraint.

We now have a banking system in which normal functioning depends upon a wide variety of money-market instruments being available for position-making. Since the end of World War II, the banking system has evolved from the simplicity of the Treasury bill's monopoly as *the* position-making instrument to a complex situation in which a representative bank juggles its government-security account or its federal-funds position, has large denomination certificates of deposit, repurchase agreements, Eurodollar borrowings (or sales), and borrowings at the Federal Reserve. The behavior of a system with such a variety of position-making possibilities is quite different from that of a simple system in which the Treasury-security market monopolized position-making activity. Furthermore, techniques for position-making are still evolving. Whenever rapid innovations in ways of buying money and in substitutes for bank financing take place, the articulation between Federal Reserve policy actions and the volume of financing available loosens. The greater the number of alternative position-making techniques available for banks and for other financial institutions, the slower the reaction of the supply of finance to monetary policy of the Federal Reserve. The lag between restrictive actions by the Federal Reserve and a supply response by banks and financial markets will take longer when evolution is occurring than when a tight and invariant relation exists. Policymakers' impatience to get results will tend to make for serious excesses and overshoots when relations have been loosened. The likelihood that policy action will result in the economy going to the threshold of a financial crisis increases with the number of markets used for position-making, and with the proportion of bank assets bought through the various markets. Thus, as the financial system evolved over the postwar period, the potential for instability of the economy increased.

What happens to banks and to the market in which banks trade assets and acquire deposits is only one side of the financial coin. When banks sell CDs or enter into repurchase agreements, a substitution of bank time deposits, or promises to pay, for demand deposits takes place. Such transactions increase the ability of the banking system to finance activity. But the financing banks provide tends to be short-term; thus, the measures that allow bank financing to grow at a rapid rate lead to an increase in the short-term financing of nonbank activity. Rapid growth of short-term financing tends to make the financial system increasingly fragile.

SECTORAL DATA OVER THE POSTWAR PERIOD

Beginning in the mid-1960s, the performance of the economy, as well as the financial structure, underwent marked changes. There is a clear tendency toward much higher rates of inflation, and unemployment has become a much more serious problem in recent year—the unemployment rates of the recessions of 1974–75 and of 1981–82 were substantially higher than during earlier years, and the minimum unemployment rate between 1975 and 1981 was higher than in previous postwar expansions.

One reason for these differences in the behavior of the economy can be found in the important changes that occurred in financial relations in the mid-1960s. In examining these changes, trends in balance-sheet data for nonfinancial corporations, households, and commercial banks—the three dominant private sectors in the American economy—need to be emphasized.

There is little doubt that the Great Depression affected views as to what was desirable in liability structures. A popular view at the time was that a bank was an institution that would lend only if the borrower did not need to borrow. In technical jargon, both borrowers and lenders were risk-averse. Because the prosperity that followed World War II was first viewed as a transitory affair, a reluctance to debt-finance continued through the early years of the postwar era.

In 1946 the balance sheets of households, businesses, and financial institutions owned a much larger proportion of government debt and owed or owned a smaller portion of private debt than had been true in the past. The federal debt was $229.5 billion, whereas total private debt of $153.4 billion was smaller than the $161.8 billion of private debt in 1929. As a result of the low level of private indebtedness and the high level of outstanding federal government debt, the balance sheets of the major sectors were dominated by the safe and secure financial assets issued by government.

Any number looked at in isolation, though, tells us little about economic relations. The distribution of various types of debt for selected years from 1946 to 1984 is shown in Table 4.3. Until the mid-1970s, federal government debt fell relative to total debt, even as the percentage of corporate debt rose. On the other hand, state and local debt as a percentage of the total grew until 1960, and then roughly stabilized at about 10 percent to 10.5 percent. A similar picture of a sharp rise until the early to middle 1960s and then stability is shown for households and noncorporate businesses. A plateau in the proportions of household and noncorporate business debt was seemingly reached.

The distribution of indebtedness has been affected by the massive contracyclical and structural deficits of 1981–84. Federal debt increased from 18.8 percent of the total in 1980 to 23.0 percent in 1984. Corporate and household debts both fell as a proportion of total indebtedness between 1980 and 1984; corporate debt fell from 23.1 percent to 21.9 percent even as household debts fell from 37.7 percent to 35.7 percent.

Table 4.3:   Distribution of Net Public and Private Debt for Selected Years, 1946–84

Year	Total Net Public and Private (Billions $)	Federal	State and Local	Corporate	Households
1943	350.4	62.8	4.4	14.1	9.8
1952	460.2	48.1	6.8	18.9	20.4
1955	544.9	41.8	8.4	19.0	25.0
1960	726.8	32.5	9.9	21.2	30.0
1965	1012.5	25.9	10.2	21.9	33.9
1970	1432.3	21.0	10.4	24.8	33.6
1975	2288.8	19.5	9.6	24.0	34.0
1980	3948.3	18.8	7.5	23.1	37.7
1981	4328.4	19.2	7.0	23.4	37.4
1982	4728.9	21.0	7.1	23.0	36.2
1983	5255.3	22.4	7.1	21.8	35.9
1984	5970.8	23.0	6.8	21.9	35.7

SOURCE: Flow of Funds Accounts, 1952–1984, Board of Governors of the Federal Reserve System, Washington, D.C., April 1985. Data from 1946 and 1950 from ibid., 1946–1975, December 1976.

After falling from its 1946 level, the ratio of total indebtedness to GNP stayed in a relatively narrow range (in the vicinity of 1.30–1.40) until the early 1960s, when a step up of debt to GNP ratio appeared. (In Table 4.4 the ratio of debt to GNP in current dollars is indicated for a number of types of debt for selected years from 1946 to 1984.) As a result of recent developments, total net public and private debt relative to GNP stood at 1.63 in 1984.

Until the deficits of the Reagan years, the ratio of federal government debt to GNP decreased; in 1946 it was 1.04, and in 1980 it was 0.28. Corporate debt showed an ever increasing ratio to GNP, until 1970 rising from 0.24 in 1946 to 0.36 in 1970. (Between 1965 and 1970 the ratio of corporate debt to GNP rose from 0.32 to 0.36.) Since 1970 the corporate debt-GNP ratio has been quite stable. State and local government debt and the debt of individuals both showed a rising trend until 1965, then stabilized within a narrow range until the mid-1970s. Since then household debts have once again risen relative to GNP.

The tapering off of the increase of state and local, household and corporate indebtedness, relative to GNP, in the 1960s and 1970s even as the decrease in the ratio to GNP of federal debt continued at a slower rate,

Table 4.4:   Net Public and Private Debt Relative to GNP for Selected Years, 1946–84 (Ratio of Debts to GNP)

Year	Total Net Public and Private (Billions $)	Federal	State and Local	Corporate	Households
1946	1.67	1.04	.07	.24	.16
1952	1.32	.64	.09	.25	.27
1955	1.37	.57	.12	.26	.34
1960	1.43	.47	.14	.30	.43
1965	1.47	.38	.15	.32	.50
1970	1.44	.30	.15	.36	.48
1975	1.48	.29	.14	.35	.50
1980	1.50	.28	.11	.35	.57
1981	1.46	.28	.10	.34	.55
1982	1.54	.32	.11	.35	.56
1983	1.59	.36	.11	.35	.57
1984	1.63	.38	.11	.36	.58

SOURCE: Flow of Funds Accounts, 1952–1984, Board of Governors of the Federal Reserve System, Washington, D.C., April 1985. Data from 1946 and 1950 from ibid., 1946–1975, December 1976.

coincided with the increased instability of financial markets. The late 1960s and 1970s also witnessed the rise in interest rates, increasing the proportion of gross business profits and household income needed to service debts. Thus the trends since the 1960s reflect the combined effect of the increases in debts that had taken place and the sharply higher interest rates.

The data on sectoral balance sheets and balance sheet-income relations indicate significant changes in financial relations in the mid-1960s. Keynes identified our economy as being characterized by a system of borrowing and lending based upon margins of safety. The margins of safety can be identified by the payment commitments on liabilities relative to cash receipts, the net worth or equity relative to indebtedness (the margin of stock market purchases), and the ratio of liabilities to cash and liquid assets, that is, the ratio of payment commitments to assets that are superfluous to operations. The size of the margins of safety determines whether a financial structure is fragile or robust and in turn reflects the ability of units to absorb shortfalls of cash receipts without triggering a debt deflation.

The nine figures presented—four that deal with nonfinancial corporations, two that deal with households, and three that deal with commercial banks—show that significant changes in the trend of financial relations occurred in the mid-1960s. The transition to turbulence and fragility is indicated in these charts.

Figure 4.1 shows the ratio of investment in fixed plant and equipment to internal funds for nonfinancial corporations. The data indicate that our sophisticated financial system accommodates the demand for funds when the desire by corporations to invest increases, because the economy did well and because of incentives to investment—such as the investment tax credit and accelerated depreciation—that increase the capacity of business to carry debts.

Figure 4.2 shows the ratio of liabilities to gross internal funds, which is an indicator, albeit crude, of the cash-payment commitments of nonfinancial corporations relative to a measure of cash flows. The indicator as presented is very conservative, since it does not allow for the increased proportion of short-term debt in liability structures that occurred over the period and is not adjusted for the rise in interest rates. The ratio showed no discernible trend until the middle of the 1960s; then it moved strongly upward. It is obvious that, from 1965 to 1974 the cash flows from operations of corporations provided a smaller cover to debt than was true earlier. Moreover, if allowance is made for the increase in interest rates, the rise in the ratios would be much sharper. In the ten years after 1955 the interest rate on long-term debt increased by about 50 percent, but in the years after 1965 interest rates more than doubled. Thus, if corporate liabilities were adjusted for changes in interest rates, the slight downward trend evident in

Figure 4.1: Fixed Investments ÷ Gross Internal Funds, Nonfinancial Corporations, 1952–84
SOURCE: Flow of Funds Accounts, Board of Governors of the Federal Reserve System.

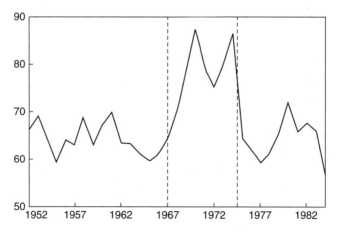

Figure 4.2: Total Liabilities ÷ Gross Internal Funds, Nonfinancial Corporations 1952–84

the chart for the first fifteen years might be wiped out and the upward thrust between 1965 and 1974 would be even greater.

Figure 4.3 indicates the trend of liabilities relative to cash assets in corporate balance sheets, a trend found for other liquid asset indicators, such as the ratio of business liabilities to holdings of no-default assets. The ratio of liabilities to demand deposits has trended upward throughout the postwar period; however, as indicated by the vertical line, the rate of growth became cyclical after 1960. The very rapid increase in the ratio of corporate liabilities to demand deposits and currency reflects the increasingly deregulated financial markets in which business "invests" in interest earning substitutes for cash. In Figure 4.4, which presents a facet of the liability structure of nonfinancial corporations, the ratio of open-market paper, plus borrowings from finance companies, to total liabilities indicates the increased recourse to exotic financing by corporations. These debts were a minor portion of total corporate liabilities prior to 1967; it is clear that they now provide substantially more funds than earlier. The dependence on exotic finance apparently increased in two steps—the first around 1960 and the second around 1969. The increase after 1969 may well reflect a view that the way in which the Federal Reserve handled the financial crunch of 1969–70—they extended protection to such liabilities—meant that they were now safer than in earlier periods.

Figures 4.5 and 4.6 show data for households; Figure 4.5 the ratio of liabilities to personal income and Figure 4.6 the ratio of liabilities to money.

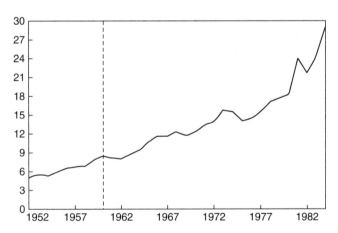

Figure 4.3: Total Liabilities ÷ Demand Deposits, Nonfinancial Corporations, 1952–84

SOURCE: Flow of Funds Accounts, Board of Governors of the Federal Reserve System.

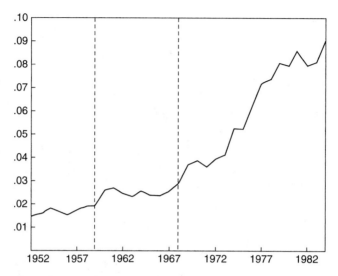

Figure 4.4: Open-market Paper and Borrowings from Finance
Companies ÷ Total Liabilities, Nonfinancial Corporations, 1952–84
SOURCE: Flow of Funds Accounts, Board of Governors of the Federal Reserve System.

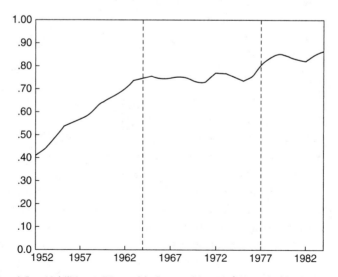

Figure 4.5: Liabilities ÷ Disposable Personal Income, Households, 1952–84
SOURCE: Flow of Funds Accounts, Board of Governors of the Federal Reserve System.

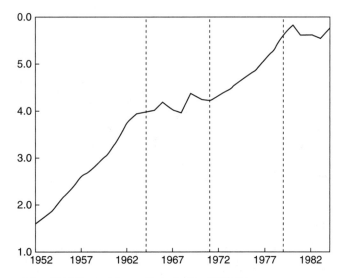

Figure 4.6: Liabilities ÷ Money, Households, 1952–84
SOURCE: Flow of Funds Accounts, Board of Governors of the Federal Reserve.

Household liabilities to personal income grew steadily until 1964, at which time, a cyclical pattern emerged. The cyclical pattern shows no trend until 1976, when a "step up" to another plateau occurred. The ratio of liabilities to money—a crude measure of liquidity—grew rapidly until 1964, at which time a cyclical pattern with no obvious trend developed. This lasted until 1971 when rapid increase took over. Since 1979 the liabilities-money ratio has shown a cyclical pattern with no obvious trend.

Figures 4.7 through 4.9 show some financial relations for commercial banking. In Figure 4.7, the ratio of financial net worth to total liabilities is shown. Between 1950 and 1960 this ratio trended upward from the neighborhood of 0.074 to 0.086; in the years since 1960 it has declined, falling to 0.056 in 1974 and stabilizing at around 6 percent since 1978. Thus, the equity protection, even as conventionally measured in commercial banking where assets are not written down to allow for interest rate increases, falls sharply. It would have fallen more sharply, however, if such revaluations were made.

Figure 4.8 portrays the ratio of protected assets to total liabilities (i.e., assets whose market value will be protected by Federal Reserve intervention), a ratio that fell sharply from just below 0.6 in 1952 until 1974, when it was 0.17. In Figure 4.9, which presents the ratio of demand deposits to total liabilities, the downward trend over the entire period can be explained by introduction of a multitude of new bank liabilities.

Figure 4.7:   Financial Net Worth ÷ Total Liabilities, Commercial Banking, 1952–84

SOURCE: Flow of Funds Accounts, Board of Governors of the Federal Reserve System.

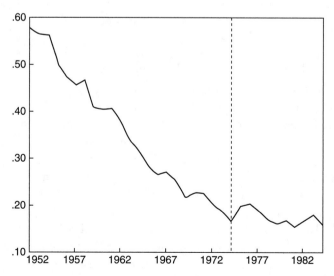

Figure 4.8:   Total Liabilities ÷ Protected Assets, Commercial Banking, 1952–84

SOURCE: Flow of Funds Accounts, Board of Governors of the Federal Reserve System.

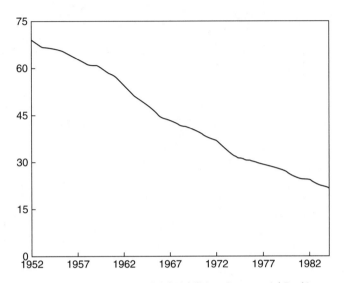

Figure 4.9:   Demand Deposits ÷ Total Liabilities, Commercial Banking, 1952–84
SOURCE: Flow of Funds Accounts, Board of Governors of the Federal Reserve System.

In these figures, a vertical dashed line is drawn at selected dates at which a change in trend or change in the mode of behavior took place in the financial structure of the economy. These changes indicate that in the early 1960s the mode of behavior of the financial system underwent significant transformation—became more speculative—and that this change tended to accelerate the trend toward fragile finance. As a result, the performance of the economy since the 1960s is more unstable than it was during the first fifteen years of the postwar era, with a tendency to much higher rates of inflation and of unemployment.

Institutional changes also contribute to the transformation of the financial structure; from 1960 to 1974 fringe banking institutions and practices—such as business lending by finance companies, the issue of commercial paper by corporations, REITs and nonmember commercial banks—have grown relative to other elements in the financial system.

As fringe banking institutions have grown, member banks—and especially the large money-market banks—have become their de facto lenders of last resort through relations that are often formalized by lines of credit. In effect, the Federal Reserve is the indirect lender of last resort to fringe banking institutions. As was evident in the REIT crisis of 1974 (see chapter 3), the hierarchical model of the National Banking System (1863–1913) has been brought into being again.

Hierarchical banking relations can be a source of weakness for the financial system as a whole. Fringe banking institutions draw upon their lines of credit at the core banks when alternative financing channels become either expensive or unusable because of some perceived weakness of the fringe banks. Inasmuch as banks hold assets that are similar to those in the portfolios of fringe institutions, some assets held by banks weaken when the losses and cash-flow shortfalls of the fringe institutions become apparent to the market. Consequently, the already weakened portfolios of some banks are made even weaker when these banks act as the proximate lender of last resort to fringe institutions. Furthermore, a succession of episodes in which giant money-market banks bail out fringe banks is likely to result in a cumulative debilitation of the giant banks; Bank of America was not necessarily strengthened when it absorbed Seafirst of Seattle in the aftermath of the Penn Square fiasco of 1982.

The potential for a domino effect, which can cause a serious disruption, is implicit in a hierarchical financial pattern. The introduction of additional layering in finance, together with the invention of new instruments designed to make credit available by tapping pools of liquidity, is evidence, beyond that revealed by the financial data itself, of the increased fragility of the system.

THE CREDIT CRUNCH OF 1966

The credit crunch of 1966 was the first difficulty since the 1930s that involved a run on a financial instrument or institution and that induced the Federal Reserve to act as a lender of last resort. Earlier postwar financial traumas had occurred because of specific failures or frauds, for example, the Billy Sol Estes affair and the salad oil scandal of 1963. These episodes led to Federal Reserve intervention to offset a specific incident. But in 1966 the Federal Reserve was a true lender of last resort, aiming to control a systemic shortcoming—a market at hazard. The credit crunch of 1966 was really a normal result of the cyclical expansion of the economy since 1961—within the context of a long postwar period without a significant recession. A crunch can occur only when margins of safety in portfolios have been eroded. The financial legacy of a Great War immediately after a Great Depression meant that robust financial markets ruled as the war ended.

As long as banks held a large volume of Treasury securities, they could adjust their needs for cash by dealing—buying and selling—those securities. Since these position-making activities were operations on the asset side, a bank's major managerial problem in the first part of the postwar period centered on managing its assets (its loans, and its investments).

As the giant banks ran out of their excess holdings of Treasury bills in the mid-1960s, they began to trade in deposits at the Federal Reserve banks; they began to borrow and lend federal funds. Such borrowing and lending supplemented and replaced dealing in Treasury bills as a position-making activity of banks. The use of federal funds to make position meant that borrowing banks increased their liabilities when they made up a cash deficiency.

The use of federal funds was but the first step in the transformation of banking into a system in which operating upon the liability side, rather than on the asset side, became the dominant position-making technique. In 1960, with Chase National Bank taking the initiative, the active pursuit of funds through CDs became the preferred way of meeting cash needed by banks to make positions. During the 1960s the rapid growth of this liability enabled banks to increase their lending at a faster rate than their reserve base. Although the Federal Reserve was pursuing a rather moderate path as measured by the growth rate of the reserve base and of the money supply (demand deposits and currency), bank lending was growing rapidly enough to fuel an inflationary boom.

As the expansion of the 1960s progressed, spending by nonfinancial corporations on physical assets increased rapidly and outpaced the growth of corporate internal sources of funds (see Figure 4.1). Consequently, as Table 4.5 indicates, the net external-funds financing of corporations rose sharply. The demand for funds from banking institutions outpaced the supply, even though the Federal Reserve was feeding reserves into the banking system at a significant rate; interest rates as well as the general level of prices rose.

In the midst of the 1966 investment boom, the Federal Reserve progressively slowed down the rate of growth of the reserve base (shown in Table 4.6) in order to fight inflation. This meant that the rate of growth of funds available for banks to use as a basis for loans decreased.

This decrease in the rate of growth of the reserve base and the boom in investment combined to bring a sharp rise in the demand by banks for funds from the money market. Even though the Federal Reserve raised the ceiling on interest rates on CDs, the market rates on commercial paper and Treasury debt rose even more. As a result, holders of large-denomination CDs allowed them to run out; this squeezed the money-market banks.

Toward the end of June 1966, the price of large CDs carrying the ceiling rate of interest went to a discount, which effectively stopped their

Table 4.5:   U.S. Investment and Internal Sources of Funds (Nonfarm, Nonfinancial Corporate Business), 1961–66 (Billions of Dollars)

Year	Purchase of Physical Assets		Internal Sources of Funds	Net External Funds	Net External Funds/Purchases of Physical Assets (%)
1961	37.0	− 5.6%*	35.6	1.4	3.8
1962	44.7	20.8%*	41.8	2.9	6.5
1963	46.7	4.5%*	43.9	2.8	6.0
1964	52.2	11.8%*	50.8	1.4	2.7
1965	61.9	18.6%*	55.3	6.6	10.7
1966	73.8	19.2%*	58.6	15.2	20.6

*[(Value year t ÷ value year t − 1) − 1] × 100 = 100.
SOURCE: Table B-69, p. 294: *Economic Report of the President*, January 1967. U.S. Government Printing Office, Washington, 1967.

issuance. Beginning in August the amount outstanding fell rapidly; what amounted to a run on the large commercial banks took place. However, the banks had loan commitments to business that, together with the run on the banks and a decline in the reserve base, made each bank individually seek more funds.

The banks took two steps to acquire reserves that spread the dislocation to other parts of the financial system. Some New York City banks—with the Franklin National in the lead—offered negotiable CDs in smaller denominations, spreading the benefits of high interest rates to the holder of small amounts of funds. These retail CDs were at a higher yield than

Table 4.6:   U.S. Money and Bank Credit Annual Rates of Change (Various Periods, December 1965–July 1967) [% per Year]

	Initial Date			
	Dec. 1965	April 1966	July 1966	Dec. 1966
	Terminal Date			
	April 1966	July 1966	Dec. 1966	July 1967
Reserves of Member Banks	6.8	2.6	−4.3	11.1
Money Stock	6.8	−3.0	1.0	7.0
Time Deposits	9.5	10.7	4.2	17.9
Bank Credit	8.0	8.0	1.5	12.4

SOURCE: Federal Reserve Bank of St. Louis, *Monetary Trends*. St. Louis, Federal Reserve Bank Monthly Issues, 1966/1967.

savings institutions were able to pay, particularly the mutual savings banks in New York City, whose portfolios were heavy with low-interest mortgages. These high interest rates on CDs induced a repatriation of funds to the East from the West Coast, where savings deposits had migrated lured by higher interest rates.

The alternative to the substitution of another liability for a liability that is running off is the sale of assets. In 1966, as the run on large-denomination CDs developed, the banks had few Treasury instruments to sell in order to make position. As a result they turned to the sale of other securities; large money-market banks began to sell off tax-exempt municipal (state and local government) bonds.

Normally, at this time commercial banks took about one-third of the new issues of municipals, but as the crunch developed, they withdrew from bidding entirely. By the end of August, as a result of the combination of commercial banks withdrawing from the new issues market and the attempt of banks to make position by selling from their holdings of municipals, the market was disorganized. The yield on high-grade tax-exempt municipals reached 5 percent, and even at these rates the market was thin.

Throughout this period the Federal Reserve, while maintaining a nominal rediscount rate of 4.5 percent, allowed but a slight increase—some $300 million during the first half of 1966—in borrowings at the discount window. During July and August, however, the window was so tightly administered that there was no increase in borrowing by member banks, and the money-market banks believed that the discount window was effectively closed to them.

By the end of August, the disorganization in the municipals market, rumors about the solvency and liquidity of savings institutions, and the frantic position-making efforts by money-market banks generated what can be characterized as a controlled panic. The situation clearly called for Federal Reserve action. A money-market panic, however, is ephemeral, the result of real liquidity stringency and a rapidly increasing precautionary demand for funds designed to protect against awesome, unknown contingencies. As was true for some of the money-market panics of the nineteenth century, the air of crisis evaporated when the authorities finally took some action.

On September 1, 1966, the twelve District Reserve Bank presidents sent identical letters to the member banks in their districts, stating that accommodations were available at the discount window to banks whose policies corresponded to Federal Reserve objectives. In particular, accommodations were available to finance current holdings of municipal securities for those banks that showed evidence that they were constraining the expansion of their business loans. In addition, the letter stated "that banks adjusting their position through loan curtailment may need a longer period of discount accommodation than would be required for the disposition of securities." The letter is important because it makes clear that the Federal Reserve was acting in defense of the municipal-security market and, by allowing municipals to be used at the discount window, was effectively setting a floor to their price. As the money-market banks had been actively trying to restrain the expansion of their business loans even before the price of the large CDs went to a discount, each bank, in its own mind, believed it was eligible for such accommodations. The discount window, previously assumed closed, was now provisionally open.

The Federal Reserve's letter of September 1, 1966, was a lender-of-last-resort act; it recognized that disequilibrating factors were dominating financial markets and provided access to Federal Reserve borrowing to refinance the positions that were being exposed by the run on bank CDs.

The opening of the discount window worked: the panic subsided. In the aftermath of the crunch, Congress passed a law allowing the Federal Reserve, the FDIC, and the Federal Home Loan Bank Board to set differential ceilings on interest rates according to size and terms of deposits for institutions under their jurisdiction.

A large decrease in investment was associated with the crunch; gross private domestic investment decreased at an annual rate of 26 percent between the fourth quarter of 1966 and the second quarter of 1967. This decline in private investment did not lead to a fall in aggregate income, however, because spending on the war in Vietnam increased just as civilian investment expenditures tapered off. A recession was prevented by an inadvertent but apt use of fiscal policy. The crunch of 1966 was the first serious financial disruption of the postwar era. The Federal Reserve's action seemed to assure the money market that banks would be protected against a run. It legitimized the use of negotiable CDs by banks and the juggling of liabilities to make position. Because the difficulties were papered over with the cosmetic changes that allowed interest rate ceilings to vary with the size of the deposit, the crunch was not interpreted as a signal that there were serious weaknesses in the financial structures.

THE LIQUIDITY SQUEEZE OF 1970

The second postwar financial disturbance that required lender-of-last-resort intervention occurred in 1970. This time the market in distress was the commercial-paper market. The intervention of the Federal Reserve took the form of (1) opening the discount window so banks could acquire funds to refinance a run on commercial paper, and (2) encouraging banks to form syndicates to refinance organizations such as finance companies that did not have statutory access to the discount window.

Whereas in the early 1960s the bank negotiable CD was the "new" instrument that financed expansion, commercial paper was the new instrument of the late 1960s. Commercial paper is the unsecured note of a business corporation that is issued for a set period of time—say 90 or 180 days. While large finance companies—such as General Motors Acceptance Corporation—place their own commercial paper, smaller companies use dealers.

At the beginning of 1966 about $10 billion of commercial paper was outstanding. By midyear 1968 the figure had doubled to $20 billion, and by the end of May 1970 some $32 billion of such paper was outstanding.

In the beginning of 1969, when Nixon took office, the unemployment rate was 3.5 percent and the CPI for the year just ended had risen 4.2 percent. Corporation investment increased by 5.0 percent in 1968 over 1967, and was to increase by 11.6 percent in 1969. As the internal funds generated by corporations remained essentially static, the net external financing of investment rose, and the percentage of corporate investment that was financed by external funds rose from 13.9 percent to 27.5 percent (see Table 4.7).

In the midst of this explosion in the external financing of investment, the Federal Reserve undertook to fight inflation by monetary policy. The rate of growth of bank credit was cut from about 10 percent in 1968 to 5 percent in the first half and 3 percent in the second half of 1969 and the first part of 1970. As a result, the sensitive federal-funds rate rose from 6 percent at the end of 1968 to 9 percent by midyear 1969, where it stayed into early 1970, when it began to decrease. Other interest rates also rose.

In this tight-money situation, the Penn-Central Railroad filed for bankruptcy and defaulted on some $82 million in outstanding commercial paper. This default led to a run on the commercial-paper market; some $3 billion—about 10 percent—of the outstanding commercial paper ran off in a three-week period. The Federal Reserve Bank of New York and the Federal Reserve Board of Governors intervened by assisting in the formation of syndicates of commercial banks, which refinanced the organizations affected by the run on commercial paper. During July member bank borrowings at the Federal Reserve discount window rose by $1 to $2 billion,

Table 4.7:   Investment and Internal Sources of Funds (Nonfarm, Nonfinancial Corporate Business), 1967–70 (Billions of Dollars)

Year	Purchase of Physical Assets		Internal Source of Funds	Net External Funds	External Funds as % of Physical Assets
1967	$71.4	−3.36%*	61.5	9.9	13.9
1968	$75.0	5.04%*	61.7	13.3	17.7
1969	$83.7	11.60%*	60.7	23.0	27.5
1970	$84.0	0.40%*	59.4	24.6	29.3

*[(Value year t ÷ value year t − 1) − 1] × 100 = 100.
SOURCE: Flow of Funds Accounts, 1946–1975, December 1976, Board of Governors of the Federal Reserve System,Washington, D.C., 1976.

and the Federal Reserve pumped additional funds into the banking system by means of open-market operations.

By these actions the Federal Reserve protected the commercial-paper market. As result of the commercial-paper crisis of 1970, a standard procedure was institutionalized whereby companies who issue commercial paper would have unused lines of credit at banks that are sufficient to pay off their outstanding commercial paper if the need arises.

By this usage, commercial paper became a covert liability of commercial banks: an increase in bank liabilities took place, but the additional liabilities did not appear on banks' balance sheets. This practice introduced an additional component to the effective money supply that was not constrained by the traditional powers of the Federal Reserve.

No reform of banking was undertaken in the aftermath of the liquidity squeeze of 1969–70, even though the 1969–70 period was a bona fide recession. At the end of 1970, unemployment was 6 percent—and the GNP deflator rose by 6 percent. This 6 percent inflation, 6 percent unemployment rate marked the emergence of stagflation—high unemployment associated with rising prices—as a characteristic of the American economy. The emergence of stagflation was further evidence that the economy's behavior no longer conformed to the pattern that ruled in the 1950s and early 1960s.

With the recession, the federal government budget position went from a surplus of $8.5 billion in 1969 to deficits of $11.9 billion in 1970 and $21.9 billion in 1971. These deficits not only sustained income and employment but, as indicated in Table 4.8, also led to an increase in the cash flows to the

Table 4.8:   Corporate Cash Flows and Federal Government Budget, 1968–72 (Billions of Dollars)

Year	Federal Government Budget Position	Corporate Gross Profits after Taxes
1968	−6.5	61.7
1969	+8.1	60.7
1970	−11.9	59.4
1971	−21.9	69.9
1972	−17.5	77.5

SOURCE: *Economic Report of the President*, 1976, U.S. Government Printing Office (1976), and Flow of Funds Accounts, 1946–1975, Board of Governors of the Federal Reserve System, 1976.

corporate sector. In the years 1971 and 1972 cash flows increased to $69.9 billion and $77.5 billion from the approximately $60 billion plateau that characterized 1968–70. Paradoxically, recessions are good for corporate gross profits after taxes in an economy with Big Government.

Although the 1969–70 crisis in the commercial-paper market led to a serious recession, the combination of prompt intervention by the Federal Reserve as a lender of last resort and the emergence of what was then a massive government deficit in 1970, 1971, and 1972 contained the recession. But the rapid increase in corporate cash flows in the years after the near crisis set the stage for another burst of expansion and external finance in the years that followed.

The policy of using monetary constraint to control inflation was not a great success in 1969–70. The policymakers had assumed that constraint upon the rate of growth of the money supply would lead to a smooth decrease in business and household spending and this would remove some of the excess demand that contributed to inflation. In the world in which we live, however, monetary policy does not directly affect demand; it first affects financing and refinancing conditions and the prices of instruments traded in financial markets. Consequently, monetary constraint leads to financial-market disruption even though income, employment, and prices continue to increase; before demand is finally lowered, a financial crisis is induced. However, the success of monetary constraint in triggering financial traumas that threatened a deep depression in 1966 and again in 1970 meant that it was sure to be the principal weapon of an anti-inflationary policy in 1973–74 and 1980–81.

The familiar pattern of explosive growth in corporate investment and its external financing (see Table 4.9) after 1971 meant that there was upward pressure on market interest rates. The abrupt removal of price controls in early 1973 by the victorious Nixon administration, following the easy-money policy of the election campaign, led to a virulent inflation that helped strip units of their liquid-asset margins of safety. A boom in housing and commercial investment was facilitated by the emergence of REITs, which were the new miracle financial child of the early 1970s. Once again high interest rates emerged, and again financial institutions, which depended upon refinancing their positions, were placed in great difficulties. In particular, virtually all the REITs became walking bankrupts in 1974. These years saw an epidemic of bank failures.

The 1974–75 debacle conformed to the pattern of the episodes of 1966 and 1969–70. In both cases, a run on some institutions or instrument required Federal Reserve action to abort what looked like the beginnings of a financial crisis. In each case, the deficits of Big Government sustained income, generated conditions conducive to business profits, and fed secure instruments into portfolios.

Table 4.9:   Investment and Internal Sources of Funds (Nonfarm, Nonfinancial Corporate Business), 1971–80 (Billions of Dollars)

Year	Purchase of Physical Assets		Internal Source of Funds	Net External Funds	External Funds as % of Physical Assets
1971	$ 87.2	3.8%*	68.0	19.2	22.0
1972	102.5	17.5%*	78.7	23.8	23.2
1973	121.5	18.5%*	84.6	36.9	30.4
1974	125.9	3.6%*	81.5	44.4	35.2
1975	99.9	−7.9%*	124.4	−24.5	−24.5
1976	139.0	39.1%*	142.9	−3.9	−2.8
1977	169.8	22.1%*	166.3	3.5	2.1
1978	195.9	15.3%*	186.8	9.1	4.6
1979	220.9	12.7%*	218.1	2.8	1.2
1980	216.9	−9.8%*	230.0	−13.1	−6.0

*[(Value year t ÷ value year t − 1) − 1] × 100 = 100.

SOURCE: Flow of Funds Accounts, 1946–1975, Board of Governors of the Federal Reserve System, Washington, D.C., December 1976, and later releases of Flow of Funds Accounts.

THE LESSONS FROM THE RUNS

In the years following 1965, at least four serious runs occurred on financial markets or banks. In each case, an instrument or an institution that had grown rapidly over the preceding boom was the focal point of the disturbance, and each time, the Federal Reserve intervened to facilitate the refinancing of the threatened position. In 1966 and 1970 only minor institutional and usage reforms were suggested; no serious effort at reform of the overseas operations of U.S. banks occurred after the 1974 Franklin National fiasco; and nothing was done after 1974 to prevent the emergence of new financial institutions that, like the REITs, are based upon covert bank liabilities.

Every time the Federal Reserve protects a financial instrument it legitimizes the use of this instrument to finance activity. This means that not only does Federal Reserve action abort an incipient crisis, but it sets the stage for a resumption in the process of increasing indebtedness—and makes possible the introduction of new instruments. In effect, the Federal Reserve prepares the way for the restoration of the type of financing that is a necessary, but not a sufficient condition, for an investment boom that is brought to a halt by financial crises.

The deficits of Big Government are the sufficient condition. By sustaining aggregate demand, they sustain corporate profits and feed secure assets into portfolios. These effects of Big Government mean that an investment boom will occur quite soon after a recession, and the investment boom generates the demand for finance that leads to another bout of inflation and crisis.

What we seem to have is a system that sustains instability even as it prevents the deep depressions of the past. Instead of a financial crisis and a deep depression being separated by decades, threats of crisis and deep depression occur every few years; instead of a realized deep depression, we now have chronic inflation. In terms of preventing deep depressions, we have done better than in earlier epochs. This is not a trivial gain. But the instability and the deteriorating performance mean that we need to search for something better.

ECONOMIC
THEORY

PERSPECTIVES
ON THEORY

In all disciplines theory plays a double role: it is both a lens and a blinder. As a lens, it focuses the mind upon specified problems, enabling conditional statements to be made about causal relations for a well-defined but limited set of phenomena. But as a blinder, theory narrows the field of vision. Questions that are meaningful in the world are often nonsense questions within a theory. If such nonsense questions are *often* posed by developments in the world, then the discipline is ripe for a revolution in theory. Such a revolution, however, requires the development of new instruments of thought. This is a difficult intellectual process.

Within today's standard economic theory, which is commonly called the neoclassical synthesis, the question "Why is our economy so unstable?" is just such a nonsense question. Standard economic theory not only does not lead to an explanation of instability as a system attribute, it really does not recognize that endogenous instability is a problem that a satisfactory theory must explain.[1]

---

1. Robert E. Lucas, Jr., recognizes this problem. In the conclusion to his influential paper, "Expectations and the Neutrality of Money," *Journal of Economic Theory* 4 (April 1972), pp. 103–24; reprinted in Robert E. Lucas, Jr., *Studies in Business-Cycle Theory* (Cambridge: MIT Press, 1981), he states that "This paper has been an attempt to resolve the paradox posed by Gurley" (from J. G. Gurfey's review of M. Friedman, "A Program for Monetary Stability," *Review of Economic Statistics* 43 [1961], pp. 307–08) in his mild but accurate parody of Friedmanian monetary theory: "Money is a veil, but when the veil flutters, real output sputters." In order to show that business cycles are compatible with neoclassical theory, Lucas constructs an elaborate schema in which systematic inability to understand signals leads to business cycles. The Keynesian formulation which emphasizes the market processes that lead to capital asset prices and financing decisions is much more straightforward.

Economists who offer policy advice are neither fools nor knaves. Knowing instability exists, they nevertheless base their analysis and advice upon a theory that cannot explain instability, because this theory *does* provide answers to deep and serious questions and *has had* some success as a basis for policy. Before abandoning or radically revising neoclassical theory, therefore, it is necessary to understand the significance of the deep and serious questions that this theory does answer and why any alternative economic theory must come to grips with the questions that neoclassical theory addresses.

THE IMPORTANCE OF THEORY

Understanding the strengths and weaknesses of standard economic theory is particularly important now that active economic policy is the norm rather than the exception. Indeed, in a world with active policy the content of economic theories and the significance of differences in theory for policy are of special interest. James Tobin, who was a member of the Council of Economic Advisers during President Kennedy's first two years in office and who received the Nobel Prize in 1982, noted that "The terms in which a problem is stated and in which the relevant information is organized can have a great influence on the solution."[2] But the way "a problem" is stated and the identification of "relevent information" reflect the economic theory of the policy adviser. That is, the game of policymaking is rigged; the theory used determines the questions that are asked and the options that are presented. The prince is constrained by the theory of his intellectuals!

Today's standard economic theory is largely a creature of the years since World War II. It integrates some aspects of Keynes's theories with the older classical analysis that he believed he was replacing.[3] This neoclassical synthesis now guides economic policy.

---

2. James Tobin, *The Intellectual Revolution in U.S. Policy Making*, Noel Buxton Lectures (Essex: University of Essex, 1966).
3. John Maynard Keynes, *The General Theory of Employment, Interest and Money*, vol. 7, *Collected Writings of John Maynard Keynes* (London: Macmillan, for the Royal Economic Society, 1973), p. 383. Dan Patinkin's *Money, Interest and Prices*, 2d ed. (New York: Harper and Row, 1965), is an early and classic statement of the neoclassical synthesis.

It is ironic that an economic theory that purports to be based on Keynes fails because it cannot explain instability. The essential aspect of Keynes's *General Theory* is a deep analysis of how financial forces—which we can characterize as Wall Street—interact with production and consumption to determine output, employment, and prices. One proposition that emerges from Keynes's theory is that, from time to time, a capitalist economy will be characterized by persistent unemployment. The neoclassical synthesis accepts this result, even though a deeper consequence of the theory, which is that a capitalist economy with sophisticated financial practices (i.e., the type of economy we live in) is inherently unstable, is ignored. Keynes's analysis that leads to this deeper result provides the foundation for an alternative economic theory that leads us to an understanding of instability.[4]

Essentially, the neoclassical synthesis says that fiscal and monetary policy measures can eliminate persistent unemployment and that there are self-correcting forces within decentralized markets that set the economy at full employment. The neoclassical synthesis, however, speaks with a forked tongue: on the one hand, interventionist policy can eliminate persistent unemployment or chronic inflation, and on the other, if nothing is done, in time and of its own workings, the economy will sustain stable prices and full employment.

This neoclassical synthesis will no longer serve. It cannot explain the business cycles with regular incipient crises that we are now experiencing as a result of the internal operation of the economy. Unless we understand what it is that leads to economic and financial instability, we cannot prescribe—make policy—to modify or eliminate it. Identifying a phenomenon is not enough; we need a theory that makes instability a normal result in our economy and gives us handles to control it.

Thus, in the light of the behavior of the economy in the years since the mid-1960s, any economic analysis that claims to be relevant needs to address:

1. How the ruling market mechanism achieves coherence in particular outputs and prices,

---

4. This is the essential line of argument of the so-called post-Keynesian economists. See Paul Davidson, *Money and the Real World* (New York: Wiley, 1972), and Hyman P. Minsky, *John Maynard Keynes* (New York: Columbia University Press, 1975).

2. How the path of incomes, outputs, and prices is determined, and

3. Why coherence breaks down from time to time: that is, why is the economy susceptible to threats, if not the actuality, of deep depressions?

Furthermore, these questions need to be answered in the context of the institutions and financial usages that actually exist, not in terms of an abstract economy. It may be that what the neoclassical theory ignores, namely institutions, and in particular financial institutions, leads to the observations it cannot explain. A fundamental question that economic policy analysis must confront is whether, and over what domain, market processes can be relied upon to achieve a satisfactory economic performance. The general view sustained by the following analysis is that while the market mechanism is a good enough device for making social decisions about unimportant matters such as the mix of colors in the production of frocks, the length of skirts, or the flavors of ice cream, it cannot and should not be relied upon for important, big matters such as the distribution of income, the maintenance of economic stability, the capital development of the economy, and the education and training of the young. In what lies ahead, we will develop a theory explaining why our economy fluctuates, showing that the instability and incoherence exhibited from time to time is related to the development of fragile financial structures that occur normally within capitalist economies in the course of financing capital asset ownership and investment.

We thus start with a bias in favor of using the market mechanism to the fullest extent possible to achieve social goals, but with a recognition that market capitalism is both intrinsically unstable and can lead to distasteful distributions of wealth and power.

THE CURRENT STANDARD THEORY: THE PRE-KEYNESIAN LEGACY

During the 1970s American economists engaged in what might have been taken to be a serious controversy between Keynesians and monetarists.[5] The

---

5. The literature is immense, and any full citations would be book-length. The key names for monetarism are Milton Friedman and the joint and separate products of Karl Brunner and Alan Meltzer, Paul Samuelson, Franco Modigliani, and James Tobin are names in the neoclassical Keynesian camp, although from time to time Tobin shows signs of being a Keynesian rather than a neoclassical Keynesian.

participants and the press made it appear that a deep debate was taking place. In truth, the differences were minor—as the competing camps used the same economic theory. Furthermore, the public policy prescriptions do not really differ. The debate was largely academic nitpicking, and the public controversy was largely created by the press and by politicians. In this debate, monetarists emphasized that changes in the money supply destabilize the economy, and Keynesians argued that fiscal variables can be used to stabilize the economy. Until late in the 1970s, and even into the first years of the Reagan administration, both believed that with correct (that is, their) policy the economy could be fine-tuned so that full employment without inflation would be achieved and sustained. Both schools hold that the business cycle can he banished from the capitalist world; and neither school allows for any within-the-system disequilibrating forces that lead to business cycles. Neither Keynesians nor monetarists of the policy establishment are critical of capitalism as such; at most they are critical of some institutional or policy details.

Both monetarists and Keynesians are conservative in that they accept the validity and viability of capitalism. Neither are troubled by the possibility that there are serious flaws in a market economy that has private property and sophisticated financial usages. The view that the dynamics of capitalism lead to business cycles that may be thoroughly destructive is foreign to their economic theory.

The economic theory that is common to the Keynesians and the monetarists is the neoclassical synthesis. Keynes held that his new theory of 1936 marked a sharp break with the economic theory that then ruled; the neoclassical synthesis, however, integrates strands of thought derived from Leon Walras—a nineteenth-century economist—with insights and apparatus derived from Keynes. The dominant view among contemporary economists was expressed by Gardner Ackley—a member and then chairman of the Council of Economic Advisers in the Kennedy-Johnson era—when he held "that Keynes' work represents more an extension than a revolution of 'Classical' ideas."[6]

The process of assimilating Keynes's *General Theory* to the previous tradition began with the early reviews and academic interpretations. In this process, important aspects of Keynes's theoretical structure, which lead to revolutionary insights into the functioning of capitalism and to a serious critique, were ignored. This is why Joan Robinson called standard Keynesianism "bastard Keynesianism." As far as an understanding of

---

6. Gardner Ackley, *Macroeconomic Theory* (New York: Macmillan, 1961), p. vii.

Keynes by policy-advising economists and their political patrons is concerned, the Keynesian revolution is still to come.

The elements of Keynes that are ignored in the neoclassical synthesis deal with the pricing of capital assets and the special properties of economies with capitalist financial institutions. These elements can serve as the foundation for an alternative economic theory that is a better guide to interpreting events and is more relevant for policymaking than current standard theory. Indeed, these forgotten parts lead to a theory that makes instability, which has been of increasing importance since the mid-1960s, a normal consequence of relations that reflect essential attributes of a capitalist economy.

The view that instability is the result of the internal processes of a capitalist economy stands in sharp contrast to neoclassical theory, whether Keynesian or monetarist, which holds that instability is due to events that are outside the workings of the economy. The neoclassical synthesis and the Keynes theories are different because the focus of the neoclassical synthesis is on how a decentralized market economy achieves coherence and coordination in production and distribution, whereas the focus of the Keynes theory is upon the capital development of an economy. The neoclassical synthesis emphasizes equilibrium and equilibrating tendencies, whereas Keynes's theory revolves around bankers and businessmen making deals on Wall Street. The neoclassical synthesis ignores the capitalist nature of the economy, a fact that the Keynes theory is always aware of.

The Walrasian input to the neoclassical synthesis starts with a discussion of an abstract exchange (barter) economy: the analogue may be a village fair. Results are obtained by analyzing a model that does not allow for capital-intensive production, capital assets as we know them, and capitalist finance. Using an artificial construction of trading relations, the theory demonstrates that a decentralized market economy achieves a coherent result.[7]

Standard economic theory then goes on to show that the property of coherence also carries through for an economy that produces, but only under heroic assumptions about the nature of capital and time. In further extensions, the analytical apparatus of the neoclassical synthesis is applied to problems of aggregate income, money prices, and economic growth. In particular, supply and demand relations for labor are derived, and it is

---

7. Gerard Debreau, *Theory of Value* (New Haven: Yale University Press, 1959).

assumed that a price-level-deflated wage will adjust so that labor supply and demand are equal. The theory is set up in such a way that any deviation from the labor supply–labor demand equality will be removed by market interactions; that is, the theory holds that full employment is achieved by means of the internal operations of the economy. The theory does not explain, however, how any initial deviation is brought about: unemployment as the result of economic processes is unexplained. The emphasis is upon the interactions that make for equilibrium and not upon endogenous disequilibrating processes.

In the neoclassical synthesis, capital accumulation and the rate of growth of the labor force determine the rate of growth of output. The savings ratio yields the proportion of income that is accumulated. The neo-classical theory treats household savings propensities as the tune-caller, determining investment and, in turn, investment is the determinant of growth. The theory has no room whatsoever for institutions that finance investment and, in so doing, force saving.

Neoclassical theorists do short-run analysis—where inflation and unemployment exist—on the basis of a theory that does not allow for inflation or unemployment except as the result of outside forces. The monetarists identify an outside force—inept changes in the money supply—as the cause of unemployment and inflation. Neoclassical Keynesians do not have a consistent explanation of how unemployment and inflation are brought about. Their short-run theory is a muddle: they believe that the economy will not sustain full employment, but they do not identify the mechanisms that lead to unemployment and inflation.

In addition to demonstrating that decentralized market processes lead to coherent results, the tools and techniques of the neoclassical synthesis are used to demonstrate that a decentralized competitive market mecha-nism achieves an optimal result. The optimum that is derived is of a very special character: it rules out interpersonal comparisons of well-being and ignores the equity of the initial distribution of resources (and thus of income). Inasmuch as our aim is to indicate how we can do better than we have, and as the best is often the enemy of the good, we can forget about the optimum. Even though a tendency toward coherence exists because of the processes that determine production and consumption in market economics, the processes of a market economy can set off interactions that disrupt coherence. Accordingly, the flaws that lead to instability make ques-tions as to the optimality of the results of the market mechanism irrelevant.

Current theory makes an economy a lifeless arena in which depersonalized agents play abstract auctioning or recontracting games.

In our world of imperfect knowledge and imprecise actions, standard theoretical analyses posit either perfect knowledge or a fantastic capacity to compute. Nevertheless, these models (which are now highly mathematical) are interesting because they show that coherence is possible. But what practical people need to know is the extent to which market processes can be used to achieve desired results. The practical problem of economic policy is to identify the sources of instability and to determine policy interventions that constrain the emergence of incoherence, even as policy abstains from intervening in those markets whose internal operations tend to yield coherent results.

Coherence and Policy

A system is coherent if the connections among variables are stable enough that the reactions of the system to external changes are predictable. In an economy, coherence implies that a close approximation to equality between quantities supplied and demanded of the various commodities and services (including labor) almost always rules, and that such virtual equality is achieved and sustained by minor adjustments withim the economy. Planning, interventions, regulation, or controls are not required.

We know, however, that from time to time the coherence of the market system breaks down: the Great Depression of the 1930s is one example. Economic theory must, therefore, explain both the coherence of the pricing process and allow for the possibility of a breakdown. One way to do this is to build a theory that does not allow incoherence to be a result of the internal process of the economy, but that allows the pricing process to collapse when an unusual shock or some institutional aberration occurs. Occasional disorder is consistent with underlying coherence, if outside forces are responsible for the disorder.

For the neoclassical synthesis to be valid, apparent incoherence must be explained by external factors, such as imperfect institutions or errors of human judgment. Intervention in economic affairs by an outside party, such as a central bank (Federal Reserve System), is an obvious scapegoat for observed incoherence; other possible outside parties are trade unions, giant firms that have market power, foreign cartels, and government. Many of the explanations of the Great Depression, the inflation of the 1970s, and the depression of 1981–82 are in terms of just such outside influences.

For markets in which the future is important it is difficult to show that the reactions required for coherence will take place; the decentralized pricing process may sustain coherence in some markets, while in others, processes will be at work that will, in time, disrupt coherence. If this is the nature of the economy, then it is necessary to inquire if policies can be adopted or institutions created that are able to constrain or offset the processes that would lead to incoherence.

If the pricing mechanism of a decentralized capitalist economy can lead to coherent results *only if* proper policy or institutions rule, then intervention is necessary even though the market mechanism can be relied upon to take care of details. Once such conditional coherence is accepted as a characteristic of a capitalist economy, blind faith in and acceptance of the results of market processes can no longer be sustained. Moreover, in an economy that is conditionally coherent, legislated and evolutionary institutional changes affect the policy actions needed to sustain coherence. Policy cannot be a once-and-for-all proposition: as institutions and relations change so does the policy that is needed to sustain coherence.

Furthermore, for coherence to rule in a set of markets a substitution principle must apply. One facet of this principle is that if supply conditions change so that the price of a commodity (or service) used in consumption or production rises (or falls) relative to other prices, the quantity taken will decrease (or increase); this means that demand curves are usually negatively sloped. The second facet is that if the price of a commodity rises (falls), the quantities that will be taken of other commodities at a fixed price will tend to increase (decrease). That is, the quantities demanded of the commodities whose relative prices rise tends to decrease, whereas the quantities demanded of those commodities whose relative prices fall tends to increase. The principle states that higher relative prices tend to discourage and lower relative prices tend to encourage the use of a commodity or service.

If the principle of substitution is sufficiently strong, then decentralized markets are reliable tools for allocating output to households and input to businesses. However, in financial and capital-asset markets, in which speculative and conjectural elements are powerful, the principle of substitution does not always apply. A rise in the relative prices of some set of financial instruments or capital assets may very well increase the quantity demanded of such financial or capital assets. A rise in price may thus breed conditions conducive to another such rise.

Demonstrating that an exchange economy is coherent and stable does not demonstrate that the same is true of an economy with capitalist financial institutions; the wage and price changes brought about by unemployment do not always lead to the increase in investment needed to eliminate unemployment. External controls and coordinating mechanisms may be needed in a capitalist economy. Indeed, central banking and other financial control devices arose as a response to the embarrassing incoherence of financial markets, an incoherence that indicates that free markets will not do as a *universal policy prescription* for economies with capitalist financial institutions.

ROOTS OF THE NEOCLASSICAL SYNTHESIS: PRICES AS PARAMETERS

The basic constructs of the Walrasian or price-theoretic core of the neoclassical synthesis are preference systems of households and production functions for plants. The units of the theory are households and business firms.[8] The behavioral assumptions are that households try to maximize their well-being as defined by their preference systems under a budget—or total spending—constraint and firms try to maximize profits with defined production possibilities.

The task of neoclassical theory is to demonstrate that profit-maximizing firms, which are characterized by production functions, and utility-maximizing households, which are characterized by preference systems, interact in markets so that coherence results. To this end, supply and demand curves are determined by entering underlying preference systems and production functions with given prices of commodities and productive inputs. In competitive markets, each individual decision maker is assumed to take the price of all he sells and buys as given. Thus, each and every participant is powerless; the market is a thoroughly imperial and majestic instrument of control.

This is an impressive and beautiful result. Each person is powerless before the impersonal market, yet the prices that control behavior in the

---

8. We note an inconsistency here that is usually glossed over: production functions refer to plants, and the behavioral unit that corresponds to the production functions are firms. Plants are technological units, whereas firms are financial and managerial units. Plants exist in all economies, whereas the firm that is a financial unit exists only in capitalist economies.

market are market-determined transformations of individual behavior. If one set of prices leads to supplies not equaling demand in all markets, then prices will change: some prices, those of output with excess supply, will fall, and others, those with excess demand, will rise. Each new set of prices will affect demand, supplies, and incomes in such a way as to improve the coordination of the system. Excess supplies and demand therefore are transient phenomena, and the market mechanism is an efficient adjustment mechanism. In effect, the laws of supply and demand provide all the planning that a market economy requires.

If, with each unit behaving as if the prices that now rule have always ruled and will always rule, the system of markets is not fully coordinated, then prices will change. If units, in spite of price changes, continue to behave as if the new set of prices always ruled and will continue to rule— changes are never extrapolated—then the adjustments will be such that coordination of the system will improve. No one calls signals, no one runs drills, nevertheless each unit behaves as if it were a perfectly disciplined and extraordinarily well-trained member of a team. Any economy in which each individual unit has no option but to act in its own best interest, on the assumption that existing prices will always rule, will achieve a well-coordinated set of outcomes; units without power and units behaving with present prices as parameters guarantee coherence.[9]

The analysis of firms with market power and markets in which units have power is foreign to the essential core of the neoclassical theory. Too much monopoly, and monopolies confronting one another, can lead to a breakdown of the ability of the market to achieve coherent results.

In addition, if units act as if today's prices need not be tomorrow's prices, and decisions take into account what may happen in the future, then the market can also break down as an effective coordinating device. By their very nature, capital-asset and financing decisions involve action over calendar time; yesterday, today, and tomorrow exist. Of necessity, capital-asset decisions need to take into account what can happen over the life of projects; present decisions must allow for the future, and what happens today is the future for some prior decisions. It is impossible to sustain a naive argument that all such decisions are made on the expectations that what is will rule forever or, alternatively, that rational

---

9. Oscar Lange, "On the Economic Theory of Socialism," *On the Economic Theory of Socialism*, ed. Benjamin E. Lippincott (Minneapolis: University of Minnesota Press, 1938).

agents make capital and financial decisions assuming they know the future.[10]

Where monopoly power exists and when financing and investment are undertaken, present prices are not parameters for decisions. In these cases prices either vary with the unit's own decisions or the future enters in a significant way in determining behavior. Under these conditions markets can fail to be effective control and coordinating mechanisms.

We are left, then, with a split attitude toward the market. On one hand, the market is a very effective control and coordinating device if units are forced to take prices as parameters and to behave as if current prices will exist forever. On the other hand, the market can fail to achieve coherent results in situations in which units know either that their actions will have an appreciable effect upon prices or that current prices will not necessarily rule forever.

In market economies prices distribute outputs among households, and they allocate productive resources, which have alternative uses, to the production of various outputs. The price system therefore has distributional and allocational functions in the world of the neoclassical price theorists. In a world with capitalist institutions, however, prices will or will not validate past financing and capital-investment decisions as well as distribute income to workers and to owners of capital assets. But the relation between capital-asset compensation and the allocation of capital-asset services to various outputs is not as direct and simpleminded as the relation between labor compensation and the allocation of labor services to various productions. Time, investment, and finance are phenomena that embarrass neoclassical theory; once the problems associated with capital accumulation in a capitalist environment are introduced, the theory breaks down.

In essence, then, the valid part of neoclassical theory boils down to visualizing the economy as an interrelated set of supply and demand curves.

---

10. The "rational expectations" school holds that agents do not know the future, but they formulate their expectations on the basis of a satisfactory knowledge (i.e., a theory) of how the economy functions. If we add propositions to the effect that each agent's decisions are based on its maintained theory of system behavior, that general equilibrium theory is an apt representation of the world, and that those whose behavior is consistent with this apt theory will be successful, then an equilibrium and equilibrating view of the economy emerges. (See Robert E. Lucas, Jr., op. cit.) If the economy does not conform to the general equilibrium theory, if it is endogenously unstable, and if units behave accordingly, then rational expectations will exacerbate instability.

For each commodity a supply and demand curve is defined. These curves link the quantity of the commodity to the price of the commodity and to other prices; price in the neoclassical theory is the signal that determines quantities offered or taken. This way of looking at the economy is good enough for consumer spending out of income where the purchase is not only a repetitive act but also is not an overwhelming part of the total budget, but it breaks down where the purchase is a unique act, has consequences over a period of time, and involves large-scale financing that carries future commitments, that is, where the budget constraint on spending is not independent of financial-market decisions.

The interdependent supply and demand curves combined with the dynamic assumption that the system will move around until it reaches the sets of prices that simultaneously has supply equal demand for *all* markets is *the* Law of Supply and Demand that is so beloved of writers of editorials and conventional textbooks. But the validity of this law is restricted to a domain of markets in which the ability to spend is governed by some predetermined budget. Once the budget equations, which enter into the determination of demand curves, are affected by financing conditions and ruling expectations about the future, then the assumption that the interrelated supply and demand curves wiggle around until equilibrium is achieved is no longer valid. Markets involving finance and investments can achieve prices, quantities, and payment commitments that may not be sustained by future demand or profits.

The visions, constructs, and results of neoclassical price theory are all pre-Keynesian in the sense that the problems and the insights that Keynes introduced into theory are nowhere evident. The neoclassical synthesis is, however, an amalgam of the pre-Keynesian theory with ideas and constructs derived from Keynes's great work. The amalgamation does not take place in price theory; it takes place when the domain of economic analysis is extended to include the determination of employment, money wages, and prices in money terms. Accordingly, although today's aggregate theory is different from the pre-Keynesian aggregate theory, much of the aggregate theory of the neoclassical synthesis exists in a form that ignores Keynes's contributions.

NEOCLASSICAL AGGREGATE THEORY: THE PRE-KEYNESIAN BASIS

Neoclassical aggregate theory is an extension of the constructs and methods of analysis of neoclassical price theory to the determination of employment, output, accumulation, and the price level. It rests upon the heroic assumption that once relative prices and quantities are determined by the relations and processes examined in neoclassical price theory, then output and employment are also determined. The only problem that neoclassical aggregate theory has to address is the determination of prices measured in terms of money.

Aggregate production functions and collective-preference systems are the key construct of neoclassical aggregate theory. From the aggregate production function a relation between employment and output, the demand curve for labor, and a demand curve for increments to the stock of capital assets (a demand curve for investment) are derived. The collective-preference system yields the supply curve for labor and a supply curve for savings. Both the demand and the supply curves of labor are functions of a price-level-deflated money wage—what is called the real wage. The intersection of the supply and demand curves for labor determines this real wage and employment. Thus, the economy is placed at full employment, for that is what the situation determined by the intersection of labor demand and supply curves signifies. Once employment is determined, the production function yields output.

Neoclassical price theory, when used as a basis for aggregate analysis, leads to the labor market dominating in the determination of aggregate output. As some of Keynes's ideas were assimilated in the neoclassical synthesis, the real wages and employment of the intersection of the demand and supply curves for labor became the goal or objective that market processes achieved. In neoclassical theory, if labor demand is less than labor supplied (i.e., if unemployment exists), then an external barrier is preventing the attainment of the real wages and employment of the intersection, or some time-consuming process is under way that will, eventually, lead to full employment. If unemployment persists, it must be because the real wage of labor is too high and barriers in the form of union pressures or legislation prevent the real wage from falling, or because the equilibrating process is at work but takes a long time to achieve the equilibrium.

Supply and demand analysis is also used to derive savings, investment, and interest rates. The supply curve of savings reflects an assumption that consumption will he forgone only if there is a promise that future consumption will be larger. The increment to future consumption is discounted back to today at a discount rate, which makes that which is forgone now equal to that which is attained in the future. The preference system is assumed to be such that increasing doses of future consumption are needed to compensate for incremental sacrifices of current consumption.

In this way the savings out of current income are a rising function of the interest rate.

Investment is much like savings in that it involves a present sacrifice for a future benefit. Investors exchange the present costs of the investment output for a future income that will accrue as the investment output is used as a capital asset in production. If the present cost and future incomes are known, a discount of interest rate can be calculated for each investment project.

The amount of savings-investment that takes place and the interest rate are determined by assuming that savings are a function of the interest rate, that investment is a function of the interest rate, and that the interest rate varies so that saving equals investment. Savings, investment, and interest rate determination are thus no different from that of any other price.

The rate of accumulation that rules depends upon thrift, as a characteristic of preference systems, and productivity, as revealed by production functions. Money, bonds, and other financial instruments—and financial markets—do not enter into the determination of interest rates. In neoclassical theory, the connection between the fluctuating interest rates as observed in bond and stock markets and the obviously slowly moving—if it moves at all—productivity of capital assets as revealed by production functions is not explored. In neoclassical theory, if investment decreases rapidly—as it did between 1929 and 1933—it must be because of a sudden exhaustion of the technical ability of increments to the stock of capital assets to aid production or of a sudden increase in the future payoff required to compensate for forgone consumption. *In the neoclassical view, speculation, financing conditions, inherited financial obligations, and the fluctuating behavior of aggregate demand have nothing whatsoever to do with savings, investment, and interest rate determination.*

In neoclassical theory, the only way a present demand for future consumption can be realized is by storing some of current output, either in the form of the commodities to be consumed or as productive capacity. The supply of savings must become a demand for inventories and additional capital assets. Nowhere do money and finance affect the real variables—output, employment, and the division of output between current consumption and investment. The interest rate, also, is independent of money, reflecting thriftiness and productivity.

But money exists and is an economic phenomenon; furthermore, the prices we pay are money prices. Economics must come to grips with money, even though the subject is foreign to the village-market perspective and distasteful to the pure theorist because when money is recognized institutional detail intrudes upon the purity of generalized abstract reasoning.[11]

THE QUANTITY THEORY OF MONEY

Money enters into neoclassical theory because of the need to transform real wages and the relative prices of commodities into the wages and prices we observe, that is, wages and prices denominated in money. In neoclassical theory, money does not have any significant relation to finance and the financing of activity. Even though money becomes the fixed point, and other prices, as well as index numbers of prices, move relative to the value of the money unit, money in the neoclassical theory is, by definition, sterile. Money yields no income, and in the neoclassical view it only yields benefits in terms of facilitating transactions involving goods and services. Inasmuch as there is no uncertainty in the neoclassical world, the possession of money does not yield a subjective benefit in the form of protection against uncertainty.

Money is sometimes called a store of value because it is a way of carrying command over goods and services from one time to another. However, in neoclassical arguments that equate saving and investment, capital assets are the way in which consumption is carried from today into the future. Money as a store of value is inconsistent with interest rates adjusting to assure that investment equals full-employment savings.

In an economy in which money is used, the value of money paid equals the value of money received; the value of commodities and services bought equals the value of those sold. These identities state that the two sides of any exchange are equal in dollar terms: the money turned over equals the value of goods, services, or assets bought and therefore sold.

In order to utilize an identity in the construction of a theory, behavioral relations have to be established for the variables in the identity. The identity is the equation of exchange which, following Irving Fisher,[12] is conveniently written as $MV = PT$, where M is the money supply, V is the

---

11. "The most serious challenge that the existence of money poses to the theorist is this: the best developed model of the economy cannot find room for it. The best developed model is, of course, the Arrow Debreu version of Walrasian general equilibrium." Frank H. Hahn, *Money and Inflation* (Cambridge: MIT Press, 1983), p. 1.

12. Irving Fisher, *The Purchasing Power of Money* (New York: Macmillan & Co., 1911).

velocity or turnover of money, P is the price level, and T are the transactions. The relations that are assumed in transforming the identity into the quantity theory are:

1. M is assumed given from outside by the "authorities"

2. V is institutionally determined by the existing integration of production, payment conventions, and so on

3. P is the price level, which is to be determined by the quantity theory

4. T is the output as determined by the supply and demand for labor and the production function (when so defined, O for output replaces T for transactions in the equation).

When the quantity theory of money is added to (1) the labor market determination of income, (2) the saving-investment determination of the interest rate, and (3) the consumption–investment division of output, a precise theory emerges that determines the price level and its change over time. "Money is neutral" is the conventional phrase: it is an assertion that money does not matter, except for the determination of the price level.[13]

As a result, in the quantity theory of money, the general level of wages and prices are made a function of an exogenously determined money supply, but the institutional arrangements by which money is created are not considered to be important. In a world in which money is mainly demand deposits at commercial banks, much of the financing of business involves the creation of money—as debts are entered upon the books of banks—and

---

13. One way of interpreting Keynes is that in Keynesian theory money is never neutral. In Wassily W. Leontief's comment on the *General Theory* ["The Fundamental Assumption of Mr. Keynes' Monetary Theory of Unemployment," *Quarterly Journal of Economics* 51 (Nov. 1936)], he pointed out that Keynes's system was not neutral. In his rebuttal to Leontief and others ["The General Theory of Employment," *Quarterly Journal of Economics* 51 (Feb. 1937)], Keynes argued that the assumption of neutrality made the classical economics a very special case. AntiKeynesians such as Milton Friedman (see "The Role of Monetary Policy," *American Economic Review* 56 (March 1968), pp. 1–17), and Robert E. Lucas, see *Studies in Business Cycle Theory* (Cambridge: MIT Press, 1981), adopt various expedients to achieve transitory nonneutrality of money even as they assert that longer-run neutrality reigns.

the destruction of money—as debts are repaid. The effect of money upon the behavior of the economy has some connection with the processes by which it is created and destroyed. But in the quantity theory of money, what follows after an increase in the money supply is independent of whether the money enters the economy by means of loot from the Incas, a pirate's raid, the financing of business activity, or the purchase of government bonds by banks from prior holders. Such considerations are irrelevant: how money is created and the complex nature of money in a sophisticated capitalist economy are ignored.

NEOCLASSICAL AGGREGATE THEORY: A SUMMING UP

Neoclassical aggregate theory is a hierarchical system: labor demand and supply determine employment, the real wage, and, by entering employment into the production function, output. The consumption and investment allocation of this output reflects the reconciliation of productivity and thriftiness by means of the interest rate, which is determined in the saving and investment process. The quantity theory of money determines prices, but the determination of the real variables—production, employment, techniques of production, investment, and so forth—is independent of monetary influences.

Neoclassical aggregate theory is an extension of the model that is used to explain relative prices and output. Each commodity and its market can be treated as a separate entity, and the system can be required to satisfy *simultaneously* the clearing conditions for each commodity market as well as for money. In this formulation, money enters as a substitute or a complement with other specific commodities; however, in the aggregate an excess supply of money needs to generate an excess demand for commodities. But an excess demand for commodities leads to a rise in the market-clearing money price of commodities. Higher prices, in general, reduce real or price deflated wages for a given money wage. In this way a general model of interdependence can be set up in which a quantity theory of money is added to the relative price-determining system.

The neoclassical model is a full employment model; all who want to work at the prevailing price-deflated wage are employed. The dynamics of the aggregate model are predominantly particular market dynamics. Disequilibrium in a particular market—be it for underarm deodorants, labor, or savings-investment—is presumed to be resolved mainly by its own market dynamics. How an equilibrium is attained if the initial condition is not an equilibrium is discussed, but how the economy through its own processes would get to such an initial condition is foreign to the analysis.

In neoclassical theory, markets absorb disturbances from outside and transform them into displacements from equilibrium and determinants of a new equilibrium. Perhaps the fundamental difference between that viewpoint and the financial instability hypothesis—the theoretical core of what follows—centers on the notion of disequilibria and how they are generated. To the neoclassical synthesis, deviations from a full employment–stable price level equilibrium have to be explained by shocks; strong deviations, such as the Great Depression of the 1930s, the chronic and accelerated inflation of the mid-1960s through the 1970s, and the serious recession of 1974–75 and 1981–82, have to be explained by strong shocks. Thus, in the neoclassical view "outside" disturbances are responsible whenever the performance of the economy is unsatisfactory. The usual villains are the monetary system and the government. Depressions and inflations are due to some combination of the structure of monetary institutions, the operations of monetary policy, and government policies that affect institutions or change the level of government activity. In particular, any inquiry into what goes wrong in the monetary system need look no further than the behavior of the quantity of money. No differential effects of monetary changes depending upon the behavior and evolution of money institutions and markets is allowed—in particular the causation always runs from money to economic disturbances rather than from changing economic circumstances to monetary changes.

The neoclassical model is a weak intellectual and logical reed to lean on in explaining the behavior of and in formulating policy for our economy. Too much is either ignored or posited out of consideration. The neoclassical theory—as well as the neoclassical synthesis that is built upon it—does have one important and valid contribution to make to economic policy. The demonstration, albeit under strict conditions, that a competitive market mechanism can do the job of guiding production to conform to consumer's demands means that, for those subsystems of the economy where conditions are apt, the market can be relied upon, particularly if the market is *not* relied upon for (1) the overall stability of the economy, (2) the determination of the pace and even the direction of investment, (3) income distribution, and (4) the determination of prices and outputs in those sectors that use large amounts of capital assets per unit of output or per worker. The last point follows from the peculiar way in which the pricing of capital assets and their returns enters into the neoclassical theory when compared with the actual way returns to capital assets are determined in our economy.

Thus, a major theorem—the proof of the possibility of coherence—of the classical theory remains valuable. The demand curves of the economy reflect consumer preferences—once income distribution is taken for granted and allowance is made for the cultural determination of preference systems. Coherence will be sustained even as excise taxes and subsidies are used to both constrain and expand various outputs. Laissez-faire is not resurrected, however, by the realization that coherence can rule; what is valid is that intervention into the details of the game might be unnecessary once the aggregate outcome of the game is rigged.

THE CURRENT
STANDARD THEORY:
THE AFTER-KEYNES
SYNTHESIS

The fundamental neoclassical perspective is, as stated by Milton Friedman: "Despite the importance of enterprises and money in our actual economy, and despite the numerous and complex problems they raise, the central characteristic of the market technique of achieving coordination is fully displayed in the simple exchange economy that contains neither enterprises nor money."[1] In this view, "money has been introduced as a means of facilitating exchange, and of enabling the acts of purchase and sale to be separated into two parts."[2] The models that economic theorists constructed demonstrate that it is theoretically possible, albeit under restrictive circumstances, for markets without overt control to achieve a coherent result, and furthermore such abstract economies do not contain internal processes that can disrupt coherence. The incoherence that an economy exhibits during the downward spiral of a debt deflation or during an accelerating inflation is, therefore, foreign to neoclassical economic theory.

The inherited economic theory as of say, 1930, could not explain what happened in the Great Depression. From the perspective of neoclassical theory, a large shock would be necessary to cause such a large decline, and no proximate large shock, except for the stock market collapse, had

---

1. Milton Friedman, *Capitalism and Freedom* (Chicago: University of Chicago Press, 1962), p. 14.
2. Ibid. "Introduced" refers to the theory rather than to the world.

occurred.[3] Furthermore, standard economic theory offered no explanation of the stock market crash, of the subsequent debt deflation, and how a stock market crash could cause a deep depression. Even though business cycles, financial crises, and deep depressions occurred through the nineteenth and early twentieth centuries, the neoclassical theory sketched in the last chapter could not explain these events. The great decline of the American economy from 1929 to 1933 involved a sequence of crises in financial markets and an explosion of bankruptcies and unemployment. In these years a steady rain of failures of banks, other financial institutions, and corporations was punctuated by intervals in which a torrent of failures occurred. As a result, it became evident to economists that a better understanding of why our type of economy was so given to fluctuations was needed. Business-cycle research had been a major activity through the 1920s, and a variety of approaches to the analysis of business cycles appeared. A race was on for a new theory—a race won by Keynes.[4]

In August 1931 Keynes stated a view of how money enters into and affects our economic life that is in striking contrast to neoclassical views:

> There is a multitude of real assets in the world which constitute our capital wealth—buildings, stocks of commodities, goods in the course of manufacture and of transport, and so forth. The nominal owners of these assets, however, have not infrequently borrowed *money* in order to become possessed of them. To a corresponding extent the actual owners of wealth have claims, not on real assets, but on money. A considerable part of this "financing" takes place through the banking system which interposes its guarantee between depositors who lend it money, and

---

3. Peter Temin, *Did Monetary Forces Cause the Great Depression?* (New York: W. W. Norton, 1976), and Milton Friedman and Anne Schwartz, *A Monetary History of the United States 1867–1960* (Princeton: Princeton University Press, 1963), are briefs for the proposition that a significant prior disturbance did occur. To Temin, the prior disturbance was a drop in the consumption; to Friedman and Schwartz, the prior disturbance was a decrease in the money supply. To them, the Great Depression was not a normal outcome of economic processes.

4. Keynes wrote to George Bernard Shaw, on a post card, "I believe myself to be writing a book on economic theory that will largely revolutionize . . . the way the world thinks about economic problems." Cited in Roy F. Harrod, *The Life of John Maynard Keynes* (New York: Harcourt Brace, 1951).

its borrowing customers to whom it loans money wherewith to finance the purchase of real assets. The interposition of this veil of money between the real asset and the wealth owner is a specially marked characteristic of the modern world.[5]

In this view, money is created in the process of financing investment and positions in capital assets. An increase in the quantity of money first finances either an increase in the demand for investment output or an increase in the demand for items in the stock of capital or financial assets. As money is created, borrowers from banks enter upon commitments to repay money to the lending banks. In its origins in the banking process, money is part of a network of cash-flow commitments, a network that for the business side of the economy ultimately rests upon the gross profits, appropriately defined, that firms earn. In an economy in which government is small, which was true in 1931 when Keynes wrote the above, the money supply increases when bankers and their business customers are willing to increase current indebtedness. This will occur only because they both believe that future business revenues will finance the payments due on debts.

On the other hand, the money supply decreases as bank loans are reduced. A net decrease occurs when a significant portion of bankers and of (potential) borrowing businesses believe that future profits would not validate the commitments that would be embodied in new debts. Banks fail because cash due to them on their assets is not forthcoming, because assets they offer to sell to yield cash have fallen in price, or because they cannot place (sell) their liabilities. Bankers' expectations about the ability of business to validate debt reflect their experience with existing loans as well as their expectations of how the economy will behave. Successful fulfillment by business of commitments to banks increases the money supply because it encourages debt financing, and the failure of business to fulfill commitments decreases the money supply because it leads to a reluctance by bankers to debt-finance business. Thus, the money supply is very much determined within the economy, for changes in the money supply reflect profit anticipations of business and bankers' expectations of business conditions.

---

5. John Maynard Keynes, "The Consequences to the Banks of the Collapse in Money Values," *Essays in Persuasion: Collected Writings of John Maynard Keynes*, vol. 9 (London: Macmillan, St. Martin's Press, for the Royal Economic Society, 1972), p. 151.

In Keynes's view, money is related to the way ownership and control over capital assets are financed; the terms upon which money is created and held, therefore, are part of the mechanism by which today's views about the future affect current behavior. When the money supply due to business borrowing is increasing, both bankers and their borrowing business customers have favorable views about the future, whereas unfavorable views lead to bankers and their business customers contracting loans. This tends to decrease the money supply. Shifts from favorable to unfavorable views about the future take place in response to phenomena, internal to the operation of the economy, that affect realized and expected profits and terms on financing contracts. Most concretely, an increase in debtors who find it difficult or impossible to fulfill their commitments on debts will induce bankers to be skeptical of new proposals for debt financing, even as nonfulfillment of debt contracts by business decreases available bankers' funds.

To Keynes, bankers and their borrowing customers remember the past, try to evaluate the present, and recognize that the future can be unlike either. Successful bankers are not automata that treat present prices and cash flows as if they always existed and will rule forever. Because both bankers and their borrowers are aware of time, they recognize that their current decisions are made in the face of uncertainty. Calendar time and commitments denominated in bank liabilities (i.e., in money) are of vital importance in an economy with banking and in which debt financing of positions in capital assets takes place. The Friedman view, as cited at the head of this chapter, is thoroughly inconsistent with Keynes's view as to how our economy works and with simple observations on our economy.

As the Great Depression worked its malevolent will upon the world economy, it became evident that a theory aiming to explain the behavior of the economy would need to integrate monetary and financial variables into the explanation of why coherence does or does not rule. The split between what was taught in pure theory and what was taught in money and banking courses in the graduate schools of economics became untenable.[6]

Keynes's theory of a capitalist economy integrates the operations of Wall Street into the determination of what happens in the economy. One of the peculiarities of the neoclassical theory that preceded Keynes and the neoclassical synthesis that now dominates economic theory is that neither

---

6. Paul A. Samuelson, "What Classical and Neo-Classical Monetary Theory Really Was," *Canadian Journal of Economics* 1, no. 1, pp. 1–15. In Clower, ed., *Monetary Theory* (Harmondsworth, England: Penguin, 1969).

allows the activities that take place on Wall Street to have any significant impact upon the coordination or lack of coordination of the economy.

Keynes redefined the problem: economic theory had to explain why our economy is so given to fluctuations rather than being content with abstract arguments that a decentralized market system can yield coherence. Keynes's explanation of the performance of a capitalist economy emphasized investment, the way in which investment is financed, and the effects of financial commitments. The core of Keynes's analysis integrates the profitability of existing capital assets, the financing conditions for investing and holding capital assets, and the supply conditions of investment into a theory of effective investment demand. In this theory investment is a time-consuming process that rests upon profit expectations, so that the decisions to invest are always made under conditions of uncertainty. Because of uncertainty, investors and their financiers seek asset and liability structures that provide protection against unfavorable contingencies and adjust their portfolios as history unfolds and their views about the likely development of the economy change.

Keynes's *General Theory* was written in the aftermath of the Great Depression, during which a financial collapse as well as an enormous downward movement of output, employment, and asset prices took place. An analysis of investment under conditions of uncertainty and with capitalist financial usages is the core of his theory. Unfortunately for the development of economic theory, for an understanding of how our economy works, and for the design of policy to improve the performance of our economies, Keynes's investment theory of business cycles and his financial theory of investment in the face of uncertainty were lost as the standard interpretation of Keynes's *General Theory* evolved into today's orthodox theory. What had started as an inspired flash of understanding into basic relations guiding our economy was reduced by the interpreting economists who followed into a banal set of prescriptions for guiding aggregate output.[7]

In the standard interpretations, Keynes has been integrated with classical theory (see chapter five) to form what is called the neoclassical synthesis. Whereas Keynes in *The General Theory* proposed that economists look at the economy in quite a different way from the way they had, only those parts of *The General Theory* that could be readily integrated into the old way of looking at things survive in today's standard theory. What was

---

7. This is the theme of Hyman P. Minsky, *John Maynard Keynes* (New York: Columbia University Press, 1975).

lost was a view of an economy always in transit because it accumulates in response to disequilibrating forces that are *internal* to the economy. As a result of the way accumulation takes place in a capitalist economy, Keynes's 1935 theory showed that success in operating the economy can only be transitory; *instability is an inherent and inescapable flaw of capitalism.*

The view that survived is that a number of special things went wrong, which led the economy into the Great Depression. In this view, apt policy can assure that it cannot happen again. The standard theory of the 1950s and 1960s seemed to assert that if policy were apt, then full employment at stable prices could be attained and sustained. The existence of internally disruptive forces was ignored; *the neoclassical synthesis became the economics of capitalism without capitalists, capital assets, and financial markets.* As a result, very little of Keynes has survived today in standard economics.

CHRONOLOGY OF THE KEYNESIAN INPUT

To understand the interpretations and the influence of Keynes's *General Theory* it is useful to keep some dates in mind. In the United States, the contraction and collapse phases of the Great Depression took place between late 1929 and early 1933. The economy did not fully recover until very late in the 1930s, when arms expenditures, after the start of World War II in Europe, increased rapidly.

Keynes's revolutionary theory, *The General Theory of Employment, Interest and Money*, appeared in 1936. (The preface is dated December 13, 1935.) The reviews and the formal, often quasi-mathematical, expositions of what *The General Theory* is about began to appear in 1937.

The reform and recovery efforts that began in 1933, when Roosevelt began his first term, preceded the appearance of *The General Theory*: Roosevelt's second term began in January 1937. After *The General Theory* appeared, some of its ideas were used to rationalize the effects of the government deficits that occurred during the recovery years. However, the programs of the first years of Roosevelt's New Deal were mainly motivated, rationalized, and defended on humanitarian grounds. The unemployed needed income so as not to starve, and work was the way to provide income; the idea that money income could be distributed independently of work by means of a dole was anathema to both Roosevelt and the country. The idea that a government deficit would increase output and employment in the private portions of the economy was not advanced as the reason for the government spending programs, even though some not well-formulated ideas that pump priming was a good thing were advanced.

The New Deal was a reform effort as well as a recovery program. The main structural reforms of Roosevelt's first term, 1933–37, were in place before the ideas in *The General Theory* could have any influence. Many of the reforms were an attempt to arrange things so that a Great Depression could not occur again, and thus they reflected an explanation of the Great Depression. The reforms of the New Deal years mainly treated price deflation as the major cause of the Great Depression and looked with favor upon government and private interventions that constrained downward price flexibility. From the theory of *The General Theory*, however, price deflation was a symptom and part of the process that led to the severity of a depression; it was not the cause of a depression. From the perspective of *The General Theory*, the structural reforms of 1933–37 treated a symptom but not a cause of the great decline.

The recession of 1937–38 was largely imputed to price increases that occurred in markets where administered price ruled as the partial recovery took place. Economists newly converted to Keynes, such as Alvin Hansen of Harvard University, emphasized as causes of the 1937–38 recession the fiscal push from the veterans' bonus of 1936, the fiscal and monetary constraint as the economy moved toward a balanced budget in 1937, and Federal Reserve action to offset what was viewed as an inflationary potential.

The recession of 1937–38 led to the creation of the Temporary National Economic Committee,[8] which initially held the view that the exercise of monopoly power and administered prices was responsible for the incomplete expansion and the recession. Hansen's testimony to the commission was important in introducing Keynesian ideas into the policy discussions; however, it was not until the expansion of government activity as a result of World War II that a significant number of economists who had been influenced by Keynes became active in government and affected policy.

Keynesian ideas had some influence in the late 1930s because the theory, even in the bowdlerized form in which it became known, held that the market mechanism was not necessarily a self-correcting system that sought out and sustained full employment. In the 1930s it was self-evident that the

---

8. The Temporary National Economic Committee (TNEC) was organized in 1938 to make a thorough study of the concentration of economic power. See Ellis W. Hawley, *The New Deal and the Problem of Monopoly* (Princeton: Princeton University Press, 1966). The TNEC became the forum in which alternative views as to the causes and cures of recessions and depressions contended.

market was a fallible coordinator of economic activity. Even if market processes tended to correct deviations from full employment, the evidence of the 1930s was that correction did not take place quickly. The time it took for the internal adjustment processes to lead the economy back to full employment after a great recursive decline like that of 1929–33 was too long and too costly to be acceptable politically; at a minimum, market processes needed help from appropriate policy.

The 1930s were replete with various suggestions for reforming or helping the market mechanism. Keynes was interpreted by Hansen and others to mean that a close approximation to full employment can be achieved and sustained by an appropriate use of fiscal and monetary policy regardless of the structure and the institutional organization of labor and product markets.[9] This meant that the politically touchy problems of the structure of industry and the extent of market power could be largely ignored in formulating policy. It was argued that recovery and sustaining full employment did not require constraint upon the market powers of giant firms and the emerging unions. Monopoly and cartel policies were not considered vital, for their potentially adverse effects upon employment could be offset by an appropriate fiscal policy.

LABOR MARKET: DOMINANT OR DEPENDENT

A characteristic of Keynes's thought is that the level of employment is not determined by the internal working of the labor market. In the story told by classical aggregate models, as indicated previously, supply and demand conditions in the labor market determine employment and price-deflated wages. This equilibrium employment reflects production characteristics of firms and preference systems of households. In this theory the labor market is treated very much as if it were a market for peas or peashooters. The

---

9. Alvin Hansen, *Monetary Theory and Fiscal Policy* (New York: McGraw-Hill, 1949), is a mature statement of Hansenian Keynesianism. Alvin Hansen, *Fiscal Polity and Business Cycles* (New York: Norton, 1941), is an earlier statement. The review article by Henry C. Simons, "Hansen on Fiscal Policy," *Journal of Political Economy* L, no. 2 (April 1942), pp. 161–96; reprinted in *Economic Policy for a Free Society*, op. cit., is a model of an "attacking review." Simons's review can be read with pleasure for both its rather unfair attacking style and as a sophisticated attack on the interventionist economy.

assumed dynamics are that if a disequilibrium appears, in the form of either excess supply or demand for labor, changes in the price-deflated wage will eliminate the disequilibrium. Once employment is given, production characteristics of the economy determine output.

In place of the above classical scenario, Keynes's tale begins with the determination of the demand for output: the demand for output by households and business are taken up in the pure model, the demand for output by government is added in the policy model, and total demand is the sum of these sectoral demands. Employment equals the demand for labor as derived from output, provided the labor demanded is equal to or less than the quantity available at the ruling set of money wages. In Keynes's view, it is possible for the supply of labor at a ruling money wage to exceed demand and for the processes set in motion in response to unemployment to be ineffective in eliminating the excess supply. Keynes characterized this situation with involuntary unemployment as an equilibrium. It obviously is not a no excess supply/no excess demand situation, and it does not preclude falling money wages; it is an equilibrium only in the sense that the market reactions to the excess supply will not eliminate the excess supply efficiently.

In considering the processes that are set off by excess supply or demand, it is useful to distinguish between own-market and intermarket reactions. The own-market reactions include the movement of the price and quantity of the commodity or service itself. The intermarket reactions depend upon how changes in own-market variables affect supply or demand conditions in other markets, and the feedbacks from changes in other markets to the ownmarket. In the labor market, the own-market variables are the money wages of labor and the amount of labor actually employed. By the dynamics Keynes introduced, an excess supply of labor leads to a fall in the money wage; a fall in the money wage lowers supply prices of output and the incomes of the employed workers; the lower incomes lower money demand for output and thus for labor. At the lower money wages, both the supply and demand for output will decrease, thus lowering prices; there is no presumption that a fall in money wages will lower price-level-deflated wages. Thus, the effects of changes in labor market variables upon the labor supply and demand relations are such that an initial excess supply of labor may not be eliminated.

Even though a fall in prices and wages may not eliminate excess supply of labor through own-market reactions, it may by way of its effects upon other markets. Within Keynes's framework, this question is transformed into "How do falling money wages and output prices affect consumption and investment expenditures?" A decline in money wages leads to lower interest rates by increasing the price level deflated money supply. This effect is likely to be of limited power in removing the excess supply in the face of falling wages and prices. Furthermore, a fall in money wages and prices makes things worse initially by decreasing the cash flows that are available to households and business to meet commitments on inherited debts.

The essence of the neoclassical synthesis is to accept Keynes's formulation that aggregate demand determines a demand for labor independent of the price-level-deflated money wages; and then to show that market processes will, in time, assure full employment. If an excess supply of labor exists, then for this to happen market processes must shift the demand for output so that the demand curve for labor shifts upward. As a result, the excess supply is, in time, eliminated; the quantity of labor demanded increases because aggregate demand increases.

The main theorem of the neoclassical synthesis—that the market mechanism will lead to full employment equilibrium from initial situations in which unemployment rules—is powerful. The developers of the neoclassical synthesis granted Keynes a great deal—the basic analytical apparatus and the initial situation of unemployment equilibrium conform to Keynes's views. They also granted that because wages are both a cost and an income, labor market processes were ineffective in eliminating unemployment and accepted that the path from wage declines through interest rate declines (by way of increases in price-adjusted money) to investment can fail to achieve a close approximation to full employment. Nevertheless, by making a reasonable assumption that with the same income a wealthier consumer will spend more than a less wealthy consumer, the neoclassical synthesis was able to show that a market economy contains an internal mechanism that in theory assures that the demand curve for labor will intersect the classical supply curve for labor at full employment. This internal mechanism operated by having the consumption-income relation so depend upon the price-level-deflated quantity of money that a fall in prices would tend to shift the consumption-income relation upward and increase demand for any given level of investment. This real balance effect upon aggregate demand makes the labor market ultimately dominant; although there may be a transition in which the labor market equilibrium level of employment is not achieved.

This neoclassical result is sharply at variance with the Keynes result. In the Keynes scheme, the labor market does not determine employment and output. The money wage enters the cost and therefore the supply conditions of output from outside; money wages have a major role in determining the output price level. In Keynes's argument, money prices and relative prices are determined simultaneously in interacting labor and product markets.

THE HANSEN-KLEIN TRADITION: THE KEYNESIANISM OF ELEMENTARY TEXTBOOKS, ECONOMETRIC FORECASTING, AND POLICY SIMULATIONS

In Keynes's view, employment depends upon the interaction of aggregate demand and aggregate supply. In the standard interpretations, Keynes's theory of aggregate supply is largely ignored. In Keynes the determination of aggregate supply under capitalism is not simply a transformation of production possibilities as standard theory holds. In a capitalist economy, output is supplied and labor is demanded as a byproduct of the pursuit of profits; profit expectations determine output plans and employment offered by business. Actual profits are earned from the use of labor and existing capital assets, which use, argued Keynes, depended upon short-run profit expectations. Short-run profit expectations from producing consumption and investment outputs, which determine aggregate supply, depend upon the expected effective demand for consumption and investment. Long-run profit expectations enter into the determination of the demand price of investment. Time enters into supply calculations by way of the short-run profit expectations from producing investment outputs whose demand depends upon long-term expectations. Furthermore, under capitalist circumstances, aggregate supply depends upon the costs of the financing that must be undertaken if output is to be produced and labor is to be hired. The theory of supply under capitalist circumstances, therefore, cannot ignore the way production is financed. In particular, the payment commitments imposed by financing conditions determine available internal finance and the conditions for financing investment.

The standard, or orthodox, interpretation of Keynes emphasizes the view that, up to some full employment level, the supply price per unit of output will tend to be constant or slowly changing. This is so because only if aggregate demand exceeds the full employment aggregate supply at inherited wages and prices will wages and prices tend to rise. If aggregate demand falls short of the full employment level by some modest amount, then prices and wages will not fall or will fall but slightly. This gives rise to a theory in which prices do not change much for some range of aggregate demand, tend to increase if aggregate demand exceeds some level, and tend to fall if aggregate demand falls below some level.

The movement of wages and prices in general is determined by processes that are analogous to that which determines movement of particular prices. These orthodox Keynesian wage and price assumptions assume that supply in specific markets becomes inelastic as demand exceeds some level; that is, as aggregate demand rises the prices for some commodities will rise, because the quantity supplied does not change proportionally to demand.

Given the specification of aggregate supply in the orthodox Keynesian literature, employment depends upon aggregate effective demand. Up to some full employment barrier, a rise in aggregate demand leads mainly to a rise in employment; beyond that barrier it leads mainly to a rise in prices. For purposes of analysis, private domestic demand is broken down into homogeneous components. Households are one homogeneous class; they have incomes and buy consumption goods. Another homogeneous class consists of business firms, which have current and anticipated profits, own capital, and usually have liabilities outstanding that require either cash for servicing or that lead to some financial market transaction. Investment is the component of aggregate demand that is due to business demand.

Foreign demand and government demand also enter into total aggregate demand. Total aggregate demand equals total output, which is called gross national product (GNP) and is equal to the sum of consumption, investment, the excess of export over imports, and government outputs. Consumption demand is a function of income after tax adjustments. Because of this behavioral specification—that consumption depends upon income after taxes and transfers—arithmetically income becomes a multiple of the sum of investment, foreign, and government demand. In this version of Keynesian theory—as developed mainly by Alvin Hansen—the aggregate demand for output and thus for labor is a multiple, which is derived from the relation between consumption and income after taxes, of investment, exports minus imports, and government spending. In this view, any shortfall or excess of income from some target level can be offset by an appropriate change in government expenditure or taxes; fiscal policy becomes a device for steering the economy.[10]

In the simple case (no foreign trade) the argument boils down to the proposition that income is some constant (called the multiplier) times investment and government spending. Furthermore, this constant is the

10. Alvin Hansen, *Monetary Theory and Fiscal Policy*, op. cit. See also A. P. Lerner, "Functional Finance and the Federal Debt," *Social Research* 10 (Feb. 1943).

reciprocal of the ratio of an increment to saving to an increment to income; this ratio is called the marginal propensity to save.

The idea that saving out of income has to be offset by investment and government expenditure and the idea that more investment (or government spending) leads to higher incomes that generate the offsetting savings are clearly stated in this simple, one-function Hansen model. Conservative businessmen, politicians, and public figures who argue that the tax system should be adjusted to increase incentives for business to invest, because more investment means higher incomes and employment, are implicitly accepting the validity of this simple Hansen model.

This argument that employment, and therefore supply, are functions of the incentives for business to invest, was the basis for tax incentives and investment credits during the Kennedy-Johnson era. This Keynesian conservatism differs from the supply-side conservatism of Reagan in that Kennedy-Johnson focused on corporations' inducement to invest, whereas the later Reagan policies focused on household incomes and inducements to save. The earlier programs, though deeply conservative, implicitly recognized that excess desire to save had negative influences on the incentives to invest, whereas the later supply-side conservatism almost explicitly assumed that no matter what the saving relation may be investment will be sufficient to offset full employment saving.

Soon after the outbreak of World War II in September of 1939, Keynes and some of his Cambridge students were ensconced in the government. As it turned out, thinking in terms of the aggregates of the simple Keynesian theory proved useful in war planning. During a serious war, investment on private account, largely as a result of government controls, diminishes to the vanishing point: government demand and consumption make up aggregate demand. Taxation and rationing are used to constrain and control consumer spending and thereby free resources for the war. In these circumstances, the conundrums that concerned Keynes about investment, the financing of investment, and the relation between financial flows and system coherence or stability were irrelevant.

As World War II progressed, increasingly complicated models based upon the consumption function and exogenously determined or controlled investment and government spending were developed, and became a basis for planning for demobilization and the return to a civilian economy.[11] It

---

11. Nicholas Kaldor, "The Quantitative Aspects of the Full Employment Problem in Britain," Appendix C in *Full Employment in a Free Society*, ed. William H. Beveridge (New York: Norton, 1945), pp. 344–401.

therefore is no surprise that, in the early postwar years, analysis of the private economy and techniques for forecasting based upon the consumption function emerged. These models, however, either ignored monetary and financial relations or introduced monetary and financial relations in a very primitive way. A leading player of this model-building game was and is Lawrence Klein.[12]

Forecasting models were first developed as academic exercises and later became instruments used in policy analysis. By breaking variables like consumption and investment into component parts and by introducing sectors such as state and local government and financial institutions, income and employment were made to depend upon a complex system of empirical equations and relations.

It is quite common to set up the models in terms of markets—such as durable goods, services, labor—and to treat aggregate demand as if it were the result of the behavior in these markets. But these are pseudo-markets, for there are no markets for durable consumer goods; there are only various kinds of durable goods, and each kind is produced by firms and sold by retail outlets in markets with particular institutional characteristics. The structural models of the economist cannot be compared with the models that aeronautical engineers test in wind tunnels or by computer simulations. They are not miniature replications of what goes on in the economy; the structural models of the forecasters are disaggregations of the larger aggregates used in simple, Hansenian theory.*

Forecasting models based upon the consumption function survive in various government agencies, the Federal Reserve System, and a good number of commercial services, and are continuously updated to take into account emerging data. Their existence as up-to-the-minute forecasting tools depends heavily upon the capabilities of computers, which allow experimentation with different forms and different variables for the

---

12. Lawrence Klein of the University of Pennsylvania, a Nobel laureate, spawned a variety of econometric models that were complex in the detail they encompassed, even though they were, and remain, analytically simple. See Lawrence R. Klein and Arthur S. Goldberger, *An Econometric Model of the United States, 1928–1952* (Amsterdam: North Holland Publishing Company, 1955).

* By disaggregating and introducing additional variables, each of which requires further explanation, it is possible to make the forecasting format as complicated as is desired, even though the intellectual sophistication of the work never goes beyond that of the simple consumption function or multiplier model.

equations that summarize experience. This experimental approach means that the structure of forecasting models changes by modifying existing equations and, as a result, are a hodgepodge of often inconsistent pieces. Even economists who are sympathetic to the use of econometric models are unhappy about the relations that are implicit in these models.

Forecasting involves feeding policy items such as government spending and taxing formulas and Federal Reserve operations into a model that consists of equations representing the components of aggregate demand. The various equations have parameters that were derived empirically. Each structural model is transformed into solution equations for the system-determined variables that concern the forecaster. The model then gives values of variables for a particular date as a function of the past of the system. If the model is well behaved, the forecast values of the variables can be used as past values to get even further into the future. By such recursive computations, a time series—a run of the model—can be generated; multiple runs can be generated by varying the policy premises and the behavior of unexplained variables. If these runs vary in their policy assumptions, they are policy simulations. Policy evaluations such as, "if we give each person a $50 tax rebate, then real income will be 4 percent higher and inflation will be 2 percent higher than otherwise" are the result of simulations of the economy by runs with forecasting models.[13]

Policy simulations can also be made by varying the fitted or estimated parameters in structural models to probe the effects of changes in legislation, for example, changes in the minimum wage or institutions. However, the simulation cannot be better than the model, and the econometric model cannot be closer to reality than the economic theory of the model builder. In particular, instability generated from within the workings of the economy is not caught by models that do not include strong links with the financial structure.

As the 1970s progressed, it became clear that models that ignored financial relations did not work well as forecasting instruments, and they were modified so that the money supply—as an exogenous factor—became of greater importance in the forecasting process. We now have forecasting models that combine ideas drawn from Keynesian aggregate-demand theory

13. Daniel B. Suits, "Forecasting and Analysis with an Econometric Model," *American Economic Review* LII (March 1962); reprinted in Robert A. Gordon and Lawrence R. Klein, *A.E.A. Readings in Business Cycles* (Homewood, Ill.: Richard D. Irwin, Inc., 1965).

and the classical quantity theory of money. Such models are internally inconsistent; whatever success they enjoy is due to the way in which they extrapolate past values of variables into estimates of near-term future values. Their success, such as it is, demonstrates that the economy has a good deal of momentum.

The simple Hansen consumption-function model was the backbone of an entire generation of economics textbooks and the rock upon which the fiscal policy approach to fine tuning the economy was based. It was durable because it was the intellectual basis of apparently successful policy as well as of the forecasting and policy-simulation models. As policy has become less successful, the Hansen model lost its popularity. Nevertheless, the econometric models, which are very complex structures built upon an extremely simple theoretical input, have survived as a tool of policy analysis.

Financial instability was an evident trait of the economy after the mid-1960s. The models derived from the Hansen and Klein formulation are incapable of generating financial instability by their internal processes. Policy decisions on the basis of simulations with such models, therefore, reflect the explicit assumption that financial instability cannot occur or is not relevant. Consequently, such decisions ignore a major part of reality and will often result in the economy missing the policy objectives.

The line of development from Hansen's simplification of Keynes's concepts to the forecasting and simulation models based upon the consumption function provided economists with a simple, powerful, and relevant way of looking at our economy—as long as financial and monetary factors could, for the most part, be disregarded. The early postwar period was marked by such financial and monetary tranquility, but that tranquility has been replaced by turbulence since the mid-1960s, and with turbulence the reliability of the models derived from Hansen and Klein has declined. Forecasts and simulations with such models have accordingly been. poor guides to policy: recent experience has shown that the economy does not behave as it is supposed to.

THE HICKS VERSION

The formulation of Keynes put forward by John R. Hicks in 1937[14] goes beyond Hansen's simple consumption-function model. Hicks recognized

---

14. John R. Hicks, "Mr. Keynes and the 'Classics': A Suggested Interpretation," *Econometrica* 5 (1937).

one essential point of Keynes's theory, namely, that financial and monetary variables must be integrated into the explanation of aggregate demand. Hicks interpreted Keynes as allowing for two sets of interdependent markets, one for commodities and the other for money or finance (bonds). In each set of markets Hicks derived the interest rate and level of income combination consistent with equilibria. He identified the problem as set up by Keynes as the determination of the simultaneous equilibrium in both sets of markets. Hicks has aggregate output and interest rates settling at the level that simultaneously satisfies the equilibrium conditions in the commodity and the money sets of markets.

Hicks therefore treated the determination of aggregate demand as if it were a supply and demand problem; he argued that there are combinations of interest rates and incomes that would equate supply and demand in both commodity and money markets. As in Hansen, private domestic demand for commodities is made up of two parts: the demand for consumption and the demand for investment. Consumption demand was taken to be a function of income and the interest rate. The use of income as a variable is a bow toward Keynes, while the use of the interest rate as a determinant of consumption is a bow to classical views of saving.

Hicks took investment to be a function of the interest rate and the level of income (mainly as an afterthought). At this point Hicks made a major step toward forcing Keynes into the classical model, for he interpreted the relation between investment demand and interest rates as reflecting the marginal productivity of capital. This identification of the interest rate with a production-function attribute meant that Hicks was implicitly assuming that the economy gravitated to some unique full employment income level. In an economy in which the level of employed to employable labor varies, the profits earned by capital assets depend upon the extent to which aggregate demand leads to scarcity of capital-asset services. A steel mill is just as productive *technologically* when it is working well below capacity as when it is working at capacity, although it is much more *profitable* at capacity output than at lower operating levels.

Income equals consumption plus investment, and as income minus consumption also equals saving, saving equals investment. Both saving and investment depend upon the interest rate and income. Therefore, there is a two-dimensional curve that gives the interest rate and income combinations for which savings and investment are equal, albeit at a different level for each combination. Along this curve a lower interest rate is associated with higher investment and therefore higher income: the curve slopes downward.

In a neoclassical framework, the rationalization for a lower interest rate implying more investment is that lower interest rates with given money wages lead to the use of production techniques that use more capital relative to labor, and the greater the desired capital/labor ratio the higher the rate of investment. The greater the rate of investment then, by the multiplier relation, the greater the level of income.

The argument advanced for the interest-investment relation used in the Hicks formulation, and in most formulations that stick to an orthodox view of investment, is mainly a hand wave. Even if it is accepted that lower interest rates imply that production is best carried on with higher capital output ratios, investment, which is the time rate of change of capital assets, need not increase. A desire for a larger capital stock does not necessarily mean that the capital stock will increase at a more rapid rate.[15]

Money is demanded for its ability to expedite transactions that enter into current output, and as an asset that offers an in-kind yield as a protection against unfavorable contingencies.[16] Because money is demanded to facilitate exchanges that involve current income, income is a variable in the demand for money. As the yield in kind from money must be worth as much as the return on bonds for money to be held, the interest rate is a variable in the demand for money. This means that if income is given, the greater the amount of money the lower the interest rate. Furthermore, for any given quantity of money, a higher income is associated with a higher interest rate. Thus, for any given supply of money, a set of interest rate and income combinations exists at which the demand for money equals the supply; these combinations are alternative equilibria in the money market.

Ignoring everything Keynes wrote about the way in which the money supply of a capitalist economy is created in the process of financing activity, the Hicksian tradition assumes that the money supply is determined by the authorities (the Federal Reserve in the United States); that is, the quantity of money is a policy variable. The authorities can use changes in the money supply to determine the interest rate-income combination that will rule. For a given money supply, a higher income is associated with a higher

15. In his 1937 article, Hicks offered no argument for the way he stated his investment function; indeed the long discussions about investment and capital-asset prices in Keynes's *General Theory* were ignored.

16. Hicks and Patinkin and the other economists of the neoclassical synthesis have a problem at this point. Because they do not recognize the importance of Keynes's hypothesis with respect to uncertainty, there is no return that they can identify with the in-kind yield of money.

interest rate, for the value of money to facilitate transactions increases the more transactions that have to be facilitated.

In Hicks's argument one curve, the loci of investment-saving equilibria, slopes downward, and the other, the loci of money equilibrium, slopes upward. Furthermore, the interest rates and incomes in both curves are positive. With both income and interests constrained to the first quadrant and appropriately placed, the two market-equilibrium curves will intersect. There is one unique interest rate and income combination that simultaneously satisfies the equilibrium conditions in the money and in the commodity markets. If the quantity of money changes, then the equilibrium curve for the money market may change, and thus the intersection with the commodity-market-equilibrium curve will change.

Once income is determined, the level of employment is also determined. Let us assume employment is below the full employment level. In these circumstances, an increase in money may lower the interest rate and raise the income level—thus tending to decrease unemployment. In this Hicks formulation, therefore, it appears possible for money to call the tune: seemingly there exists an appropriate quantity of money that will lead to a full employment income level.

In order to get unemployment as an equilibrium position that is independent of the amount of money supplied by the authorities within the Hicks model, it is necessary to introduce appropriate specifications of the shape or position of the commodity or the money-market-equilibrium curves. One way this can be done is by an exhaustion of investment opportunity specification of the investment function. What if the amount of investment at a zero interest rate is insufficient to generate full employment, given the nature of the consumption-income relation? That is, no matter how low the nonnegative interest rate may be driven by increasing the money supply, investment cannot be large enough to offset full employment savings.

If investment insufficiency is the cause of the unemployment equilibrium, then policy aimed to increase employment can go one of three ways: government spending can be added onto income; investment can be increased by government subsidies and guarantees; or the cost of investment can be lowered relative to the stream of anticipated profits. The first route leads to government tax and spending programs (including transfer payments) that raise the consumption-income relation so that the employment level compatible with any investment level increases.

The second path, government guarantees of returns on investment projects, has been traveled in the United States during peacetime mainly with government guarantees on mortgages, a variety of agriculture programs, and some defense and other public-function spending.

A third direction policy can take is to lower the price of investment goods or raise the stream of anticipated profits. Starting with the Kennedy-Johnson years, the policy diagnosis has usually been that more investment is needed to achieve both full employment and faster growth. As a result, a wide variety of tax credits and income tax adjustments have been used to reduce the net price of investment or to increase profit flows.

Unemployment would be unresponsive to changes in the supply of money within the Hicks formalization if the interest rate is independent of the money supply. This is the famous liquidity trap—which holds that an increase in the quantity of money for certain ranges of income does not lower the interest rate.

The liquidity trap renders monetary policy ineffective. Such a trap is possible in the aftermath of a financial crisis and will be characterized by low interest rates on default-free securities and substantial interest premiums on riskier securities. But in the Hicks formulation monetary policy that changes the money supply remains effective in affecting income so long as interest rates are not too low.

The Hicks formulation was and continues to be the basis for textbook expositions of the Keynesian model. The curve of the equilibrium interest rates and incomes in the commodity market is usually labeled IS, and the curve of the equilibrium interest rates and incomes in the money market is usually labeled LM. The Hicks formulation is known as the IS-LM model.[17]

The IS-LM formulation is not the neoclassical synthesis, although it paved the way for the neoclassical synthesis. The money demand equation is stated in such a way that it can be interpreted as a quantity theory of money equation with a variable velocity that is a function of the interest rate. It also embodied a classical view of the investment function. The Hicks formulation did not contain a mechanism by which an excess of labor supply necessarily leads to reactions that increase the demand for labor. Although it goes quite a way toward the classical view, the Hicks model does not achieve the labor-market-dominated equilibrium that characterizes classical thinking.

---

17. Martin Bronfenbrenner, a well-known economist of wit, has labeled the Hicksian model the world of ISLAM.

THE PATINKIN RESOLUTION: THE TRIUMPH OF LABOR MARKET DOMINANCE

To the established economists of his day, Keynes's results flew in the face of the standard wisdom that the economy was a self-equilibrating system. Keynes's theory implied that market processes guaranteeing that the economy will achieve full employment equilibrium may not exist and that the internal processes of a decentralized market economy can be disequilibrating. In effect, Keynes argued that the coherence result of classical theory was not in general valid for capitalist economies because the financial and monetary systems could not be relied upon to be well behaved.

Keynes's results meant that there was a prize awaiting any academic who could upset the heresy. The game was to show that, even if Keynes is granted his assumptions and postulates, the normal processes of a decentralized market mechanism will attain and then sustain full employment unless they are prevented from operating.

Part of the success of Keynesian analysis—and also one reason why the full scope of Keynes's economic theory was not recognized—was due to the development, almost concurrently with the publication of *The General Theory*, of a system of national income accounts. This system of accounts, largely developed by Simon Kuznets,[18] treated income in ways that are compatible with the breakdown of demand into homogeneous behavioral classes as postulated by Keynes. It was but a small logical step to use the apparatus as developed by Hansen and Hicks to explain the national income accounts. A symbiotic relation developed between national income accounting and the standard Hicks and Hansen interpretation of *The General Theory*.[19]

---

18. Preliminary results of Kuznets's research were available to Keynes as he wrote *The General Theory*. On pages 102–04, Keynes used data drawn from Kuznets's preliminary results as reported in Bulletin 52, National Bureau of Economic Research, 1935.

19. National income accounting was relevant because of the analysis derived from *The General Theory*, and *The General Theory* led to metrical statements about the economy because of the existence of national income data. Without national income data the Klein type of model building could not have taken place.

Kuznets's research on national income and its components showed that there was a difference between the short-run—or cyclical—and the longrun—or secular—behavior of the consumption-income ratio. In the short run—or over a business cycle—the ratio of consumption to income varied: it was higher in recessions than in prosperity, but in the long run, where the impact of business cycle stages are averaged out, the ratio of consumption to income seemed to be almost constant.

A rise in the saving ratio during a cyclical expansion means that investment increases at a faster rate than income as the economy expands toward full employment. At the investment-to-income ratio that is required as an expansion matures it becomes difficult to sustain the expansion. The behavior of the consumption-income ratio apparent in the Kuznets data gives credence to views that the cyclical behavior of saving is an element determining the cyclical behavior of the economy.

The apparent paradox, in which the secular consumption-income ratio is constant whereas the cyclical ratio is variable, is the type of problem that academic researchers like. Those who played the game of finding resolutions of the paradox tend to fall into two groups: one offered explanations that tried to explain the observations by referring to social and psychological phenomena; the other presented explanations that referred to the economic phenomena of the valuation of capital and accumulation.

One set of social and psychological explanations argued that it takes time to adjust to increases in income, and that once a consumption level is attained, it will be defended even if it involves decreased saving or selling assets.[20] Thus, when income is reduced in a recession, consumption tends to be sustained. Another set of social and psychological explanations argued that consumers looked at their lifetime or permanent income.[21] Consumption; in this view, is based either upon the present value of all future incomes, where a unit is in its life cycle, or upon the permanent income that a unit expects to receive. In principle, the lifetime and the permanent-income concepts assume that a consuming unit has a trade or skills, that

---

20. James Duesenberry, *Income, Savings and the Theory of Consumer Behavior* (Cambridge: Harvard University Press, 1949).

21. Milton Friedman, *A Theory of the Consumption Function* (Princeton: Princeton University Press, 1957). France Modigliani, "Fluctuations in the Savings-Income Ratio: A Problem in Economic Forecasting," *Studies in Income and Wealth*, vol. 2 (New York: National Bureau of Economic Research, 1949), pp. 371–443.

these skills fit the unit into production functions, and that the marginal product of its skills or trade determines its income. From time to time, deviations from this income will arise, but these deviations will not affect consumption. In depressions this income deviation is negative, and in good times it is positive; thus, in depressions the ratio of consumption to income is high, and in prosperity it is low.

A second explanation for the difference refers to the accumulation of wealth. When our economy does well, investment takes place and presumably useful capital assets are accumulated: the average per capita wealth increases. If we make the assumption that the greater the value of wealth relative to income the smaller the incentive to save, then there will be an upward drift in the consumption-income ratio as accumulation takes place. If, over a business cycle, wealth and income increase and if the wealth-income ratio remains about the same, then the incentives for saving will be unchanged, even though income per capita has increased. These considerations point to the view that in the longer run the savings-income ratio will tend to be constant.[22]

Two major steps in the development of the neoclassical synthesis out of the Hicks model are (1) the proposition that the longer-run savings-income ratio does not change very much as income per capita increases and, (2) the explanation of this proposition by an assumed effect of increased wealth upon the consumption-income ratio. To complete the neoclassical synthesis, a way is needed for the processes presumably set in motion by the insufficient investment that leads to unemployment to induce to a rise in the consumption income relation. A rise in this relation means that for every level of investment the equality of saving and investment will be achieved with higher income and employment.

A basic proposition in economics is that in the absence of market power excess supply in a market leads to a fall in the price of the traded item. Excess supply of labor (unemployment) will therefore mean that money wages will fall. A fall in money wages leads to a fall in the supply prices of output, so that the money wage rate adjusted for price level changes need not fall. If the price-level-deflated money wage is the determinant of both the demand and supply of labor, no reduction in unemployment need occur when wages and prices fall. To get a reduction in unemployment,

---

22. Tibor Scitovsky, "Capital Accumulation, Employment and Price Rigidity," *Review of Economic Studies* 7 (1940–41), pp. 69–88. Arthur C. Pigou, "Economic Progress in a Stable Environment," *Economica* 14 (1947).

a decline in money wages and supply prices would have to increase either consumption or investment demand. However, it was accepted that the path to increased demand by way of interest rate declines that lead to increased investment was barred by adverse expectational effects when prices are falling. The only way for price deflation to increase aggregate demand is thus by way of increased consumption.

If falling prices bring about an increase in wealth per capita, then consumption per unit of income is likely to increase. Wealth mainly consists of capital assets, which have value solely because of the cash flows or profits they are expected to generate. Since a general decline in wages and prices is likely to lead to an equal or greater decline in the cash flows or profits that capital assets earn, the value of capital assets will go down as fast, or faster, than the price level of output. When money prices fall, the change in the price-level-deflated values of real capital assets cannot lead to a wealth effect that increases consumption.

But the owners of wealth do not own only capital assets, they also own money and government bonds. Presumably, the price-level-deflated value of money and bonds will rise with falling prices: this should help push consumption demand upward. In any event, since bank money is typically offset by debts by private individuals and business, the burden of the payments required by debts increases as price deflation takes place. As a result, the expansionary effects upon consumption caused by the rise in the price deflated value of money will be offset by the effect upon both investment and consumption caused by the increased burden of servicing debt as prices fall. The desired shift in aggregate demand will not take place as a result of a wage and price deflation so long as capital assets, private debts denominated in money, or money that rises from private debts are the only assets—real and financial—in the economy.

However, the debts of banks that make up the money supply are offset by three classes of bank assets: private debts, interest-bearing government debts, and gold or fiat currency issued by governments. A fall in prices will tend to increase the price-deflated value of government debt held by a bank or by households and businesses, the price-deflated value of money that is offset by bank-held government debt, and the price-deflated value of gold or fiat money. (A debate, mainly unresolved, exists whether a price-level-deflated rise in taxes to service government debt offsets all or part of the impact of government debt.)

This real-balance effect—that an increase in the price-deflated appropriately defined money supply will increase the consumption-income ratio for every income—is the rock upon which the neoclassical synthesis is founded.[23] If as a result of unemployment, wages and prices fall, creating a rise in the price-deflated money supply, then the increased wealth will raise the ratio of consumption to income. If wages and prices fall as long as labor supply exceeds labor demand and if falling prices increase the consumption income ratio, then, in time, the labor supply will no longer be excessive (full employment will be achieved), and the decline in prices will cease.

Once demand for labor derived from the sum of investment and consumption passes through the intersection of the labor demand and supply curves, then the price and wage deflation ceases. In this view the classical labor market is dominant, for the system settles at an income level given by the full employment of labor. Once output is given, then the saving and investment functions determine the interest rate, and once the interest rate is given, then velocity or the cash balance is determined. With output and velocity determined, the demand and supply of money determines the price level. Once the real-balance effect is introduced, the classical result is achieved from Keynesian beginnings.

The trick of introducing the price-deflated value of the portion of the money stock that does not reflect private debt into the consumption function is mainly credited to Don Pafinkin: hence this real-balance path to achieve the demand consistent with labor-market equilibrium is often labeled the Patinkin resolution.[24] If we start with a Patinkin equilibrium and change the quantity of the relevant type of money, then a disequilibrium will be set up along with various destabilizing and equilibrating processes. Eventually, it is argued, the equilibrating process will take over and will lead to a price level that stands in the same ratio to the initial price level as the new quantity of relevant money stands to the initial quantity. At this new equilibrium, all the variables of the system other than the money supply and the price level will be exactly as they were in the initial equilibrium. The Patinkin resolution reestablishes the quantity theory of money—except that the proportionality between the price level and the money supply holds only at equilibrium positions. Out-of-equilibrium positions are characterized by deviations from this equilibrium ratio between money and money prices.

23. Milton Friedman, *A Monetary Framework*.

24. Don Patinkin, *Money, Interest and Prices: An Integration of Monetary and Value Theory*, 2d ed. (New York: Harper and Row, 1965).

With the Patinkin resolution we have achieved the neoclassical synthesis. The fulcrum used to move the world to its full employment equilibrium is the excess demand (or supply) for commodities or services that exists whenever there is an excess supply (or demand) of money. The Patinkin resolution is more than the quantity theory of money, for it achieves the labor-market dominance that characterizes neoclassical economics as a theorem rather than as an assumption.

But the Patinkin resolution proves too much. It leaves the neoclassical synthesis with no explanation of how an economy can get into an initial unemployment or inflationary position. Once the economy is out of equilibrium, the Patinkin resolution shows how equilibrium can be established, but it cannot generate the initial disequilibrium.

Furthermore, within the world of the Patinkin resolution the appropriate money supply is not the money supply as reported by the Federal Reserve; it is, rather, the money supply that is not offset by private debts to the banking system. In many ways the Patinkin resolution operates as if the entire money supply were gold and the nominal value of gold were fixed.

However, today's world is not a gold-coin world. The essential money-creating act involves the financing of investment or positions in assets. In this world, price deflation increases the burden of indebtedness of capital-asset-owning units, which tends to constrain investment and employment. If the Patinkin effect is relevant it is only in the long haul and after a large price is extracted in lost output and employment.

THE REDUCTION OF THE KEYNESIAN REVOLUTION TO BANALITY

A fundamental shortcoming of the neoclassical synthesis is that it does not explain how an economy gets into the unemployment equilibrium trap from which the real-balance effect is to induce a recovery. This shortcoming exists because the neoclassical economic theory, which is constructed to demonstrate that a decentralized market mechanism yields a coherent result, does not allow for disruptive internal dynamic processes. Neoclassical theory also assumes that the apparatus of constructs developed to show how a decentralized trading economy can achieve coherence can be applied to answer questions about the behavior of an accumulating capitalist economy and to explain observed differences in well-being among economies. In particular, the doctrine that household demand brings forth the production of commodities so that the consumer is sovereign is extended to the treatment of savings. In the neoclassical view household savings seemingly draw forth investment. Questions as to how economic institutions operate so as to create, extract, and allocate a surplus are foreign to the neoclassical formulation of economic analysis.

Within the neoclassical theory, fluctuations, disequilibrium, and financial trauma can only occur because of shocks or changes imposed from outside the system. Thus, a great deal of what happens in history is explained as the result of institutional failures in unique historical circumstances. Dominant events such as the Great Depression of the 1930s cannot be explained as the result of systemic characteristics so long as the world is viewed through the blinders imposed by neoclassical theory.

Because the neoclassical synthesis does not allow for internal destabilizing forces and has no view of historic time, it needs to explain the existence of persistent disequilibrium by processes that block the workings of the equilibrating mechanisms within the system. In particular, for the real-balance effect to work it is necessary for an excess supply of labor to lead to a fall in money wages and prices. If, with excess supply, traditions and imperfect markets lead to wages and prices not declining or not declining fast enough, unemployment will persist. This makes the persistence of unemployment the result of perverse behavior by labor. In particular, it is the handiwork of a villain—the trade unions. Note that in this argument the proximate victims of unemployment (workers) cause unemployment to persist; it thus appears as if the market mechanism not only yields a coherent result, but also retributive justice.

As the neoclassical synthesis mainly compares positions of equilibrium, the economy it models does not exist in historic time but in a timeless vacuum. Because private financial commitments exist, the burden of inherited debt increases with wage and price deflations. A rise of the burden of debt when price deflation occurs makes borrowers and lenders alike wary of the debt-financing of private spending, and in particular of investment. A decline in investment is a reaction to price deflation. Even as a theoretical construct it is not until investment virtually disappears that the money–price level effect upon consumption emphasized by Patinkin can tend to stabilize and then increase demand. Unemployment is likely to become worse before it gets better once price deflation takes hold, and it may be worse for an uncomfortably long period. Unless we can identify who gets hurt and for how long, and are willing to say it is good and proper for those who get hurt to pay the price, it is rather cavalier to assert that the neoclassical mechanism of price deflation should be allowed to operate if there are alternatives. If an economy is not doing all that poorly, even if it is not doing as well as the best possible, then the chance that things will get and stay worse if wage and price deflation is allowed to rule acts as a barrier to using price deflation as a conscious policy.

Theory lends legitimacy to policy. The neoclassical synthesis puts blinders on policy makers by restricting the legitimate options to manipulating government spending and taxation and operating upon the money supply. At present there is considerable controversy about the details of fiscal actions and whether the Federal Reserve should operate upon the money supply alone or should consider interest-rate effects in determining its behavior. But, to the neoclassical synthesis, the pricing of capital assets in markets in which today's views about the future and today's financing possibilities are vital is not an issue for policy. The possibility that the instability so evident in our economy is due to the behavior of financial markets, asset prices, and profit flows is foreign to the neoclassical synthesis.

Furthermore, the neoclassical synthesis holds out the promise that a close approximation to full employment at stable prices can be achieved and sustained by manipulating monetary and fiscal policies. As a result, the neoclassical synthesis enables economists to ignore the effects of industrial structure and income distribution upon overall economic performance.

Prior to the victory of the Hansen and Hicks versions of Keynes, it was widely held that the structure of industry and finance is at least in part responsible for instability. The neoclassical synthesis and various models based upon the standard interpretation of Keynes, however, made this view obsolete. It became possible to be conservative on industrial organization and liberal on full employment policies. Keynes's *General Theory* could have been the base of a thorough revolution in economic thought; its basic argument pointed to essential flaws in the capitalist modes of organizing accumulation and how policy can cope with these flaws. But the interpretation of Keynes that followed the Hicks-Hansen lines of thought has led to the neoclassical synthesis, and the banal proposition that all would be well if a proper mix of monetary and fiscal policies can be achieved.

As instability became evident and as inflation and unemployment coexisted during the late 1960s, 1970s, and early 1980s, it became apparent that the neoclassical synthesis did not provide a guide to relevant policy. If we are to do better in policy, we have to dig deeper into the processes at work in our economy than the neoclassical synthesis permits.

CHAPTER 7

PRICES AND PROFITS
IN A CAPITALIST
ECONOMY

Neoclassical theory does not deal with the full set of relations that must be satisfied for a capitalist economy with a complex financial system to be coherent. Neoclassical price theory is limited to explaining how relative prices of currently produced goods adjust so that markets are cleared; the financial and capital-asset price-validating relations that must be satisfied if the economy is to be coherent are ignored. In particular, the role of prices as the carrier of profits is not a central concern of the theory.

In the neoclassical view, the functions of prices are (1) to state the terms upon which alternatives are available[1] and (2) to determine claims upon output. In this formulation, the only function of the price mechanism is to ration output and allocate resources. Absolute prices, that is, prices in dollars, are irrelevant for the heart of the theory because debts and other contracts denominated in dollars are ignored. The view that capital assets as used in production are analogous to money today/money tomorrow financial contracts is not central to neoclassical theory. Accordingly, in neoclassical theory the course of money prices and money profits over time is not an essential determinant of the behavior of the economy.[2]

However, the economy we live our lives in is a capitalist economy that invests. In such an economy, the financing of investment and of ownership

---

1. Oscar Lange, "On the Economic Theory of Socialism," *On the Economic Theory of Socialism*, ed. Benjamin E. Lippincott (Minneapolis: University of Minnesota Press, 1938), pp. 60–61. Lange is citing Philip H. Wicksteed, *The Common Sense of Political Economy*, 2d ed. (London: 1937).
2. This is where Frank Hahn begins his analysis in *Money and Inflation* (Cambridge: MIT Press, 1983).

of the stock of capital assets leads to commitments to make money payments, that is, to contractual cash flows. In essence, a financial paper world of interrelated cash flows is fully integrated with what neoclassical economists call the real world of production, consumption, and investment; what happens is the result of combined financial and "real" influences upon economic behavior. As a result, if the economy is to be coherent, prices must accomplish not only the resource allocation and output-rationing functions but also assure that (1) a surplus is generated, (2) incomes are imputed to capital assets (i.e., profits), (3) the market prices of capital assets are consistent with the current production costs of outputs that become capital assets, and (4) obligations on business debts can be fulfilled.

The price system of a capitalist economy must carry the carrots that induce the production of the physical resources needed for future production. To do this it is necessary that the present validate the past, for unless the past is being validated and the future is expected to validate present investment and financing decisions, none but pathological optimists will invest.

Past investment outputs must be justified by the incomes received by owners of capital assets. Because the past financing of investment output left a legacy of payment commitments, which become current as time goes by, the income of debtors must be sufficient to fulfill these commitments. In other words, the price system must generate cash flows (profits, quasi-rents), which simultaneously free resources for investment, lead to high enough prices for capital assets so that investment is induced, and validate business debts. For a capitalist system to function well, *prices must carry profits.*[3]

Prices are also vehicles for recovering costs. In a capitalist economy the costs that need to be recovered include financial, overhead, and ancillary costs, as well as the costs of the technologically determined operating costs for labor and purchased materials and services. Firms try to build into their supply prices an excess of cash flows over operating costs so they can fulfill their outstanding financial contracts and sustain the value of their

---

3. There is a remarkable essay by Dudley Dillard, "The Theory of a Monetary Economy," in *Post-Keynesian Economics*, ed. Kenneth K. Kurihara (London: George Allen and Unwin, 1955), which is most insightful about the relations between prices and profits. Much of what goes by the label post-Keynesian economics is in this essay of thirty years ago.

capital assets. This building takes the form of markups on technologically determined costs; a firm can control these markups to the extent that it has market power. These markups, if realized on enough output, enable a firm to validate its debts and the prices that were paid for its capital assets. The markups will also yield the cash that covers the business style of the firm, that is, that validate overhead and ancillary costs.

To understand how coherence normally rules in a capitalist economy and why it sometimes breaks down, prices cannot be treated as though their only function is to allocate resources and distribute income. Prices also must be related to the need for cash flows to validate the capital assets, financial structure, and business style of the economy.[4] The cash flows that prices carry enable debts to be paid, induce and partially finance investment, and enable new financial obligations to be accepted.

The distribution of cash flows among firms—which can be viewed as the outcome of a competition among capitals for profits—depends upon the behavior examined in microeconomic analysis, but the macroeconomic state of the economy determines the totality of such cash flows. That is, the individual prices, outputs, and allocations are determined under conditions that reflect the macroeconomic state of the economy. Even relative prices, the main province of neoclassical theory, are not independent of how total demand is divided among investment, consumption, and government; they are not set by technology and preferences alone.

The following discussion of how consumer goods prices are determined will show that the markups on labor costs contained in prices reflect the investment and government financing that takes place. The argument shows that we cannot understand how our economy works by first solving allocation problems and then adding financing relations; in a capitalist economy resource allocation and price determination are integrated with the financing of outputs, positions in capital assets, and the validating

---

4. That prices must support the business styles of an economy means that the costs of advertising on television must show up in revenues received by the advertiser, just as an excise tax must be recouped in prices. On the cost structures due to business style, see Myron K. Gordon, "Corporate Bureaucracy, Productivity Gains, and Distribution of Revenue in U.S. Manufacturing, 1947–1977," *Journal of Post-Keynesian Economics* 4, no. 4 (Summer 1982), pp. 483–96; and Paola Sylos-Labini, "Prices and Income Distribution," *Journal of Post-Keynesian Economics* 2, no. 1 (Fall 1979), pp. 3–25.

liabilities. This means that nominal values (money prices) matter: money is not neutral.[5]

There are really two systems of prices in a capitalist economy—one for current output and the other for capital assets. When the price level of capital assets is high relative to the price level of current output, conditions are favorable for investment; when the price level of capital assets is low relative to the price level of current output, then conditions are not favorable for investment, and a recession—or a depression—is indicated. Business cycles result from a dance of these two price levels, even as the price of a unit of money is fixed at one. One key problem of economic policy is to fix the economy so that the two price levels are such that there is an appropriate amount of investment: this requires that both realized and expected profit flows be high enough so that capital-asset prices exceed the supply prices of investment output. "What determines profits?" is a key question for understanding how our economy works.

MACROECONOMIC PRICE RELATIONS: THE SIMPLEST CASE

Any investing economy generates and allocates a surplus. In a simple or skeletal investing economy, in which all of labor is employed to produce consumption or investment goods, the market price of a representative consumption good must be greater than the wages of the labor required to produce a unit of the good, because consumption goods have to be rationed among all workers. The workers who produce consumer goods and those

---

5. On the neutrality of money, see John Maynard Keynes, "The General Theory of Employment," *Quarterly Journal of Economics* 51 (1936–37), pp. 209–23. This essay includes a rebuttal to Wassily W. Leontief, "The Fundamental Assumption of M. Keynes' Monetary Theory of Unemployment," *Quarterly Journal of Economics* 51 (1936–37), pp. 192–97. Monetarists such as Milton Friedman ["The Role of Monetary Policy," *American Economic Review* 58 (March 1968), pp. 1–170], and the new classical economists such as Robert E. Lucas, Jr. ["Expectations and the Neutrality of Money," *Studies in Business Cycle Theory* (Cambridge: MIT Press, 1981)], construct elaborate and artificial devices to achieve transitory nonneutrality of money even as they retain the essential system in which money is neutral.

who produce investment goods spend their wages on consumer goods. Under the heroic assumption that all of wage income is spent on consumption goods and none of profit income is so spent, the sum of the realized markups (profits in a very gross sense) on the technologically determined direct labor and material costs of producing and distributing consumption goods equals the wage bill in investment goods production. Given that profits in the production of investment goods and, as in our heroic case, that total revenue from investment is split into wages and profits, total profits equals the investment that takes place. The simple equation *"profits equals investment"* is the fundamental relation for a macroeconomics that aims to determine the behavior through time of a capitalist economy with a sophisticated, complex financial structure. Furthermore, it is financed investment that forces the surplus.

In a complex market economy, household income that results from employment by the state, transfer payments, salaries to overhead and ancillary labor, and the ownership of wealth (dividends and interest) will finance the purchase of consumption goods and thus generate profits. The simple proposition, that *profits equals investment*, and the causal connection that financed investment forces the economy to operate so that profits and a surplus are generated, needs to be modified to allow for a variety of spending that leads to a markup on technologically determined costs of output and thus to profits and a surplus.

For output to be produced over a succession of periods, prices must exceed the per-unit costs of those inputs that directly vary with production. This is so because there are inputs into production whose costs are financed by the excess of revenues over out-of-pocket costs: These include the services of capital assets and overhead labor. If we ignore purchased nonlabor inputs, in competitive markets direct labor costs determine how supply varies with price; but for continued normal functioning of firms—or the economy—the realized excess of revenues over direct labor cost must be sufficient to finance overhead costs and payment commitments on liabilities.

There are different ways of rigging an economy to attain a global profit target. But the way the economy is rigged affects relative prices, the money price level, the distribution of income, the stability of the economy, and the economy's future resources. Because it is helpful to use and manipulate simple equations and diagrams to lay out how prices and profits behave in a capitalist economy, in the following a little bit of algebra and simple graphics will be used to isolate and identify how market processes and economic policies affect prices and profits.

Let us write P_C as the price and Q_C as the quantity of a (representative) consumer good. $P_C Q_C$ summed over all goods, then, is consumption. We also write W_C as the money wage rate in the production of consumer goods and W_I as the money wage rate in the production of investment goods. Employment is N_C in consumption goods and N_I in investment goods; $W_C N_C$ is the wage bill in consumption goods and $W_I N_I$ in investment goods. It should be noted that these wage costs are of labor that is required by the production and distribution of commodities and services; in other words, these are the labor costs that are mandated by technology. The cost of overhead labor is not included; total employment in the private economy is greater than the sum of $N_C + N_I$.

Let us assume that there are only workers, whose labor is directly related to the production of consumer and investment goods, and profit receivers (i.e., no overhead labor). Further, let us assume heroically that workers spend all of their income on consumption goods and profit receivers spend none of theirs. Hence the demand for consumption goods is the total wage bill; profit income does not yield a demand for consumer goods.[6]

If only consumption goods were produced, the total wage bill would be $W_C N_C$ so that

$$P_C Q_C = W_C N_C, \text{ which gives us} \tag{1}$$

$$\pi_C = P_C Q_C - W_C N_C = 0 \; (\pi \text{ is profits in} \atop \text{the sense of gross capital income}). \tag{2}$$

Since the difference between total spending on consumption goods and the wage bill is profits, in a world in which artisans produce with found capital, profits are zero.[7]

---

6. This way of looking at prices is largely traceable to Michael Kalecki, op. cit.; Sidney Weintraub, *Keynes, Keynesians and Monetarists* (Philadelphia: University of Pennsylvania Press, 1978) and *Classical Keynesianism: Monetary Theory and the Price Level* (Westport, Conn.: Greenwood Press, 1961); and Jan A. Kregel, *The Reconstruction of Political Economy* (London: Macmillan, 1973), look at prices in an analogous way.

7. Nothing essential follows from this assertion; what follows is ease of exposition. In the interpretation that follows, the consumption ratio out of profits is identified with the spending financed by wages paid to overhead, finance, advertising, etc.

However, if $W_I N_I$ is the wage bill in the production of investment goods, then

$$P_C Q_C = W_C N_C + W_I N_I, \text{ so that} \tag{3}$$

$$\pi_C = P_C Q_C - W_C N_C = W_I N_i. \tag{4}$$

Thus, profits in consumer goods equals wages in investment goods.

Demand for investment goods is $P_I Q_I$, which equals the wage bill and the profits in investment goods production. As the wage bill in investment goods is the profits in consumer goods, simple arithmetic and extreme behavioral assumptions lead to the strong proposition that profits equal investment.*

This proposition states a powerful truth: in an investing market economy prices and income distribution are such that resources are made available for investment. The workers who produce investment goods have to be fed, and this is achieved by not allowing the workers who produce consumer goods to eat all they produce. In our economy the not allowing is enforced by the price system.

Given the assumptions, the result is obvious; realized investment equals the realized surplus, and profits are the form in which the surplus appears. Furthermore, financed investment determines aggregate income, its distribution between wages and profits, and the aggregate markups that are realized. Investment that is financed forces the surplus by affecting prices.

Investment and financing are undertaken only in the expectation that profits over a run of future periods—years—will reach or exceed some level. But profits equal investment. Thus, in a capitalist economy, investment takes place now because it is expected that investment will take place in the future.

The profits equation of our simple model leads to a view of how prices are formed. From

$$P_C Q_C = W_C N_C + W_I N_I \text{ we get by simple algebra} \tag{7}$$

$$P_C = \frac{W_C N_C}{Q_C}\left(1 + \frac{W_I N_I}{W_C N_C}\right) \tag{8}$$

---

* $I = P_I Q_I = W_I N_I + \pi_I$ and $W_I N_I = \pi_C$ we have $\tag{5}$

 $I = \pi_C + \pi_I = \pi$ $\tag{6}$

Furthermore, $Q_C/N_C = A_C$ the average productivity of labor in the production of consumer goods. As a result we have

$$P_C = \frac{W_C}{A_C}\left(1 + \frac{W_I N_I}{W_C N_C}\right).$$

(9)

If it is assumed that $W_C = W_I$ this becomes

$$P_C = \frac{W_C}{A_C}\left(1 + \frac{N_I}{N_C}\right).$$

(10)

We see that the price level of consumer goods is positively related to the money wage rate (W_C) and the ratio of labor employed in the production of investment goods to those employed in consumption goods $\left(\frac{N_I}{N_C}\right)$, and inversely related to the average productivity of labor in the production of consumer goods (A_C). Thus, if wages and employment in investment goods industries rise relative to wages and employment in consumption-goods industries, the price level rises, and as the average productivity of labor in the production of consumer goods increases, the price level falls.

The equation $P_C = \frac{W}{A_C}\left(1 + \frac{N_I}{N_C}\right)$, is a transformation of the equation $P_C Q_C = W_C N_C + W_I N_I$, using the additional assumption that wages in the two outputs are the same. This price level equation makes explicit that in the simplest formal case the proximate determinants of how our economy works are the subsystems that determine (1) money wages, (2) the average productivity of labor, and (3) the ratio of investment employment to consumption employment.

The short-run stability of the variables determined by these subsystems differ; the most variable of the determinants of prices in a simple capitalist economy is investment (see chapter 8). Investment variability is the dominant determinant of industrial fluctuations in a small government capitalist economy that is not dominated by international economic relations. The U.S. economy in the 1920s is an approximation to such a simple system.

Explanations of inflation are usually in terms of either too rapid an increase in money, a budget deficit, or wages rising too fast. Our analysis will be extended to include more than the skeletal relations. In the more complete case, the government budget position will be seen to affect relative prices, money prices, and the movement of prices. The money supply does not appear in the price level equation; the quantity theory is not visible. Money appears in the subsystems that determine realized investment and the financing of government deficits. In particular, money affects total demand and the course of prices through the banking mechanisms that finance activity and control over capital and financial assets.

MACROECONOMIC PRICE RELATIONS: ALLOWING FOR GOVERNMENT

We will now allow for a government that spends and taxes. In this extension, it will become evident that the economic relations that make a debt deflation and a long-lasting deep depression like that of the 1930s unlikely in a Big Government economy can lead to chronic and, at times, accelerating inflation. In effect, inflation may be the price we pay for depression-proofing our economy. If government is taken into account and the heroic assumption that workers (and transfer-payment recipients) spend all their receipts on consumption goods and profit receivers do not consume is retained, the demand for consumer goods equals after-tax income of wage earners and transfer-payment recipients. It can be shown that in this case pre-tax profits equal the sum of investment, the government deficit, and taxes on profits.* If investment and the deficit are unchanged and profits are taxed, then pre-tax profits will rise by the amount of the taxes on profits. Furthermore, if the government deficit increases when investment and thus income declines, then profits will not fall as they would in the absence of the government deficit. In effect, Big Government rigs the economic game

---

$$*P_C Q_C = W_C N_C + W_I N_I + \overline{W_G N_G} + T_r - T_w (W_C N_C + W_I N_I + \overline{W_G N_G}), \quad (11)$$

where $\overline{W_G N_G}$ = direct and indirect wage bill of government, T_r = transfer payments and T_w is the tax rate on wage income. The budget deficit, Df, is

$$Df = \overline{W_G N_G} + \pi_G + T_r - T_w (W_C N_C + W_I N_I + \overline{W_G N_G}) - T_\pi(\pi), \quad (12)$$

where T_π is the tax rate on profits, and, π_G is the profits earned in producing for the government. Substituting 12 in 11 yields

$$P_C Q_C = W_C N_C + W_I N_I + Df - \pi_G + T_\pi(\pi), \text{ which yields} \quad (13)$$

so that profits are sustained; by sustaining profits, government deficits can prevent the burden of business debt from increasing during a recession. Furthermore, if the deficit is large enough the burden of business debt may decrease during recessions.

From the equations it is clear that the sum of wages in investment goods, the government deficit, and taxes on profits determines the markup on unit labor costs. If the wage bill in consumption and investment production decreases because investment decreases, then in today's economy transfer payments increase and the tax take from wages drops, thus raising the deficit. If the increase in the deficit offsets the fall in the wage bill in investment goods production, then the unit markup on labor costs for the smaller consumption output will rise even as employment falls. As a result, profits and prices both may rise even as employment declines; this happened in 1975 and in 1981–82.

In our economy, business also makes profits from selling to the government. If the sum of private investment and the government deficit is unchanged, then the more profitable the production for government, the less profitable the production of consumer goods. Only to the extent that profits in producing for the government increase the deficit will profits in the production of private goods be unimpaired.

The deficit is the excess of government spending over tax receipts. Government spending for this purpose consists of direct government employment, transfer payments, and government purchases of goods from private business, while taxes consist of income taxes and excise or sales taxes. The spending excludes the purchase of preexisting assets, and the taxes exclude wealth transfers like death duties and capital levies.

$\pi_C = W_I N_I + Df - \pi_G + T_\pi(\pi)$; as

$\pi_I = I - W_I N_I$ and

$\pi_G = \pi_G$ we get

$\pi = \pi_C + \pi_I + \pi_G = I + Df + T_\pi(\pi)$. As after-tax profits are   (14)

$\pi^* = \pi - T_\pi(\pi)$ we get

$\pi^* = I + Df$. After-tax profits equals investment plus the government deficit. This is the fundamental equation for a skeletal capitalism with a government.

Equation 13 can be transformed into

$$P_C = \frac{W_C}{A_C}\left(1 + \frac{W_I N_I}{W_C N_C} + \frac{Df - \pi_G}{W_C N_C} + \frac{T_\pi \pi}{W_C N_C}\right) \qquad (15)$$

It is usually assumed that government expenditures and transfer payments are inflationary and taxes, however raised, are deflationary; but taxes also show up in prices. The price level equations include demand and supply conditions: thus, $\left(\dfrac{W_C}{A_C}\right)$ is a supply condition once W_C is defined as labor costs rather than as a worker's wages subject to tax. Consequently, the employer's contribution to Social Security must be included in labor costs, and the tax on wages will include employers' as well as employees' contributions. Because employers must recapture their costs, employers' contributions to Social Security show up in prices. As a result, a rise in transfer payments, such as Social Security, accompanied by a rise in the sales tax on labor (the so-called employer contribution) raises the demand price on consumers' goods and the supply price of all goods. A rise in prices that is independent of any rise in profits or the deficit will follow upon such tax and spending programs.

It should also be stressed that, although the government directly affects profits through its deficit, taxes that have differential effects upon the supply price of different outputs affect *relative* prices. A sales tax on labor therefore raises the relative supply price of outputs that use labor-intensive means of production. The decrease in labor-intensive ways of doing things has been aided and abetted by Social Security and other taxes on the use of labor.

One set of effects of government on the economy depends upon how specific government taxes and spending programs affect prices. Government programs affect the flow of profits, the price level, relative supply prices, and the choice of production techniques. This side of government was emphasized by the supply-siders in Reagan's first term. In addition, the effect of government depends upon its size relative to the size of the economy. If government is small, the deficit that can be attained may not have an appreciable effect in stabilizing profits or on prices. Contrariwise, a government that is large enough to stabilize profits will put upward pressure on prices even as employment falls: inflation is one result of the mechanism by which we have successfully avoided deep depressions since World War II.

MACROECONOMIC PRICE RELATIONS: ALLOWING FOR FOREIGN TRADE

The balance of trade also affects profits and prices. A trade deficit absorbs profits and constrains or lowers the domestic price level, while a surplus increases domestic profits and raises prices. The favorable balance of trade sought by mercantilist economic policies helps raise profits even as it raises prices.

Once again a little algebra is necessary.* The result of the algebra is

$$\pi = I + Df - BTDf + T^\pi \text{ or} \tag{16}$$

$$\pi^* = I + Df - BTDf. \tag{16a}$$

A balance-of-trade deficit lowers the profits associated with any given level of investment and government deficit. Since domestic profits validate debt and asset prices and are the carrot that induces investment, a structure of demand that leads to a large trade deficit at full employment makes it difficult to realize and to sustain full employment.

Because a balance-of-trade deficit tends to constrain profits, an economy in which imports react strongly to income—as is now true of the United States—will experience constrained increases in profits when the domestic economy expands. This effect weakens the expansion and increases the investment and government deficit needed to achieve and sustain full employment.

The price level of consumer goods, once the balance-of-payments deficit is taken into account, is

---

* All symbols are as earlier with $P_X Q_X$ = exports, $P_M Q_M$ = imports and BTDf = balance-of-trade deficit.

$$P_C Q_C = \frac{W_C N_C + W_I N_I + \overline{W_G N_G} + W_X N_X + Tr - T_W}{(W_C N_C + W_I N_I + \overline{W_G N_G} + W_X N_X) - P_M Q_M} \tag{17}$$

and the balance of trade deficit (BTDf) is

$$BTDf = P_M Q_M - P_x Q_x = P_M Q_M - W_X N_X - \pi_X, \text{ for } P_X Q_X = W_X N_X + \pi_X. \tag{18}$$

The above equations yield

$$BTDf + P_C Q_C - W_C N_C + \pi_X = W_I N_I + Df + T_\pi \pi - \pi_G. \tag{19}$$

$$\text{As } P_C Q_C - W_C N_C = \pi_C, BTDf + \pi_C = W_I N_I + Df + T_\pi \pi - \pi_G - \pi_X.$$

As $W_I N_I = I - \pi_I$ and $\pi = \pi_C + \pi_I + \pi_G + \pi_X$ we get that

$$BTDf + \pi - T_\pi \pi = I + Df \text{ or} \tag{20}$$

$$BTDf + \overset{*}{\pi} = I + Df; \text{ or } (16a)\overset{*}{\pi} = I + Df - BTDf. \tag{20a}$$

$$P_C = \frac{W_C}{A_C}\left(1 + \frac{W_I N_I}{W_C N_C} + \frac{Df}{W_C N_C} - \frac{BPDf}{W_C N_C} + \frac{T_\pi \pi - \pi_G - \pi_X}{W_C N_C}\right) \quad (21)$$

A balance-of-payments deficit tends to constrain the price level of domestically produced consumer goods. This result is obvious because a portion of domestic income is not used to buy domestic goods and generate domestic prices.

The remainder of this chapter drops foreign trade from consideration. Because the basic equations are linear—that is, parts or phenomena are added one onto another—we can subtract and add subsystems and not get misleading results.

MACROECONOMIC PRICE RELATIONS: CONSUMING OUT OF PROFITS AND SAVING OUT OF WAGES

Profits equal investment is a profound insight into how a capitalist economy works. It leads to the proposition that the surplus is forced by the investing process and that the distribution of income between wages and profits is determined by the economic process and not by technology. The analysis that leads to the proposition that profits equal investment also shows that the price level is determined by money wages and the way resources are allocated among investment, consumption, and government. This precise and strong result, however, is due to the heroic assumption that all of wage income and none of capital income (profits) are spent on consumer goods. It is obvious that workers may save and capital-income receivers consume.

If we allow for saving out of wage income and consumption out of profits $(C\overset{*}{\pi})$, then the simple domestic economy demand for consumer goods becomes*

---

*$P_C Q_C = W_C N_C + W_I N_I + W_G N_G - T_w(W) + c\overset{*}{\pi} - s\overset{*}{W}$, $P_C Q_C = W_C N_C + \pi_C$,

$W_I N_I = I - \pi_C$,

$Df = W_G N_G + \pi_G - T_w(W) - T_\pi(\pi)$, $\pi = \pi_C + \pi_I + \pi_G$ and $\overset{*}{\pi} = \pi - T_\pi(\pi)$

Substitution of above in 22 yields 23 and 24.

$$P_C Q_C = W_C N_C + W_I N_I + W_G N_G - T_W(W) + c\dot{\pi} - s\dot{W} \qquad (22)$$

which leads to

$$\pi = I + Df + T_\pi + c\dot{\pi} - s\dot{W} \qquad (23)$$

$$\dot{\pi} = I + Df + c\dot{\pi} - s\dot{W}. \qquad (24)$$

Accordingly, profits become higher when the ratio of consumption to after-tax profits increases and become lower when workers' saving out of after-tax wages increases.

The proposition that capitalists get what they spend, therefore, has two meanings. In one, capitalist spending on investment goods leads to profits; in the other, the spending of incomes derived from profits on consumption goods increases profits. On the other hand, workers' saving, that is, not spending wages on consumption goods, decreases profits. As profits affect investment and determine the ability of business to validate debts, frugality by capitalists and workers diminishes investment. In the same way, high-living capitalists and workers are conducive to high profits and high investment.

One route by which profits affect investment is by way of the prices of common shares that are traded on the exchanges. During a run of good times, the well-being of share owners improves because dividends to share ownership increases and share prices rise to reflect both the higher earnings and optimistic prospects. This rise in stockholders' wealth leads to increased consumption by dividend receivers, which leads to a further rise in profits. This relation between profits and consumption financed by profit income is one factor making for upward instability.

In our affluent economy, the ratio of savings out of after-tax wage income also fluctuates. During good times, employment is high and layoffs are short. This leads to workers buying big-ticket items on installment; this decreases the savings ratio out of wages. But when employment is slack, workers with jobs pay off their installment debt, even as the rate at which new installment contracts are opened decreases. This pay-down increases the savings ratio out of wages. Thus, a low ratio of savings to wages characterizes expansions, and a high ratio characterizes contractions and depressions. But a high savings ratio out of wages diminishes and a low ratio increases business profits: the behavior of saving out of wages amplifies the effect on profits of increases and decreases in investment. If a rise in the savings ratio out of wages occurs when investment drops, then the decline in profits will be amplified; symmetrically if the savings ratio falls when investment increases, the rise in profits will be amplified.

The price equation, consequently, is affected by workers' savings and capitalist consumption:

$$Pc = \frac{W_C}{A_C}\left(1 + \frac{W_I N_I}{W_C N_C} + \frac{Df}{W_C N_C} + \frac{T_\pi \pi}{W_C N_C} + \frac{c\overset{*}{\pi}}{W_C N_C} - \frac{s\overset{*}{W}}{W_C N_C}\right) \quad (25)$$

The price level of consumption goods is increased by consumption out of profits and is decreased by savings out of wages. Even if $c\overset{*}{\pi}$ and sW were equal to zero, a rise in investment would tend to raise prices. However, if consumption out of profits increases and savings out of wages decrease when investment increases, then the rise in the markup that accompanies a rise in investment will be amplified.

THE MEANING OF CONSUMPTION SPENDING OUT OF PROFITS INCOME

The proposition that consumption spending out of profits feeds back to and augments profit margins integrates the complex cost structure of a modern corporation with the generation and allocation of an economy's surplus. As business costs reflect the organizational and institutional arrangements under which output is supplied, the cost structure of firms determines the market prices that make for the normal functioning of the economy.

In the initial discussion of the surplus, it was assumed that by and large the surplus is allocated to the production of capital assets. But an economy's surplus need not be allocated to the construction of capital assets that are effective in increasing the average productivity of labor (the A_C of the price formulas). A surplus can be allocated to the building of Versailles, the maintenance of a court, the support of a military establishment, or the bloating of corporate bureaucracies.

That high living by the rich and affluent, financed by profits and rents, generates jobs even as it augments profits was understood by the classical economists: it was a major theme of Thomas Malthus. When a prince has a court or when a corporation has a bureaucracy, the incomes of courtiers or bureaucrats are allocations of the surplus, although the retainers of the prince and the corporation alike receive their incomes as wages and enter the data as gainfully employed. As this wage income is spent on consumer goods, it increases the aggregate realized margin between sales proceeds and the out-of-pocket costs that are dictated by the technique of production. In essence, the allocation of part of the surplus to wage incomes that are spent on consumption increases the aggregate surplus by raising realized profits.

In neoclassical theory, the production function is used to generate a technological theory of relative prices and of income distribution. As pointed out earlier, the economic theory built upon this use of the production function is not valid for the economy in which we live, even though using production function ideas to trace out the relation between out-of-pocket costs and output when capital assets (plant and equipment) are given is valid. In this valid application, the production function is used to trace the way output changes as labor and purchased materials and services are varied. These output-input relations for given capital assets yield the total variable cost of each output and are a solid basis for the analysis of supply. This application of the production function does not lead to a technological theory of relative prices and income distribution; with capital assets fixed, capital income depends on the scarcity of production facilities as determined by aggregate demand, not upon the technical conditions of production.

In a closed economy, the costs of purchased inputs can be broken into labor costs that are technically needed for production, purchased goods and services, and the markup. Over the entire closed economy, final sales proceeds are divided into the direct and indirect labor costs required for production with the existing capital assets and gross profits. Gross profits are divided into gross retained earnings, taxes, dividends, interest payments, rents, and the wages of overhead labor; all of these are an allocation of profits.

In the GNP accounts, GNP is separated into wages and salaries on the one hand and gross capital income on the other. The constructs introduced here look at the same total but break it down in another way. *The wage and salary incomes of those who do not furnish labor required by the technology embodied in capital assets are viewed as an allocation of profits.* Even though overhead and management employees, who work in advertising, sales, marketing, research, and so forth, receive wages and salaries, their income here is taken as an allocation of profits.

The surplus is much greater in our economy, therefore, than is indicated by measured profits or investment. Not only are the tax revenues of the state a part of the surplus, but a good portion of the wage and salary payments by private units are allocations of the surplus. The institutional structure and business style that mandate that resources be used for sales, administration, and promotion require a large surplus, not all of which shows up as measured profits.

Only a portion, and in many cases only a small portion, of the cost of doing business reflects labor and purchased inputs that are technologically necessary. The labor employed in executive offices, advertising, marketing, sales, lobbying, research, product development, corporate lawyers, and so forth is not required by the technology embodied in capital assets. The services supplied by this labor may be vital to the functioning and survival of the organization in a given business environment, but in no sense are these costs technologically determined. Whereas one steel, oil, or garment firm will be quite like another in its technical input-output relations, it can differ markedly in the structure and weight of overhead and ancillary costs and services.

The difference between the sales price per unit of output and the technologically determined average cost of output is a markup per unit of output. The firm is free to allocate this markup to taxes, retained earnings, dividends, interest, rents, the purchase or hire of overhead services, and executive compensation. Various expenses, such as interest on debt, the hire of ancillary and overhead labor, and the purchase of business services are allocations of profits, a use of the surplus.

In a modern economy the surplus can far exceed investment. Taxation and government deficits appropriate resources for both welfare-enhancing and welfare-diminishing government programs. In addition, part of the surplus is allocated to the wages and salaries of overhead and ancillary labor. The largely white-collar workers who receive this income are perhaps more affluent than the blue-collar workers who are technically required for production, but their wage income, like that of the blue-collar workers, will be mainly spent on consumption. Consequently, employee consumption, which is financed by profits in the *extended* sense, will increase profits in the same sense. Consumption financed by income received for employment as ancillary labor may account for a larger portion of the difference between the extended and the narrow profit concept than consumption financed by dividends.

Profits allocated to overhead and ancillary expenses are not reported as profits in a corporation's income statement or to the income tax authorities. They are, except for some research and product-development costs, interpreted as costs of doing business. The wages of overhead labor are treated in the same way as the wages of the assembly-line worker; advertising agency services are purchased inputs fully equivalent to the steel an automobile manufacturer buys. As a result, reported profits of the business sector underestimate the surplus being generated in our economy.

The greater the ratio of wage income from ancillary and overhead services to wage income that is determined by technology, the higher the demand price per unit of output relative to technologically mandated production costs. If all the overhead and ancillary service costs are wage costs and all of such wages are spent on consumer goods, then profits in the extended sense will rise by the amount of such wages. Consumption spending by ancillary labor validates in the aggregate the employment of ancillary labor.

If the ratio of overhead and ancillary wages to technologically determined wages is higher for every output, then the markup and the price of the product will be greater for every level of output than in the absence of such spending. An increase in corporate advertising, executive payrolls, product research, and so forth will finance consumption demand without increasing the output per unit of labor technologically necessary for production; this will tend to raise prices.

If competition among firms by means of sales, marketing, advertising, and research leads to wage and salary income derived from these functions increasing relatively to the wage and salary income derived from labor that is technologically determined, there will be upward pressures on prices. Consequently, an increasing dominance of markets by firms with market power due to and sustained by advertising, product development, and sales efforts produces inflationary pressures.

Even though the wages and salaries of overhead and ancillary service employees are best treated as an allocation of the surplus, these wages, salaries, and purchased services are costs to the individual firm that must be recovered in prices. Furthermore, in the firm's view the cash required to fulfill financial commitments on debts and to validate the capital assets owned by the firm is a cost. A minimum price necessary to validate a firm's past investment decisions, its liability structures, and its way of doing business for each output is determined by adding the technologically determined costs and the sum of the ancillary, overhead, financing, and capital costs per unit of output and allowing output to vary. In a modern corporate economy in which the firms that produce and sell output have large bureaucracies, engage in extensive product development, and advertise their products, prices must not only cover technically determined labor costs and validate past investment decisions, but must also cover the costs of these activities.

Overhead and ancillary expenses take the form of wage income even though they are allocations of an exceedingly gross profit concept. As wage incomes they are mainly spent on consumption, but, as we know, consumption out of profits raises profits. In the aggregate, but not of course for any particular firm, spending on consumption out of the profit margin increases unit profit margins. Consequently, in a closed economy aggregate corporate spending on advertising, research, development, administration, and other such overheads and nontechnologically determined business purposes returns to corporations in the form of an increase in the aggregate of markups on out-of-pocket or technologically determined costs. Such costs lead to a form of self-fulfilling prophecy: in the aggregate the greater the amount of such spending, the more firms can afford to spend in this way.

As the wage and salary incomes of overhead and ancillary workers are typically larger than the wages and salaries of workers required by the production technology, it is likely that some of these earnings will be saved. Wages that are saved lower profits. The savings of overhead and ancillary wage income make the feedback from such expenditures a not quite self-fulfilling prophecy. In addition, savings out of these high incomes offset some of the profits that would result from investment and the government deficit. As a consequence, the greater the income of the managerial, technical, and professional labor force—and the greater their savings—the lower the cash flows available for capitalist and rentier income.

As has been pointed out, the cash flow to capitalists and rentiers is a determinant of expectations of future profits and provides the carrot that induces investment. As long as the receivers of profit flows as wages spend their income, the existence of such allocations of profits is benign insofar as investment is concerned, but once savings out of these high-level wage incomes take place, then the cash flow recognized as profits in the conventional analysis will decline. For every level of investment and for every size of the government deficit, the profits available for meeting commitments on debts, dividends, and retained earnings will be lower the larger the aggregate spending by business on overhead and ancillary services. The low and apparently declining rate of profit of American industry may not be due to any declining technological productivity of capital; it may be due largely to the increase in the socially determined allocation of profits to overhead and ancillary functions and the workers' savings that arise out of these, on the whole, larger wage incomes.

In order to cover costs and leave an adequate amount for capital income, a modern corporation, with its bureaucracy and expenditures on services such as advertising, requires a large markup on its technologically determined labor costs. Furthermore, a big corporation is likely to use a goodly amount of capital-asset services per unit of output. As a result, the cash flow required to validate past investment decisions is a significant part of the total cash flow. These capital-intensity and ancillary-cost characteristics of large corporations open up a large amount of cost space for simpler or leaner organizations.

Adam Smith remarked that the "division of labor is determined by the extent of the market" and that the division of labor increases output per technologically determined worker. Smith's propositions, which have been the basis of the optimistic belief that investment and ingenuity will lead to ever improving standards of life, did not take into account the possibility that the organizational style of industry may frustrate these tendencies toward increasing well-being by imposing costs that overpower the progressive influence of accumulation and ingenuity.

If we combine the above with the differential between the wage rates paid by the large, capital-intensive, high-overhead firms and the statutory minimum wage at which alternative labor-intensive organizations can staff, there is a substantial potential for increasing output, employment, and well-being by developing institutions that facilitate alternatives to giant corporations.

SUPPLY PRICE

In our economy, supply price reflects the cost structure of firms and their market power. In the abstract, there are two types of supplying units. One type produces outputs and takes whatever price the market allows. Competitive, price-taking, or flexible-price are some labels used for these markets. Agriculture, before the days of government intervention, was characterized by this type of market, as are some of the basic minerals. In the second type of market, a firm sets a price and varies output produced according to demand. Although such price-making, market-power, or fixed-price firms dominate in utilities and manufacturing, they differ greatly in their ability to maintain their price when demand varies.[8] The achievement of market power is a major proximate goal of firms.

For fixed-price, output-variable firms the target offer price is determined by combining various explicit cash payments due to labor and material costs and contractual financial commitments with an implicit need for cash to validate the price paid for capital assets and provide a margin of

---

8. In recent writings, Hicks has made much of this two-way classification of units. See John Hicks, *Economic Perspectives* (Oxford: Clarendon Press, 1972).

safety to debt owners. The explicit and implicit needs for cash yield an average cost curve that defines the combinations of price and quantity needed to validate fully the production technique, financial structure, and business style of the firm. A target offer price is determined by combining technologically determined costs and various fixed costs. If an appropriate quantity is realized, the target price leads to cash flows sufficient to make investors in the equity shares of the firm content with their position. If a segment of a negatively sloped demand curve confronting the firm is inside the set of prices and quantities that fully validate costs (i.e., the firm has market power), then the firm has freedom to choose the price of its output. Shifts in the demand curve, due to overall economic conditions and product-market forces, will change the quantity sold at the price fixed by units with market power.

There are therefore two types of revenue-cost relations. In the fixed price-variable output case, the individual firm has market power that enables the firm to construct a complex cost structure upon the base of the technologically determined costs, which it uses to set its prices. The firm with market power offers to supply what the market is willing to take at a price that, for a significant range of outputs, covers the full per-unit costs and leaves a margin for safety. Price-taking firms, on the other hand, use the technologically determined costs to determine their output—taking a market-determined price, which their own action with respect to the amount supplied cannot affect, as given. The margin between price and the average technologically determined costs yields the per-unit cash flow that is available to cover the other costs—such as contracted financial charges and various overheads.

Inasmuch as overhead, ancillary, and capital costs are fixed sums in the short period, the total costs, inclusive of these costs, can be represented by an upward shift of a technologically determined total cost curve. The set of total cost curves that result are shown in Figure 7.1. The revenues that would validate the firm's organization, financial structure, and capital-asset position lie above the line CA-CA; this line reflects the full costs of output for the given technique, organization of the firm, and liability structure. If revenues are at or above the CA line, the firm's management and equity owners can be satisfied with past decisions.

The total cost curves as sketched in Figure 7.1 transform into one marginal cost curve and a series of nested average cost curves. The marginal cost curve reflects the technology of production, as does the average cost curve derived from the lowest of the total cost curves. The other average cost curves are the sum of the unit's technologically determined costs and

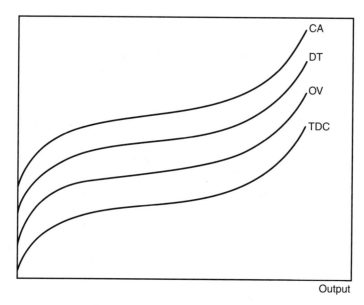

Figure 7.1:   Total Costs Allowing for the Composition of Costs
TDC = Technologically determined costs, given prices and wages of inputs
OV = Technologically determined costs and overhead
DT = OV + funds needed to validate debts
CA = DT + funds needed to validate prices paid for capital assets
Revenues > CA fully validate past investment and financing decisions
CA > revenues > DT debts can be validated but the full price paid for capital assets cannot

various items of overhead, ancillary, and capital costs. Each of these average cost curves, in turn, has its minimum point on the unique marginal cost curve. These average and marginal cost curves are sketched in Figure 7.2.

Any price and output combination within the cup AVCA-AVCA will satisfy the total revenue requirements of the firm. If price set by the firm is P_O and output is greater than O_1 and less than O_2, there will be a margin of safety, that is, revenue requirements will be more than satisfied. For a regulated industry such as utilities and for much of transportation before the mania for deregulation took hold, the cup AVCA-AVCA is determined in rate-setting negotiations before a variety of boards, and P_O is determined by bargaining about anticipated output. For an industry that is oligopolistic in structure because it is capital-intensive, the bankers and financiers implicitly insist that price competition be constrained so that, when there is a

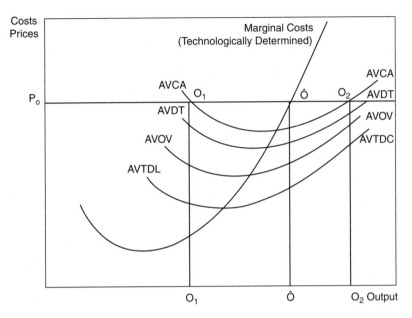

Figure 7.2: Price Setting
AVTDC = Average technologically determined costs
AVOV = AVTDC + average overhead costs (overhead costs per unit of output)
AVDT = AVOV + average debt payment (debt payment per unit of output)
AVCA = AVDT + average canital asset price validation

shortfall of demand, price does not collapse along the marginal cost curve, as it would under competitive market conditions. If a firm reacts to changes in demand by lowering price, so that the price/quantity combinations trace out the marginal cost line, the bankers correctly fear that relatively slight declines in demand may strongly compromise the market values of equities and debts.

To a banker, a situation such as that sketched in Figure 7.2 provides a much desired margin of safety. As drawn, O_1 is approximately 60 percent of $\hat{O}$ and 50 percent of O_2. If $\hat{O}$, the profit-maximizing output with $P = P_O$, is considered as capacity (at outputs above $\hat{O}$ both measured and extended profits fall as output is increased), then a sizable fall in market demand will not compromise the financial viability of the organization.

Certain aspects of our economy can be explained by the cost-price situation of Figure 7.2. If the quantity demanded at P_O falls from, say, $\hat{O}$

toward O_1 layoffs will occur in the technologically determined labor force. Overhead, advertising, research and development expenditures, and staffs will be protected until output approaches and even falls below O_1. In fact, sales, marketing, product-development and advertising expenditures might even increase as the firm struggles to improve demand and protect its market power. This reaction raises the set of average cost curves and the minimum output at which total costs can be covered at P_O. A conventional reaction of firms with market power to a fall in demand can thus lead to exacerbated difficulties if the initial shortfall of demand persists and increases.

If output is sustained close to $\hat{O}$, cash flows exceed the amount required by out-of-pocket costs and financial obligations by a good margin. These cash flows and the pressure of sales upon capacity make the firm willing to invest. Furthermore, the cash flows enable the firm to finance internally a good part of investment and sell debt to finance the rest. With outputs close to or below O_1 the willingness and ability to invest attenuates. The cost and revenue situations that make a firm willing to invest do not operate smoothly and continuously with variations in output, but in a discontinuous way.

The relative amount of debt and equity financing used by firms reflect the cyclical past of the economy. In Figure 7.2, the cup AVDT-AVDT gives the minimum price/output combinations that enable a firm to fulfill commitments on outstanding debt—including whatever requirements there may be for repaying the debt.* If the firm's debt rolls over from period to period or has a floating interest rate, then a change in financial market conditions will affect cost curves. For example, an increase in interest rates will raise AVDT-AVDT and AVCA-AVCA; it will shift O_1 to the right and O_2 to the left. If the markup at capacity or target output on AVCA-AVCA is to be maintained, then price must rise. If sales commitments at price P_O have been made, however, profits per unit of output as conventionally measured will erode. If AVDT rises above P_O because interest rates rise, the firm may not be able to meet all of its financial commitments.

---

* If there are purchased inputs, such as cloth to a garment manufacturer, the AV + debt curve includes the flow of cash needed to pay the principal and the interest of the debt used to finance the purchase of the cloth. If durable capital assets include a use component (user costs), then the user cost component of total revenues will be in the marginal and AV + debt curves.

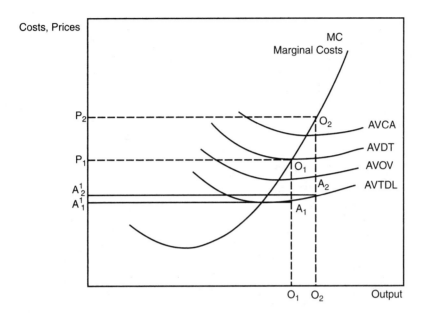

Figure 7.3:   Price Taking

Price-taking firms react to changes in demand by adjusting output along their marginal cost curve. Even though such firms own and operate capital assets and have debts, they do not have the power to set their price according to what they need to satisfy such costs; instead, they are forced to accept what they can get; they take price as a parameter and set output along their MC curve.

In Figure 7.3, profits, in the fullest sense that the term is used here, for a price-taking firm, will be $P_2O_2A_2A_2'$ with price P_2. A deterioration in demand can lead to profits of $P_1O_1A_1A_1'$ for such a firm. As sketched P_2 is not too much greater than P_1, but as the AVDT-AVDT illustrates, a modest decline in demand may make the cash flows too small to enable the firm to fulfill all of its commitments and debts. If Figures 7.2 and 7.3 reflect some truths about our economy, price-taking firms will tend to have smaller overhead and validating costs of capital per unit of output than price-making firms. *Market power, which allows a firm to constrain price movements when demand falls, may be a prerequisite for the use of expensive and highly specialized capital assets and large-scale debt financing.*

As has been shown, for the economy as a whole profits are determined by investment, the government deficit, the balance-of-payments deficit, and the consumption out of profits-savings out of wage relations. Consumer preferences and the nature of investment distribute demand among various outputs. Given the state of demand as determined by spending flows that lead to profits, employment is determined by the condition that

$$I + Def + \cdots = \sum_{i=1}^{i} \pi_i P_i \, Q_i; \quad (\pi \text{ is the profit coefficient in prices, the}$$

proportion of the price of outputs that is profits), where in some cases $\pi_i P_i$ is fixed and Q_i varies and in other cases $\pi_i P_i$ varies and Q_i is essentially fixed. Thus, investment, government deficits, and overhead costs that finance consumption out of profit incomes show up in prices, for they determine the total of the unit markups that can be achieved. If overhead costs increase, supply prices will be adjusted where firms have market power; in price-taking markets, the initial effect of rising costs will adversely affect profits. Since World War II, social and economic policy seems to have tilted or biased the economy in favor of the market-power segment by mandating overhead costs and favoring capital-intensive production techniques.

Any increase in the margin of safety, by raising prices so that costs (including the return on capital assets) are covered at smaller outputs, will lower the employment resulting from any given aggregate profits. As is well known, a number of economists imputed the recession of 1937–38 to price increases that took place as steel and other industries raised prices in an endeavor to improve profit margins so as to lower the output at which full costs were recovered.[9] Standard economics of the postwar era has, however, neglected the price level and the employment effects of the exercise of market power. Once firms with market power are an appreciable part of the economy, the division between expanding output and raising profit margins of a rise in investment, government deficits, and so forth depends upon the behavior of such firms; indeed, the efficacy of fiscal and monetary policies are conditioned by the reaction of profit margins to increased demand.

Prices, consequently, reflect market structures and the way in which demand is generated. A high-investment, Big Government economy will have a different set of relative prices than an economy in which investment and government are small. Relative prices also reflect differential market power and the business style of the economy. Advertising, administration, research expenditures, and the compensation of executives show up in the

---

9. The question of administered prices and the aggregate course of the economy was central to the TNEC investigation. See Ellis Hawley, *The New Deal and the Problem of Monopoly*, op. cit., pp. 460–65, 467.

supply prices of firms with market power. And both price-taking and price-fixing firms must recover these costs in prices: gross profit margins—as we have defined them—are equivalent to taxes, and like taxes they finance a use of resources by firms with market power that might be labeled inefficient.

Thus, cost conditions determine supply prices; however, the costs that determine supply conditions differ as the market power of firms differs. How profit margins are distributed among firms and how they enter particular prices are not determined solely by technology and consumer preferences; supply conditions reflect market power. As a result, relative prices are the result of how market power over price is exercised; in a world in which firms have market power, the "optimality" of market-determined prices is a figment of the imagination of neoclassical economists.

TAXES AND GOVERNMENT SPENDING

As we have shown, the government deficit (or surplus) affects aggregate profits and relative prices. Taxes, like profits, are a mechanism for forcing a surplus, and government spending is an allocation of the surplus.

As after-tax profits in the simple versions equal investment plus the government deficit, then if the sum of investment and the government deficit is unchanged, pre-tax profits must rise if taxes on profits increase. An equal rise in government expenditures and profit taxes will lead to a rise in pre-tax profit flows. In particular, the offer prices of producers who have market power will increase to account for the increase in anticipated taxes. Price takers, however, cannot adjust their prices to reflect an increase in anticipated profit taxes, but their prices will rise as the profits due to the increased government spending show up as an increase in the realized pre-tax markup per unit of output.

Excise taxes also enter supply prices. The employer's contribution to Social Security, which is an excise tax on labor hired, for example, affects the technologically determined costs of output. These costs rise whenever Social Security taxes increase. The fixed overhead and ancillary expenses also rise, for these costs are largely labor costs. The increase in such costs imply that the supply price that fully validates debts and capital assets rises for both price-takers and price-makers.

There are expenses mandated by business practices and labor market usages that are equivalent to taxes and labor costs—for example, fringe benefits such as health and pensions. These enter into the determination of the supply price of firms with market power and the realized markup for other firms, to the extent that such benefits finance demand.

In addition to profits and excise taxes, household wage and asset income is taxed. These taxes affect the supply price of outputs only as they affect the supply of labor or the flow of savings. The personal income tax assures that the after-tax income of technologically determined labor is not sufficient to buy back the output it produces even at the prices mandated solely by technologically determined labor costs.

Taxes therefore operate to generate a surplus in two ways. First, taxes assure that the disposable income per unit of output of the workers required by the technology is less than the supply price determined by the technology; second, taxes raise the supply price of output above the per-unit technologically determined costs. But profits also enter supply prices—by means of a markup on technologically determined costs. Thus, production-related taxes (Social Security, excise, value-added, corporate profits) and profits are equivalent. Taxes, however, give command over the surplus to government, whereas profit margins give command over the surplus to capital-asset owners and the management of corporations.

Government spending, regardless of how useful the output, is an allocation of the surplus, except if outputs are sold at prices that cover at least technically mandated costs. In a closed economy the sum of government spending and investment is offset by tax receipts and profits. The tax schedules and profit markups, together with the saving preferences of those who receive income, determine the level of employment at which the sum of taxes and profits is equal to the sum of investment and government spending.

Investment and government spending call the tune for our economy because they are not determined by how the economy is now working. They are determined either from outside by policy (government spending) or by today's views about the future (private investment). Although accounting relations assure that taxes plus profits equal government spending plus investment, they do not, by themselves, prove the direction of causality. A theory of the economic and political process is required before the proposition that causality runs from investment and government spending to taxes and profits can be asserted.

THE FINANCING OF BUSINESS SPENDING

As has been shown, aggregate profits depend upon investment, government deficits, the balance-of-trade position, consumption financed by profits, and savings out of wage income. In our Big Government economy, changes in investment and in the government deficit tend to offset one another; aggregate profits are thus not as volatile as in a small government economy.

For most firms, overhead and ancillary costs for any period are independent of the period's output. For any short period, interest payments, advertising expenditures, executive salaries, and principal due on debts are largely determined by prior commitments.

The cash to fulfill prior commitments will be forthcoming if the economy generates large enough profits in the extended sense. Whether prices (for the fluctuating-price firms) and outputs (for the fixed-price firms) are large enough to finance these expenditures depends, of course, upon the behavior of gross profits. But the cash payments because of prior commitments fall due regardless of current cash flows. When a shortfall of current profit occurs, the source of the funds needed to fulfill commitments is either cash on hand, borrowing, or the sale of assets.

Broadly speaking it is the banking system that makes it possible for business to fulfill payment commitments in the absence of sufficient current profits. Cash on hand and the ability to borrow, normally on the basis of previously established lines of credit, allow payments to be made in the absence of current validating cash flows.

Commitments to pay are made on the basis of anticipated revenues; if revenues are not forthcoming, then either cash on hand or short-term bank debt increases; if the latter, then payment commitments in subsequent periods increase. Such increases raise the cost curves that define the prices and outputs needed for a firm to meet payment commitments. The *financial* effect of a current shortfall in profits raises the future prices and outputs needed to validate the firm's capital assets, liability structure, and business style. Today's shortfalls make it more difficult to achieve validating cash flows in the future. Instead of a disappointment of expectations setting up forces that correct the disappointment, the financial consequences of a shortfall of profits make the achievement in the future of results that validate the cost structure more difficult.

In the short period, if revenues do not validate the firm's out-of-pocket costs, the firm will reduce output, but this reduces only the technologically determined costs. In the short-period overhead, ancillary and financial payments are mainly predetermined. Spending on advertising or interest payments on debts cannot be modified as readily as spending for shopfloor labor to produce current output. Once a firm is in debt, payments on long-term debts are changeable only by renegotiation; this may involve overt or covert bankruptcy.

The greater the cash payments due to the liability structure, overhead costs, and ancillary costs relative to the technologically determined costs, the smaller the proportion of expenses that can be quickly adjusted to short-falls of demand. Fixed payment commitments increase the likelihood that a shortfall in demand will lead to gross profits falling below payment com-mitments. When this happens a firm will be stripped quickly of its liquid-ity and subject to a rapid escalation of debt. Accordingly, situations conducive to financial stringency become more likely as financial and business-style costs increase relative to the technologically determined costs. Business failures are more likely to occur as capital-intensive production techniques, debt-financing of business positions, and business styles that lead to overhead and ancillary expenses become more prevalent in the economy.

The cash flows that validate capital assets, debt structures, and busi-ness styles result from investments, government deficits, balance-of-trade surpluses, and consumption out of incomes that are allocations of profits; these cash flows are diminished by savings out of the technologically deter-mined wage bill. A decline in the sum of investment, government deficit, balance-of-trade surplus, and consumption out of wages and profits decreases the validating cash flows. Investment spending, the balance-of-trade surplus, and consumption (savings) ratios of households are sensitive to financial market developments. A shortfall of validating cash flows rela-tive to payment commitments can set off an interactive and cumulative downward process. But in the economy as it is now constituted, a sharp decline in investment, in the balance-of-trade surplus, or in consumption out of wage and profits incomes will lead to a reduction in employment, a reduction in tax receipts, and rise in government transfer payments. This shift toward a government deficit sustains gross profits. As a result, the strip-ping of liquidity and the escalation of debt for capital-intensive and heavily indebted firms with high overhead and ancillary costs is diminished. In essence, Big Government, with all its inefficiencies, stabilizes income and profits. It decreases the downside risks inherent in a capital-intensive economy that has a multitude of heavily indebted firms.

CAPITAL INTENSITY, MULTIPLE MARKETS, AND MULTIPLE PRODUCTS

It is necessary to add an empirical characteristic of our current production. process to the fundamental conditions for the normal functioning

of a capitalist economy already examined: firms use capital-intensive production processes, produce a variety of products, and sell in a number of
different markets.

The relative capital intensity of a production process is measured by
the ratio to the technologically determined wage bill of the after-tax profits that are required to validate the prices that were paid for capital assets.
The greater this ratio, the greater the required markup on average technologically determined costs in product prices. If the aggregate achieved
markups are high enough to validate the prices of capital assets, they will
also validate past financial commitments. If the economy is running well,
current profits will, on the whole, validate past commitments in capital
assets and in financing relations.

Capital-intensive production processes imply that a substantial part
of a representative firm's total revenues needs to be allocated to servicing
debt and to sustaining the price of capital assets—this implies that the average technologically mandated out-of-pocket cost per unit of output is a relatively small ratio of the required price. In these circumstances sharp price
competition in the face of excess capacity and inelastic demand will lead to
a disastrous fall in profits.

A large gap between the price required to validate debt and sustain
asset prices and out-of-pocket costs of production means that price competition can extract a heavy penalty, first from firms and then from their
bankers. As a result, risk-averse investors and financiers require the protection of oligopolistic or monopolistic-competition arrangements before
hazarding financial resources on the specific capital assets needed for a particular capital-intensive process. Oligopoly and monopolistic competition
are the natural market structures for capital-intense industries. Since
investors and bankers demand some guarantee that price competition will
not occur, the paper-oriented world of Wall Street anathematizes price
competition among producers.

The purpose of production is to collect the difference between total
revenues and technologically determined and ancillary out-of-pocket costs.
Production is for profit, not use. If a firm's capital assets yield multiple products sold in multiple markets, the firm and its bankers are not mainly concerned about which market and which product generates the required
quasi-rents. Instead, their primary concern is that the *sum* of the quasi-rents
from the various markets be large enough to validate the organization's debts
and sustain its asset values. The maximum profits that a firm with power in
its product markets can earn is given by the full exploitation of its negatively
sloped demand curves in each market it serves. The minimum total required

profits are given by the debt structure and the cash flows required to sustain capital-asset values. If the maximum is greater than the minimum, then the firm can enjoy the luxury of not fully exploiting the profit potential of its market position. In such circumstances political considerations in addition to economic relations will determine the prices of products.

If financing techniques require that a substantial part of gross revenues be allocated to validating debt and sustaining capital-asset values and if firms typically produce multiple products and sell in many markets, then the prices of products may not reflect only economic relations. The firm really cares little about the proportions in which profits are collected from the various markets. Rather, a firm is concerned that the markups on out-of-pocket costs for various outputs in various markets yield an acceptable total of profits. In these circumstances what appears to be cross-subsidization by way of prices can arise; firms vary the markup on out-of-pocket costs among markets and products. Conventions, such as markup pricing, and regulations, such as setting a target rate of return on some value of capital assets, can and do guide price formation. Consequently, there are arbitrary political elements that affect particular prices in a capital-intensive world.

Where price includes a substantial markup on wage costs, fees paid for one commodity often provide for quite another commodity or service. For example, the American system of "free television" is financed by an allocation of part of the gross markup on technologically determined costs of advertised products; that is, part of the revenues received by producers of laundry soaps and underarm deodorants pay for entertainment. The markup on technologically required costs not only validates debts and capital-asset prices, but also supports Madison Avenue as well as an array of transfer payments (Social Security, Medicare).

As indicated earlier, the markup required to sustain the values of the capital assets used in production is related to the capital intensity of the production process; those industries and firms with the more capital-intensive processes require larger markups per unit of output. If aggregate investment or, for that matter, government employment or transfer payments rise, then aggregate profits increase. But the distribution of these profits among the various industries and firms depends upon the ratios of prices to labor costs for individual firms, which in turn depends upon the distribution of demand among products.

If relative prices of the capital assets used in the various processes of production are to remain unchanged, then the relative profits that are capitalized to yield capital-asset prices cannot change. This requires that profits in the various outputs change in the same proportion. The greater the capital intensity of output, however, the greater the percentage rise in product prices needed to support unchanging relative capital-asset values. One repercussion of an increase in the ratio of investment (and government and transfer payments) to income is that the prices of products produced by capital-intensive techniques must rise relative to the prices of products that use less capital-intensive techniques if the distribution of profits is not to change. But the pattern of demand curves that rule may make such required changes in product prices unobtainable. Furthermore, the principle of substitution will operate to shift demand toward outputs whose price has increased less rapidly, that is, those outputs that are produced by less capital-intensive production techniques. In order to sustain a high-investment economy, therefore, various interventions designed to increase cash flow or profits in capital-intensive lines of production relative to other lines may have to be inserted into the pricing system. Subsidies and taxes that favor capital-intensive production techniques, such as accelerated depreciation and investment tax credits, are part of the structure of an economy that seeks to stimulate economic growth by stimulating investments.

In a closed economy, the surplus is largely determined by investment, state expenditures, and overhead. Taxes are an instrument that allocates the gross surplus between profits and government revenue. For a given gross surplus a bigger deficit implies a greater mass of profits for business. As a result, a state with a large government and a contracyclical deficit maintains the size of the gross surplus and assures that business profits do not fall whenever business investment falls. Government policy can assure that the markup on labor costs not only does not fall but even increases during a recession.

CONCLUSION

Once the conditions that prices must satisfy include the generation of cash flows from operations that (1) validate liability structures, (2) induce desires to invest, and (3) draw forth financing for investment, the equilibrium and equilibrating story of neoclassical theory is not relevant. Furthermore, the greater the cash flows needed to validate inherited debt and capital-asset structures, the less valid the claim that market capitalism is efficient. In a world of large-scale, capital-intensive production, a major function of the pricing mechanism is to generate realized and expected gross profits large enough to keep investment on track. Investment or its equivalent in government deficits is necessary to sustain profits so that the inherited debt structure and historical capital-asset prices are validated. As such, any possible impact of accumulation or the technical productivity of capital assets is of secondary importance.

In an economy with an elaborate financial structure and complex expensive capital assets, a regime of private negatively sloped demand curves confronting output produced by capital-intensive production processes is necessary to attenuate the likelihood that competition will force prices down to marginal costs. Forcing prices down to the labor costs of production is disastrous for normal functioning of the financial markets of a capitalist economy. Strong, unregulated competition in the markets of products produced by capital-intensive processes is incompatible with the uncertainty attenuation required by financiers and bankers before they hazard substantial funds in the financing of such processes. For firms with debts and expensive capital assets, it is necessary that the mass of profits reach some target, but such firms are quite indifferent as to how gross profits are generated in the various markets in which they sell. In reality, policy and political choices enter into determining particular prices.

Because of constraints imposed by demand curves, there is a monopoly maximum that sets a ceiling to profits. A capitalist economy runs into problems when profit-maximizing behavior does not generate sufficient cash to service debt and sustain asset values. Inflation, which increases nominal cash flows, can become a policy instrument to validate debt.

In the world in which we live, impersonal genetic preferences and technologically determined production relations do not determine output, prices, and incomes. Economic policy cannot be based on an assumption that the details of the economy are determined independent of policy. How, what, and for whom are questions that have to be faced when policy decisions are made, but we are free to choose the how, what, and for whom characteristics of economic life only within limits that are given by the ability to produce. There are limits to what the economy can deliver, but within these limits we have some freedom to choose.

CHAPTER
8

INVESTMENT AND FINANCE

In a capitalist economy, profits motivate and reward business; they function to validate the past and induce the future. It was shown that today's profits depend upon today's investment; in the heroic or skeletal model, in which workers consume all their wages and capitalists save all profits, profits equal investment. When the model is fleshed out to allow for other than a skeletal structure and simple behavior, investment is still the major, although not the only, determinant of profits.

Investment outputs must be financed while being produced. Furthermore, ownership of (or positions in) capital assets must be financed. As a result, financing terms affect the prices of capital assets, the effective demand for investment, and the supply price of investment outputs.

Once the determinants of investment are understood, a full statement of the financial instability theory is possible. Investment is the essential determinant of the path of a capitalist economy: the government budget, the behavior of consumption, and the path of money wages are secondary. As we all know, the basic cyclical properties of our type of economy were evident when labor market institutions were very different and government was small. Although the behavior of money wages and government budgets can amplify or dampen economic instability, the fundamental cyclical properties of our type of economy are determined by relations among profits, capital-asset prices, financial market conditions, and investment.

Economic policy can affect the tendency toward instability by affecting the investment process, wages, and the government budget, but within a capitalist framework, instability cannot be fully eradicated. In particular, government contra-cyclical deficits now attenuate downside instability even as chronic deficits now exacerbate upside or inflationary instability.

Business investment involves spending money to produce goods that are to be used in production processes that are expected to yield revenues in excess of current or out-of-pocket costs. In our type of economy this excess is imputed to capital assets and becomes the return on investment. An investment is like a bond; it is a money-now-for-money-later exchange. An owner of capital assets has a special contingent contract with nature or the economy, a contract stating that money (profits) will be forthcoming to the capital assets depending upon how well the firm does, which in turn depends upon how well the industry and the economy do.

Investment involves using labor and machinery to build plants and equipment that may in today's economy be massively expensive and take many years to complete (a nuclear power plant is an extreme case). But the workers producing investment output and the owners of the debt instruments used to finance investment output have to be paid while the investment output is gestating. The money to make these payments by the producers of components to an investment output has to be obtained either from sources internal to the producing or investing firm or from outside sources. A company investing has to have a plan for financing the production of investment. A decision to invest—to acquire capital assets—is always a decision about a liability structure.

This and the following chapters will develop a way of looking at financial relations in a capitalist economy that integrates the cash-flow and present-value characteristics of units into a theory of investment. Cash-flow commitments, present-value calculations, and liquid-asset holdings determine how developments in financial markets affect the behavior and the viability of economic units. As a result, the stability of the economy depends upon the way investment and positions in capital assets are financed. It will be argued that instability is determined by mechanisms within the system, not outside it; our economy is not unstable because it is shocked by oil, wars, or monetary surprises, but because of its nature.

The fundamentals of a theory of financial instability can be derived from Keynes's *General Theory*, Irving Fisher's description of a debt deflation, and the writings of Henry Simons.[1] The economists who lived through the 1930s could not ignore the financial collapse and the preceding era of

---

1. John Maynard Keynes, *The General Theory of Employment, Interest and Money* (New York: Harcourt Brace, 1936); Irying Fisher, "The Debt-Deflation Theory of Great Depressions," *Econometrica* 1 (Oct. 1933), pp. 337–57; Henry C. Simons, "Rules vs. Authorities in Monetary Policy," *Economic Policy for a Free Society* (Chicago: University of Chicago Press, 1948); Charles P. Kindleberger, *Manias, Panics and Crises: A History of Financial Crises* (New York: Basic Books, 1978).

speculation in their explanation of what happened. In a work sponsored by the Twentieth Century Fund in the 1930s, Evans Clark and others developed an explanation of how debts affected system behavior that led to the breakdown of 1933 and acted as a barrier to recovery after 1933.[2]

As the standard interpretation of Keynes was assimilated to traditional economics, the emphasis upon finance and debt structures that was evident in the 1920s and early 1930s was lost. In today's standard economic theory, an abstract nonfinancial economy is analyzed. Theorems about this abstract economy are assumed to be essentially valid for economies with complex financial and monetary institutions and usages. As pointed out earlier, this logical jump is an act of faith, and policy advice based upon the neoclassical synthesis rests upon this act of faith. Modern orthodox economics is not and cannot be a basis for a serious approach to economic policy.

In some important sense, what was lost from the insights of the 1920s and 1930s is more significant than what has been retained. Keynes advanced an investment theory of why our economy is susceptible to fluctuations and a financial theory of investment that is especially relevant for our economy in our time,[3] but this theory was lost as the orthodox Keynesian theory, derived from Hicks, Hansen, and Samuelson, was developed.

The way in which a speculative boom emerges and how an unstable crisisprone financial and economic system develops are of particular importance in any description of the economic process that is relevant for this economy. Instability emerges as a period of relative tranquil growth is transformed into a speculative boom. This occurs because the acceptable and the desired liability structures of business firms (corporations) and the organizations acting as middlemen in finance change in response to the success of the economy. The spectacular panics, debt deflations, and deep depressions that historically followed a speculative boom as well as the recovery from depressions are of lesser importance in the analysis of instability than the developments over a period characterized by sustained growth that lead to the emergence of fragile and unstable financial structures.

---

2. Twentieth Century Fund, *The Internal Debts of the United States* (New York: The MacMillan Co., 1933) and *Debts and Recovery* (New York: The MacMillan Co., 1938).
3. See Hyman P. Minsky, *John Maynard Keynes* (New York: Columbia University Press, 1975); and "An Introduction to a Keynesian Theory of Investment," in G. Szego and K. Schell, *Mathematical Methods in Investment and Finance* (Amsterdam: Elsevier North Holland, 1972). Reprinted in Hyman P. Minsky, *Can "IT" Happen Again? Essays on Instability & Finance* (Armonk N.Y.: M. E. Sharpe & Co., 1982).

THE CHARACTERISTICS OF CAPITALISM: TWO PRICE SYSTEMS AND FINANCE

The fundamental propositions of the financial instability hypothesis are:

1. Capitalist market mechanisms cannot lead to a sustained, stable-price, full-employment equilibrium.

2. Serious business cycles are due to financial attributes that are essential to capitalism.

These propositions—and thus the financial instability hypothesis—stand in sharp contrast to the neoclassical synthesis, which holds that unless disturbed from outside a decentralized market mechanism will yield a self-sustaining, stable-price, full-employment equilibrium. The difference between the two views reflects the way in which finance and financial relations are specified. The financial instability view makes much of the way in which ownership or operating control of capital assets are financed, something standard theory ignores. Further, the financial instability theory points out that what actually happens changes as institutions evolve, so that even though business cycles and financial crises are unchanging attributes of capitalism, the actual path an economy traverses depends upon institutions, usages, and policies. In the final analysis, history remains history, although the range of what can happen is limited by basic economic relations.

For what follows, it is necessary to make precise what is meant by a capitalist economy. In a capitalist economy, the means of production are privately owned: the difference between total revenues and labor costs provides income to the owners of capital assets. Furthermore, capital assets can be both traded and hypothecated (pledged as collateral for loans). In addition, financial instruments resulting from hypothecating or pledging means of production or future incomes can be traded. Because capital and financial assets can be traded, they have prices.

These prices of capital assets and financial instruments, moreover, are determined in markets. As Keynes emphasized, a capital asset and a debt instrument are like annuities; both are expected to yield cash flows over some future span of time. Market processes, consequently, transform (capitalize) contractual or contingent cash flows of various capital and financial assets into a set of current prices.

Capital assets can be produced; and the production of capital assets is called investment. The price buyers are willing to pay for investment is derived from the income that the resulting capital asset is expected to yield.

The prices of capital assets and the way they are linked to the output of investment goods are critical determinants of the behavior of a capitalist economy. In a capitalist economy the expected income of capital-asset owners affects the demand price of investment output.

In an economy in which claims to the income from capital assets as collected in firms can be sold in the form of debts (bonds), the income from capital assets is divided between debt owners and the residual (equity) owners. The incomes earned by capital assets and payments on various classes of financial instruments are, as mentioned previously, cash flows. Thus, a complex network of cash flows due to contractual relations exists side by side and intertwined with the network of cash flows resulting from the production and distribution of current output.

The prices of capital and financial assets depend upon the cash flows they are expected to generate and the capitalization rate, which for each investment incorporates particular risk and uncertainty properties. As gross profits from the production and distribution of output depends upon the pace of investment, today's investment determines the cash flows available to fulfill financial contracts entered into in the past. As stressed earlier, the normal functioning of a modern capitalist economy depends upon capital income (and thus investment) reaching and sustaining a level at which capital assets earn sufficient income to validate past debts. If this situation does not prevail, the prices of capital assets and debts fall, and such a decline adversely affects investment demand.

A basic characteristic of a capitalist economy, then, is the existence of two sets of prices: one set for current output, the other set for capital assets.[4] The prices of current output and of capital assets depend upon different

---

4. In chapter 7 it was shown that supply prices (P) can be characterized by $P_O = (1 + M)W/A_C$ when W is the wage rate in money, A_C is the average productivity of labor, and M is some markup on per unit labor costs. The price of capital assets depends upon future profits that capital assets are expected to earn, Q_i and the transformation of these future profits into a present price, P_K. Thus we can write $P_K = K(\pi i)$, $i = 1 \ldots n$, where K is the capitalization function. P_K and P_O are linked, for investment goods once produced as current output becomes capital assets, but P_K and P_O change in time and the ratio of, or differential between, P_K and P_O changes. The determination of P_K and the explanation of how the relation between P_K and P_O affects investment are the subjects of this chapter.

variables and are determined in different markets. The prices however are linked, for investment output is part of current output.

Even though the technical characteristics of capital assets are the cause of basic money-now-for-money-later relationships in our economy, the existence of a complex financial system magnifies the number and the extent of money-now–money-later relations. The financial structure is a cause of both the adaptability and the instability of capitalism.

Since our economy has corporations and stock exchanges, which deal in the ownership of capital assets, the financial dimension of a corporate capitalist economy is much greater than for an economy dominated by partnerships and proprietorships. The focus of what follows is restricted to corporate capitalism, which became dominant over the past hundred years and which is more dominant now than ever before.

THE RUPTURING OF THE PATINKIN RESOLUTION

In the neoclassical synthesis it is necessary to show that normal market processes transform an initial situation of less than full employment into a close approximation to full employment. This is accomplished by assuming that an exogenously given money variable affects consumption out of income. By assuming that unemployment leads to wage and price deflation, an increase in the price-level-deflated value of money balances will take place. This, in turn, will lead to a rise in demand for consumer goods, which boosts employment. This line of reasoning, known as the Patinkin resolution, is the key to the emergence of the neoclassical synthesis.[5]

Milton Friedman argues that this Patinkin resolution validates the assertion that a capitalist market mechanism is not flawed: that is, that market processes will lead to a full-employment equilibrium.[6] Prior to the development of the Patinkin resolution, the following propositions, attributed to Keynes, were widely accepted: (1) the product market is the

---

5. Don Patinkin, *Money, Interest, and Prices: An Integration of Monetary and Value Theory*, 2d ed. (New York: Harper and Row, 1965).
6. Milton Friedman, "A Theoretical Framework for Monetary Analysis," *Journal of Political Economy* 78 (March–April 1970), pp. 193–238. Also in Robert Gordon, *Friedman's Monetary Framework: A Debate with his Critics* (Chicago: University of Chicago Press, 1974).

proximate determinant of the aggregate demand for labor, (2) at a given money wage rate demand for labor can be less than supply, and (3) a decline in money wages due to an excess supply of labor might not be efficient in eliminating unemployment.

These propositions really missed a critical point of both Keynesian theory and our economy, which is that there are forces for change—which we can call disequilibrating forces—in every particular short-run situation. These disequilibrating forces may be weak at times, but they accumulate and gather strength, so that after a while any ruling equilibrium will be disrupted.

The use of the term *equilibrium*, however, may be misleading. It may be best to borrow a term from Joan Robinson and call situations in which rapid disruptive changes are not taking place *periods of tranquility*,[7] noting that tranquility is disrupted by investment booms, accelerating inflations, financial and monetary crises, and debt deflations.

The underemployment equilibrium of the standard interpretation of Keynes's theory is not really an equilibrium. It is a transitory state following a debt deflation and a deep depression. During this state, market reactions to unemployment, which lead to falling wages and prices, are inefficient in raising employment because there are inherited private debts that can be validated only if money profits are sustained, and lower money wages and prices lead to lower profits. In other words, the cash flows required to validate private debts would be forthcoming only if profits are sustained. The efficacy of the Patinkin effect depends upon the ratio of inside business debts (whose validation depends upon the price level and the level of money profits) to outside financial assets (whose validation is independent of profit flows) being small. The Patinkin resolution ignores the effects of bankruptcy upon asset prices and the adverse effects of bankruptcy on the ability of private organizations to finance investment.

The Patinkin resolution therefore is not relevant for our economy, because of the limited set of financial relations it posits. The money wage and price declines that are the market reactions to unemployment (the substance of the Patinkin resolution) may make it impossible for private debtors to fulfill their obligations from their much lower wage and profit income.

In a thorough deflation, all private debts are eventually repudiated so that all capital assets are owned by individuals or by corporations that have only equity liabilities. While this process of debt repudiation is taking place,

---

7. Joan Robinson, *Economic Heresies* (London: Macmillan, 1971).

things are made worse by the affects of decreased profits, wages, and investment upon the validation of debts and the paralyzing effects of corporate reorganizations upon investment. Only after the financial structure is radically simplified, which may take many years, may falling prices be expansionary. In a world with complicated financial usages, if there is a road to full employment by way of the Patinkin real-balance effect, it may well go by way of hell.[8]

Moreover, as a practical matter the real-balance effect is irrelevant. The Patinkin resolution and other attempts in the literature to treat what are called disequilibrium phenomena are peculiar in that, once they achieve the so-called full-employment equilibrium, they do not ask whether the equilibrium so defined contains ongoing processes that will cause it to be ruptured. A close look at what goes on when the system achieves such an equilibrium uncovers ongoing processes that tend to make for the breakdown of full employment. The ongoing processes tend to rupture a full-employment equilibrium in an upward direction; that is, once full employment is achieved and sustained the interaction among units tends to generate a more than full-employment speculative boom.

Borrowing and lending on the basis of margins of safety are used to finance positions in the stock of capital assets as well as investment. Money is created in the process of borrowing and lending. Hence there are payment commitments to banks that underlay the money supply. When less than full employment gives way to a temporarily sustained full employment, changes take place in the relative values of various capital and financial assets that induce changes in desired financing arrangements.

In a capitalist economy capital assets are only incidentally desired because of their technical productivity; demand for capital assets is determined by their expected profitability. In an economy in which the debt financing of positions in capital and financial assets is possible, there is an irreducible speculative element, for the extent of debt-financing of positions and the instruments used in such financing reflect the willingness of

---

8. These interactions were discussed in detail in Irving Fisher, "Debt Deflation Theory of Great Depressions," *Econometrica* 1 (Oct. 1933). James Tobin in his *Asset Accumulation and Economic Activity* (Chicago: University of Chicago Press, 1980) referred to the Fisher interactions, but he seems unaware that this introduces a set of considerations that are foreign to his basic neoclassical perspective. See also Hyman P. Minsky, "Debt-Deflation Processes in Today's Institutional Environment," *Banco Nazionale del Lavoro Quarterly Review* 143 (Dec. 1982).

businessmen and bankers to speculate on future cash flows and financial market conditions. Whenever full employment is achieved and sustained, businessmen and bankers, heartened by success, tend to accept larger doses of debt-financing. During periods of tranquil expansion, profit-seeking financial institutions invent and reinvent "new" forms of money, substitutes for money in portfolios, and financing techniques for various types of activity: financial innovation is a characteristic of our economy in good times.[9]

Each new type of money that is introduced or an old one that is used to a greater extent results in the financing of either some additional demand for capital and financial assets or of more investment. This results in both a higher price of assets, which, in turn, raises the demand price for current investment, and increases the financing available for investment. Financial innovation therefore tends to induce capital gains, increase investment, and increase profits: the economy will try to expand beyond any tranquil full-employment state.

The financing of investment demand by means of new techniques means the generation of demand in excess of that allowed for by the existing tranquil state. The rise in spending upon investment leads to an increase in profits, which feeds back and raises the price of capital assets and thus the demand price of investment. Thus, any full-employment equilibrium leads to an expansion of debt-financing—weak at first because of the memory of preceding financial difficulties—that moves the economy to expand beyond full employment. Full employment is a transitory state because speculation upon and experimentation with liability structures and novel financial assets will lead the economy to an investment boom. An investment boom leads to inflation, and, by processes still to be described, an inflationary boom leads to a financial structure that is conducive to financial crises.

Therefore, in a capitalist economy that is hospitable to financial innovations, full employment with stable prices cannot be sustained, for within any full-employment situation there are endogenous disequilibrating forces at work that assure the disruption of tranquility.

---

9. Hyman P. Minsky, "Central Banking and Money Market Changes," *Quarterly Journal of Economics* LXXI, no. 2 (1957), reprinted in *Can "IT" Happen Again? Essays on Instability & Finance* (Armonk, N.Y.: M. E. Sharpe & Co., 1982), is an early discussion of the relation of financial innovations and financial and economic instability.

QUASI-RENTS AND CAPITAL-ASSET PRICES

According to Keynes, capital assets used in production are expected to yield income in the form of quasi-rents, Q_i. Quasi-rents are the difference between the total revenue from selling output produced with the aid of capital assets and out-of-pocket, running, or technically determined costs associated with producing output; they are a gross-profits concept. Capital assets yield quasi-rents because of the way the economy actually functions, not because of an abstract productivity of capital assets. As quasi-rents are identified with profits, then capital assets yield profits because the output they produce commands a price that exceeds unit out-of-pocket costs. Such a price in excess of out-of-pocket costs is due to the scarcity of the output and therefore of the capital assets needed to produce the output. As the productive capabilities of an economy are determined in the short run by the existing stock of capital assets, changes in the scarcity of capital are due to variations in demand. Investment is undertaken to alleviate a shortage of particular types of capital as made manifest by profits earned and anticipated. The level and the composition of demand determine the profits that capital assets earn, and capital assets are valuable *only* because they earn profits.

Capitalism leads to two sets of prices, one for capital assets and one for current output. These two sets of prices are linked because investment goods are a part of current output, and those investment goods that will be like some of the existing capital assets must have prices as current output consistent with their prices as capital assets.

As has been shown, prices of current output depend upon money wage rates, the productivity of labor with the existing capital assets, and the markups on technologically determined labor costs that are sustained by demand and that reflect the business style of the economy. The supply prices of various types of investment goods are a subset of the prices of current output. Capital-asset prices on the other hand are determined by supply and demand in markets in which the supply is fixed in the current period and demand reflects the value placed upon the cash (or the quasi-rent) the capital asset is expected to yield over a run of years. In order to understand how the prices of capital assets are determined, it is necessary to understand how the expected cash flows or quasi-rents are transformed into prices of capital assets.

Although the two price systems of capitalist economies are formed in quite different markets and are determined by quite different variables, they are not independent. The market price of a capital asset that is a substitute in production for an investment output must be equal to, or greater than, the supply price of the investment good if the investment good is to be produced.

In our economy there are financial assets, which are commitments to pay cash over some time period. These financial assets are much like capital assets in that ownership entitles one to a stream of cash. Moreover, like capital assets, these financial assets have current prices, which are capitalizations of the future cash flows as laid down in contracts.

The cash flows that capital assets and financial assets are expected to yield are not certain; each financial asset and capital asset has its own special set of contingencies that defines the condition under which the expected cash flows will not be forthcoming. The determination of asset prices starts with the fact that the price of a unit of money is one (be it dollar, mark, or yen). In our economy, in which banks create money by lending and in which bank deposits are the dominant form of money, debtors to banks are under obligation to fulfill contracts to pay money. As will be argued in chapter 10, it is the debtors' obligations to pay money to banks that make bank debts money.

Investment and ownership of capital assets are undertaken in the expectation that they will produce money. The old radical characterization of our economy as one in which production takes place for profit and not for use is valid. The use of capital assets in production involves the purchase of commodities and the hiring of labor. In order to purchase or to hire one must pay money to suppliers and workers. Money on hand therefore guarantees that payment commitments for the production of current output and the fulfillment of contracts will be honored.

In a world with borrowing and lending, it is sensible for anyone or any organization with payment commitments to keep some money—the item in which its commitments are denominated—on hand as an insurance policy against unfavorable contingencies. Money consequently yields a return in kind in the form of protection against contingencies. But the price of a unit of money is always a dollar, so that the price paid for the protection a dollar yields cannot vary. However, the value of the protection that a dollar yields can change. When this happens, the price of alternatives to holding money—that is, the price of other assets—must change.

Each financial or capital asset other than money yields either contractual payments or quasi-rents, and it has a value at which it can be sold or used as collateral for a loan. Some assets can be readily negotiated for money—such as Treasury securities or time deposits at banks and depository institutions—whereas others—such as partially completed nuclear power plants, oil refineries, and specialized machinery—cannot. Money is a unique asset in that it yields no net cash income, but it enables one possessed of it to meet commitments and to undertake current or spot transactions.

In a world with a wide variety of financial markets and in which capital assets can be sold piecemeal or as collected in firms, all financial and capital assets have *two* cash-flow attributes. One is the money that will accrue as the contract is fulfilled or as the capital asset is used in production; the second is the cash that can be received if the asset is sold or pledged. The ability of an asset to yield cash when needed and with slight variation in the amount is called its liquidity.

The price, P_K, of any capital asset depends upon the cash flows that ownership is expected to yield and the liquidity embodied in the asset. The cash flows a capital asset will yield depend upon the state of a market and the economy, while the liquidity embodied in an asset depends upon the ease and the assuredness with which it can be transformed into money. The price of a financial asset such as a bond or even a savings account depends upon the same considerations as the price of a capital asset: the cash flow and the breadth, depth, and resilience of the market in which it can be negotiated.

In determining asset prices, the fixed point is that the price of a dollar is a dollar, one dollar is like another, and each dollar in existence supplies liquidity. When, with a given perception of expected cash flows and uncertainties embodied in various financial and capital assets, the dollar is plentiful relative to the stock of assets, then the price of assets will be high; the prices attached to capital and financial assets will tend to be higher the greater the quantity of money (P_K (Normal) in Figure 8.1).

An exception to that rule occurs, however, whenever an increase in the amount of insurance against default on payment commitments does not lower the premium a holder is willing to pay for such insurance. Such an infinitely elastic demand for insurance arises only if the likelihood is believed to be high that cash shortfalls and default will occur. But such expectations happen only if recent and current experience is replete with shortfalls and defaults. After a debt deflation that induces a deep depression, an increase in the money supply with a fixed head count of other assets may not lead to a rise in the price of other assets. An insatiable demand for liquidity is a pathological condition, which may have been approximated in the United States at the end of the great 1929–33 collapse (Figure 8.1, P_K Post debt-deflation, 1).

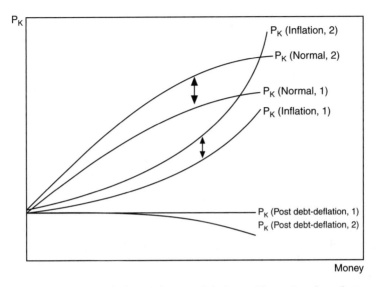

Figure 8.1:   Price Level of Capital Assets: Relation to Money Supply and Alternative Expectations Environments

Therefore, there exists a *functional* relation between the price, P_K, of a particular or a representative capital or financial asset and the quantity of money, M. Normally the price of a capital asset is a rising function of the quantity of money, for as the quantity increases the value of the insurance embodied in money decreases. As the price of money is always one, this implies that the price level of income-yielding capital assets increases. Furthermore, the functional relation has a logarithmic shape unless:

1. there exists the aforementioned infinitely elastic demand for the insurance provided by liquidity at a given fixed subjective valuation or,

2. the insurance embodied in money is deemed to be of no or decreasing value because prices are expected to rise more rapidly than the value of insurance.

In the special case of the infinitely elastic demand for liquidity as insurance, the price of capital assets may very well fall even when the money supply is increased. (There is a run to money (P_K (Post debt-deflation, 2)).) In the case of inflation expectations, however, the price of tangible assets may increase at a more rapid rate than the increase in the money supply; there is a run from money (P_K (Inflation) Figure 8.1).

But more important than the possible shapes of the relation is the fact that the function shifts as experience changes expectations of the cash flows that capital and financial assets will yield and the worth attached to holding money. (Indication by arrows in Figure 8.1.) It is not so much the movement along these curves as shifts from one of the relations that reflect normal, inflation, and depression valuations of liquidity to another that calls the tune to which the economy dances.

The effect of liquidity upon the relative prices of different capital assets and the index of capital asset prices are measured by P_{Ki}, M functions. We start with the statement that capital assets are valuable because of the quasirents, the Q_{Ki}, they are expected to earn. Let us assume an initial unemployment situation and a Patinkin process begins. As the Patinkin process increases the ratio of consumption to income by owners of monetary wealth, profits tend to rise. This is true because profits are directly related to the consumption ratio out of wage and profit income. A rise in Q_{Ki}, all other elements remaining constant, tends to raise P_{Ki}.

A rise in Q_{Ki} also eases the constraint imposed by an existing liability structure, for Q_{Ki} is the source of the funds available to fulfill contracts. A rising Q_{Ki} thus diminishes the virtue of money as the source of insurance as liquidity. As the virtue of this insurance decreases, the desired cash balance per unit of income and financial commitments also decreases, and a further rise in the price of Q-yielding assets occurs. For this to happen, money holdings need to be used to acquire nonmoney assets. Furthermore, the rise in Q_{Ki} and the capitalization ratio increases wealth, which further raises the spending-income ratio. Furthermore, an improvement in cash flows not only implies an increased ability to spend but it also augments the ability to borrow.

Both a rise in Q_{Ki} and a diminished virtue of liquidity tend to raise the price of capital assets because the capitalization rate and the expected returns tend to increase. The rise in the capitalization rate reflects a decline in the virtue of money as insurance. Once debt structures are easy to bear, then increased debt can be floated at favorable rates. Liability structures reflect the value placed upon the liquidity embodied in money at the time various items were negotiated.

A rise in the price of capital assets relative to the price of current output leads to increased consumption and investment. Furthermore, the rise in quasi-rents that accompanies such a process lowers the value of liquidity embodied in money. Although the Patinkin process may lead the economy out of a stagnation that follows a debt deflation, the result is not a movement toward an equilibrium. It may at first generate a period of relatively tranquil expansion, but tranquility diminishes the value of the insurance (liquidity) embodied in the dollar, so that a rise in the absolute and relative prices of capital and financial assets that are valued mainly for income will take place. Tranquility therefore leads to an increase in acceptable debt to equity ratios even as it raises the value of inherited capital assets.

The endogenously determined value of liquidity means that each possible equilibrium of the economy contains disequilibrating forces. Even if the neoclassical proposition that the endogenous workings of the market mechanism will lead an economy from less than full employment to full employment is valid, the processes that bring this about will not stop with full employment, but will carry the economy to a speculative boom.

INVESTMENT

The analysis of investment begins with the determination of the prices of capital assets. As sketched in the previous section, the quantity of money, the value placed upon liquidity, and the income and liquidity characteristics of the various capital and financial assets lead to the set of prices of capital and financial assets. The prices of capital and financial assets determine the demand price for investment outputs of various kinds. These demand prices are either derived by analogy—the investment is like some existing capital assets—or by capitalizing the expected cash flows and liquidity return from a project.

The demand prices for investment, however, do not determine the pace of investment. The existence of a market price for a capital asset and a demand price for comparable investments does not necessarily imply that there is an effective demand for investment; an effective demand for investment takes financing. There are three sources of such finance: cash and financial assets on hand, internal funds (i.e., gross profits after taxes and dividends), and external funds. External funds are either borrowed or acquired by issuing equities. When borrowed, their acquisition leads to payment commitments. The payment commitments determine the minimum cash flows required to satisfy the legal obligations of the unit doing the financing.

Investment—like all the other components of GNP—is a flow. Assuming that the per-unit supply price of investment rises after the flow of investment exceeds some level, there is a maximum rate of investment that will be produced at the price given by the demand price for capital assets.

The workings of the economy can be thought of as yielding a stream of capital income to business firms. This stream will be affected by the pace of investment;[10] in the simple heroic case, capital income (profits) equals investment. In a world with business debts, interest, dividend, and repayments of principal on debts come out of the flow of gross capital income. Furthermore, executive and other ancillary labor costs are largely an allocation of capital income. Thus, the aggregate funds available from internal sources to finance gross investment fall short of the financing required by gross investment.

The internal funds that are available to finance investment need to be augmented by outside funds. In the decision to invest, the availability of outside financing is a key element.

Planning an investment project involves two sets of interlocking decisions on the part of the firm that is investing. One set deals with revenues expected from using the capital asset in production and the cost of the investment. The second set deals with financing the capital asset: a decision to acquire capital assets is, basically, a decision to put out liabilities.

The costs of financing the production of investment is a cost that enters the supply price of output just like the costs of labor and purchased inputs. The fact that a firm has to borrow to pay wages raises the effective costs by the interest payments on the borrowings. The supply price of investment output thus includes interest during the gestation period, just as the normal supply price of post-harvest wheat reflects interest carrying charges on wheat in storage.

Production financing is typically short-term, and much of such financing involves bank lending. The cost of production and presumably the supply price of all output, but more particularly those outputs with significant gestation periods, includes a cost item that reflects interest charges.

Even as production financing is short-term, take-out or permanent financing is presumably long-term. The funds used in take-out financing may be obtained from the sale of bonds, mortgages, or new-equity issues as well as corporate retained earnings. In making an investment decision, where the gestation period of the investment good is not trivial, present views about the kind of permanent financing that will be used involves conjectures about the size of retained earnings and the conditions that will rule in the capital market at the time the permanent financing takes place.

---

10. See chapter 7.

The decision to invest therefore involves a supply function of investment, which depends upon labor costs and short-term interest rates, a demand function for investment, which is derived from the price of capital assets, and the anticipated structure and conditions of financing. Whereas the structure of balance sheets reflects the mix of internal funds (gross retained earning) and the external funds (bond or equity issues) actually used, the investment decision is based upon expected flows of internal and external funds. But the flows of internal funds to investing units depends upon the performance of the economy during the period between the decision to invest and the completion of the investment. Thus, there is an element of uncertainty in the decision to invest that has nothing to do with whether the investment will perform as the technologists indicated and whether the market for the product of the investment will be strong. This element of uncertainty centers on the mix of internal and external financing that will be needed; and this mix depends upon the extent to which finance for the investment goods will be forthcoming from profit flows.

Since investment deals preeminently with decisions that involve time, in order to explain investment it is necessary to come to grips with the meaning and significance of uncertainty in economics. Uncertainty deals with that class of events for which the outcome of actions cannot be known with the same precision as the average outcome at a roulette table, or even of a mortality table, is known. In a word, uncertainty in economics does not deal with risks that are insurable or analogous to gambling risks. For example, the appropriate liability structure for holding any type of capital asset cannot be known in the same sense as the appropriate technology for manufacturing. Today's appropriate liability structure for holding any capital asset can be determined only on the basis of history and conventions. In the course of history there have been significant swings in the mix of internal and external financing of investment and much innovation in liability structures. Liability structures (and asset holdings by intermediaries) that were deemed safe when entered upon may turn out to be highly risky as history unfolds.

Uncertainty is largely a matter of dealing today with a future that by its very nature is highly conjectural. In a world with uncertainty, units make do with and react to the often surprising fruits of past decisions as they ripen. One concrete manifestation of the uncertainty that rules is found in the *willingness* to lever or debt-finance positions in inherited capital assets, financial assets, and newly produced capital assets. Willingness to lever affects two sets of decision makers: the owners of capital assets, who determine their willingness to finance the acquisition of capital by means of debts, and the financial community, which determines its willingness to finance levered positions. As Keynes put it, our economy is characterized by "a system of borrowing and lending based upon margins of safety." The margins of safety required by both the borrowers and the lenders affect the extent to which positions and investments are externally financed.

As previously noted, positions in capital assets and financial instruments are financed and refinanced. Anytime capital assets change hands—such as when a home is sold or a company is taken over—the position in this particular asset is refinanced: old debt is extinguished, and new debt is created. In the world of Wall Street, every corporate takeover and merger involves a change in the liability structure for financing capital-asset ownership. If the conventional liability structure for financing positions in some capital assets changes so that more debt becomes acceptable, then the firms that financed their positions by conforming to the prior conventions acquire borrowing power: they can acquire cash by issuing more debt with the same capital assets as before. If the conventional debt-equity ratio does not change, but the market valuation of the cash flow generated by capital assets increases, then capital-asset-owning firms acquire borrowing power.

Perhaps the best example of how changes in conventions and value of assets affects borrowing power is found in the market in which proxies for residual claims to capital assets as organized into firms are traded—the stock exchange. The theoretical argument of how investment is determined involves a comparison of the price of capital assets and of investment output. In a corporate capitalist economy with a stock exchange, the market's valuation of a firm's capital assets and market position substitutes for the price of capital assets. This market valuation is the sum of the market value of the firm's common stocks and debts minus the value of the financial assets the firm owns. This valuation varies with the course of the stock market. A stock market boom leads to a higher implicit market value of the underlying capital assets of the economy; conversely, a fall in the stock market lowers the implicit value.

Ownership of common stocks and bonds is often financed by debt (a margin account leads to a levered position in stock market assets). When debt is used to finance common-stock ownership, a rise in the price of the stock will uncover an ability to borrow by the stockholders, which, in turn, can be used to finance the purchase of additional shares. An initial rise in the price of stocks can lead to a further rise in demand for stocks. Furthermore, in a bull market such appreciation in stock exchange values leads to building expected price increases into the determination, by both borrowers and lenders, of the required margin of safety.

Symmetrically, a fall in stock market valuations will decrease borrowing power and increase the burden of debt relative to asset values. As the decline in the price of common stocks gets built into the determination of the acceptable leverage ratio or the required margin of safety, the acceptable leverage ratio falls; borrowers and lenders both increase their required margins of safety.

The required margins of safety affect the acceptable financing plans of investing units. The ratio of external to internal financing that is acceptable changes over time to reflect the experience of economic units and the economy with debt-financing. If recent experience is that outstanding debts are easily serviced, then there will be a tendency to stretch debt ratios; if recent experience includes episodes in which debt-servicing has been a burden and representative units have not fulfilled debt contracts, then acceptable debt ratios will decrease.

Current views about financing reflect the opinions bankers and businessmen hold about the uncertainties they must face. These current views reflect the past and, in particular, the recent past, and how experience is transformed into expectations. A history of success will tend to diminish the margin of safety that business and bankers require and will thus tend to be associated with increased investment; a history of failure will do the opposite.

Investment therefore is a financial phenomenon. The various parts of the investment relations can be illustrated to show how different factors are interrelated and how asset prices, financing conditions, and income flows affect investment. The diagramatic exposition is illustrative; it is designed to identify the parts of the investment mechanism and to indicate how the processes of our economy interact.

The price of capital assets, either directly for those assets that have well-defined markets or indirectly for those that are proxied by the market (or the management) valuation of a firm's debts and shares, is a demand price for investment output. Given the labor force, wage rates, interest rates, and the techniques embodied in the stock of capital assets for producing investment output, there is a supply price of investment output. Because of the made-to-order nature of much of investment, these prices can be taken to be bid prices by producers. Assuming that the existing stock of capital assets and labor specialized to the production of plant and equipment sets limits to the ability to produce investment, the supply curve of investment will rise after output exceeds some norm.

A decision to invest will result in a capital asset at some date after the commitment. Given a go-ahead on an investment project, the sequence of

expenditures on labor and material for the various components of the investment good is more or less determined by the technical conditions of
production of the capital asset. This implies that investment spending
during, say, the second quarter of 1984 was largely determined prior to that
period. Furthermore, investment decisions made in the spring of 1984 will
affect income, employment, and financial markets over a varying number
of future quarters.

The material sketched so far has a demand curve for investment that
is a horizontal line at the price of capital assets and a supply curve of investment output that, after a threshold level, rises. The intersection of the two
curves leads to a quantity of investment ordered during the period and thus
to a schedule of investment spending over the time that it will take to
complete the projects set in motion (see Figure 8.2).

The above figure, however, has no place for financing: presumably
the amount of investment designated by the intersection will be ordered
independently of the financing arrangements. This is palpable nonsense.
The investment producers will not undertake their activity unless there is
some guarantee that the final purchaser will be able to pay for the completed investment good. This is where bankers, using the term broadly to
mean the financial community, come into play. Even in these days, when
giant multinational corporations do much of the investment ordering and
employ much of the capital assets of the economy, the creditworthiness of
corporations is watched and recorded by bankers, credit-rating services, and
stock market analysts. For each particular investing unit, and for investment

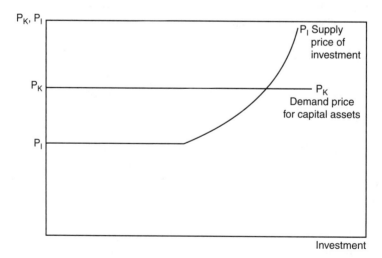

Figure 8.2:   Investment: Ignoring Financing Considerations

in general, a mix of gross retained earnings *and* external finance determines its gross investment activity. The extent of investment relative to internal financing reflects current views about the margins of safety required in financing relations. Both borrowers and lenders want protection, and the demand for protection by borrowers lowers the demand price for capital assets and by lenders raises the supply price of investment output.

During periods in which financial markets operate smoothly (i.e., when interest rates do not vary greatly, innovations in financial usages are few and small, and no traumatic threats or realizations of financial failures are evident), engineering and marketing considerations may be the dominant factors determining investment. The technical demand for capacity, as determined by extrapolations of past behavior and the profitability of existing capacity, dominate in determining investment during such periods.[11] In periods when the above does not rule, financial market conditions are of greater importance; the technical factors recede in importance.

Once a project passes the test in that the capitalized expected quasi-rents exceed the cost of the investment by a sufficient margin to compensate for the uncertainties inherent in taking positions in capital assets, the decision whether or not to invest turns upon the conditions at which the project can be financed. In the abstract, as noted briefly at the beginning of this section, three sources of financing can be distinguished. One is the cash and equivalent assets (Treasury securities, commercial paper, and so forth) on hand that are not required by current operations. Such a situation existed for many firms immediately after World War II because wartime government spending, controls over investment, and limits on dividends led to business accumulating cash and government securities. It may also occur in

---

11. It is worth noting that the period from the end of World War II until the emergence of financial tautness with the credit crunch of 1966 was just such a period of relative financial tranquility. The large number of econometric studies of investment, such as those done by Jorgenson and his associate's and which were surveyed in a number of review articles published in 1971 and 1974, use data from just such a rare period of relative tranquility in financial markets. As such, the articles surveyed and their conclusions are not worth much either as a test (or refutation) of the views put forth here or as a guide to understanding our economy. See Dale Jorgenson, "Econometric Studies of Investment Behavior: A Survey," *Journal of Economic Literature* 9, no. 4 (Dec. 1971), pp. 1111–47. Dale Jorgenson, Jerald Hunter, and M. Ishaq Nadiri, "A Comparison of Alternative Econometric Models of Investment Behavior," *Econometrica* 38, no. 2 (March 1970), pp. 187–212, and "The Predictive Performance of Econometric Models of Quarterly Investment Behavior," *Econometrica* 38, no. 2 (March 1970), pp. 213–24.

the aftermath of a great depression or a deep recession followed by a period during which business investment stagnates even after government deficits lead to improved profits; the result is an improvement in the liquidity of banks and business. As argued earlier, it took twenty years to dissipate the liquid financial structures that were the legacy of a Great War that followed hard upon a Great Depression.

A second source of investment finance is the flow of gross profits after dividends and taxes that accrue while the investment is being produced; these are the internal funds that are available to finance investment projects. Gross profits are less than gross capital income because of interest and repayment of principal on debts, as well as the allocations to dividends, taxes, and business style. A restriction of investment to what the flow of internal funds can finance leads to a sequence of decreasing investments and therefore diminishing total profits and national income. Internal finance of investment by business is consistent with sustained or expanding profits and income only if business payment commitments on debts are small and the government is running a large deficit, there is a surplus on current account on the balance of payments, or there are surplus financial assets in business portfolios that can be run off to finance investment. Once debts that require interest payments and repayment of principal are significant, external finance that sustains and even increases debts is necessary to keep profits and income from falling.

The third source of financing consists of external funds. These are either borrowed from banks or other financial intermediaries or obtained by issuing bonds or selling equities. External financing of investment and positions in capital assets is a marked characteristic of our economy.

In determining whether an investment project is worth undertaking, anticipated cash flows are compared with the cost of the project. The price of a bond is analogous to the cost of an investment project, and to the holder the interest and repayment of principal on bonds are analogous to the anticipated cash flows from owning a capital asset. The payments to the bondholder are presumably protected by an anticipated excess of earnings (cash flows) by the issuer over the payment obligations. It follows that the anticipated net earnings from an investment project must exceed the interest due on bonds if the investment is to provide a margin of safety to bondholders. Such an excess of anticipated investment income over bond interest payments is necessary if bonds are to finance investment projects.

As noted earlier, our economy is characterized by complex borrowing and lending relations based upon various margins of safety. The ratio of external to internal financing can increase only if borrowers and lenders

expect the margin of safety to increase or hold that the prior margins of
safety were excessive. The belief that prior margins of safety were too great
(or too small) reflects the experience with liability structures; the margins
of safety relevant for decision change with experience.

A buyer of capital assets that are expected to yield a given flow of profits
can increase his margin of safety to offset an increased exposure to failure
to fulfill debt contracts by lowering his demand price for capital assets to
reflect an increased dependence on debt financing. Borrower's risk shows up
in a declining demand price for capital assets.[12] It is not reflected in any
financing charges; it mirrors the view that increased exposure to default will
be worthwhile only if there is a compensating potential gain.

Internal cash flows can pay for some level of investment (for both an
individual firm and for the economy). Once anticipated internal flows (Q)
are estimated, their relation to investment output can be represented as a
rectangular hyperbola ($Q_N Q_N$ in Figure 8.3) because the internal cash
flows, or quasi-rents, Q_N are related to the price P_I and the output I_I of
investment by the formula $P_I Q_I = Q_N$. The intersection of this rectangular hyperbola with the supply price, P_I, of investment output yields I_I
(internal), the investment that can be financed by anticipated internal funds
(point A in Figure 8.3).

To finance investment in excess of I_I (internal) it is necessary either to
run down holdings of financial assets that are superfluous to operations or

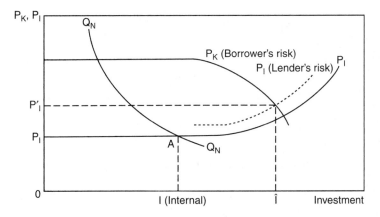

Figure 8.3:   Investment: Impact of Internal Funds and External Finance

---

12. The terms *borrower's risk* and *lender's risk* are usually associated with Kalecki,
    although the terms appear in Keynes's *General Theory*.

to engage in external finance. If financial assets are run down, then margins of safety in the asset structure are reduced. If new issues of common shares are undertaken, the issue price will have to be attractive, which may mean that present stock owners feel their equity interest is being diluted. If debts, bonds, or borrowing from banks or short-term markets are used, then future cash-flow commitments rise, which diminishes the margin of safety of management and of equity owners. In every case—running down of financial assets, issuance of new common stocks, or borrowing—borrower's risk will increase as the weight of external or liquidity diminishing financing increases. This borrower's risk is not reflected in any objective cost, but it lowers the demand price of capital assets. Although increased borrower's risk can be due to a variety of portfolio and income changes, in what follows the borrower's risk that affects investment will be treated as if this financing is debt-financing.

The supply schedule of investment goods rises after some output. However, lender's risk imparts a rising thrust to the supply conditions for capital assets independent of technological-supply conditions. This rising thrust takes a concrete form in the financing conditions that bankers set. In loan and bond contracts, lender's risk is expressed in higher stated interest rates, in terms to maturity, and in covenants and codicils. Covenants and codicils might restrict dividends, limit further borrowings, and constrain the sale of assets; they might also require the maintenance of some minimum stated net worth. Essentially, the covenants and codicils reflect negotiations about the risks and uncertainties the unit faces and the way in which these may impinge upon the lender. Although some risks faced by lenders are expressed in observable increases in interest rates, as leverage increases and the confidence in future cash flows decreases, this observed rise in interest rates is not the full picture of the rise in financing costs.

Investment will be carried to the point where the supply curve of investment, which incorporates lender's risk, intersects with the demand curve for investment, which reflects borrower's risk. This intersection yields an implicit price of the asset, but this is a price that is never observed. In Figure 8.3, the observed price per unit of investment goods is P'_I somewhat in excess of the base or slack output supply price. The quantity is $\hat{I}$ of which $O - I$ (internal) is internally financed and $\hat{I} - I$ (internal) is externally financed.

Figure 8.3 gives some, but not all, of the ingredients of what determines the pace of investment in our economy. The ingredients not included are the way in which changing long-term or take-out financing terms affect the demand price of capital assets and how changing short-term interest rates affect the base supply price of capital assets. The relative positions of the price of capital assets, P_K, and the supply price of investment output, P_I, in Figure 8.3, are not explained.

Before we discuss how P_K and P_I are affected by movements in interest rates, it is important to note that borrower's risk and lender's risk, as represented by the dotted segments P_K and P_I, are *effective* determinants of the pace of investment.

If entrepreneurs have been successful and are confident of further success, then borrower's risk will be slight and the dotted line will barely fall away from the P_K line. If few prior borrowers have failed to fulfill contracts, then lender's risk will be weak and a rising supply curve of investment due to such risk will not become evident until after considerable external financing. The pace of investment will vary as borrower's and lender's risk vary.[13]

In a world in which financing conditions do not intrude into investment decisions, the technical productivity of capital assets and their supply price would determine investment. Changes in investment would tend to be a regular, smooth phenomena. Money and finance would not enter into the determination of anything of major significance in the economy. Only a formulation of the investment process that accepts the existence of capitalist financial institutions is capable of explaining the observed instability of investment.[14]

Figure 8.4 illustrates various configurations of the investment-determining relations, along with the anticipated cash flows. If the actual cash flows ($Q'_N - Q'_N$) exceed the anticipated cash flows ($Q_N - Q_N$), then the amount of external financing actually required will be smaller than expected. When this occurs, the balance sheet with the newly acquired capital assets will be less encumbered by debt than originally anticipated. Such a better-than-anticipated balance sheet means that both the firm and its bankers view the investing unit as having unused borrowing power, and the financing conditions for subsequent investments will be more favorable than otherwise.

---

13. Robert Clower, "An Investigation into the Dynamics of Investment," *American Economic Review* XLIV (March 1954); James G. Witte, Jr., "The Micro Foundations of the Social Investment Function," *Journal of Political Economy* 71 (Oct. 1963).

14. Instability of investment within an idealized socialist regime would reflect political changes. Within actual socialist regimes instability of investment reflects the inability to execute, which is a universal attribute of any bureaucratic organization of society.

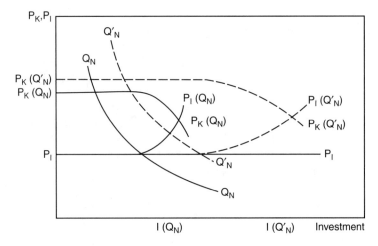

Figure 8.4: Investment Determination: Alternative Configurations of Internal and External Finance

Symmetrically, if the cash flows available for internal financing fall short of those anticipated, then the financing of, say, $I(Q'_N)$ of investment will require a greater amount of external funds than originally thought. This circumstance means that the balance sheet will be less favorable than anticipated and the financing conditions for further investment will be more demanding.

A deviation of quasi-rents, Q, from what was expected affects not only the way investment impinges upon the balance sheets of firms; it also affects the price level of capital assets. If actual quasi-rents are greater than anticipated, then the excess of profits over expected profits will raise P_K, increasing the gap between P_K and P_I. Then, for any given gradient due to borrowers' risk, the demand price at each output will be higher with the new P_K. This situation implies an increase in investment demand relative to the availability of internal finance. Profits in excess of those anticipated therefore increase the demand for investment by improving the flow of internal funds, raising the (implicit) price of capital assets and increasing borrowers' willingness to finance externally. The above relations between quasi-rents and the demand price of capital assets hold even if conditions in financial markets do not change, but changes in conditions in financial markets do occur and they affect P_K and P_I.

The extent to which internal funds or net worth is leveraged is one way, but not the only way, in which financial market conditions affect investments. Financing conditions also affect the demand price of capital assets and the supply price of investment goods; furthermore, the gap between the two prices is influenced by the level of short- and long-term interest rates.

Short-term interest rates affect the supply price of investment output. For any output that has a positive gestation period, the supply price must allow for interest on early-on costs in the production process. If the gestation period is long—and if a significant part of costs are early in the production process—then the supply price of investment goods is affected to a meaningful extent by financing charges.

Since commercial banks are specialists in the short-term financing of business activity, the financing of investment production is a major bank activity. This type of financing is basically interim, lasting until an investment project comes on-stream, at which time take-out or permanent financing occurs. Investment production therefore uses bank financing as an input, and its cost affects the supply price of capital assets. Because the items being financed by short-term debt are en route to being capital assets, they have no value until completed. Partially completed investment leads to an inelastic demand for finance; a half-finished power plant or pipeline leads to an inelastic demand for finance. Furthermore, as suppliers deliver the components for complex installations, this inelastic demand curve rises.

A rising inelastic demand will lead to a rise in the observed price unless supply is infinitely elastic at the existing price. Thus, in terms of financing investment as it is being produced, an infinitely elastic supply of finance will exist if, and only if, the banking system is *willing* and *able* to finance any amount of investment in embryo at unchanging interest rates. For a variety of reasons—the limited equity base of banks, internal and foreign drains of bank reserves, and, in modern times, central bank (Federal Reserve) actions to restrain the money supply—the supply of finance from banks eventually becomes less than infinitely elastic. This means that after favorable conditions for investment are sustained over some time, the cost of financing investment as it is being produced increases. Furthermore, the supply of finance can become very inelastic because of policy decisions or the internal processes of the banking and financial system. This means that short-term interest rates can become very high quite rapidly.

Such a rise in short-term interest rates will lead to a marked increase in the supply price of investment goods with significant gestation periods. In a modern stock market, short-term financing is used to finance some positions in equities and bonds. This means that a rapid run-up in short-term interest rates can lead to a sharp rise in long-term rates, that is, to a fall in stock and bond prices.

But rising short- and long-term interest rates have opposite effects on the demand price for capital assets and the supply price of investment. The demand price for capital assets falls as long-term interest rates increase, and the supply price of investment output rises as short-term interest rates rise. This tends to lower the price gap that induces investment demand. If the rise in interest rates is extreme, the present value of the investment good as a capital asset can fall below the supply price of the investment good as current output. Such a present value reversal, if it occurs, will bring investment activity to a halt. If the interest rate increases are sharp and are accompanied by declining estimates of the profitability of projects, even investment projects under way will be abandoned.

Although present value reversals occur—they certainly did in the 1930s and again to a much more limited extent in 1974–75 and 1981–82—the cyclical contractions and expansions of investment activity do not depend upon this extreme case. It is enough that the margin between the price of capital assets and the supply price of investment, inclusive of financing costs, varies *inversely* with interest rates. A regime of low short- and long-term interest rates will lead to a large margin between the two prices, which leads to a high ratio of external to internal finance. This increases investment and profits, and the willingness to engage in debt financing of capital asset positions. Thus, there are strong *internal* destabilizing interactions in any economy in which financial markets are part of the mechanism by which investment is determined.

As a result of the impact of financing conditions, the relation between investment and interest rates can be represented by a negatively sloped function. Because of the way in which acceptable lender's and borrower's risk varies with the behavior of the economy and the way in which investment determines profits and thus the realized extent of external finance, the negatively sloped investment–interest rate relation shifts to reflect experience with the fulfillment of commitments embodied in liabilities. The negatively sloped investment–interest rate relation is not a simple corollary of the diminishing technical productivity of capital assets and the supply price of investment goods. Rather, it summarizes the behavior of technical, marketing, and financial influences. Because financial influences are so affected by the considerations that fall under the rubric of uncertainty, if a negatively sloped function between investment and interest rates is used in an argument, it must be recognized that this function shifts as the path of the economy changes present views about future contingencies.

FINANCIAL
COMMITMENTS AND
INSTABILITY

The main reason why our economy behaves in different ways at different times is that financial practices and the structure of financial commitments change. Financing practices result in payment commitments that are embodied in contracts that reflect market conditions and expectations that ruled when they were negotiated and signed. The payment commitments come due and are discharged as the economy moves through time, and the behavior and particularly the stability of the economy change as the relation of payment commitments to the funds available for payments changes and the complexity of financial arrangements evolves.

There is no doubt that the American economy was more unstable, in the 1970s and 1980s than in the 1950s and early 1960s: in the mid-1960s an apparently significant change in the stability properties of the economy became evident. A robust financial structure—the legacy of World War II and financial conservatism induced by the Great Depression, which together were conducive to stability—was succeeded by a fragile financial structure that is instability-prone and, from time to time, requires intervention by the Federal Reserve and cooperating authorities to abort apparent incipient financial crises. The evolution from financial robustness to financial fragility did not take place in a vacuum. The sources of the change can be traced to profit opportunities open to financial innovators within a given set of institutions and rules; a drive to innovate financing practices by profit-seeking households, businesses, and bankers; and legislative and administrative interventions by governments and central bankers.

The financing of activity results in a residue of financial commitments. Investment not only affects aggregate output, income distribution, and production capacity, but in a capitalist economy it also leaves a residue in the financial structure. Furthermore, positions in the inherited stock of capital assets are financed by instruments that are entered on the liability side of balance sheets. The liability structure used to finance holdings of capital assets changes, which in turn affects the structure of financial relations and payment commitments: mergers, takeovers, and acquisitions change liability structures without changing the aggregate output or the productive capacity of the economy.[1]

Profits are available to innovators in financial structures and institutions as well as to innovators in products, production techniques, and marketing. Many of the great fortunes accrued to financial innovators, either as borrowers or lenders. Banks, other financial institutions, businesses, and households are always seeking new ways to finance activities. Successful financial innovators are rewarded by fortunes and flattered by imitators. Once an innovation proves successful, it can spread rapidly because financial innovations are almost always the application of some idea, and there is no patent constraint upon imitators.[2]

Government, which is a source of change in financial market usages and institutions, operates by way of legislation and decrees or interventions by authorities, such as central banks. Government influences the norms of financial behavior and structure. Legislation, decrees, and interventions reflect the views about how the economy is affected by financial institutions and instruments held by our rulers and their court intellectuals. Behind all but the crassest of special-interest legislation and regulation lies some theory about how markets behave and how they affect the economy

1. The income of Wall Street operators in the mergers and acquisition business is part of national income and output. Thus, while the meaning of the above is clear, it is not technically correct. In our type of economy, there is a peculiar output called mergers and acquisitions. The value of this output in national income accounts is the fees to professionals in law firms and Wall Street as well as the particular costs of firms that arise because of the possibility of mergers or acquisitions. The "golden parachutes" of the 1980s yield "incomes" that are hard to relate to the standard economic view of incomes.

2. Hyman P. Minsky, "Central Banking and Money Market Changes," *Quarterly Journal of Economics* (May 1957); reprinted in Hyman P. Minsky, *Can "IT" Happen Again? Essays on Instability & Finance* (Armonk, N.Y.: M. E. Sharpe & Co., 1982), details some implications of a money market innovation. See also Hyman P. Minsky, "Financial Intermediation in the Money and Capital Markets," in G. Pontecorov, R. P. Shay, and A. G. Hart, *Issues in Banking and Monetary Analysis* (New York: Holt Rinehart & Winston, Inc., 1967), pp. 33–56.

and therefore the common good. Legislated changes, such as the reforms that took place during the Roosevelt years and the deregulation mania of the late 1970s and 1980s, reflect some theory. If the theory is at variance with the way the economy behaves, the reforms will do little good and may do great harm.[3]

If with the passage of time the behavior of the economy changes, the intellectual foundation of particular legislation may be undermined. At that time, legislation, and the institutions and usages that it created, can lose its legitimacy. The regulated financial structure was thus legitimized by the financial debacle of 1929–33, and the deregulation mania occurred in the 1970s and 1980s after a long run without a fully realized debacle.

To analyze how financial commitments affect the economy it is necessary to look at economic units in terms of their cash flows. The cash-flow approach looks at all units—be they households, corporations, state and municipal governments, or even national governments—as if they were banks.

Traditional banking literature emphasized the need for bankers to be liquid and solvent, and this was to be achieved by banks emphasizing self-liquidating commercial loans. In this way the cash flows from business sales would lead to payments to banks; these payments would guarantee bank liquidity and solvency. In a similar way ordinary business needs to be liquid and solvent; this means that the payment commitments on debts must lie within bounds given by realized and expected cash flows.

Some of the problems that surfaced in the 1970s and the early 1980s can be traced to the neglect (or ignorance) of old textbook rules for the prudent operation of banks and businesses that were universally accepted, though often violated, in earlier days. In recent years traditional wisdom has often been ignored by the management of giant banks and the various banking authorities: this was particularly evident in the REIT problems of the 1970s, the Hunt-Bache affair of the late 1970s, and the exposure of giant banks in international finance in the 1980s. Part of this neglect is due to the giant banks' belief that the Treasury, the Federal Reserve, and other government agencies will provide them with a bail-out in order to prevent a big crash. The experience of the 1970s and early 1980s validated this belief that the giant financial institutions will be protected. Once the management

---

3. On the deregulation movement are Thomas F. Cargill and Gillian C. Garcia, *Financial Deregulation and Monetary Control* (Stanford: Hoover Institution Press, 1982).

of multibillion-dollar banks assumes that the authorities will always act to make them healthy and once the authorities validate this assumption, bankers' behavior will take the existence of the safety net of a bail-out into account.[4]

Cover-ups, however, have repercussions, as do bail-outs. Protecting and bailing out bankers affect the subsequent performance of the economy. The interventions, beginning with the credit crunch of 1966, to protect financial institutions from the life-threatening effects of their behavior have led to an economy that fluctuates, over a period of varying length, between financial crises and accelerating inflations. The authorities, frightened of the unknown consequences of the failure of giant banks, intervene to protect them when they are at hazard, which implies that the giant banks are too big for a noninterventionist, free-market economy.

One cause of the observed instability, not only of the past decade and a half but of the past century and a half, lies in the financing needs of industrial and industrializing economies. External or bankers' finance is no longer needed solely or even mainly to finance commerce and inventories; investments in and the ownership of capital assets with long lives also require external finance. This means that a lack of synchronization between contractual payments on debts and receipts from operations can be built into the banker-business relation as positions in long-lived assets are financed by short-term liabilities.

Capitalism may very well work best when capital assets are cheap and simple. Instability may very well be exacerbated as production becomes more capital intensive and as the relative cost and gestation periods of investment goods increase, for in such a capitalist economy financing arrangements are likely to appear in which debtors pay debts not with cash derived from income production but with cash obtained by issuing debt. We have to investigate the implications of debts and external financing of the financial structures we all know exist, for the stability of the economy.

---

4. The virtual failure of the Continental Illinois Bank of Chicago, where the authorities intervened on a massive scale to prevent an "open" failure, shows the extraordinary lengths the banking authorities are ready and willing to go to prevent overt bank failure. In the Continental Illinois "failure"—which stretched out over two years—stockholders, directors, management, and some employees were punished as all depositors, regardless of the size of their deposits, were protected.

A TAXONOMY OF CASH FLOWS

We can distinguish three basic types of cash flows—income, balance sheet, and portfolio.[5] Income cash flows—wages and salaries, both public and private, the payments from one stage of production and trade to another, and gross profits after taxes of business—result from the process of production. Money, in effect, goes around an income circuit; the income circuit as here defined includes all the payments for partially finished products sold by one firm to another. It is not restricted to payments that arise from the final sales of output.[6]

In addition, cash flows are mandated by existing, inherited liabilities. These cash flows, which are on account of both principal and interest, can be determined by reading the contracts that are the debt instruments. Such cash flows will be called balance-sheet cash flows; the shorter the duration of financial instruments, the greater the balance-sheet cash, flows per dollar of liability.

A third set of cash flows are portfolio cash flows. These are the result of transactions in which capital and financial assets change hands. These cash flows are the outcome of decisions to acquire or to sell assets or to put new liabilities into circulation. Some of any period's portfolio cash flows are the result of previous commitments; this is especially true of the cash flows at the completion of the production of investment output and the metamorphosis of investment output into capital assets.

There is an asymmetry about the cash flows involving investment. To the producers of investment goods the cash receipts are an income-account

---

5. The classification of cash-flow types and the relation of cash-flow types to the stability of the economy were developed over a number of years. See Hyman P. Minsky, "Financial Instability Revisited: The Economics of Disaster," Board of Governors, Federal Reserve System, *Fundamental Reappraisal of the Federal Reserve Discount Mechanism* (Washington, D.C., 1972); reprinted in Hyman P. Minsky, *Can "IT" Happen Again? Essays on Instability & Finance*, op. cit. Also see Hyman P. Minsky, "The Modelling of Financial Instability: An Introduction," *Modelling and Simulation*, vol. 5, Proceedings of the Fifth Annual Pittsburgh Conference (Pittsburgh: Instrument Society of America, 1974).
6. Frank H. Knight, "Social Economic Organizations," *Syllabus and Selected Readings for the First Year Course in the Social Sciences*, 2d ed. (Chicago: University of Chicago Press, 1933); George J. Stigler, *The Theory of Price*, rev. ed. (New York: Macmillan, 1952), chapter 1.

cash flow; the selling prices of investment goods recover the wage, financing, and material costs of production. To the purchaser of the investment good, however, the transaction is a portfolio transaction, in which the newly produced investment good is just like a capital asset or financial instrument that may be acquired from the economy's stock of assets. This asymmetry reflects one way in which the future enters into the decision to produce; investment goods are assimilated to the stock of capital assets because they are expected to generate large enough cash flows as they are used in production or trade to validate their cost of production.

It is also useful to distinguish three different types of balance-sheet cash flows: dated, demand, and contingent. Dated cash flows are easy to understand. An automobile finance contract or home mortgage requires monthly payments of a stipulated amount. These monthly payments are cash payment commitments.

Such arrangements clearly originated as a money today (the amount of the purchase price that is financed) for money tomorrow (the set of monthly cash payments) deal. If the set of monthly cash payments is discounted back to the day of the contract at the interest rate of the contract, the present value of the payment commitments equals the money today paid by the lender.

Anyone who has purchased a house or a car by borrowing knows that the contract divides each payment into a part that is interest and a part that is a reduction of principal. This is important for income tax purposes and if the contract needs to be closed out before the stated time. Thus, at each date on such conventional fully amortized contracts there is a contractual value of the outstanding principal. If the payments that still have to be made on this contract are capitalized at the interest rate at which the contract was computed, the value of the remaining payments equals the amount stated in the contract as the amount still outstanding (unless the contract has a penalty for prepayment).

If the market interest rate is different at some date into the contract from the initial interest rate, then the capitalized value of the remaining payments at this market rate will differ from the principal as stated in the contract. The capitalized value will be higher if the market interest rate is lower than the initial contractual rate, and it will be lower if the market interest rate used is higher. This inverse relation between market interest rates and the capitalized value of anticipated and contingent contractual returns is fundamental to an understanding of capitalist finance.

Two other types of dated financial contracts can be distinguished, the discounted note and the bond. In the case of the discounted note, the borrower agrees to pay a specific sum at a particular date and receives in exchange some percentage less than the amount he agrees to repay. Such discounting is of special interest because it turns up in accrual accounting, and accrual accounting is perhaps essential to the existence of nonfraudulental Ponzi finance,[7] in which the funds to pay interest and dividends are obtained by borrowing. The most widely known discount instrument is the Treasury bill. In a discounted bill, which is typically for a short period, the principal and interest are returned in one payment at a designated date. In the 1970s and 1980s private organizations began to experiment with zero coupon debts that had a deep discount because they had a long time to maturity.

A more traditional type of contract is the bond: an example might pay $100 per year for twenty-five years and $1,000 at the end of the period. The price of such a bond will rise or fall depending upon whether the current interest rate is above or below 10 percent.

The above are examples of dated contracts: in addition, we have financial contracts of indeterminate duration, which are phrased as demand contracts. The most important demand contracts are deposits at commercial banks and other depository financial institutions, such as savings banks. Of particular importance are the deposits subject to check, which are readily spent on current activity, moved from one bank to another, or exchanged for other assets. Such deposits are the principal form of money in our economy.

Demand deposits may be considered as the shortest-term financial instrument. In usual practice the demand for payment is exercised by transferring the deposit to another party. If there were only one bank issuing such deposits, no problems would arise as a result of such orders; in an economy with many banks, however, payments normally lead to transfers of assets among banks. In a well-functioning banking system there is some agreed-upon bankers' money that banks use in making payments to one

---

7. Donald H. Dunn, *Ponzi!* (New York: McGraw-Hill, 1975), is a fictionalized account of the affair that catches some of the feeling of "irresponsible" finance that is all too often practiced in more respectable surroundings. The use of the term *Ponzi* for financing relations which involve the capitalization of interest was originally a joke that became a fixture in my way of describing things. It is not meant to be "demagoguery," as Raymond Goldsmith has it. See comment by Raymond Goldsmith in C. P. Kindleberger and J. P. Laffaugue, *Financial Crises Theory History and Policy* (Cambridge: Cambridge University Press, 1982), p. 43. For an alternative terminology to my hedge, speculative and Ponzi finance, see P. Davidson, *Money and the Real World* (New York: John Wiley and Sons, 1972).

another, and there are arrangements by which banks can exchange their assets for bankers' money. Gold once served as bankers' money; in modern banking, deposits at the central bank—or at correspondent banks—serve that function: the arrangements take the forms of a money market and of access to the central bank's lending facilities.

A third class of financial instruments embodies conditional or contingent claims. One set of contingent claims arises due to endorsement by a third party of a note. The government-guaranteed Lockheed and Chrysler loans, the Moral Obligation Bond of New York State, the Federal Home Loan Banks Guarantee on mortgages, and a banker's acceptance are examples of contingent claims due to endorsements.

In addition, life, liability and accident insurance, and the common stock of corporations embody contingent claims, but these are quite different from the claims set up by endorsements. The contingent claim of the common stockholder, for example, is to a proportional share of earnings, if they exist and are distributed, or to a proportional share of the value of the company if sold or liquidated. The value of common shares therefore is intimately related to the expected course of the cash flows that will remain with a firm after payment of contractual commitments on debts.

A special type of contingent claim exists in dated bond contracts, in that if the debtor defaults on any outstanding debt, all the outstanding debt becomes due. This provision is designed to protect the rights of the holders of longdated debts. If it did not exist, the assets of an organization whose debts exceed the value of its assets could be dissipated before the date at which the long-dated debt is due.

Financial instability is linked to the relative importance of income, balance-sheet, and portfolio cash flows in an economy. Income cash flows—the wages, salaries, and payments for final and intermediate products—are the foundation upon which the balance-sheet and portfolio cash flows rest. If realized and expected income cash flows are sufficient to meet all the payment commitments on the outstanding liabilities of a unit, then the unit will be hedge financing. However, the balance-sheet cash flows from a unit can be larger than the expected income receipts so that the only way they can be met is by rolling over or even increasing debt; units that roll over debt are engaged in speculative finance and those that increase debt to pay debt are engaged in Ponzi finance. Thus, speculative and Ponzi financing units need engage in portfolio transactions—selling assets or debts—to fulfill their payment commitments, whereas units engaged in hedge finance can meet payment commitments on debts without portfolio transactions. Of course, hedge units may engage in portfolio transactions to acquire assets, but this is a business strategy and not the result of a shortfall of income cash flows relative to maturing payment commitments.

It is important to note that the need to roll over or increase debt in order to meet payment commitments and keep a business going may have been envisaged by the business and the banker when contracts were entered upon. However, whereas hedge units are not dependent upon financial market conditions in order to fulfill obligations, speculative and Ponzi financing units are. The relative weight of income, balance-sheet, and portfolio payments in an economy determines the susceptibility of the financial system to disruption. An economy in which income cash flows are dominant in meeting balance-sheet commitments is relatively immune to financial crises: it is financially robust. An economy in which portfolio transactions are widely used to obtain the means for making balance-sheet payments can be crisis-prone: it is at least potentially financially fragile.

CASH FLOWS FROM OPERATIONS AND DEBTS

A unit's cash receipt expectations are based upon its operations and financial assets. It is cash receipts earned by a business that make ownership of capital assets worthwhile. From a Wall Street perspective, capital assets are valuable not because they are productive in a physical sense but because they yield profits. To Wall Street the technical capacity of a Boeing 747 to deliver seat-miles is of secondary importance; what is important is the ability of an organization in a particular market and economic situation to operate 747s profitably. Similarly, whether nuclear power plants produce electricity, damage the environment, or are safe is not important from a Wall Street perspective; what is vital is the calculation of expected costs and revenues. As has been argued, in our economy the prospective profitability of collections of capital assets under the control of a firm is critical in determining investment, for it determines whether the production and ownership of capital assets are financed.

If it is true that capital assets are valuable because they yield profits, it follows that the market price of a capital asset depends upon current expectations of future profits and the way expected profits are transformed into a present value. There are, however, two valuations in addition to the capitalization of future incomes that can be put upon capital assets—the supply price of investment goods that can be substituted

HEDGE, SPECULATIVE, AND PONZI FINANCE

In our economy, characterized as it is by borrowing and lending based upon margins of safety for both the borrowers and lenders, positions of firms in capital assets, which are expected to yield cash flows as they are used in production, are financed by combinations of equity shares and debts. Similarly, positions in collections of financial instruments owned by commercial banks, insurance companies, savings banks, and so forth are financed by combinations of capital and surplus and debts. The debts of financial institutions may be demand or time deposits, cash surrender values, and so forth. The financial assets are expected to yield cash flows as stated by their contracts.

There are three types of financing of positions in assets that can be identified in the financial structure of our system: hedge, speculative, and Ponzi finance. These financing regimes are characterized by different relations between cash payment commitments on debts and expected cash receipts due to the quasi-rents earned by capital assets or the debtor contractual commitments on owned financial instruments.

Hedge-financing units and their bankers (those who arrange financing even though they may or may not own the instruments used) expect the cash flow from operating capital assets (or from owning financial contracts) to be more than sufficient to meet contractual payment commitments now and in the future. Consequently, a hedge-financing unit cannot have a large volume of demand debt. Contingent debts, unless the contingency follows some well—known actuarial rules—as is true for insurance—also cannot be a large part of the liabilities of a hedge unit. A commercial bank cannot be a hedge-financing unit.

Speculative-financing units, and their bankers, expect the cash flows to the unit from operating assets (or from owning financial contracts) to be less than the cash payment commitments in some, typically near-term, periods. However, if cash receipts and payments are separated into income and a return of principal components (as, for example, monthly payments on a fully amortized home mortgage are separated), then the expected income receipts exceed the income (interest) payments on existing commitments in every period. Cash-flow deficiencies arise because there are commitments to pay cash on the account of principal that are greater than the receipts on principal account during these periods. Speculative financing involves the rolling over of maturing debt.

A unit (and its bankers) that engages in speculative finance expects the cash receipts in later periods to exceed the cash payment commitments in those periods due to debts now on the books. Speculative finance involves the short financing of long positions. Commercial banks are the prototypical speculative financial organization. A hedge unit can become a speculative unit if there is a shortfall of income, and a speculative unit a hedge unit if there is a surge of income or if debts are "funded."[10]

A Ponzi-financing unit is similar to a speculative financing unit in that, for some near-term periods, the cash payment commitments exceed the expected cash receipts on account of owned assets. However, for at least some near-term periods, the cash payment commitments on income account exceed the expected cash payment receipts on income account. Whereas the shortperiod cash flows for speculative units are such that financing costs do not increase outstanding debt, for Ponzi finance units financing costs are greater than income, so that the face amount of outstanding debt increases: Ponzi units capitalize interest into their liability structure.

Debtors and bankers engaged in speculative and Ponzi finance expect payment commitments on debts to be met by refinancing, increasing debts, or running down superfluous stocks of financial assets. Whereas hedge finance units are vulnerable to difficulties in fulfilling outstanding financial commitments only if receipts fall short of expectations, speculative- and Ponzi-financing units are vulnerable to developments in financial markets. Both speculative- and Ponzi-financing units have to meet changing financial-market conditions, whereas a hedge unit will be impervious to such changes.[11]

Ponzi financing is quite often associated with fringe or fraudulent financial practices, even though the intent is not necessarily to cheat. Interest- and dividend-paying units that borrow to pay for investments and that accrue income engage in a variety of Ponzi financing. A speculative financing arrangement can be transformed into a Ponzi finance scheme by a rise in interest or other costs or a shortfall in income.[12] On the other hand, if earnings are better or costs, especially interest rates, fall, Ponzi financing

---

10. Bankruptcy is one way of transforming speculative and Ponzi units into hedge and speculative units.

11. By this criterion, a unit that borrows at floating rates is engaged in a form of speculative finance, even though at ruling interest rates it is engaging in hedge financing.

12. This is of course what happened to the thrifts as they moved toward universal insolvency in the early 1980s.

may be transformed into speculative financing. Refinancing, which changes the time pattern of payments, can change the balance-sheet posture of a unit.

Debt restructuring is often an effort to transform speculative into hedge financing, and concessions in financing terms by lenders may be made in an effort to transform Ponzi units into speculative units. The refinancing and restructuring of debt of entities as diverse as Chrysler, New York City, Baldwin-United, and Brazil that have taken place in the past decade are efforts to shift the financing of particular organizations toward the hedge side of the spectrum of financing relations.

The Weight of the Types of Finance

Hedge-financing arrangements are such that contractual commitments will be fulfilled unless the quasi-rents earned by capital assets fall below expected levels. A hedge-financing unit is vulnerable only to cost escalation or to revenue declines, for its balance-sheet payment commitments will not be directly affected by developments in financial markets. A speculative-financing unit needs to raise funds in various financial markets to fulfill payment commitments on outstanding debt. Speculative units, therefore, are not only vulnerable to product- and factor-market developments—as is true of hedge-financing units—but also to financial-market developments. As a result, interest rate increases and changes in market credit standards can affect the viability, as measured by both cash flows and present values, of units engaged in speculative finance.

A Ponzi unit is not only vulnerable to developments that would affect a speculative unit, but its balance sheet deteriorates as interest or even dividends are paid by increasing debts. Thus, the cash flows that must be earned for the financial commitments to be fulfilled become greater, and the equity-debt ratio on the balance sheet deteriorates. The conditions for full debt validation become stricter, and the shortfall of earnings or the rise in interest costs that makes it highly unlikely that payment commitments will not be fulfilled becomes smaller. Although periods of Ponzi finance may be part of the normal cyclical experience of firms, being forced into Ponzi-financing arrangements by income shortfalls or interest costs escalation is a systemic part of the process that leads to widespread bankruptcy.

The mixture of hedge, speculative, and Ponzi finance in an economy is a major determinant of its stability. The existence of a large component of positions financed in a speculative or a Ponzi manner is necessary for financial instability. A question that needs to be addressed is, What determines the changing proportion of units in each financing mode? In order to answer this question, it has to be broken into two elements: what determines desired, and what determines actual or realized financing modes?

Desired and actual financing postures for a unit differ because receipts and payments in any period are largely the results of commitments and activity of past periods. Once financial, capital-asset, and investment commitments are made, they cannot be undone except at some, perhaps large, cost.

Financial commitments and financial practices are linked to the real resource commitments made in capital-asset ownership and investment production. In the aggregate, the prospects of the financial assets in an economy can be no better than the financial prospects of the underlying units—households, business firms, and governments. However, the critical private debt-financing is linked to the ownership and creation, through investment, of capital assets. The time series of cash flows that capital assets are expected to yield as they are used in the production of income is an underlying determinant of the time dimensions of financial instruments.

The robustness or fragility of the financial system depends upon the size and strength of the margins of safety and the likelihood that initial disturbances are amplified. Hedge, speculative, and Ponzi financing units alike are vulnerable to economic developments that reduce the cash flows from assets. A decrease in income from operations or a default on debts owed to a hedge unit can transform it into a speculative unit. For things to go wrong with a hedge unit, something first had to go wrong someplace else in the economy—unless the hedge characteristics of the initial financing were based upon unrealistic euphoric expectations with respect to costs, markets, and their development over time. Note that for hedge units, even the euphoric expectations deal with product and factor markets.

On the other hand, speculative- and Ponzi-finance units are vulnerable to changes in interest rates—that is, to financial-market developments—as well as to product and factor market events: increases in interest rates will raise cash-flow commitments without increasing prospective receipts. Furthermore, as they must continuously refinance their positions, they are vulnerable to financial-market disruptions. The greater the weight of speculative and Ponzi finance, the smaller the overall margins of safety in the economy and the greater the fragility of the financial structure.

The Thrust toward Speculative and Hence Ponzi Finance

Experience indicates that our economy oscillates between robust and fragile financial structures, and financial crises require the prior existence of a fragile financial structure. We need to explain how fragility emerges and how robust situations are reconstituted.

In a system dominated by hedge finance, the pattern of interest rates (short-term rates being significantly lower than long-term rates) are such that profits can be made by intruding speculative arrangements. The intrusion of speculative relations into a system of mainly hedge financing of positions increases the demand for assets and therefore raises asset values—that is, it leads to capital gains. A regime in which capital gains are being earned and are expected is a favorable environment for engaging in speculative and Ponzi finance. Profit opportunities within a robust financial structure make the shift from robustness to fragility an endogenous phenomenon.

In the aftermath of a financial crisis, bankers and businessmen who have been burned shy away from speculative and Ponzi financing. In today's economy after a crisis, income, employment, and business profits are maintained by government deficits, so that business profits increase relative to business investment. This decreases the weight of external financing of capital-asset positions, even as refinancing operations at lower post-crisis interest rates fund short-term debts into equities and long-term debts. Simultaneously, because of the deficit, government debt is fed into the portfolios of banks and other financial units, which decreases the exposure of the banking and financial systems to default. The economy emerges from a recession that follows a financial crisis with a more robust structure than it had when the crisis took place.[13]

In our economy an overwhelming proportion of the capital assets are owned by corporations. The equity shares, bonds, and short-term indebtedness of corporations are financial assets that households own either directly or through intermediaries. The quasi-rents earned by capital assets depend upon the performance of the economy; as a result, realized quasi-rents can make a unit's cash receipts–cash commitment relation different from what was anticipated. Actions to adjust to this difference lead to changes in portfolios and in orders for the production of investment output. Furthermore, the cash payment commitments that are acceptable change as the performance of the economy affects views as to how the economy will behave. In a world dominated by hedge finance and in which little value is placed on liquidity because it is so plentiful, the interest rate structure yields profit opportunities in financing positions in capital assets by using short-term liquid liabilities. This interest rate structure will exist if the inherited asset structure is heavily weighted by money or liquid assets or if

---

13. See Appendix A For a full discussion of these terms.

the government deficit is large enough to generate high quasi-rents relative to the current expenditures on capital assets. If investment and the government deficit generate ample profits in an economy with a robust financial structure, short-term interest rates on secure instruments will be significantly lower than the yield from owning capital. Furthermore, interest and principal payments on longer-term private debts, which are synchronized in their pay-outs with the quasi-rents that capital assets are expected to yield, will be low relative to these quasi-rents. The interest rate used in capitalizing the payment commitments of a hedge firm on its debts will be lower than the interest rate used in capitalizing the quasi-rents of a capital asset. In addition, the interest rate on short-term money-like liabilities of firms and financial institutions will be lower than on the longer-term liabilities used in hedge-financing positions in capital assets. There are profit prospects that induce units to engage in speculative finance.

With such a rate pattern, one can make on the carry by financing positions in capital assets by long- and short-term debts, and positions in long-term financial assets by short-term, presumably liquid, debts. Hence a double set of profit opportunities exists. Our financial institutions and usages are such that the financing available for investment and capital-asset holding is within significant limits determined by portfolio decisions of profit-seeking bankers. The existence of a wide spectrum of financial instruments by which bankers can raise money means that bankers are able to finance capital-asset holdings and investment whenever the structure of asset prices and interest rates makes it profitable to do so. In a world dominated by hedge finance, profit opportunities exist for both borrowing units and banks to shift to a greater use of short-term debt to finance positions in capital assets and in long-term debt.

The existence of profit opportunities does not necessarily mean that fragile financing patterns will emerge immediately. Cash payment commitments on private debt and the quasi-rents that capital assets are expected to earn are less assured than the cash flows that are embodied in money and other shortterm financial debts. The ruling borrower's and lender's risk sets limits upon the rapidity with which the opportunities for profits through liability management are exploited.[14]

---

14. *Borrower's and lender's risk* are terms coined by Michael Kalecki, *Selected Essays on the Dynamics of the Capitalist Economy* (Cambridge: Cambridge University Press, 1971), and John Maynard Keynes, *The General Theory of Employment, Interest and Money* (New York: Harcourt Brace, 1936). See also Hyman P. Minsky, *John Maynard Keynes* (New York: Columbia University Press, 1975).

Another barrier to the quick exploitation of interest rate differentials in the aftermath of a financial trauma lies in the need to develop institutions that can absorb the preferred liabilities of holders of capital assets and emit instruments that satisfy the need of wealth owners or other financial institutions for liquidity or value assuredness. Bankers—using the term generically to include various financial-market operators—are always seeking to innovate in financial usages. But orthodoxy and conservatism can form a barrier to the assimilation of innovation at any time by acting as a "governor" constraining the rate of transformation.

A third barrier to the immediate emergence of fragile financing patterns once profit opportunities from speculative and Ponzi finance exist is the need for assured refinancing by organizations engaging in speculative finance. The assured refinancing can take the form of a deep and wide market for an instrument or of lines of credit from banks or other institutions. It takes time for a usage and institution to spread throughout a market. The speed at which financial innovations such as commercial paper occur and spread is a governor that regulates the pace of movement out of hedge and into speculative finance.

Additionally, the interest rate conditions conducive to an increase in speculative financing can rule without such a movement taking place because of an unwillingness of market participants to believe optimistic forecasts of profit potentials. Keynes, in *The General Theory*, observed that the willingness of businessmen to borrow after a financial difficulty will recover before the banker's willingness to lend. This banker's reluctance slows the transition to a regime dominated by speculative and Ponzi finance.[15]

In the process of generating increased financing by instruments that embody some new practices, an endogenously determined increase in money and liquid assets occurs. Bankers respond to optimistic views about the viability of debt structures by financing positions with an increase in their own liabilities—money. Instruments such as commercial paper enable the volume of near money to grow faster than the quantity of money.

---

15. Just as Joan Robinson wrote of an inflation barrier, so we might think of a financial orthodoxy barrier. A period of success of the economy, during which losses on financial instruments are clearly due to special circumstances, will lead to a lowering of the financial innovations barrier, whereas a period of bankruptcies and lender of last resort has the potential for raising the financial innovation barrier.

Endogenous increases in money and liquid assets raise the price of capital assets relative to money and current output prices. This increases the difference between capital-asset and investment-good prices. In a robust financial structure, the supply of short-term financing responds to demand, so that invesment will rise, increasing the yield of the existing stock of capital assets. Thus, not only does the price of a capital asset for a given set of quasi-rents increase, but on the average the quasi-rents increase as well. This means that the internal financing through retained earnings is greater than anticipated, and the push toward a greater use of short-term debt in liability structures is frustrated. The rise in profits and in internal funds available for the financing of investment is another reason why it takes time for a robust financial structure to be transformed into a fragile structure. This is especially true as the rising profits that are the mirror image of an investment boom increase the apparent debt-carrying capacity of profit-earning firms. Once a shift toward increased external and speculative financing develops, market reactions validate the decision to engage in such financing.

Acceptable financing techniques are not technologically constrained; they depend upon the subjective preferences and views of bankers and businessmen about prospects. With the financial structure that ruled in the 1950s, it was correct for businessmen and bankers to increase short-term indebtedness. However, success breeds a disregard of the possibility of failure; the absence of serious financial difficulties over a substantial period leads to the development of a euphoric economy in which increasing short-term financing of long positions becomes a normal way of life.[16]

As a previous financial crisis recedes in time, it is quite natural for central bankers, government officials, bankers, businessmen, and even economists to believe that a new era has arrived. Cassandra-like warnings that nothing basic has changed, that there is a financial breaking point that will lead to a deep depression, are naturally ignored in these circumstances. Since the doubters do not have fashionable printouts to prove the validity of their views, it is quite proper for established authority to ignore arguments drawn from unconventional theory, history, and institutional analysis. Nevertheless, in a world of uncertainty, given capital assets with a

---

16. See Hyman P. Minsky, "Financial Instability Revisited: The Economics of Disaster," reprinted as chapter 6 in *Can "IT" Happen Again? Essays on Instability & Finance,* op. cit.; Charles P. Kindleberger, *Manias, Crashes and Panics* (New York: Basic Books, 1978).

long gestation period, private ownership, and the sophisticated financial practices of Wall Street, the successful functioning of an economy within an initially robust financial structure will lead to a structure that becomes more fragile as time elapses. Endogenous forces make a situation dominated by hedge finance unstable, and endogenous disequilibrating forces will become greater as the weight of speculative and Ponzi finance increases.

THE FINANCING OF INVESTMENT

Investment is a process in time, and investment typically involves a large number of firms that produce inputs into the finished capital assets. Investment thus involves a complex of payments, which need to be financed. These payments need to be made even though investment projects yield no revenue to the final holder until they go on-stream. The value of the investment project depends upon the prices put on the resulting capital assets, which in turn depend upon the expected quasi-rents and how positions in newly produced capital assets can be financed. Investment in our economy is a money-now-in-exchange-for-money-later transaction. In this sense it is like a bond or the purchase of an annuity. However, the money-later from an investment depends upon the fortunes of often a quite specific endeavor—the particular profits are contingent upon performance.

Investment is a peculiar activity in that labor, steel, and so forth are bought at current market prices and put together into something—a capital asset that has value only as it generates quasi-rents. Both investing, which has a gestation period, and owning capital assets, which yields income over a span of time, are economic activities inescapably linked to time.

The price of capital assets, which depends upon the quasi-rents that are expected, enters into the determination of the demand price (and pace) of investment. The gestation period of and the production capacity for investment set limits on how high the price of capital assets can go relative to the price of output, for ultimately capital assets can be made available at the supply price of investment. An increase in liquidity-yielding assets or the impact of experience upon preferences that lowers the subjective value of liquidity will raise the price of capital assets, but not necessarily to the full extent that would occur if investment could not take place. It is investment that makes the prices of produced capital assets behave differently from land prices as envisaged by classical economists.

Whenever the price of a capital asset exceeds the cost of investment, an implicit capital gain is realized at the moment an investment project is fully assimilated to the stock of capital assets. Such capital gains serve as a lure that induces investment activity.

The instability of a financial regime heavily weighted by speculative and Ponzi finance is due to the impact of changing interest rates that develop as an investment boom matures. As financial and product markets react to profit opportunities in an investment boom, the demand for financing increases interest rates. As a result, the margin between the present value of assets and the price of investment output decreases. If carried far enough a present value reversal occurs: that is, the value of capital assets falls below the supply price of investment. Rising interest rates diminish or eliminate the margins of safety that make the financing of investment possible. This tends to force units to decrease investment or sell out positions. Whenever the need to try to make position by selling out positions becomes prevalent, the price level of capital assets and financial instruments break, so that the prices of capital assets fall relative to the production costs of investment. Such a sharp decline in asset prices is what occurs in stock market crashes. Downside instability of asset prices can lead to a spiral of declining investment, declining profits, and declining asset prices.[17]

Historically, an extremely robust financial system, dominated by hedge finance and with a surfeit of liquid assets in portfolios, is created in the aftermath of either a wave or a traumatic debt deflation and deep depression. Experience since the mid-1960s shows that massive government deficits and Federal Reserve lender-of-last-resort intervention increase the robustness of the financial system. That is, in the modern economy the job that was done by deep depressions can be accomplished without the economy going through the trauma of debt deflation and deep depression. However, the government deficit and lender-of-last-resort interventions that abort the consequences of fragile financial structures lead in time to inflation. Inflation enables firms, households, and financial institutions to fulfill commitments denominated in dollars that they could not fulfill at stable prices.

Investment, its financing, and its validation (first by take-out financing and then by earned quasi-rents) are keys to the performance of our economy.[18] Investment affects the financial structure of the economy in two ways; projects need to be financed and investment activity generates

---

17. The Hunt-Bache silver affair in the spring of 1980 is a classic example of the instability of speculative finance. See Stephen Fay, *Beyond Greed* (New York: Penguin, 1983).

18. See Appendix A for a treatment of investment and finance.

corporate profits—the quasi-rents upon which the viability of private financial commitments depend. An investment project is equivalent, in terms of cash-flow commitments, to the acceptance by a number of organizations of debts that are due at more or less precisely known dates: the amount due will vary as material, labor, and financing costs change. The funds to pay these debts can come from inside—as allocations of the gross profits after taxes—or outside—as exchange for liabilities such as newly issued equities and debts to individuals, banks, or other financial institutions. Debts to suppliers—the organizations that produce the components of investment outputs—also enter the picture.

The payments to suppliers—who finance the increase in their accounts receivable by some combination of internal funds and debts—and to labor are made before the investment good is able to yield useful output, in many cases years before. As a result, investment leads to an initial increase in the demand for consumer goods without any offsetting increase in the ability to supply: this leads to higher profit margins.

An increase in investment leads to a rise in short-term payment commitments. The impact of investment, beyond that which can be financed by gross profits after taxes and dividends, upon financial markets is equivalent to outstanding debt that has to be refinanced. The overall financial impact of investment in excess of internal funds is equivalent to an increase in the weight of speculative and Ponzi finance in liability structures. As the relative extent of speculative and Ponzi finance determines the fragility and hence susceptibility to financial instability, a rise in the ratio of investment to corporate internal funds increases the fragility of financial structure. The excess of investment over corporate internal funds leads to an increase in indebtedness. However, if some of the investment is financed by internal funds, the balance sheets will show that net worth is increasing.

Ongoing investment projects lead to a very inelastic demand for funds with respect to interest rates. This is so because a partially completed investment has no value as determined by future profits unless the project is completed and goes on stream. The various steps of the project must be paid for and financed on schedule. Delays are expensive because the liabilities used to finance investment are accruing interest. With compounding, changes in interest rates affect the costs of projects with significant gestation periods by more than the simple change indicates. Thus interest rate changes have a greater impact upon investment in projects with a significant time to completion and a long expected useful life than upon short-term investments. The sunk costs increase as interest is imputed. The income stream that the project is expected to yield as it is used in production has to be large enough for its capitalized value to exceed the cost of the completed project, including such interest payments.

Interest rates thus enter in both the cost of the project and the value of the capital asset. The present value of expected quasi-rents determines the maximum price the completed project could bring if it were sold; it also is the base for any mortgage. For a project to be financially feasible the present value of the quasi-rents must exceed the cost of the project.

Consequently, once an investment project is under way the cost of the project and the present value of the future quasi-rents (and hence its financial feasibility) are affected by changes in interest rates. The total costs and the present value of a project are calculated at some current and expected interest rates to determine whether the project should be undertaken. Once begun, if interest rates fall, the cost of the completed project is lower and the present value of the project is greater than the initial computations indicate, and if rates rise, the reverse is true.

If an investment is being internally financed by an ongoing corporation, the out-of-pocket costs do not rise as interest rates increase. In this case the present value may not be recomputed as market interest rates change. As a result, a continuing firm with positive profits is not forced to recognize that a project has become a bad deal. However, if the funds for a project are raised in financial markets and the repayment of the short-term financing used for construction depends upon take-out financing, increases in interest rates while projects are in process can transform an initially viable project into one that must be aborted.

Two margins of safety for a firm that finances investment externally are the liquid assets held in portfolios and the excess of the present value of the expected quasi-rents from the project over the full costs of its completion. The prospective capital gain is what makes it possible for the investing unit to raise funds for the project. The size and the assuredness of the margins of safety determine the risk class of borrowers. The explicit or implicit rating of a firm and the bank loan officers' classification of a credit in terms of its premium over prime and collateral requirements depend upon perceived need for margins of safety. For an investment project, a rise in interest rates decreases the capital gain that can be realized upon completion. This is a systemic factor that diminishes the creditworthiness of firms with ongoing investment projects; this may further increase financing costs and lower even further the present value of the implicit capital gain upon completion. Financial-market reactions to a decrease in margins of safety further decrease the margins of safety. A rise in interest rates and the constraints imposed upon borrowing following a revaluation of risks are like a self-fulfilling prophecy in that they induce changes that further increase financing costs.

During an investment boom material and labor costs also rise. Furthermore, shortages—or bottlenecks—develop, delaying the completion of projects. The obvious effect of a rise in material and labor costs is that the costs of a completed project rise; the more subtle effect is that the expected capital gain upon completion decreases. The margins of safety, which help determine a project's risk class and financing conditions, are diminished and may even disappear.

As interest rates, costs of inputs, and delays increase the costs of the investment, the ratio of available internal funds to the cost of the project will decrease, even if the flow of internal funds remains constant. However, an investment project that has internal funds available must be a project begun by a going concern, which has debts that are independent of the investment project. If these debts are short-term or are based on a floating interest rate, their carrying costs will increase as market interest rates rise. Thus, the amount of debt-financing of an ongoing project increases, and the ratio of the total that can be financed by internal funds decreases as interest rates rise during a maturing expansion.

When this occurs, firms will use their "cash kickers," that is, funds kept for emergency purposes, to meet increased costs. Such stripping of liquidity from units is a crucial way in which a rise in cash payment commitments (due to rising financing costs of ongoing investment projects) leads to an increase in the fragility of the financial and economic system.

To sum up, a marked increase in the fragility of an economy occurs as an externally financed investment boom takes place. The financing relations assure that an investment boom will lead to an environment with increased speculative financing of positions, which in turn will lead to conditions conducive to a crisis. That is, a financial structure in which a debt deflation can occur and events that trigger the start of a debt deflation are normal results of the financing relations that lead into and take place during an investment boom.

FINANCIAL MARKETS AND FINANCING REGIMES

When investment projects with significant gestation periods are undertaken, financial officers and bankers alike need believe that the required funds will be forthcoming from internal and external sources. For speculative financing of positions and deficit financing of investment to be chosen, businessmen and bankers must assume that financial markets will be functioning so that debts can be issued or assets can be sold at terms which do not make the cost of investment greater than the value of the resulting capital asset.

Since financial innovation is a striking attribute of a capitalist economy, a significant part of the financial evolution of an economy centers on the development of instruments and markets that enable higher levels of activity to be financed. These markets create instruments that seem to assure both those who use and those who supply short-term financing that money will be available when needed as long as they hold appropriate assets or have good enough profit prospects. The effectiveness of this assurance depends upon financial markets functioning normally; financial innovation results in there being both asset holders and potential borrowers who depend upon the continued normal functioning of some new financial market or institution.

Standard economic theory assumes that the demand for money is related to the level of income because it bridges the intervals between income receipts and purchases. In the conventional view, money is valuable because it obviates the need for a double coincidence of wants for transactions to take place. We live in a world, however, in which capital assets exist, can be traded, and are financed by some combination of debt and equity instruments. Since there is an extensive network of payment commitments resulting from the direct and indirect financing of positions in assets and investment, there is a demand for money to make payments on financial contracts. Because the cash flows that capital assets yield are uncertain, that is, depend upon developments in the economy and in markets, money and easily negotiable financial instruments are desired to provide a margin of safety to assure the fulfillment of contracts. The margins of safety carried in the form of liquid assets, so that commitments can be fulfilled even though surprises occur, need not be in either currency or in demand deposits: they can be in instruments exchangeable for currency or demand deposits on short notice or as needed.

Because speculative financing leads to a need for precautionary balances, there is a demand for instruments that can be readily negotiated. A profit opportunity in financing exists whenever liquidity is plentiful even as capital assets yield high returns. Any set of financial instruments or market organizations that can finance positions in capital assets and can offer a good measure of the protection offered by money holdings can borrow low and lend high: that is, can make on the carry. As capitalism abhors unexploited profit opportunities, market instruments and usages develop to exploit interest rate gaps.

Thus, a hierarchy of liquid assets comes into being; for example, a dealer may borrow from a finance company to hold its inventory of automobiles, the finance company may use commercial paper to borrow from an insurance company, which has outstanding commitments on take out mortgages, and so forth. As a result, an elaborate network of financial commitments exists whose viability depends upon the ability of units to borrow at rates that are consistent with the underlying profitability of capital assets.

The financing relations can be characterized as juggling acts in which normal functioning depends upon the belief—and the reinforcement of belief by performance—that refinancing of short-term debts will be available. Once an investment boom starts, the volume of funds demanded increases as projects move toward completion. If at some stage the elasticity of supply of funds decreases because the growth in the volume of financing available from commercial banks slows, then a sharp increase in interest rates will occur.

Since the financial institutions that generate liquid assets often engage in speculative finance, a rise in the interest rates they pay will cause a decrease in their net worth as asset values fall and profit on the carry decreases or disappears. The pressures on speculative finance in the face of rising interest rates are often acutely felt by financial intermediaries, and a deterioration in their ability to make position will adversely affect the balance sheets of their liability holders. A potential for contagion exists, which was most acutely realized in the wave of bank failures in the 1929–33 collapse. Intervention by central banks, including deposit insurance organizations, serves to abort such contagious developments.

CONCLUSIONS

Our economy is unstable because of capitalist finance. If a particular mix of hedge and speculative financing of positions and of internal and external financing of investment rules for a while, then there are, internal to the economy, incentives to change the mix. Any transitory tranquility is transformed into an expansion in which the speculative financing of positions and the external financing of investment increase. An investment boom that strips units of liquidity and increases the debt-equity ratios for financial institutions follows. Margins of safety are eroded even as success leads to a belief that the prior—and even the present—margins are too large.

A break in the boom occurs whenever short- and long-term interest rates rise enough so that attenuations and reversals in present-value relations take place. Often this occurs after the increase in demand financed by speculative finance has raised interest rates, wages of labor, and prices of material so that profit margins and thus the ability to validate the past are eroded.

Whether the break in the boom leads to a financial crisis, debt deflation, and deep depression or to a nontraumatic recession depends upon the overall liquidity of the economy, the relative size of the government sector, and the extent of lender-of-last-resort action by the Federal Reserve. Thus, the outcome of a contraction is determined by structural characteristics and by policy.

But the tendencies toward speculative finance and toward debt financing of investment are themselves the result of institutional structures and policy expectations. It is possible that with other institutional organizations and policy systems the susceptibility of our economy to financial crises can be lower than at present.

The evidence indicates that since the mid-1960s a progression in the seriousness of financial crises has taken place. Policy, if it is to be effective, must reflect an understanding of why this trend exists.

PART 4

INSTITUTIONAL
DYNAMICS

BANKING IN
A CAPITALIST
ECONOMY

Business cycles are "natural" in an investing capitalist economy, but to understand why this is so it is necessary to deal with the financing of investment and positions in capital assets explicitly. Financing other than through retained earnings involves contracts denominated in money and banks are organizations that arrange for and engage in the financing of business. Banking therefore takes in more than the organizations that are chartered as banks. The line between commercial banks, whose liabilities include checking deposits, other depository thrift institutions, miscellaneous managers of money (like insurance companies, pension funds, and various investment trusts), and investment bankers is more reflective of the legal environment and institutional history than of the economic function of these financial institutions.

The clear distinction between commercial banks and investment banks that ruled in the United States over the post–World War II era was a creature of the reforms that followed the Great Depression. This distinction is currently breaking down, and it never really existed in other capitalist economies such as Germany's. Furthermore, as the financing of activity and asset holdings as well as the management of money have become more sophisticated in response to the turbulent era since the 1960s, the line between commercial banking, other depository institutions, and money managers of various kinds has become blurred.

We can envisage an evolution of banking in which the multiple product characteristics of banking in the asset, liability, and fee-for-services dimensions are fully realized. Individual banks will be located in a spectrum that stretches from universal banks to highly specialized, almost one-dimensional organizations. (A Citicorp will coexist with a Lazard Freres.)

However, as banking is presently organized, there is one set of banks—the commercial banks—that remain of special importance because of their aggregate size and because their liabilities constitute a large part of the money supply. In a capitalist economy money is tied up with the process of creating and controlling capital assets. Money is not just a universal ration coupon that makes trading possible without a double coincidence of wants: it is a type of bond that arises as banks finance activity and positions in capital and financial assets. Because of the special import of the relation between banks and money in our economy, these deposit banks will be emphasized in this chapter, with side remarks on nonbank financial intermediaries and investment banking.

In 1931, as the Great Depression was working its way through the capitalist world, Keynes stated that the banking system interposes "its guarantee between its depositors who lend it money, and its borrowing customers to whom it loans money wherewith to finance the purchase of real assets.... [T]his veil of money ... is a specially marked characteristic of the modern world."[1] Money is created as bankers go about their business of arranging for the financing of trade, investment, and positions in capital assets. An increase in the quantity of money through bank lending to business transforms a desire for investment or capital assets into an effective demand; the creation of money is part of the mechanism by which a surplus is forced and allocated to the production of particular investment outputs.*

When money is created a borrower enters upon a contractual commitment to pay money to the lending bank in the future. The ability of business borrowers to satisfy these commitments ultimately rests upon the quasi-rents that capital assets earn when used in production, although the proximate source of cash may be rollover borrowing by the debtor or borrowing by a unit that buys from the debtor. Normal functioning of a capitalist economy depends upon the income-producing system generating profits that service loans and the financial system making loans that lead to investment and therefore to profits.

Banks whose liabilities are money are unlike money lenders whose financing activities are restricted to the contents of their strongbox. Banks

---

* The above is strictly true for a no-government/no-household debt-closed economy, that is, for the basic skeletal capitalist economy.

1. John Maynard Keynes, *Essays in Persuasion: Collected Writings of John Maynard Keynes*, vol. 9 (London: Macmillan, St. Martin's Press, for the Royal Economic Society, 1972), p. 151.

lend by taking on an obligation to make payments on behalf of a borrower in the future, confident that when the time comes they will obtain the asset needed to fulfill these obligations either as a result of flows in their favor by prior borrowers or by dealing (borrowing, selling) in some market. This characteristic of banking provides flexibility to the financial structure; it allows business commitments to be undertaken in the face of uncertainty with respect to cash receipts from assets or operations.

Prior to the emergence of modern industrial capitalism, bank money was mainly created in financing commerce, namely, goods in the process of production and distribution. The label *commercial banks* reflects the original dominance of this type of financing in the business of banks.[2] In such bank financing the near-term sale of goods furnished the cash needed to pay the bank debt.

In the modern economy there is a much greater need than in earlier epochs to finance durable fixed capital assets, both as they are produced and as they are used. The greater the use of capital in production, the larger the volume of money today–money later commitments per unit of output: durable capital is analogous to a bond in that past spending is transformed into future income. Investment bankers arrange the financing of investment and capital-asset ownership by underwriting and distributing new security issues and making markets, as brokers and dealers, for existing securities. The reforms of the 1930s separated investment and commercial banking for private debt so that, with few exceptions, an organization is now not

---

2. Prior to the development of the current money view of banking, a commercial-loan or real-bills theory of banking was dominant. This theory held that commercial banks should restrict their leading to instruments that represent goods in the process of production (inventories) and that if the banks did this, then the correct amount of money would be in existence. Regardless of the validity of this theory, both the commercial-loan and the money view of banking tend to ignore the role of banking in the financing of capital-asset ownership and investment output. As such, these traditional views of banking are complementary to neoclassical economic theory, which emphasizes transactions in newly produced output and virtually ignores the existence of capital assets. The commercial loan view of banking and the village market perspective on the economy are logical partners. Definitive works on these issues are contained in Jacob Viner, *Studies in the Theory of International Trade* (New York: Harper, 1937), especially chapters 3, 4, 5; and Lloyd Mints, *A History of Banking Theory in Great Britain and the United States* (Chicago: University of Chicago Press, 1945).

allowed to engage in both types of business.[3] This division between commercial and investment banking is artificial, and has been breaking down rapidly in recent years as banks finance positions in fixed capital assets, and investment bankers develop deposit-type liabilities that indirectly furnish funds to finance business.

In the neoclassical synthesis banking, especially commercial banking, is mechanical, static, and passive; it has no significant impact upon the behavior of the economy. In this theory, the effects of banking are fully captured by the money supply, changes in the money supply, and transitory movements of interest rates. This view also holds that the Federal Reserve can guide or control the money supply by controlling bank reserves and interest rates.[4]

In truth, the Federal Reserve's control over banks is imprecise.[5] Banking is a dynamic and innovative profit-making business. Bank entrepreneurs actively seek to build their fortunes by adjusting their assets and liabilities, that is, their lines of business, to take advantage of perceived profit opportunities. This banker's activism affects not just the volume and the distribution of finance but also the cyclical behavior of prices, incomes, and employment.

The narrow view that banking affects the economy only through the money supply led economists and policymakers to virtually ignore the composition of bank portfolios. Throughout the first decades after World War II, the banking authorities—the Federal Reserve, Comptroller of the Currency, and Federal Deposit Insurance Corporation—neither controlled nor had strong views about bank assets, other liabilities, and the ratio of bank assets to equity (leverage). As banking innovation accelerated in the 1960s and 1970s, it became apparent that there are a number of different types of money, and that the nature of the relevant money changes as institutions evolve. Money, banking, and finance cannot be understood unless allowance is made for financial evolution and innovation: money, in truth, is an

3. Commercial banks were allowed to continue to underwrite and distribute state and municipal securities. Perhaps the difficulties of New York City, which were so prominent in 1975, can be laid to the continued dominance of banks, and in particular the giant banks, in this business.

4. Chester Arthur Phillips, *Bank Credit* (New York: Macmillan, 1931); Karl Brunner, "A Scheme for a Supply Theory of Money," *International Economic Review* II (Jan. 1961), pp. 79–109; and Albert E. Burger, *The Money Supply Process* (Belmont, Calif.: Wadsunta Publishing Company, 1971).

5. Sherman Maisel, *Managing the Dollar* (New York: Norton, 1973).

endogenously determined variable—the supply is responsive to demand and not something mechanically controlled by the Federal Reserve.[6]

Changes in the quantity of money arise out of interactions among economic units that desire to spend in excess of their income and banks that facilitate such spending. The essential spending in excess of income (deficit financing) in a capitalist economy is done by business for investment and the acquisition of capital assets, although as is evident some households and governments deficit-finance. The viability of debts due to household deficit spending depends upon the behavior of employment and money wages. Prior to the Reagan administration, significant peacetime deficit spending by the federal government was largely a recession phenomenon reflecting the dependence of taxes and spending on the performance of an unstable economy: the Reagan tax measures of 1981 seem to have made government peacetime deficits a permanent or structural feature. It is an open question how the cash flows to validate the government's debts—which are exploding because of the structural deficits—are going to be generated; one obvious way is through income and therefore tax revenue inflation.

State and local government indebtedness has always been tied to revenue expectations. Shortfalls of revenue due to changes in global or local economic conditions have been the usual sources of debt problems for such local governments.

As has been shown, in the simple parable of an accumulating economy in which only consumption and investment goods are produced, the markup on labor costs for consumer goods is the wage bill in investment goods; thus, profits in consumer-goods production depend upon investment-goods production.[7] The markup on labor costs in investment-goods production depends upon the demand for protection by those who finance investment production and market conditions in the production of investment goods. The demand for investment depends upon the excess of the capitalized value of future expected profits over the supply price of investment output and financing conditions.

The demand price for investment goods changes as views about the future change. Nevertheless, an increase in the demand price will not result in a rise in investment unless financing is forthcoming. We have to

---

6. Basil Moore, "The Endogenous Money Stock," *Journal of Post-Keynesian Economics* II (Fall 1979), pp. 49–70.
7. See Appendices A and B of chapter 9 for the relations that give insight into how markets work in a capitalist economy.

understand how the banking and financial system works so that an increase in the demand for financing of investment leads to an increase in the supply of financing in dollar terms, and how an increase in the ability and willingness of banks to acquire assets leads to an increase in investment. Money, as bank liabilities, emerges out of the processes by which investments and positions in the stock of capital assets are financed.

Financial markets and banking affect investment because the current value of capital assets and thus the demand price for investment output are determined in financial markets, because the amount of investment that will be financed depends upon banking processes, and because the supply price of investment depends upon the costs of finance.

The peculiar circularity of a capitalist economy—that sufficient investment to assure the economy does well now will be forthcoming only as it is believed that sufficient investment to assure the economy does well will be forthcoming in the future—has a banking and financial-system corollary. Not only must the banking and financial system maintain favorable asset prices and conditions for investment financing now, but the banking and financing system also must be expected to maintain favorable asset prices and conditions for investment financing in the future. Because such normal functioning of the banking and financial system is a necessary condition for the satisfactory operation of a capitalist economy, disruption of the system will lead to malfunctioning of the economy.

Dependence upon investment for normal functioning is also dependence upon external finance. If the demand for external finance exceeds the supply at given financing terms, then financing terms, that is, what is written on the contract in which money is exchanged for promises to pay money in the future, will rise. Financing terms include provisions for collateral, maintenance of net worth, and the coverage of debt payments that must be satisfied before dividends can be paid as well as interest rates. The existence of codicils that state the other terms makes interest rates, by themselves, a misleading indicator of conditions under which investment can be financed. Analytically, these codicils are largely designed to protect financing units from the dissipation of assets by debtors. Money contracts used to finance asset holding and investment contain clauses that protect financing units against the moral hazard of borrowers conveying assets.

A rise in current financing terms means that the prices of inherited financial and capital assets fall. This lowers the demand price for investment. A delicate mechanism controls the amount of investment that takes place. A rise in the demand price for investment increases the demand for financing, and unless the supply of finance is elastic, this increases financing terms, thus lowering capital-asset prices and the demand price for investment.[8]

Since we live in a world of uncertainty and current views about the future affect capital-asset prices, the governor mechanism by way of financing terms is often dominated by positive, disequilibrating feedbacks. An increase in the demand prices for capital assets relative to the supply prices of investment output increases investment, which increases not only profits but also the ratio of profits to payment commitments on outstanding debts, the amount of financing available from banks and financial markets at any set of terms, and businessmen's willingness to invest. Because bankers live in the same expectational climate as businessmen, profit-seeking bankers will find ways of accommodating their customers; this behavior by bankers reinforces disequilibrating pressures. Symmetrically, the processes that decrease the prices of capital assets will also decrease the willingness of bankers to finance business.

The view of money, banking, and financial markets consistent with the investment-financing perspective presented here clearly differs radically from the standard view, which divorces how money affects the economy from any consideration of the specific transactions by which money is created. Both the monetarist and standard Keynesian approaches assume that money can be identified quite independently of institutional usages. But in truth, what is money is determined by the workings of the economy, and usually there is a hierarchy of monies, with special money instruments for different purposes. Money not only arises in the process of financing, but an economy has a number of different types of money: everyone can create money; the problem is to get it accepted.

The portfolio preferences of banking and financial institutions determine capitalization rates for different types of capital assets and financing terms for various types of investments. Our world is characterized by heterogeneous capital assets, techniques of production that require extensive financing, and a variety of organizational forms for business and finance. In such a world financial advantages and disadvantages can offset production advantages or disadvantages. The successful can be technologically inferior if they have a large enough offsetting financial advantage.

In order to understand our economy it is necessary to take a critical, nononsense look at banking. It is a disruptive force that tends to induce and

---

8. A symmetric mechanism holds for a fall in the demand price for investment.

amplify instability even as it is an essential factor if investment and economic growth are to be financed.

THE BUSINESS OF BANKING

Banking is not money lending; to lend, a money lender must have money. The fundamental banking activity is accepting, that is, guaranteeing that some party is creditworthy. A bank, by accepting a debt instrument, agrees to make specified payments if the debtor will not or cannot. Such an accepted or endorsed note can then be sold in the open market. A bank loan is equivalent to a bank's buying a note that it has accepted.

The commercial-paper market illustrates how bank promises to lend affects credit and economic activity. It is standard practice for a unit that issues commercial paper (a corporation's unsecured promise to pay) to have unused bank lines of credit that equal or exceed its outstanding commercial paper. The buyer and seller of commercial paper both know that, if necessary, the funds are available from a bank to cover maturing paper. The guarantee of bank refinancing makes the commercial-paper market viable, for it makes commercial paper as good as a dated bank deposit to the lender.[9]

When a banker vouches for creditworthiness or authorizes the drawing of checks, he need not have uncommitted funds on hand. He would be a poor banker if he had idle funds on hand for any substantial time. In lieu of holding non-income-earning funds, a banker has access to funds. Banks make financing commitments because they can operate in financial markets to acquire funds as needed; to so operate they hold assets that are negotiable in markets and have credit lines at other banks. The normal functioning of our enterprise system depends upon a large array of commitments to finance, which do not show up as actual funds lent or borrowed, and money markets that provide connections among financial institutions that allow these commitments to be undertaken in good faith and to be honored whenever the need arises.

Banks and bankers are not passive managers of money to lend or to invest; they are in business to maximize profits. They actively solicit borrowing customers, undertake financing commitments, build connections

---

9. By late 1977 the growth of the commercial paper market was so great that the giant banks—which are the primary suppliers of the guaranteed refinancing— were complaining of the growth of their unused lines of credit.

with business and other bankers, and seek out funds. Their profits result from charging for funds they make available, even as they pay for funds. Banks, in effect, lever their equity base with other people's money, and profits are derived from fees for accepting debts, committing funds, and miscellaneous services—as well as the spread between the interest rates they charge and they pay.

Banks have three basic types of overt liabilities—demand deposits (checking deposits), dated debts, and owners' equity—along with contingent or covert liabilities such as acceptances, letters of credit, open lines of credit, and responsibilities due to customer connections. A bank's overt assets are various forms of money, loans, and securities; covert assets are the liabilities of those who have lines of credit or whose debts have been endorsed as well as the bank's own lines of credit—including its connections with the central bank.

Loans represent payments the bank made for businesses, households, and governments in exchange for their promises to make payments to the bank at some future date. Securities, or investments, reflect purchases from financial markets using funds on hand or acquired through markets; these securities are also promises to make payments at various future dates.

Loans, unlike securities, involve a customer relation, in which banks use private knowledge willingly given by the borrowing units. An implicit commitment for continuing relations may exist for a loan customer, whereas no such continuing commitment exists for securities. Because of the private knowledge involved in bank lending, loans are presumably not transferable without the bank accepting a contingent liability. An initial purpose of the discount windows at Federal Reserve banks was to improve the negotiability of loans.

Since a loan contract commits borrowers to making payments to banks, banking gives rise to two flows; an initial flow from the bank (a loan) sets up later flows to the bank (the repayment). What exactly flows to and from the bank, and to whom and from whom are these flows?

The payments banks make are to other banks, although they simultaneously charge the account of a customer. In the receiving bank, the payments are credited to a depositor's account. These payments are from the account or line of credit of some customer at the paying bank and are credited to a particular account at the receiving bank. As individuals, corporations, and government units make payments one to the other, they set in motion transfers among banks.

For member banks of the Federal Reserve System, the interbank payments lead to deposits shifting from the account of one bank to the account of another at Federal Reserve banks. For nonmember banks, another bank—called a correspondent—intervenes, so that the transfer at the Federal Reserve banks are for the accounts of correspondents. Whereas business, households, and state and local governments transfer deposits on the books of commercial banks, payments among member and nonmember banks transfer credits on the books of Federal Reserve banks. Whereas the public uses bank deposits as money, banks use Federal Reserve deposits as money. This is the fundamental hierarchical property of our money and banking system.

In our system payments banks make for customers become deposits, usually at some other bank. If the payments for a customer were made because of a loan agreement, the customer now owes the bank money; he now has to operate in the economy or in financial markets so that he is able to fulfill his obligations to the bank at the due dates. Demand deposits have exchange value because a multitude of debtors to banks have outstanding debts that call for the payment of demand deposits to banks. These debtors will work and sell goods or financial instruments to get demand deposits. The exchange value of deposits is determined by the demands of debtors for deposits needed to fulfill their commitments.

Bank loans, while ostensibly money-today for money-later contracts, are really an exchange of debits from a bank's books today for credits to a bank's books later.[10]

Let us assume a 100 percent loan/demand deposit ratio, a month with twenty business days, and all loans made for one month. On the average, 5 percent of the outstanding loans become due each business day and are repaid by canceling demand deposits on the books of banks. For these demand deposits to be there the borrowing customer need have operated in the economy after his loan was entered upon the books so as to build up his deposit to the required amount. In effect, the borrower's sales and revenues build up a deposit sufficient to repay the loan; the borrower's operations during the month lead to a net gain of Federal Reserve deposits by the lending bank.

---

10. In an economy where government debt is a major asset on the books of the deposit-issuing banks, the fact that taxes need to be paid gives value to the money of the economy. The virtue of a balanced budget and a surplus insofar as the commodity value (purchasing power) of money is concerned is that the need to pay taxes means that people work and produce in order to get that in which taxes can be paid.

In our example, the borrowers will operate in the economy over a month in such a way that the bank receives Federal Reserve deposits equal to the value of outstanding loans plus interest due. If the bank is to remain fully loaned up, it will make loans or investments equal to the amount repaid even as the interest received is mainly used to pay the bank's costs of money, labor, etc.

In the United States member banks of the Federal Reserve System are required to keep some specified fraction of deposit liabilities that are on their books on deposit at a Federal Reserve Bank or in currency. Bankers pay bankers by means of these deposits—they are money to bankers—whereas other units pay by means of checks drawn on banks or by currency (which flows into and out of banks).

As checks flow into and are presented for payment to a bank, they are credited or debited to the account of the bank at the Federal Reserve. (For nonmember banks the crediting and debiting take place on the books of a correspondent bank.) The net difference between the amount added to and subtracted from the account is a change in the bank's reserve position. Position making is the bank activity that either brings the bank's reserve account up to the amount required as reserves by selling assets or borrowing or uses any excess to repay debts or to acquire assets.

Demand and time deposits are funds that the bank owes to others. The difference between total assets and borrowed funds is the book value of the bank's equity, a measure of the investment of the owners in the bank. In the United States in 1983, the ratio of book value to assets was about 3 percent for some of the very largest banks, about 8 percent for many of the large banks, and up to 12 percent for smaller banks. That is, for every dollar of assets owned by a bank some eighty-eight to ninety-seven cents was financed by borrowed money. The ratio at the end of 1983 ran from 2.8 percent for the most highly levered of the giant banks (Bank America and Banker's Trust) to only 5.9 percent for a more modestly levered giant bank (Mellon Bank).

Bankers make money by earning more on assets than they pay for funds, and assets that yield income to banks are loans and investments. The line of commerce in which banks have the greatest comparative advantage is in lending, especially to business. Under one label or another banks have "business development" departments whose main purpose is to find and solicit business borrowers.

A bank's lending function has three facets: soliciting borrowers, structuring loans, and supervising borrowers. Bankers, in seeking profits, need to structure the loans they make so that the borrowers are almost always going to fulfill their contractual obligations. Before a banker lends, he needs to have a clear vision of how the borrower will operate in the economy to get the money to repay the loan.

Debtors have three sources of the money they need to fulfill their payment commitments: cash flows from operations, refinancing or rolling over debts, and selling assets or net borrowing. A well-structured bank loan should be good both for the borrower and for the banker; this means that the proceeds of a loan will be used to yield the borrower an expected income (cash) that is more than sufficient to fulfill the commitments on the contract.

The bank officers who structure and supervise loans are loan officers. Loan officers are the key to successful banking. A professional loan officer knows that he is a partner of the borrower: a loan officer is a success if his borrowing customers are successful. Furthermore, a borrower who makes money using bank loans will prosper and return for future loans: continuing relations are profitable for banks. Thus, loans that finance activities that yield more than sufficient cash to meet contractual commitments are best from both the banker's and the customer's viewpoints. If loans are structured so that anticipated cash flows fulfill the contractual commitment, then the borrowers and the lenders are engaged in hedge finance. The traditional commercial loan, in which the sale of or stock of goods yielded cash to repay debt, was an example of hedge financing.

The issuance of new debt is another source of cash to meet commitments. In a continuing operation, such as manufacturing, batches of purchased materials proceed through various tranformations to become output. In such a process, the debts associated with the first batches may be paid off even as new batches are financed by debt. This sequential arrangement can be replaced by a variable total debt, in which maturing debts are paid off even as new debts are issued.

Debts that are not tied to a particular input in the production process but that are tied to the general profitability of a business organization open the way for speculative financial relations. The financing of positions that include assets that yield returns over an extended period of time by short-term debts will build the need to refinance into business liability structures—a characteristic of speculative finance. The viability of speculative financial structures depends both upon profit flows sufficient to pay interest on debts and the normal functioning of financial markets in which such debts can be negotiated. Loan officers will go along with such floating debt-financing relations in the expectation that refinancing will be available as long as the underlying profits are adequate.

The sale or pledging of assets is a third source of the cash needed for the fulfillment of contractual obligations. Loans based on the value of pledged collateral are different in kind from loans based on the value of the cash flows that are expected from income-earning operations. True, in structuring a loan that is mainly based on prospective cash flows the loan officers may insist on a margin of safety in the form of pledged collateral. But this would not be the primary consideration: cash-flow-oriented loans are made on the basis of the prospective value added of some business endeavors. The viability of loans mainly made because of collateral, however, depends upon the expected market value of the assets that are pledged.

In cases such as a collateralized security or land loans, the income the pledged asset earns, while it is held, is not enough for the interest on the loan. Construction projects do not earn any income until the asset is completed. Loan officers will enter upon such arrangements because they expect that the underlying asset can be sold at a price that covers the amount lent and the accrued interest. (For a construction project the take-out financing will cover the cost plus the capitalized interest.) Such loans impart a Ponzi flavor to the financial structure. Furthermore, Ponzi-type loans may be imposed upon a bank because income earned falls below expectations or interest rates rise on speculative rollover financing beyond levels anticipated by the borrower and lender alike. Thus, whereas capitalization of interest financing (borrowing to pay interest) is part of the normal financial structure, bankers and businessmen can be forced into such financing by adverse developments. When this happens the weight of Ponzi finance in the structure increases.

Thus, the overall fragility-robustness of the financial structure, upon which the cyclical stability of the economy depends, emerges out of loans made by bankers. A cash-flow orientation by bankers is conducive to sustaining a robust financial structure. An emphasis by bankers on the collateral value and the expected values of assets is conducive to the emergence of a fragile financial structure.

THE PROFIT EQUATION OF BANKS: LEVERAGE, THE EARNINGS ON ASSETS, THE COST OF LIABILITIES

Leverage

Net profits are the income that accrues to the owners of an organization; the net profit rate or profitability is net profit as a ratio to owner's investment. Profitability can be treated as the product of two components: the net profits per dollar of assets and the ratio of assets to the owner's investment.

Owner's investment is defined as the difference between the value of assets and debts. The assets of a bank—and other financial institutions—consist almost entirely of financial instruments, which have both a face and a market value. In a regime of stable financial conditions, during which interest rates and other financing terms do not change much and financial instruments can readily be negotiated, the market value of securities will approximately equal their face value, and loans will yield their face value when they mature. Under these conditions, the market and book value of bank assets and therefore of owner's equity are approximately equal.

By the conventions of bank accounting, loan loss reserves are off the books; they are subtracted from loans outstanding rather than added to the equity account. Banks tend to value real estate conservatively. As a result, during periods of economic tranquility the market value of a bank as measured by the value of its shares might well be more than its book value. Nevertheless, the book value of a bank during a period of financial tranquility is more likely to reflect what its assets are worth in the market than does the book value of an ordinary business, for depreciation charges can have little or no relation to the economic value of the asset. However, when interest rates increase and loan losses, renegotiations, and restructuring are common (as in 1975 and 1982–83), the book value of a bank becomes as much a matter of convention and creative accounting as the book value of an ordinary business, for individual assets are *not* revalued when interest rates change.

The market value of a bank as of all other profit-oriented entities is the capitalized value of future earnings, and the capitalization rate reflects the market interest rate and the presumed assuredness and expected growth of earnings. The difference between the market and the book value of shares is an indicator of whether investment in an organization is worthwhile. The excess of market over book valuation indicates that a capital gain—above and beyond the value of retained earnings—is available if security markets capitalize retained earnings at the same rate as existing equity.

Bank leverage, the ratio of assets to equity, can be taken to indicate how much of other units' debts a bank can make generally acceptable by pledging its "good name." Alternatively, leverage can be interpreted as the use of other people's money to acquire assets. For nonbank financial institutions—life insurance companies, REITs, mutual funds—leverage clearly reflects the ratio of borrowing to owner's investment. For banks, which pledge their credit in a variety of covert ways, however, the leverage ratio, as shown by liabilities on their books, underestimates the extent to which the equity or owner's investment provides guarantees to other units.

If a bank shows $25 billion in assets and $1.25 billion of capital, surplus, and undivided profits, the assets/owner's investment ratio is 20. Further, if the bank makes $187.5 million in profits after taxes and allowance for loan losses, the ratio of profits to assets will be 0.75 percent and the yield is 15 percent on owner's equity. Assuming this bank paid one-third of earnings in dividends, retained earnings will be 10 percent of the owner's investment, and its equity will increase at 10 percent per year.

Supposing that another bank, which is just as profitable in managing assets, has an assets to owner's investment ratio of twelve. Such a bank, with about $25 million in assets and $2.085 million in stockholders' equity, will earn $187,500 (0.75 percent) on assets or 9 percent on owner's equity. If its dividend is 5 percent, retained earnings will be 4 percent of owner's equity. Thus, the first bank, the more highly levered one, will be able to grow faster, even though both banks are equally efficient in terms of net earnings per dollar of assets managed.

The increase in book value due to retained earnings indicates that there is an internal dynamic in banking making for the growth of successful units. But aggregate retained earnings can lead bankers to aim at a rate of growth of bank assets and liabilities that may be incompatible with the potential for overall, real economic expansion. For instance, an assumption underlying many of the standard policy arguments about monetary growth is that the real growth potential of the economy is at most 4 percent per year. To many standard economists this implies that a steady 4 percent increase in the money supply will lead to noninflationary growth if velocity is constant.[11] In our example, the bank that earns 15 percent on equity will endeavor to grow at 10 percent per year, whereas the bank that earns 9 percent will endeavor to increase at 4 percent per year. If the world is populated with banks that earn 15 percent and distribute one-third of earnings as dividends, then a need for bank assets to rise at 10 percent per year to sustain the assets equity ratio and bank profitability will introduce a tension into the economy; banks will try to grow at 10 percent per year while the authorities try to constrain the growth of bank liabilities to 4 percent per year.

Bank assets do not represent a commitment of physical resources (the often pretentious palaces that banks inhabit and the collection of fancy electronic gadgets that amuse bank functionaries are ignored). The owner's investment is mingled with borrowed funds and is used to finance business,

---

11. Milton Friedman of Chicago is renowned for this family of policy proposals.

government, and household activity. To a stockholder, however, the alternative to investing in the shares of a bank is owning shares in some other business. To attract funds, private portfolio investment in bank shares must be as profitable in banking as in other business. After allowing for such differentials as risk or prestige, the profit rate on bank capital has to be as large as on other forms of capital assets. If earnings per dollar of investment in ordinary business is 15 percent, competitive market forces would expand or contract investment in banking as banks earn more or less than 15 percent on equity.

A bank that increases leverage without adversely affecting profits per dollar of assets increases its profitability. The combination of retained earnings and the profitability of increased leverage can make the supply of financing from banks grow so fast that the prices of capital assets, the prices of investment output, and, finally, the prices of consumption output all rise.[12]

Earnings of banks result from interest and discounts on loans and investments, fees charged for acceptances, loan commitments, foreign exchange fees, paper processing, and so forth, minus the cost of liabilities and the costs of labor, facilities, and management. A bank attempts to maximize revenues even as it minimizes costs. On the revenue side, new and more profitable assets and additional ways to charge fees are always sought. A banker operates to control operating costs and to acquire funds at favorable terms. On the liability side the relation between profits and the asset-equity ratio implies that new ways to borrow are always sought.

A banker is always trying to find new ways to lend, new customers, and new ways of acquiring funds, that is, to borrow; in other words, he is under pressure to innovate. The retention of earnings leads to a minimum target growth rate of profits. For a bank's profit rate to be sustained, if the profits per dollar of assets do not change, then assets and nonequity liabilities must grow at the same rate as the book value of equity.

---

12. In our perspective, the effort to have bank assets grow at 10 percent leads to an increase in the investment/consumption ratio, which implies that prices of consumption goods will rise (see chapter 7). In standard quantity theory reasoning, a rate of growth of money that is greater than output leads to a rise in prices. Our argument leads to a consideration of the financing banks do, whereas quantity theory reasoning concentrates on one or more bank liabilities.

If we assume that operating costs are under control, a bank's profit rate will increase if either net earnings per unit of assets or the ratio of assets to owner's investment increases. The first implies a search for ever larger spreads between interest rates on liabilities and assets. The spread among rates reflects relative riskiness and the time to payment, which can be reduced to a risk factor. To increase earnings on assets, a banker will be tempted to reach for yield by accepting either longer-term or higher-risk assets.[13] To decrease the rate paid on liabilities for any level of market interest rates, a banker endeavors to give ever greater promises of safety to depositors. This is done by shortening the term of liabilities and by providing special assurances. The attempt to increase the spread between asset and liability interest rates leads banks to improve the services they provide to depositors and borrowers by creating new types of paper; new financial instruments result from pressure for profits.

The impact of increased leverage on bank profits is impressive: if a bank that makes 0.75 percent on assets decreases the ratio of capital to assets to 5 percent from 6 percent, the profit rate on book value will be 15.0 percent rather than 12.5 percent. If such an increase in leverage takes place over several years, the profit rate will rise each year. With a constant dividend on book value ratio, this implies that the growth rate mandated by retained earnings will rise from 7.5 percent to 10 percent. Per-share earnings will rise, and the stock market valuation of the shares will reflect this growth of earnings.

In the aggregate between 1960 and 1974, the period over which inflation and financial instability became major concerns, the leverage ratio for banks increased about 50 percent. This rise was part of the change in the financial environment, which included an increase in the weight of speculative and Ponzi finance in the liability structure of business. The higher leverage ratio of banks was part of the process that moved the economy toward financial fragility because it facilitated an increase in short-term borrowing (and in leverage) by bank customers: the leverage ratio of banks and the import of speculative and Ponzi financing in the economy are two sides of a coin.

---

13. One measure of the riskiness of financial instruments is the expected source of the funds that are needed to fulfill financial contracts. Banks that seek increased spread will accept speculative cash flow relations and loans that are based upon the value of collateral rather than upon expected cash flows. Profit-seeking banking can induce speculative and even Ponzi financing by bank customers.

Bank Management Motivation

The rise in bank share prices that follows a growth in profitability is particularly important in a world of professionally managed institutionalized banks. The typical professional bank president is not a rich man when he starts his career. As a bank president he is a hired hand trying to achieve a personal fortune. But given the tax structure, it is difficult to accumulate a fortune by saving out of income; the most efficient route for a business executive is by way of stock options and the capital gains that accrue as the stock market price per share rises.[14] As holders of stock options, bank management is interested in the price, on the exchanges, of their bank's shares.

The price of any stock is related to the earnings per share, the capitalization rate on earnings of the bank's perceived risk class, and the expected rate of growth of such earnings.[15] If bank management can accelerate the growth rate of earnings by increasing leverage without a decrease in the perceived security and safety of the bank's earnings, then the price of shares will rise because both earnings and the capitalization rate on earnings that reflects growth expectations rise. In a capitalist society with institutionalized organizations and tax laws such as ours, fortune-seeking by the managers of institutionalized enterprises leads to an emphasis upon growth, which in turn leads to efforts to increase leverage. But increased leverage by banks and ordinary firms decreases the margins of safety and thus increases the potential for instability of the economy.

Prudence and Surveillance

Banking literature posits the concept of the *prudent banker*: a banker who accepts just the right amount of risk. To a banker risk results from the

---

14. Preferential taxation of capital gains in a world of high income taxes and institutionalized corporations is a way of enabling corporate management to become rich, not a way of rewarding thrift. Some scheme involving stock option and preferential capital gains treatment is necessary if a bureaucratic corporate capitalism is to be steered toward efficient production, product choice, and financing by the self-interest and fortune seeking of managers.

15. If a stock earns 15 percent on book value and the capitalization rate is 15 percent, then the share prices will equal book value. If the capitalization rate, however, is 10 percent, then the market value will exceed the book value; if the capitalization rate is 20 percent, then the market value will fall short of the book value. Furthermore, if the earnings per share are expected to grow, then the capitalization rate of current earnings will be the reciprocal (for a perpetuity) of the nongrowth capitalization rate minus the expected growth rate of profits.

selection of assets, liabilities, and leverage, that is, from the composition of the balance sheet. But the risks bankers carry are not objective probability phenomena; instead they are uncertainty relations that are subjectively valued. Furthermore, the acceptable risks for a unit to carry at any moment of time reflect experience and, predominantly, quite recent experience. Before the early 1960s, banks improved their profitability by changing the structure of their assets by substituting loans for government debt, whereas after the mid-1960s banks sought profits by changing the structure of their liabilities and increasing their leverage ratios. The profit drive—a fixed factor in banking—takes different forms at different times, but throughout the post–World War II era a common thread has been a trend of increasing exposure to risks associated with the cyclical performance of the economy.

Traditionally bank exposure to risk was constrained, albeit imperfectly, by customer and collegiate surveillance. In a regime in which banks can and do fail and in which bank failure imposes losses upon depositors, stock owners, and borrowing customers, sophisticated users of bank services reacted to the portfolio and leverage properties of their banks. In the era since World War II, customer surveillance has diminished in importance as deposit insurance and Federal Reserve interventions have tended to protect all nonequity liability holders rather than just small depositors. Although by law only a limited value per account—rising from an initial $5,000 to $100,000—is insured, the FDIC has financed the merger of bankrupt banks rather than closing and liquidating them. As a result, all of the nonequity liabilities of almost all failing banks have been validated. The deposit insurance for the thrift organizations has operated in a similar way.*

This technique of managing bank failures, together with the belief that the Federal Reserve will cooperate with the deposit insurance organizations to prevent a wholesale closing of banks, means that a depositor does not need to be concerned about the viability of a bank with which he deals. As a result, depositors' surveillance, which would lead to deposit losses, interest rate disadvantages, and borrowers seeking alternative sources of financing, does not currently constrain bank leverage and asset-liability structures. The presumption is that the protection from the regulatory authorities makes private surveillance unnecessary.

---

* The open-ended liabilities of the Penn Square bank, which failed in 1982, meant that the FDIC refused to validate all of its liabilities. The Continental Illinois case in 1984 was so big that the FDIC and the Federal Reserve were "forced" to announce that they would validate all deposit liabilities even as they were sticking to the legal $100,000 deposit insurance protection at some smaller banks.

Collegiate surveillance is the control that other banks and money-market institutions impose as they set terms upon the financial instruments exchanged among banks. Since reserve deficiencies and shortages are first handled by the lending or borrowing of federal funds, collegiate surveillance appears in the forms of differentials in the willingness to lend or in the terms of lending to a particular bank. When difficulties emerge for particular banks or classes of banks, rate differentials appear so that banks in doubtful positions pay premium rates on money-market borrowings.[16] A bank seen as having difficulties may be unable to sell CDs or borrow federal funds; it is forced to borrow at the Federal Reserve's discount window.

Bank Examination

With the attenuation of customer and collegiate surveillance as a result of the risk absorption by broadly defined central banking, bank examination becomes increasingly important as an instrument for constraining the exposure to risk of banks. Bank examination is largely perfunctory—the domain of accountants who look for proper procedures, documentation, and obvious fraud—rather than an inquiry into the economic viability and the exposures to risk of banking organizations. Although an examiner can understand the operations and deals of a modest $20 to $100 million bank, the existing examination procedures are not a serious substitute for customer and collegiate surveillance for giant banks with complex asset and liability structures. In the 1970s and 1980s the increase in the number and complexity of problem banks was largely a result of the increased risk exposure of banks in an increasingly cyclical environment.

The lack of power of examinations is evident from the problem that banks had with REITs in 1974–76 and their foreign loans in the early 1980s. Both sets of problems were legacies of credit practices that were put in place well before the crisis. Examiners had no power, even if they had understood the problems, to constrain the credit policies of giant banks. In our present institutional arrangements the only recourses of the examining authorities are the appointment of a conservator and the withdrawal of deposit insurance. A threat by examiners to request a conservator for the resources of,

---

16. In the New York City crisis in late 1975, New York City banks lost their preferred position in the CD market. As early as the spring of 1974 Franklin National Bank was paying premium rates to borrow.

say, the Chase Manhattan Bank because of the bank's exposure to real estate or South American credits is not credible, although examiner threats are effective for small banks.

In addition to the lack of credible power—and just as important—the bank examination procedure reflects a lack of understanding of banking. A bank is a cash-flow machine. Deposits and withdrawals are cash flows, and assets are valuable only as they set up cash flows. Assets can set up cash flows by means of the fulfillment of the contract by the debtor or by their sale or hypothecation. For the sale or pledging of an asset to be a realistic possibility, it is necessary for some financial markets to function in an appropriate way. For contractual cash flows to a bank to be realized, the debtor's cash receipts must fulfill some minimal expectations. But a business debtor's cash receipts available to fulfill payments on debts depend upon gross profits as measured in the currency of denomination of the debts, a government debtor's cash receipts depend upon tax expectations, and a household's cash receipts depend mainly upon wages and salaries.

Examiners have to be cognizant of the underlying prospective cash flows that debtors must earn if a bank's anticipated cash receipts are to be realized. Bank examination must become a conditional economic analysis of the bank's operations if it is to function as a substitute for customer and collegiate surveillance. In the absence of effective controls on bank risk exposure, bankers' efforts to achieve profit growth by increasing their leverage will lead, from time to time, to wholesale cash-flow difficulties. As a result, the deposit insurance organizations and the Federal Reserve will be forced to intervene to protect banking organizations from defaulting on their liabilities. Such bail-outs, which are necessary to prevent deep depressions, serve to validate financial practices that contributed to both the debt burdens of business, governments, and households and the exposed position of banks. As a result of the need to offset consequences of the inability of bank regulators or market organizations to prevent pre-crisis situations from developing, rates of growth of bank reserves that are not warranted by the potential growth of output are forced upon the Federal Reserve. The monetary input to inflation is in part a result of the inability of the authorities to control banking by regulatory interventions and the open market/discount rate manipulation available to the Federal Reserve system.[17]

---

17. Hyman P. Minsky, "Suggestions for Cash-Flow Oriented Bank Examination," *Proceedings of a Conference on Bank Structure and Competition*, Federal Reserve Bank of Chicago, 1975.

Overt and Covert Costs of Bank Liabilities

Demand and time deposits and funds borrowed from various markets are the nonequity overt liabilities of banks, and the costs of these liabilities—explicit interest charges, services rendered in lieu of paying explicit interest, and forgone earnings because of assets that a bank is required to keep in order to have particular types of liabilities—are a major expense of banks.

Time deposits, CDs, repurchase agreements, and federal funds carry explicit interest costs. Banks will advertise, give gifts, call on potential depositors, and use the services of money brokers to acquire such deposits. CDs, especially large-denomination negotiable CDs, are a major tool of liability-management banking, which is the aggressive pursuit and juggling of liabilities to acquire funds to finance positions.

The payment system consists mainly of checks, which are costly to process. Although computer-linked electronic devices have mechanized bank operations, signature verification requires labor. Banks either charge service fees for processing checks and deposits or they absorb these costs in lieu of paying full market interest on checking deposits. (Interest on checking deposits was forbidden by law from the Great Depression until 1982–83.) It has been estimated that processing costs run about 3.5 to 4.5 percent of the dollar volume of deposits subject to check per year. This implies that, when interest rates are substantially above 6 percent, banks will tend not to have service charges and will be willing to pay interest on deposits subject to checks and that, when interest rates are lower, service charges will be levied.

Banks are required to keep cash reserves against demand and time deposits. These cash reserves are either in the form of vault currency or deposits at the Federal Reserve banks (for member banks) or at ordinary banks (for nonmember banks). Vault cash and reserves do not earn income, which means there is a covert cost for such cash holdings in the interest income forgone. The various types of liabilities absorb reserves in different proportions: traditionally demand deposits absorb more reserves than time deposits and liabilities, like repurchase agreements, Eurodollars, and federal funds do not absorb reserves at all.

As reserves represent forgone income and as various liabilities eat up reserves in different proportions, bank management will try to substitute liabilities with low-reserve absorption for those who consume more reserves until overt costs offset the differences in covert costs in the form of required reserves. Whenever interest rates rise, the overt cost of liabilities increases and banks try to substitute low-reserve absorption liabilities for high-reserve absorption liabilities. As demand deposits traditionally were the

high-reserve absorption liability, banks attempted to substitute other liabilities for demand deposits when interest rates rose. This leads to banks invent-
ing new forms of liability and paying higher rates on existing liabilities that
economize on reserves.

Coda

In the standard view of banking, reserves determine the aggregate nonequity liabilities of the banking system, but a given volume of reserves can
sustain different amounts of liabilities depending upon the composition and
reserve absorption of liabilities. If the absorption of different liabilities
remains invariant, then as interest rates rise there will be a substitution
toward reserve-economizing liabilities: the total assets compatible with any
volume of bank reserves will rise. Conversely, as interest rates fall, the higher
reserve-absorption liabilities can be expected to increase as a proportion
of liabilties.

As a unit of reserves can carry different amounts of bank liabilities,
the financing available from banks is responsive to the demand for financing; it is not mechanically determined by Federal Reserve action. Bank
profit-maximization efforts and the changing cost of reserves as interest
rates rise and fall make the supply of bank finance responsive to the demand.
Once the behavior and motivations of bankers are taken into account,
changes in bank liabilities are not the result of the passive reaction by banks
to Federal Reserve initiatives: money, in the sense of bank liabilities subject
to check, is endogenously determined.

Monetary policy attempts to determine the rate of growth of bank
assets and liabilities by controlling the growth of bank reserves. Since the
rate of growth of bank assets desired by bank management and mandated
by retained earnings can be substantially larger than the rate of growth of
bank reserves monetary policy aims to achieve, during good times, when
banks are confronted with a large demand for accommodation by apparently creditworthy clients, the banking system is characterized by innovations that try to circumvent Federal Reserve constraint. That is, bankers
aim at having assets and nonequity liabilities grow at least as fast (if not
faster) than bank equity, whereas the Federal Reserve tries to have bank
liabilities subject to check grow at a slower rate than bank equity.

In a world without central bank protection of bank liability holders,
the tendency to increase leverage was constrained albeit imperfectly by
customer and collegiate surveillance. In a world in which central banking
and deposit insurance gives almost perfect protection to holders of bank
nonequity liabilities, surveillance by customers and colleagues atrophies.

As a result, there are no effective market barriers to bank expansion and thus to the destabilizing impact of banks upon demand. Whenever the authorities act to constrain monetary growth during a strong expansion, dangers of financial crises appear and the authorities are forced to intervene to protect the viability of the banks. This intervention leads to a rate of infusion of reserves into the banking system that exceeds the rate that is compatible with noninflationary economic expansion. In this way banking forces the hands of the monetary authorities; monetary growth that will support inflation is a result of the way the thrusts to debt deflation are aborted.

To control the disruptive influence that emanates from banking, it is necessary to set limits upon permissible leverage ratios and to constrain the growth of bank equity to a rate that is compatible with noninflationary economic growth. This principle should guide policy, but in an economy in which new financial usages and institutions appear in response to profit opportunities, it is a principle that is much easier to state than to translate into practice.

THE PROFIT EQUATION OF BANKS: RESERVES AS COSTS AND THE EVOLUTION OF FINANCIAL PRACTICES

The return on assets, the cost of liabilities, operating costs, and the leverage on stockholders' equity determine the profitability of banks, and profit-seeking bankers operate on all these factors. The leverage factor clearly affects the volume of bank financing available. Although the Federal Reserve tries to control bank credit and money by governing the reserves available to banks, the authorities historically did not control the leverage ratio. The Federal Reserve controls the availability and the efficacy of the reserves that are required for specific liabilities, but controlling the total volume of bank credit (let alone total credit) by these means is an impossible task. At best the authorities can hope to set limits to overt bank liabilities in this way: the covert liabilities, largely in the form of guarantees and commitments, escape control through reserves.

The Federal Reserve attempts to determine bank credit and deposits by varying the amount of reserve money in existence, setting the ratio of reserves to specified liabilities that a bank must hold, and fixing the interest rate at which banks can acquire reserves by borrowing (at the Federal

Reserve discount window) in order to control the economy by controlling money markets. Thus, it sets the environment within which banks seek profits. The reserve-availability constraint operated by the Federal Reserve, however, is not a precise determinant of reserves available for demand deposits. What the Federal Reserve controls is the volume of its own liabilities outstanding and the terms upon which member banks and other units, under special circumstances, can borrow at the Federal Reserve.

The amount of currency in circulation is determined by the demand for funds in this form. In spite of the existence of deposit insurance and the use of credit cards, the ratio of currency to total money supply has increased in recent years. A rise in the currency ratio lowers the amount of bank earning assets that a given amount of Federal Reserve liabilities can sustain. During periods of uncertainty and financial instability, a rise in the currency ratio reflects a heightened importance of liquidity.

Another point to consider is that nonmember banks have grown much faster than member banks during the postwar era.[18] Nonmember banks use deposits at other commercial banks as their reserve deposits. At the end of 1976 there was $618.7 billion of deposits at member banks and $257.9 billion of deposits at nonmember banks. If we assume a 10 percent reserve requirement against deposits at nonmember banks, then some $26 billion was required for reserve deposits by nonmember banks; $26 billion is only 4.2 percent of $618.7 billion. Thus, the potential bank reserves for nonmember banks was virtually infinite compared with the funds they actually used. Reserve availability therefore is not an effective constraint upon nonmember banks.

Whenever interest rates increase, the covert costs of reserve deposits at Federal Reserve banks increase. As a result, the higher the interest rate the greater the disadvantage of membership in the Federal Reserve System. The more the Federal Reserve endeavors to constrain inflation by holding down the growth of reserves, the greater the competitive advantage of nonmember banks who have a huge untapped reservoir of potential reserves. As nonmember banks can use deposits at nonmember and member banks

---

18. Noninsured nonmember banks have grown even faster than nonmember insured banks in the recent past. This increase is due largely to the opening of branches of foreign banks. Because loans negotiated in New York or Chicago can be booked in Amsterdam, Frankfurt, Tokyo, or the Bahamas, the ability to finance these nonmember/noninsured banks is much greater than their assets and equity indicates.

as reserves, the growth of large multi-million-dollar nonmember banks further increases the availability of reserve deposits.

As the absolute size of nonmember banks and the proportion of bank assets and deposits they hold grows, the banking system increasingly takes on a hierarchical cast in which member banks use Federal Reserve deposits and currency as reserves and nonmember banks use bank deposits and currency as their reserves. The thrust toward this hierarchical structure depends upon the growth of nonmember banks either through *de novo* chartering or shifts of membership. At the end of 1960 there were some 13,500 banks in the United States, of which 6,900 (51.1 percent) were nonmember banks. At the end of 1976 there were 14,671 banks, of which 8,914 (60.8 percent) were nonmember banks. As the growth in nonmember banks is pro-cylical and responsive to the demand for financing, nonmember banking is a further factor making the supply of finance responsive to demand.[19]

The ability to create substitutes for reserves and to minimize reserve absorption is an essential property of a profit-maximizing banking system. If the thrust to financial fragility is to be constrained, then constraint on bank leverage ratios and internal growth of stockholder's equity through retained earnings may be necessary. The emphasis on the control of banking by controlling the ratio of cash assets to deposit liabilities is misplaced.

THE PROFIT EQUATION EXTENDED TO NONBANK FINANCIAL INSTITUTIONS

In addition to commercial banks, financial intermediaries such as savings and loan associations, mutual savings banks, life insurance companies, sales and consumer finance companies, REITs, and money-market funds are sources of credit. Even though some may be organized as mutuals, they are highly levered profit-seeking organizations. They supply finance in response to profit opportunities.

These nonbanking financial intermediaries, together with commercial banks, assure that the supply of finance will be responsive to demand in credit markets. Specialized financial intermediaries were often closely related to particular industries: sales finance companies to automobiles,

---

19. John T. Rose, "Federal Reserve System Attrition," Ph.D. diss., Washington University, St. Louis, 1973.

savings and loan associations to single-family housing, and REITs to large-scale commercial and residential construction. Others were mainly devices for raising funds from some particular source. Pension funds, insurance companies, and money-market funds are thus tied to a particular way of raising money: pension funds and insurance companies receive funds on a predetermined schedule and have considerable flexibility in their assets; money market funds compete with depository institutions for financial resources. Unlike commercial and savings banks, however, money-market funds do not have a constituency that supplies them with assets.

As Table 10.1 shows, the ratio of financial net worth to total assets for commercial banks and major nonbank financial intermediaries fell—sharply for all except savings and loan associations—during the decade ending in 1974. Between 1974 and 1978 there was a slight increase in the financial net worth ratio of all organizations, again with the exception of the savings and loan organizations. Between 1964 and 1978 the leverage ratio (the reciprocal of the ratios given above) increased for all the listed sets of institutions.

Finance companies—both those that primarily finance the purchase of automobiles and consumer durables and those that mainly make loans to households—actively manage their liabilities. They finance their positions by issuing bonds and commercial paper and borrowing from banks. Inasmuch as sales finance operations use a point-of-sales originator of their assets, they tend to be organizations that respond to a demand for credit by acquiring funds. (They are like commercial banks in that they first make loans and then find funds.)

For finance companies, a rise in demand will initially lead to a rise in bank borrowing, followed by a rise in commercial paper. The standard

Table 10.1:   Financial Net Worth as a Percentage of Total Financial Assets

	1964	1974	1978
Commercial banks	7.27	5.82	6.14
Savings and loan associations	6.62	6.23	5.54
Mutual savings banks	9.35	7.89	8.62
Life insurance companies	7.57	4.35	5.04
Finance companies	7.64	2.60	3.15
Commercial banking	7.09	5.55	5.74

SOURCE: Flow of Funds Accounts, Board of Governors Federal Reserve System: 1964–December 1976 supplement; 1974, 1978–September 1979 supplement, Flow of Funds Accounts.

procedure in commercial-paper financing calls for open lines of credit at banks to equal or exceed outstanding commercial paper. Thus, a strong expansion of commercial paper will run up against the limits set by lines of credit. When this happens, finance companies issue bonds to free lines of credit. Accordingly, the short-term expansion of finance companies is limited by bank lines of credit, while the longer-term limit to expansion is set by the ability to sell bonds.

Finance companies are rather unconstrained financial organizations that can operate nationally and are flexible in the assets and liabilities they use. In Table 10.2 the asset and liability structures of finance companies in 1964, 1974, and 1978 are laid out. As is evident, the liability structure was shortened between 1964 and 1974: in 1964 permanent financing (equity and bonds) was 44 percent of assets; in 1974 it was but 32 percent of assets. (By 1978 longer-term financing had recovered to 35 percent.) The dependence on open-market paper financing increased from 18 percent in 1964, to 29 percent in 1974, and to 33 percent in 1978. As a result of this increased dependence on short-term money market financing, finance companies are more vulnerable to sharp increases in interest rates.

The composition of their assets also changed, particularly the proportions of consumer (household) and business loans: in 1964, of the total assets of finance companies, 57 percent were in household loans and 29 percent were business loans; in 1974 household loans represented 46 percent and business 39 percent; and in 1978 household loans were still 46 percent of assets, but business loans were 43 percent.

Table 10.2: Finance Companies, Structure of Assets and Liabilities

	1964	1974	1978
Demand deposits and currency	4.51	3.85	3.02
Home mortgages	9.87	11.03	7.41
Consumer credit	56.55	46.41	46.05
Loans to business	29.13	38.71	43.45
Financial net worth	13.96	2.60	3.16
Corporate bonds	30.38	29.14	35.21
Bank loans NIC	24.35	21.64	14.28
Open-market paper	18.43	28.51	32.53

SOURCE: Flow of Funds Accounts, Board of Governors, Federal Reserve System, 1964–December 1976; 1974, 1978–September 1979.

Although household loans were the original special business of these organizations, as acquired skills enabled them to play financial markets efficiently they were able to increase their asset-equity ratio from seven in 1964, to fourteen in 1974, and to more than thirty in 1978, even as they shifted toward business loans.

Our complex financial structure consists of a variety of institutions that lever on owners' equity and normally make on the carry, that is, borrow at a lower rate than their assets earn. In order to make on the carry, their liabilities have to be viewed as embodying more of Keynes's liquidity premium than their assets. If the likelihood of financial difficulties is excluded, such financial intermediaries raise their asset–net worth ratio without lowering the liquidity of their liabilities over periods in which their cash receipts enable them to fulfill commitments on liabilities. The increase in the dependence upon open-market paper (e.g., commercial paper) by firms and financial institutions leads to prices of capital assets and equity shares that are vulnerable to an unfavorable reevaluation of the liquidity component of such liabilities that would raise open-market interest rates and therefore reduce the ability of such institutions to make on the carry. Indeed, the depressed stock market and investment of the late 1970s and early 1980s can be viewed as a reaction to the change from a world in which financial difficulties were deemed not likely to occur to one in which they are deemed likely. This increases the value of liquidity embodied in default-free assets and lowers the liquidity return of many private debts; it also leads to a fall in the value of capital assets and equity shares.

THE RESPONSIVENESS OF THE SUPPLY OF FINANCING TO DEMAND

The standard version of banking and financial theory holds that the Federal Reserve, by controlling the reserve base, effectively controls the amount of demand deposits and bank financing. Bank and financial intermediary profit-seeking behavior, however, leads to growth rates of finance different from that desired by the Federal Reserve.

The effect of financed investment on the economy cannot be understood by narrowly focusing on the supply of the means of payment as the carrier of the impact of banking. Money is one of several instruments that imposes a financing veil between the proximate and the ultimate owner of capital assets: liabilities of other financial institutions, commercial paper, and corporate bonds and equity shares also interpose a financing veil.

Money is unique in that it is created in the act of financing by a bank and is destroyed as the commitments on debt instruments owned by banks are fulfilled. Because money is created and destroyed in the normal course of business, the amount outstanding is responsive to the demand for financing. Banks are important exactly because they do not operate under the constraint of a money lender—banks do not need to have money on hand in order to lend money. This flexibility of banks means that projects that need funds over an extended period of time can arrange for such funds to be available as needed. A line of credit and a commitment by a bank are as good as the possession of funds.

The investment process depends upon the flexibility banking gives to the financial system. But bankers and other money market operators, being profit-minded, are always seeking new ways to turn a dollar. It is necessary for the financial system to be responsive to changing business demands for financing, but if financial innovation and aggressive seeking of borrowers outpaces the demands for funds for investment financing, excess funds will be available to finance demand for existing bonds, common stock, and capital assets. This leads to a rise in the price of capital assets relative to the supply price of investment output. This, as has been explained, increases investment activity and thus profit—leading to a further rise in the price of capital assets and long-lived financial instruments. The behavior of financial markets, then, can trigger a boom from seemingly stable expansions.

Although financial innovations are common, their acceptance depends upon an attenuation, however trivial, in the subjective evaluation of the liquidity premium embodied in holding money. A period of successful functioning of the economy leads to a decrease in the value of liquidity and to an acceptance of more aggressive financing practices. Banks, nonbank financial institutions, and money-market organizations can experiment with new liabilities and increase their asset-equity ratio without their liabilities losing any significant credence. In these circumstances the readily available supply of finance from aggressive financial institutions raises capital-asset prices and induces short-term (i.e., speculative) financing of capital-asset positions and investment.[20]

Banking and finance can be highly disruptive forces in our economy, but the flexibility of finance and its responsiveness to business, which are needed for a dynamic capitalism, cannot exist without the banking process.

---

20. In 1974–75 the selling of financing to developers by REITs and of credit to
     REITs by banks was one element making for the financial fragility that emerged.

The destabilizing aspect of banking should not be surprising—after all, bankers are specialists in providing short-term financing to business, government, and households, and the banker sells his services by teaching customers how to use bank facilities. Bankers cannot make a living unless business, government, and households borrow; they are merchants of debt.

BANKING AS AN ENDOGENOUS DESTABILIZER: THE CENTRAL BANK AS THE LENDER OF LAST RESORT

The standard analysis of banking has led to a game that is played by central banks, henceforth to be called the authorities, and profit-seeking banks. In this game, the authorities impose interest rates and reserve regulations and operate in money markets to get what they consider to be the right amount of money, and the banks invent and innovate in order to circumvent the authorities. The authorities may constrain the rate of growth of the reserve base, but the banking and financial structure determines the efficacy of reserves.

This is an unfair game. The entrepreneurs of the banking community have much more at stake than the bureaucrats of the central banks. In the postwar period, the initiative has been with the banking community, and the authorities have been repeatedly "surprised" by changes in the way financial markets operate. The profit-seeking bankers almost always win their game with the authorities, but, in winning, the banking community destabilizes the economy; the true losers are those who are hurt by unemployment and inflation.

It is the self-interest of the butcher and the baker that leads to the provision of meat and bread. This dictum, propounded by Adam Smith, has led to the proposition that the pursuit of self-interest leads to the achievement of market equilibrium; the neoclassical results follow from the effects in markets of action based on self-interest. It is in the self-interest of bankers to make loans, to spread the use of their services, and it is in the self-interest of investors to use bankers' services as long as the price of capital assets exceeds the supply price of investment goods. Whereas in commodity production the process of supply generates incomes equal to the market value of supply, in financial markets with responsive banking the demand for finance generates an offsetting supply of finance. Furthermore, if the supply of finance exceeds the demand at the current relative price of capital assets and investment output, the excess supply will push up the price of capital assets relative to the supply price of investment output, and this will increase the demand for investment and therefore finance.

In a world with capitalist finance it is simply not true that the pursuit by each unit of its own self-interest will lead an economy to equilibrium. The self-interest of bankers, levered investors, and investment producers can lead the economy to inflationary expansions and unemployment-creating contractions. Supply and demand analysis—in which market processes lead to an equilibrium—does not explain the behavior of a capitalist economy, for capitalist financial processes mean that the economy has endogenous destabilizing forces. Financial fragility, which is a prerequisite for financial instability, is, fundamentally, a result of internal market processes.

The regime of regulation by the authorities, chartering restrictions, and central bank determination of the volume and effectiveness of bank reserves is intended to control the destabilizing forces inherent in banking and finance. The dominant economic theory, however, leads to the view that regulatory arrangements reflect primitive superstitions and ignorance, because the phenomena that central bank regulations and discretionary power are designed to deal with do not exist in nature. This view holds that instability—booms, inflation, crunches, recessions, and depressions—are mainly due to the ill-advised efforts to contain and offset instability.

Institutions such as the Federal Reserve, which were introduced in an effort to control and contain disorderly conditions in banking and financial markets, are now slaves of an economic theory that denies the existence of such conditions. Today's standard theory argues that the authorities should focus on the money supply and should operate to achieve a constant rate of growth of this construct. The authorities, in large part, accept the validity of this view. As a result, the officials making monetary policy wear blinders that restrict their vision, so that they tend to ignore the financing relations by which monetary phenomena affect activity.

The money-supply blinders worn by the authorities in effect dismiss the ways in which portfolio transformations occur and how they affect the stability of the economy. The erosion of bank equity bases, the growth of liability management banking, and the greater use of covert liabilities are virtually ignored *until* financial markets tend to break down. At this time the Federal Reserve's original reason for being comes into play—and the Federal Reserve, acting as a lender of last resort, pumps reserves into the banking system and refinances banks in order to prevent a breakdown of the financing system.

Whenever the authorities act as a lender of last resort, they increase the reserve base of banks and validate threatened financial usages. Also, whenever they have been forced to intervene as lenders of last resort, many financial institutions, in addition to those that are in immediate danger of failing, are in taut positions; they fear they will be next. As a result, a successful lender-of-last-resort intervention is followed by a period of financial retrenchment and conservatism as taut units try to improve their financial posture. In a capitalist economy with Big Government, automatic and discretionary fiscal stabilizers lead to a large deficit that sustains profits and employment. Because of the large deficit and the lender-of-last-resort intervention, the downward spiral so common in history is aborted.

The lender-of-last-resort actions combined with the huge government deficit increases the reserve base and the government debt holdings of the banking system. The banks, in effect, are able to shore up financing ability for a future business expansion during and in the immediate aftermath of a recession. Because the interventions lead to a quick halt to the downturn, financial disturbances, which force lender-of-last-resort intervention by the authorities, no longer lead to sustained price decreases; instead, the actions that are taken to prevent a debt deflation and a depression set a groundwork for a subsequent burst of expansion followed by inflation.

Over an expansion, new financial instruments and new ways of financing activity develop. Typically, defects of the new ways and the new institutions are revealed when the crunch comes. The authorities intervene to prevent localized weakness from leading to a broad decline in asset values; this intervention takes the form of the Federal Reserve accepting new types of instruments into its portfolio or acquiescing in refinancing arrangements for new institutions and markets. Since the intervention by the authorities tends to validate the new ways, the central bank sets the stage for a broader acceptance and use of the new financial instruments in subsequent expansions.

If the disrupting effects of banking are to be constrained, the authorities must drop their blinders and accept the need to guide and control the evolution of financial usages and practices. In a world of businessmen and financial intermediaries who aggressively seek profit, innovators will always outpace regulators; the authorities cannot prevent changes in the structure of portfolios from occurring. What they can do is keep the asset-equity ratio of banks within bounds by setting equity-absorption ratios for various types of assets. If the authorities constrain banks and are aware of the activities of fringe banks and other financial institutions, they are in a better position to attenuate the disruptive expansionary tendencies of our economy.

Bankers supervise borrowers and holders of lines of credit. Once a line of credit is opened, the banker has a continuing concern about the affairs of the borrower and about business and financial developments that can affect the customer's viability. Given his behavior as a lender, a banker as a borrower naturally accepts supervision from its actual or potential lenders. However, because of deposit insurance and the merger technique of dealing with distressed banks, depositor surveillance has disappeared. Bank examination by the insuring or chartering agency is now a substitute for depositor surveillance; thus, the insuring authority should have power to constrain and control business practices of its policy holders. Where deposits are uninsured, depositors will walk away from banks with low equity ratios and suspect assets. The regulating and insuring authorities, as substitutes for depositor surveillance, must be able to constrain bank asset-equity ratios and asset structures.

Commercial bank reserves mainly result from the ownership of government securities by the Federal Reserve. The government security/open market technique of supplying reserves to the banking system is not the only way reserves can be furnished. Prior to the Great Depression, a major part of reserves that were not based on gold were based on borrowings by banks at the discount window. The resurrection of the discount window as a normal source of bank reserves is a way of tightening Federal Reserve control over commercial banks. If commercial banks normally borrow at the Federal Reserve discount window, they will necessarily accept and be responsive to guidance by the Federal Reserve.

As long as bank reserves are mainly the result of open-market purchases of government securities, the giant banks are virtually immune to Federal Reserve pressures. If normal functioning requires banks to borrow at the discount window, then the capital adequacy and asset structure of banks will be under Federal Reserve supervision. A shift to a greater use of the discount window as a normal source of bank reserves should diminish the destabilizing influences in our economy that are the result of too rapid an expansion of bank financing of business and asset holdings.

INFLATION

Since the mid-1960s consumer prices have behaved quite differently from the way they did earlier in the postwar period (see Figure 11.1). The nature of inflation, which was mild and episodic before 1967, has changed; it has become more severe, quite clearly following a cyclical pattern. In particular, the aggravated inflation of the recent past can be linked to the financial crises that now periodically occur. In today's economic structure, financial instability, which historically was associated with deep depressions, seems to be tied to the emergence of aggravated cyclical inflation.

In chapter 5, it was shown that prices in our accumulating economy are the carriers of profits and vehicles by which a surplus is forced. Furthermore, the profits that prices carry either do or do not validate the liability structures and the prices business paid in the past for capital assets. The total markup on labor costs that are realized was shown to depend upon the financed demands for output, and this markup carries the cash flows that both validate past financing and make new financing available. The argument reveals that absolute prices (i.e., the observed result of market processes) and relative prices (i.e., the terms upon which alternatives are available) emerge simultaneously; one is not more real or basic than the other.

Using the skeletal price equation, $\left[P_C = \dfrac{W_C}{A_C}(1+\mu) \right]$ the rate of change of consumer prices (i.e., inflation) is equal to the rate of increase of wages minus the rate of increase of labor productivity plus the rate of increase of the markup.[1] The simplistic propositions to the effect that wage

---

1. $P_C = \dfrac{W_C}{A_C}\left(1 + \dfrac{W_1 N_1}{W_C N_C} + \cdots \right)$

$$(1)$$

which for our purposes can be written as

$P_C = \dfrac{W_C}{A_C}(M)$

$$(2)$$

where M is one plus the markup and reflects the structure of final demands and institutional characteristics. From (2) we get by changing to logarithms and differentiating

$\dfrac{dP_C}{P_C} = \dfrac{dW_C}{A_C} - \dfrac{dA_C}{A_C} + \dfrac{dM}{M}$

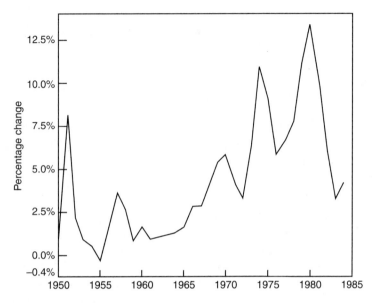

Figure 11.1:   Time Series of Rates of Changes in CPI
SOURCE: Economic Report of the President, February 1985, U.S. Government Printing
Office, Washington, D.C., 1985, Table B 56, p. 296.

increases in excess of productivity lead to inflation are captured in the first
part of this relation. Such simple statements of the wage-price relation,
however, ignore the effect of changes in the markup on prices. The view put
forth here emphasizes the central role of the markup in the inflationary
process of Big Government capitalism.

My theory emphasizes the composition of financed demand and the
spending of incomes that are allocations of profits as the determinants of the
prices of consumption goods. It is compatible with the multiplier analysis in
orthodox Keynesian theory. In the skeletal orthodox Keynesian model,
incomes earned in the production of investment combine with those earned
in the production of consumer goods to finance demand for consumer goods.
The resulting prices yield gross profits (i.e., gross capital income) in the production of consumer goods that are equal to the wage bill in investment
goods if heroic assumptions about spending behavior are made. The money
wage rate enters into the normal supply price of output, but if a rise in money
wages is to be sustained, investment (and government) demand at supply
prices that reflect these higher costs must be financed. Even in a world with
trade union power, where money wages are set by bargaining, wage increases
must be ratified by financing from the banking and financial system.

The determination of employment, wages, and prices starts with the profit calculations of businessmen and bankers. This proposition is in sharp contrast to the views of neoclassical monetarist theory. Monetarists such as Milton Friedman hold that "real" economic results—employment, its distribution among outputs, relative prices, including wages and interest rates—are "ground out by the Walrasian system of general equilibrium equations, provided there is imbedded in them the actual structural characteristics of the labor and commodity markets, including market imperfections, stochastic variability in demands and supplies, the cost of gathering information about job vacancies and labor availabilities, the costs of mobility, and so on."[2] In this glib handwave by Friedman, the real results are determined independently of money and financing phenomena; given the way monetarists set up the analysis, the rate of growth of money can only affect the behavior of the price level.

Monetarist inflation theory rests upon the quantity theory of money, whereby the money supply transforms the relative prices determined by neoclassical price theory into money prices; money is not a factor in determining relative prices and the outputs produced, consumed, and invested.

Bankers are in business to accommodate customers. A rise in business demand for financing of production or investment will thus lead to a rise in bank holdings of business assets and in bank liabilities outstanding, that is, in money. In particular, an increase in investment production will require either a rise in bank credit, and thus in bank liabilities outstanding, or an activation of previously idle money balances. What happens to the money supply as velocity increases is part of an inflationary process, not the cause.

In our economy the causal chain that leads to inflation starts with rising investment or government spending, which leads to increases in markups; an increase in the money supply or in money velocity usually is associated with the rise in investment or government spending. Investment

---

2. Milton Friedman, "The Role of Monetary Policy," *American Economic Review* 58, no. 1 (March 1968), pp. 1–17; p. 8 for quotation. Professor Friedman's assertion as to what the Walrasian system of general equilibrium equations tells us is a great big "handwave." "The Walrasian system of general equilibrium equations" does not grind out outputs, employment, and relative prices—market processes determine economic reality. The Walrasian system of general equilibrium equations is an attempt to model reality; it is not reality. Furthermore, the existence of a consistent solution to the Walrasian model has not been shown to occur for a meaningful sample of the institutional relations identified by Professor Friedman, let alone the "handwave" of "and so on."

demand rests upon the availability of financing. As the supply of financing through banks is responsive to demand, the money supply changes to accommodate the activities that determine the demand for financing.

MONEY WAGES AND PRICE-DEFLATED WAGES

The literature and the press distinguish between real wages and nominal—or money—wages. This terminology reflects the view that the economically relevant wages are determined by the real output that labor produces and that wages can buy.

The proposition that labor supply and demand depend upon the ratio of wages to prices is not a conclusion of economic theory. It is, rather, an assumption: the axiom of reals is a postulate of orthodox theory.[3] In order to prove that a decentralized market leads to a coherent result, it is assumed that an increase in the supply of labor will be forthcoming only if wages rise relative to prices.

This focus on wages relative to prices is not sufficient to explain how wages affect what happens in an economy in which investment takes place and capital assets and financial contracts denominated in money exist. Money wage rates and money profit flows determine whether payment commitments on debts can be fulfilled. The ability of workers with mortgage and installment debts fixed in dollars to fulfill their obligations improves when money wages increase, even if current prices rise and fall with money wages. Business is concerned with the flow of gross money profits; to a firm, a rise in money wages means that the same percentage markup will yield a larger money flow. In a simple model, gross money profits in the production of consumption goods rise when total wages in investment goods production rise, and fall when total wages in investment goods production fall.

---

3. Frank H. Hahn, *Money and Inflation* (Cambridge: MIT Press, 1983): "The objectives of agents that determine their actions and plans do not depend on any nominal magnitudes. Agents care only about real things, such as goods (properly dated and distinguished by states of nature), leisure, and effort. We know this as the axiom of the absence of money illusion, which it seems impossible to abandon in any sensible analysis" (p. 34). See also Hyman P. Minsky, "Frank Hahn's Money and Inflation: A Review Article," *Journal of Post-Keynesian Economics* 6, no. 3 (Spring 1984), pp. 449–57.

In a broader view, the ability of producers of consumer goods to meet financial obligations depends upon those wage and other incomes that determine realized aggregate markups.

Prior to the development of price-support programs, the relation between the ability to fulfill commitments on debt and prices was clearly exhibited in agriculture. Decreased demand for or increased supply of agricultural output would lead to a fall in prices that quite often led to an inability of farmers to fulfill debt commitments. The decline in dollar agricultural prices associated with the return to the gold standard after the Civil War led directly to William Jennings Bryan's Cross of Gold speech.

In a world with intertemporal contracts denominated in money, the path of money wages and prices determines whether such contracts are fulfilled. If money wages and prices change by the same percentage, the "real" wages of neoclassical theory do not change—but the cash flows available to meet payment commitments do. Nominal magnitudes matter.

A labor compensation system does not set all wages and salaries in money. Employees usually receive some compensation in goods and services. The health benefits provided to employees, for example, are often fixed in terms of the services to be made available, not the costs to be borne. These agreements to provide a fixed packet of goods and services make employers' cash flows vulnerable to increases in costs.

Because most labor remuneration is in money terms, the part of well-being determined by purchased commodities depends upon what wages will buy. Whereas wage bargains are struck in money terms, what wages will buy is determined by the way prices behave. Even though labor contracts and government actions affect money wages, the command of a money wage over goods and services is determined by market developments. Labor contracts only set a process in motion; they do not establish a result. Myriad adjustments stand between a wage contract and a realized standard of living. Legislation and collective bargaining that affect wages can only start a process within the institutional setup: collective bargaining may propose, but market processes dispose.

Referring to our skeletal model of the economy (see Appendix B), the purchasing power of money wages is directly related to the output of consumer goods and inversely related to employment and wage rates in investment and consumption goods. If the ratio of output to employment in consumption goods production is unchanged, then the purchasing power of money wages in consumption-goods industries decreases whenever employment in investment goods increases relative to employment in consumption goods. Thus, given the skeletal specifications, inflation can be slowed or stopped by increased production of consumer goods: if the output of consumer goods increases at a faster rate than the wage bill, the price level will tend to fall.

Increasing investment imparts an inflationary push to an economy. As relative wage rates reflect market demands or differential union strength, rising investment increases the demand for the specialized skills needed for the production of investment goods. In an economy that emphasizes investment, wages in investment-goods industries will tend to rise relative to wages in consumption-goods industries. This increase in relative wages will tend to boost the price level of consumer goods by increasing the markup per unit of output.

If we examine more complex relations, allowing for government, consumption out of profits, and savings out of wages, we find that the course of the purchasing power of money wages depends upon the size of the demands for consumption goods financed by income other than that derived from the production of consumer goods. Accordingly, a rise in consumption demand financed by profits will raise prices. What firms spend on employee medical care, advertising, product development, and so forth can be interpreted as an allocation of broadly defined profits. Such spending raises both the costs that have to be recovered and the demand for consumer goods, as the fees and wages paid for these activities become wage income. In the aggregate such business-style spending becomes a self-fulfilling prophecy, for it raises both unit costs and realized output prices; prices rise with the spending on these activities. Unless shopfloor productivity improves, increases in those incomes that can be viewed as allocations of profits to wages and salaries for ancillary business functions produce inflationary pressures.[4]

There are, essentially, two types of inflation. In one, prices rise even as increases in money wages lag behind prices; in the second, prices rise as money wage increases keep up with or even lead prices. When the determinants of the markup rise relative to the output of consumer goods, then prices rise relative to wages and the purchasing power of wages falls. This type of inflation does not feed on itself. If the fall in the purchasing power of wages is sufficiently great, union militancy, union-aborting wage increases by employers, or government interventions (such as raising minimum wages or legislated indexing of wages) will occur. When this becomes

---

4. See Appendix B for the equations and a discussion of the relations between money and wages, prices, and profits in consumption goods production.

the norm, the economy moves to the second type of inflation—an open inflation in which rising prices induce rising wages, which leads to further rises in prices.

The point at which rising money wages are triggered by falling price-deflated money wages depends upon the institutional arrangements, political climate, the size of the fall, and whether inflation is a regular or an occasional phenomenon. Once inflation becomes expected, the organization of the labor market and the political climate will evolve so that some sort of indexing is institutionalized. A modest, irregular, and unexpected fall in price-deflated wages will not trigger a rise in money wages. The sluggish response of labor markets provides a barrier against open inflation. This barrier means that small and transitory changes in the wage bill in investment goods relative to that in consumer goods industries, within an economy in which government wages, transfer payments, and consumption financed by profits are small or do not change, will not lead to increases in money wage rates. However, marked and sustained increases in the demand for consumer goods financed by incomes that do not result in consumption-goods output will break through the inflation barrier, thus leading to the type of inflation that is associated with increases in money wages.

Prior to World War II contra-cyclical economic policies were ineffective or nonexistent. Until the New Deal and the post–World War II eras, government was a small part of the economy, and there was little effective government or private effort to stabilize the system. Peacetime inflations were associated with business-cycle expansions. As such inflations were of limited duration, a rise in prices did not lead to expectations of a continued rise in prices. Only if it is believed that the fall in the purchasing power of money wages is part of a continuing process will institutions appear that have the effect of indexing wages.

Since World War II government has been a big part of the economy. Government wages, purchases, and transfer payments generate demand for consumption goods, even as they do not augment directly their supply. Any increase in the ratio of the demand for consumer goods to the output of consumption goods is inflationary; transfer payments in particular tend to raise this ratio.

Any rise in the ratio of consumption spending financed by profits to the wage bill in the production of consumer goods tends to lower the purchasing power of wages. In a simple sense this includes consumption financed by dividends, interest, and capital gains. In our economy, however, a large proportion of gross capital income—revenues minus technologically determined labor and material costs—is distributed in the form of wages and salaries to workers involved in administration, marketing, advertising, and other ancillary business functions. These wages and salaries finance spending on consumer goods, raise the markup on technologically determined costs, and lower the purchasing power per dollar of wage income.

The course of prices therefore is mainly determined by the way the economy is run (in the sense of the composition of final demands and the sources of incomes that are available for spending on consumer goods relative to the wage incomes arising in the direct production of consumer goods), and the course of money wages, which are either technical costs of production or allocations of profit. Whether money wages do or do not react to a decline in the purchasing power of wages determines whether inflation becomes open-ended, that is, whether the inflation barrier holds.

As mentioned above, each economy has an inflation barrier in that, beyond some point, price increases will lead to parallel increases in money wages. The location of the inflation barrier determines whether, or at what stage, money wage increases become a major determinant of inflation. One specific determinant of the transition to an open inflation, in which money wages, money investment, government deficits, and prices chase one another, is the existence of large and growing demands for consumer goods that are financed outside of wage incomes received in direct productive channels. War and defense spending, a system of indexed transfer payments, government policies to induce investment, the complex of advertising, marketing, and administration in business, and credit purchases of consumer goods all finance such demand.

In an economy with the complex corporate and government structure that now exists, the course of money wages is not the triggering factor in inflation. Inflation is, first of all, the result of financing too many claims on the supply of consumer goods at the inherited set of prices. Any restriction on the supply of consumer goods—such as occurs in wartime or as the result of a drought—or any expansion of incomes that will be available to finance the demand for consumer goods, without any concomitant increase in supply, will lead to rising prices.

In this view, the behavior of money wages once the inflation barrier is pierced is more a defensive reaction than a cause. When the financing of consumer demand by investment, government transfer payments, business-style expenditure, and consumer debt increase the demand for goods relative to the supply, then prices rise so that the price-level-deflated wage decreases. Open inflation occurs when market conditions are conducive to rising money wages, that is, when employment is relatively full and business profits are high. What trade unions do is speed up the money wage response, lowering the inflation barrier; a strengthening of trade unions lowers the inflation barrier and a weakening raises it.

The new thing in the past two decades is that inflation—including increases in money wages—persisted in times of high unemployment. These stagflations have taken place in an era in which transfer payments increased rapidly, in which government deficits persist through business-cycle expansions and exploded when unemployment increased, and government wage rates and wage bills increased rapidly. Both business gross profits and consumer prices were sustained and even increased during the recessions of the late 1960s, 1970s, and early 1980s. Government policies that sustained profits enabled business and the banks to survive the financial traumas of 1966, 1969–70, 1974–75, 1979–82, and 1983–84; the result was a markup inflation.

Price-deflated money wages tended to fall during recessions in recent decades because government deficits that support profits sustain and increase markups. As a result, pressure to raise money wages became evident once employment was stabilized and began to increase. Wage increases, which occur even in periods of labor-market slack, are best interpreted as defensive or institutionalized reactions to profit-generating government deficits that result in rising markups and price increases during recessions.

MONEY WAGES

Soon after World War II it became clear that there was a hole in the standard version of Keynesian theory—it did not really explain prices. This vacuum was filled with work by Phillips, Phelps-Brown, and Samuelson and Solow, who argued that there is an inverse relation between money wage changes and the unemployment level and that this relation leads to an inverse relation between the unemployment rate and price-level changes.[5]

This inverse relation has been enshrined in the doctrine of the trade-off, a proposition that inflation is the price the economy must pay for low

---

5. Alban W. Phillips and Ernest H. Phelps-Brown, "The Relation between Unemployment and the Rate of Change of Money Wage Rates in the United Kingdom, 1862–1957," *Economica* 25 (Nov. 1958), pp. 183–99; and Paul A. Samuelson and Robert M. Solow, "Analytical Aspects of Anti-Inflationary Policy," *American Economic Review* 50 (May 1960), pp. 177–94.

unemployment. In later literature the unemployment rate associated with stable prices has been identified as a "natural" rate that will be the actual rate whenever inflation is fully anticipated, regardless of the rate of inflation. The natural-rate theorists argue that the trade-off only exists for transitory and surprise rates of inflations.[6] In this view the trade-off depends upon a bluff; the unemployment rate can be lowered only if the workers believe that the inflation rate will be lower than it will in fact be, even as employers have a correct perception. The unemployment rate always tends toward the rate that would rule with stable prices and the absence of monetary or fiscal policies to reduce unemployment. This position is the modern statement of the classical view that supply and demand for labor, which reflects workers' preferences and productivity, determine employment and the real wage.

Figure 11.2 shows that there is no obvious consistent relation in the United States between the rate of inflation, as measured by changes in the CPI, and unemployment. During the Kennedy–Johnson years (1961–69) there is a nice inverse relation between unemployment rates and inflation, which seems to indicate that unemployment rates below 4 percent lead to accelerated inflation without any further lowering of the unemployment rate.

If we identify the vertical or backward-bending portions of the chart with the inflation barrier, then in 1955–57 and 1968–69 the barrier was at a 4 percent unemployment rate (but at lower inflation rates in 1955–57 than in 1968–69); in 1972–74 it was at 5 percent, and in 1978–79 it was at 6 percent. The chart shows that a wide range of inflation rates are compatible with any particular unemployment rate.

Phillips's seeming corroboration of the trade-off hypothesis with British data covering 1862–1957 and the apparent contradiction of the

---

6. Milton Friedman, "The Role of Monetary Policy," *American Economic Review* 58 (March 1968). Edmond S. Phelps, *Inflation Policy and Unemployment Theory: The Cost-Benefit Approach to Monetary Planning* (New York: Norton, 1970). For example, when stable prices are anticipated, a zero rate of price inflation may be associated with a 5 percent unemployment rate and a 4 percent unemployment rate with a 2 percent unanticipated inflation rate. After policy achieves 4 percent unemployment and 2 percent inflation rates, a 2 percent anticipated inflation rate will be built into the system. As this is taking place the unemployment rate will creep to 5 percent; stimulus beyond that which leads to a 2 percent inflation rate is needed for an unemployment rate of 4 percent. Such stimulus may lead to a 4 percent inflation rate. Thus, the inflation rate associated with unemployment below the natural rate increases.

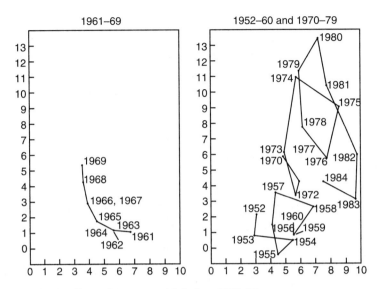

Figure 11.2:   Unemployment and Inflation, 1952–84

SOURCE: Economic Report of the President, February 1985, U.S. Government Printing Office, Washington, D.C., 1985, Table B 56, p. 296, and Table B 29, p. 266.

hypothesis by the U.S. data for the postwar period call for a theory that can accommodate the fact that a trade-off does not necessarily occur. Furthermore, since 1966 there has been a sharp increase in the tendency for prices to rise; an inflationary thrust developed in the age of instability.

The British data used in the trade-off argument were taken from trade union records over a period encompassing many business cycles. Over this time, business-cycle expansions were marked by a rise in wages even as contractions saw wages fall. Expansions were characterized by increases in investment and favorable foreign balances and contractions by corresponding decreases. Thus, fluctuations in the price level reflected changes both in money wages and in the composition of output.

In the price formula of the skeletal model,[7] an increase in payrolls for producing investment goods while labor markets are slack will increase both employment and output by producers of consumer goods. When this happens, a rise in consumer goods prices would reflect increases in productivity-adjusted wages. As the productivity of labor usually rises

---

7. $P_C = \dfrac{W_C}{A_C}\left(1 + \dfrac{W_I N_I}{W_C N_C}\right)$

during early stages of expansion, prices do not increase very much, if at all, as an expansion gets started. Once labor markets tighten, however, an increase in employment in investment-goods production will not be associated with a comparable increase in employment in consumer-goods production, and as a result, the markup and money wages increase; inflation takes place. Thus, inflation is larger when expansions lead to labor shortages.

Inflations also differ according to the nature of market organizations. If price flexibility is dominant, then a rise in investment will lead to higher prices that may precipitate wage pressures. On the other hand, if supply increases as demand increases, then the markup need not increase. Only after labor shortages appear will increases in investment employment lead to demand conditions conducive to increased unit markups and higher wages.

The observed trade-off between unemployment and inflation in the British data reflected the behavior of wages and prices in an institutional setup that differs markedly from our own. The U.S. economy is now characterized by: (1) effective partial trade unionism; (2) a Big Government that has sustained profits even in serious recessions; (3) the great weight of industries using expensive and relatively long-lived capital assets. All of the above were missing or took quite different forms in England when the data supporting the trade-off were collected.

When trade unions cover part of the labor forces, slack in the economy will not lead to falling money wages in the occupations and industries where they are effective. The downward pressure on labor costs and prices will be attenuated.

Big Government deficits during recessions sustain—and may actually increase—the realized markup on unit labor costs. By taxes and regulatory programs, government mandates costs; it also generates income that helps validate these costs. If Social Security taxes and Social Security benefits are raised, then the rise in labor costs is matched by expenditures financed by Social Security receipts. In such programs, every time government taxes raise the supply price of output, government spending generates incomes that can validate the higher price. It is not just the government deficit that generates inflation; if government expenditures are rising relative to the output of consumer goods, even a balanced government budget will result in rising prices.

As previously mentioned, the U.S. economy has been more unstable since the credit crunch of 1966 than it was in the earlier years of the post-World War II era. Aggregate demand has been sustained by the government fiscal posture even as financial-market conditions and the prospective profitability of investment thrust the economy into a recession. The profits that government deficits sustained and even increased during recessions appeared as higher unit markups on the smaller recession volume of consumer-goods output; that is, inflation resulted from the way depressions were contained. A commitment to full employment in a financially unstable economy means that both unemployment and inflation rates are likely to show a secular upward drift.

An increase in the significance of capital-intensive modes of production increases the importance of stability in the cash flows carried by markups on labor costs. If the wage rate in investment goods increases when investment employment is maintained or increased, the markup on unit labor costs in consumption production will increase. Wage increases in investment make it easier for firms producing consumer goods to validate their debts. Once increased markups force a decline in the purchasing power of wages, the stage is set for an open inflation that requires increases in money wages.

As money wages in investment production and government increase, the cash flow per unit of consumption output available to validate debt increases. Markup inflation eases the cash payment commitments due to debts and thus, with a lag, is favorable for investment. An expansion generates conditions conducive to further expansion, which will then continue until the cost and financing terms of investment are affected. But if it is believed that money wage increases are likely to be reversed quite soon, then the wage and price increases of an expansion will not induce further investment spending and further wage and price increases.

However, if money wage increases are expected and thought likely to continue, then investors, particularly investors in financial instruments, will seek out those ventures—whether they finance output or not—that are expected to maintain or improve their price-level-deflated capital value. Various commodity and artifact bubbles will ensue—be they housing, gold, stamps, diamonds, or even collectibles—and financing terms will be modified to allow for anticipated inflation. Once interest rates adjust quickly to reflect anticipated inflation, the weight of financial obligations will not be eased when an inflation occurs, and the inflationary process will not lead to further investment. Anticipated inflation means that the connections between investment activity, employment, and price increases are ruptured; the rate of inflation is no longer inversely related to the unemployment rate. Inflation can accelerate even as unemployment increases if money wages have a built-in momentum and the fiscal posture increases the markup on money wages.

The Phillips Curve of Phillips and Phelps-Brown was a valid generalization of historical observations, reflecting the institutional conditions of a specific era. In the current economy, the close link between inflation and investment by way of markups has been broken. Inflation has become a secular rather than a cyclical phenomenon as the secular increase in government and business-style spending has led to a secular increasing price level.

In summation, there are a variety of inflations: inflation can reflect open wage increases or the financed composition of demand. This view is in sharp contrast to the simple assertions that inflation is everywhere a monetary phenomenon, or is caused by government, or is the result of wage increases exceeding productivity increases. Both monetary and the wage/productivity phenomena occur in observed inflations; both are parts of the inflation process, but they are neither the originating nor the entire mechanism. Furthermore, controlling the money supply or money wages only addresses symptoms, not causes, of the inflation disease.

THE FINANCING OF WAGES

Workers are compensated by money wages and other considerations as determined by tradition or by bargaining between employers and employees. A large proportion of the bargaining negotiations are between collectives, such as trade unions and organized employers, rather than between individual workers and atomistic employers. Furthermore, limits are set on the conditions of employment by legislation dealing with wages, hours of work, and various conditions in the shop.

The cost of labor covers not only pre-tax pay but also costs that are mandated by government, trade union contracts, or an employer's interest in constraining turnover. As a result, the wage level that enters into discussions on inflation is an average of many items, and any change is made up of movements in the different components of employee compensation.

Our model of price determination allows for specific wage movements in consumption-goods production, investment-goods production, and government employment. In this model, the possible disparate movements of these components are natural subjects of attention.

An increase in the general level of money wages starts with increases in particular wages. For wages to increase, the contracting parties must believe that funds to pay the higher wages will be forthcoming. Because the implication of higher money wages is higher technologically determined average and incremental costs, the arithmetic of costs and revenues shows that either prices will be higher or unit markups will be lower. However, because the validation of liability structures and business styles sets a minimum to required cash flows, there is a minimum difference between sales revenues and technologically mandated costs that must be maintained if commitments are to be fulfilled. Wage increases that guarantee to bankrupt the employer are rarely negotiated, and wage contracts that seem to lead to bankruptcy will be renegotiated.*

If nothing else changes, a rise in price usually decreases sales. For increases in money wages and prices not to impair the viability of a firm, the rise in prices cannot lead to a percentage fall in sales that exceeds the percentage rise in the markup. This condition implies that product demand cannot be elastic.

If demand is elastic, the gross flow of profits to firms that raise wages and prices will be compromised. A rise in wages that leads to a much lower output will lead to a fall in anticipated profit flows and in the market valuation of firms. Firms cannot cavalierly accept such developments. Firms that lead in increasing money wages cannot be selling in markets that conform to the elastic demand that is assumed to rule for individual units in competitive markets.

A demand curve that is not infinitely elastic for a particular firm defines monopoly or oligopoly: the firm has market power. If a firm is a constrained monopolist, so that it has unexploited monopoly power, a rise in wages as a result of a union contract may relax the constraint so that previously unexercised monopoly power can be used. Thus, firms will agree to raise wages when there is unused market power or if an increase in market power is anticipated. Simple wage-push inflation can only occur if constrained monopoly power exists and wage increases relax the constraint. Because wages are costs that business must recover, there is a symbiotic relation between firms and trade unions in industries dominated by a few units; wage increases are grounds for the firms to exercise market power in political situations in which the existence of power has to be camouflaged.

Higher money wages may not compromise gross profit flows if demand increases, as is true when a particular output is gaining market acceptance. Firms that are successfully introducing new products enjoy both rising and inelastic demand and need additional labor. As a result, they offer higher wages and improved terms of employment so that they can reap the benefit of their often transitory advantages.

---

* This became evident in 1982–83 when Continental Airlines sought the protection of bankruptcy in order to break its union contracts.

Money wage increases also may reflect the increase in particular demands during a business cycle expansion. In Big Government capitalism, the dimensions that lead in an expansion often reflect policy measures and not infrequently are associated with institutional changes. Economic policy and evolving economic and financial institutions cause differential changes in money wages and employment during expansions.

The eras of tranquility (1946–65) and turbulence (1966 to date) have witnessed shifting patterns of government intervention, spending programs that start up and fade away, and the spread of institutions and usages that finance particular outputs, industries, and incomes. The shifting patterns affect what expenditures can be financed and thus make variations in relative wages possible. As a result, in our decentralized wage-determination process the skills and industries that gain because of government programs often become the leading sectors in the propagation of wage inflation.

In private businesses, sales revenues finance wages paid in producing output. If the output is a consumption good, then the sales revenue will, in turn, be mainly derived from wage income. If the output is an investment good, then sales revenue will be financed initially by some interim construction debt and then by the take-out instrument of the final user of the asset. This financing is available because profit flows are expected to validate the debt instruments. The costs that are recaptured in sales revenues include the profits that will validate debts; expected profits set a limit to the prices and financing terms for capital assets and investment output.

Wages in the production of investment goods are limited by the available interim (construction) and take-out financing; financing breaks down into internal and external financing. The rise of wages in investment goods production is limited by the price that business can pay for capital assets, which, in the first instance, is limited by available financing. Furthermore, available financing is restricted by bankers' views as to the cash flows that the investment goods, once they become capital assets, are expected to generate. Present views of future profits and financing costs determine demand prices for capital assets.

In a business-cycle expansion, the demand for investment goods increases. A greater demand for labor to produce investment goods increases employment and, in turn, wages, profits, and prices. Once investment employment rises, then the demand for consumption goods, for consumption-goods output, and for employment in consumption-goods production increases; as a result, the gross profits of consumption-goods producers increases. Thus, an initial increase in investment-goods employment and wages leads to rising employment, wages, and prices in consumption goods. This process, however, is limited by financial-market reactions to increased financial layering and the emergence of fragile financial structures conducive to crises and cyclical downturns. Available finance, in effect, sets limits to the increase in wage rates in investment-goods production. A strong sustained inflationary thrust is not possible if the cash to finance ever more expensive investment production is not forthcoming from the banking system. A lack of finance will reflect a lack of faith by bankers and financiers that the cash flows needed to validate more expensive investment outputs will be forthcoming.

Furthermore, in every capitalist economy a substantial number of people live on fixed or politically determined incomes, such as the military, civil servants, and recipients of entitlements. If pensions and government employee salaries do not rise with private wages, then money demand for current consumption output will fall relative to the technologically determined costs. This lowers the profits that will be forthcoming to validate capital-asset prices and leads to doubts that the profits will be forthcoming to validate investment at the current high prices. Open inflation is a self-limiting process in a predominantly private economy that accepts cyclical declines in the purchasing power of government wages and pensions and other fixed incomes.

While the ability of the banking system to finance investment in process and positions in capital assets is limited, these limits are flexible. They depend upon the efficacy of innovations in stretching the financing available to business by banks and nonbank institutions and the course of bank reserves. Because of the limits due to private financing of investment activity and capital assets, in the era of small government a strong expansion with considerable price increases occurred only as the memory of past debt deflations became dimmed by time. The succession of minor and major business cycles reflected this financing limitation.

A central bank that is conscious of the potential instability of a financial structure in which units have been largely stripped of their liquidity may be reluctant to slow down the rate of growth of bank reserves. The central bank is often confronted with a choice between possibly triggering a financial crisis or going along with inflation. Even though the central bank is accommodative in furnishing reserves, the investment cost, financing conditions, expected price and profit conditions, and augmented uncertainty will lead to a slowdown of investment after a bout of inflation. Once again the expansion and inflation have self-limiting properties even if there is an accommodative central bank.

Thus, in an economy with small and passive government, the feedbacks in the debt-validation processes limit the likelihood of an open inflation.

For an open inflation to be more than a transitory phenomenon, the constraining feedbacks due to financial relations have to be overridden, as they are, for example, in wartime by the government's insatiable demand for output. In Big Government capitalism, the constraining feedbacks are thwarted by the various and sundry government programs that subsidize and sustain investment output, and the various ways in which the incomes of direct and indirect civil servants and recipients of transfers are indexed. When government undertakes to supply some fixed quantity of diet, medical care, defense, or living standards of the retired without setting limits on supplier prices, the potential for government-financed expenditure to sustain and even lead an uncontained inflation is circumscribed only by the extent of government and the willingness and ability of the government to run a deficit.

Open inflation is largely the result of rupturing the inflation barrier after a shortage of consumer goods relative to the financed demand for consumer goods leads to inflation. If inflation is to be constrained without recessions, the output of consumer goods needs to be increased as the financed demand for consumer goods increases. The key to successful policy to constrain inflation lies in knowing that the output of consumer goods is deflationary, whereas investment and government spending are inflationary. Attempts to control inflation through control of the money supply or money wage rates can enjoy but transitory success in a Big Government market economy in which the sustaining of a reasonable approximation of full employment is a dominant aim of policy and the techniques used by government to maintain employment do not lead to an expansion of useful output. Economies in which government is big because of transfer payments and military expenditures are susceptible to uncontained inflation.

GOVERNMENT AS AN ENGINE OF INFLATION

The inability to externally finance an ever increasing share of private investment in total output makes inflations in a capitalist economy with a small government self-limiting. Inflations in such an economy depend upon the impact of innovations in finance upon asset prices and investment and whether speculation infects businessmen and bankers. Because of the upward instability of the investment-financing-profits interactions, from time to time fragile financial structures emerge. Fragile financial structures regularly break, which sharply reduces investment spending. Sometimes the end comes with a whimper and a recession results; at other times the end comes with the bang of a financial crisis, and a deep depression follows. Small-government noninterventionist capitalism therefore is not hospitable to protracted, prolonged, and chronic inflation, but it is susceptible to debt deflations and deep depressions.

Peacetime Big Government capitalism matured after World War II, and its success was followed by the emergence of a fragile financial structure and a combination of sharp cycles, seemingly chronic inflation, and bouts of persistent unemployment. When lender-of-last-resort refinancings and massive government deficits abort debt deflations and sustain profits they also sustain, with a lag, the ability to finance spending at higher prices. The inflationary impact of investment is augmented by the inflationary consequences of government intervention. The financial and profit repercussions of government interventions to prevent deep depressions override the limitations on inflation caused by the inelasticity of finance and by the uncertainty, with respect to validating profits, that constrain private investment.

The accelerated though cyclical inflation of the years between 1966 and 1982 can be imputed to the rapid growth of transfer payments, state and local expenditures, and bursts of military spending. These became so large relative to GNP that a noninflationary economy can be achieved only if their rate of increase becomes less than or, at most, equal to the rate at which GNP grows in the absence of inflation.

But government intervention in the economy is not limited to purchasing goods and services and transfer payments; it also takes the form of encouraging particular outputs by endorsement of obligations and special tax treatments. One attribute of such programs and interventions is that they often set specific numerical targets: a number of housing units to be built, a particular set of medical services to be delivered, a man to be put on the moon by a particular date.

Such numerical targets determine an inelastic demand curve, for specific outputs or services, which rises with prices. This results in inelastic and rising demand curves for particular kinds of labor. Such target policies enhance the market power of producers and of labor specialized to these outputs. Government quantitative targets, together with the belief that the government will finance the achievement of these targets, are a grant of market power to both the suppliers and the laborers responsible for these outputs. History and theory indicate that market power will not go unused, especially if the government does not also set the purchase price for outputs it buys or the amount suppliers can pay their labor. Thus, in a military buildup profits and wages in defense production are likely to lead the inflationary process, and a commitment by government to pay for medical services for the aged will lead to an explosion in the cost of medical services.

The inflationary effect of a rapidly growing government does not depend solely upon the government's being in deficit. For the budget to be balanced, if not now then eventually, as government spending increases, revenues must increase. Unless taxes are levied on a pure residual claimant (which really does not exist) or income taxes are designed to have no effect upon the supply of labor (which really is an impossible design problem), they will affect supply prices. To achieve a close approximation to full employment, expansionary monetary (and fiscal) measures must offset the effects that taxes have on supply prices. But the offset is limited by the fear of accelerating inflation and that taxation will stifle supply. Fiscal policy and deficit financing are easy roads to a noninflationary expansion only in the aftermath of a financial crisis and debt deflation when business, households, and financial institutions all desire the liquidity and safety that government debts and bank money that reflects bank ownership of government debt provide.

Government spending financed by taxes has much the same effect upon prices as the financing of consumption by profits. In the consumption case, prices rise so that profits net of consumption spending are at the targeted level; in the tax case prices rise so that after-tax profits equal the level determined by investment, the government deficit, and the other determinants of profits.

Inflation has accompanied wars. The government's ability to commandeer resources, so that the proportion of demand for goods financed by income other than that derived from the production of consumer goods rises, is the cause of wartime inflation. During peacetime, however, transfer payments and state and local expenditures also commandeer resources, which leads to increases in the ratio of the financed demand for consumer goods to the technologically determined costs of producing consumer goods. It does not matter if the budget is balanced during wartime: the real resource costs of war lead to inflation. Similarly, there are real resource costs to state and local government spending, transfer payments, and defense spending during peacetime, and these costs show up in inflationary price pressures.

COMPONENTS OF THE MARKUP

Having taken up the role of government and investment, we now turn to other determinants of the markup. Basically, inflation is the result of the course of productivity-adjusted wages and markups. The markups that can be realized depend upon consumption spending financed by various wage and nonwage incomes.

In the price formula[8] consumption spending financed by after-tax profits increases the markup because profits, net of taxes and of consumption spending financed by profits, are the major source of the savings offset to investment. If capitalists live high on the hog, the markup on technologically determined labor costs will reflect this spending. Consumption out of profits—profits being defined as the difference between sales revenues and technologically determined costs—is not, however, restricted to consumption financed by dividend income or capital gains; it also includes consumption financed by wage incomes that arise out of business styles.

Data on the breakdown of labor income between the workers who are mandated by technology and those whose employment is ancillary are not available, but the breakdown between production and nonproduction workers in manufacturing is available. The higher the proportion of nonproduction workers to total employment, the higher the consumption financed by profits and thus the higher the markup on technologically determined costs that will be realized. An increase in the ratio of nonproduction workers to total employment will lead to a rise in the markup by units with market power that set prices to recapture costs.[9] For units without market power, the consumption financed by the distribution of profits as wages will lead to an increase in the average realized gap between price and technologically determined costs. Thus, if there is a trend in the proportion of the total wages and salary bill that goes to workers who are not mandated by the technology of production, there will be upward pressure on prices, relative to the course of productivity-deflated money wages.

Technical progress increases labor productivity and in a competitive economy would impart a downward trend to prices. In the 1950s a doctrine emerged to the effect that money wages should rise by some productivity coefficient each year; it has since become a fixed point in policy. This

8. $P_C = \dfrac{W_C}{A_C}\left(1 + \dfrac{W_I N_I}{W_C N_C} + \dfrac{C\overset{*}{\pi}}{W_C N_C}\right)$

9. Myron J. Gorden, "Corporate Bureaucracy, Productivity Gains and Distribution of Revenue in U.S. Manufacturing, 1947–77," *Journal of Post-Keynesian Economics* 6, no. 4 (Summer 1982); and Paolo Syles-Labini, "Prices and Income Distribution," *Journal of Post-Keynesian Economics* 2 (Fall 1979).

doctrine reflected the belief that, for firms with market power, increased productivity will not lead to falling prices; thus, the only way the purchasing power of wages can improve is if money wages rise as prices remain roughly constant. If money wages rise to reflect productivity increases and if the percentage of workers employed in ancillary activities increase, then prices must increase if firms are to earn the cash needed to cover expenses.

Table 11.1 shows how the percentage of nonproduction workers to total employment in manufacturing has increased. An era of relative tranquility, such as 1952–66, is conducive to an increase in the ratio of

Table 11.1: Nonproduction Workers as a Percent of Total Employment in Manufacturing

Industry	1952	1966	1976
Durable Goods	19.2	25.8	25.6
Lumber and Wood	9.2	13.1	15.2
Furniture and Fixtures	14.4	17.1	18.1
Stone, Clay and Glass	14.9	19.7	20.3
Primary Metals	15.4	18.6	21.7
Fabricated Metal	19.6	22.1	24.6
Machinery, except Electrical	23.3	29.7	35.1
Electrical Equipment	23.2	30.6	34.6
Motor Vehicles	20.4	22.2	22.5
Aircraft	25.6	40.3	48.4
Instruments	24.7	36.1	38.7
Miscellaneous Manufacturing	15.5	20.2	23.4
Nondurable Goods	20.2	25.3	27.7
Food and Kindred	27.2	33.6	32.2
Tobacco Manufacturing	8.0	14.8	17.0
Textile Mill	7.8	10.9	12.9
Apparel	10.6	11.1	13.9
Paper and Allied	16.2	22.3	24.8
Printing and Publishing	34.6	36.4	43.2
Chemicals and Allied	30.7	40.3	42.4
Petroleum and Coal	28.0	37.7	35.6
Rubber and Plastics	20.2	22.1	22.9
Leather and Leather Products	10.4	12.4	13.6

SOURCE: *Employment and Training Report of the President*, 1982, U.S. Government Printing Office, Washington, D.C., 1982.

nonproduction to production workers. In the aggregate, if nonproduction workers spend their wage and salary incomes on consumption, the markup on technologically determined costs that will be realized for consumption goods will reflect this demand. Inasmuch as laborers in ancillary functions are employed by producers of both consumer goods and investment goods, profits—net of technologically determined labor costs in the production of consumer goods—will rise as such incomes rise. That is, in a no-government economy for consumer goods we have (assuming all of wages and salary incomes and only such income is spent on consumption goods):

Consumption Goods, Total Revenue =	Technologically determined wages in the production of consumer goods + overhead wages in the production of consumer goods + technologically determined wages in the production of investment goods + overhead wages in the production of investment goods
Out-of-pocket Costs =	Technologically determined wages + overhead wages in the production of consumer goods
"Conventional" Gross profits =	Technologically determined wages + over head wages in the production of investment goods
Adjusted "Gross Profits" =	Technologically determined wages + overhead wages in the production of investment goods + *overhead* wages in the production of consumer goods

For investment to take place, the present value of the income expected from capital assets must exceed the supply price of investment. This is a necessary condition for investment; however, the necessary and sufficient condition for investment to take place adds that *financing must be available* to the necessary conditions. In a tranquil age the market value of unchanging future incomes increases, for tranquility attenuates uncertainty. Attenuated uncertainty also changes the portfolio preferences of banks, private owners of financial assets, and borrowing units so that the supply of financing increases even as the demand price for investment increases raises the demand for finances. A rise in investment results. Once investment supply becomes less than perfectly elastic, a rise in the markup on labor costs in the production of investment goods takes place.

The allocation of part of profits to the wages of ancillary functions (research, development, sales, and marketing) leads to a greater rise in profits in consumer goods than would have occurred in the absence of such spending. Similarly, in an era in which capital-asset prices and stock market valuations of firms rise, profits in the production of consumer goods will increase because the appreciation of assets leads to a decline in the saving ratio of wage and profit incomes.

A rising markup on technologically determined labor costs because of demand financed by wages from ancillary functions lends an inflationary bias to a tranquilly expanding economy, such as that which ruled between 1952 and 1966. However, the increase in the ratio of nonproduction workers to total employment is a slow process: the rise from 19.2 percent to 25.8 percent in this ratio for durable-goods manufactures took fourteen years. Part of the inflationary pressure in 1952–66 can thus be imputed to the changing composition of wage incomes, but the annual shift was small enough that the increased productivity of the technologically required labor was able to largely offset the inflationary thrust.

In the years of financial turbulence between 1966 and 1976 the percentage of nonproduction workers rose to 28.7 percent in durable-goods production and to 27.4 percent in nondurable-goods production. Thus, there was a significant slowdown in the shift toward overhead and ancillary labor. However, expenditures on such labor are not readily adjusted to changes in production. The increased instability of private output and employment in the 1970s increased the variability of the ratio of fixed to variable labor costs. The increased downward instability of total employment meant that the markup on the technologically determined part of labor costs needed to increase in order to protect firms against the consequences of anticipated cyclical declines in output. Such "perverse" price increases can occur only if the selling organizations have some unused market power.

The increase in the ratio of nonproduction to production workers has increased instability because it raises the cash payments that are not linked to output by technology. The structure of employment that ruled in 1976, for example, makes business much more dependent upon the continued maintenance of income and employment than that which ruled in 1952. Our economy is now hooked on Big Government to sustain cash flows, but government's built-in response to recessions means that inflationary processes are maintained during business-cycle contractions.

The course of money wages in the different segments of the economy depends upon what can be financed by product prices, taxes, and debts. The various wages did not move in the same proportion either in the period of relative tranquility prior to 1966 or the more turbulent years that followed.

The era of relative tranquility, 1952–66, was characterized by comparatively small increases in money wages and large increases in price-level-deflated wages. In 1952–66 average spendable weekly earnings (a concept of income that allows for the tax take from the pay packet) for the private economy rose at an annual rate of 3.05 percent, whereas in the 1966–76 period average spendable weekly earnings rose by 4.57 percent per year. Once the money incomes are adjusted for price changes, however, the rate of increase of spendable weekly earnings was 1.61 percent per year in 1952–66 and 0.06 percent per year in 1966–76. Over the fourteen years from 1952–66, the representative workers' command over goods and services increased by 25.1 percent, whereas in the period from 1966 to 1976 the American economy did not deliver any significant improvement to workers.

Among the private industries, the highest rate of increase of spendable earnings in 1952–66 was for contract construction; in contract construction,

Table 11.2:   Spendable Weekly Earnings, Average Weekly Earnings, and Weekly Compensation (Current Dollars)

	Rates of Growth per Year		
Item	1952–66	1966–76	1952–76
Average Spendable Weekly Earnings			
Total Private	3.05	5.68	4.15
Mining	3.35	7.08	4.91
Contract Construction	3.47	6.28	4.80
Manufacturing	3.26	5.96	4.38
Wholesale and Retail Trade	2.90	5.43	3.96
Finance and Insurance	2.96	5.45	3.99
Average Weekly Earnings			
Durable and Manufacturing	3.71	6.12	4.72
Machinery	3.80	5.59	4.54
Nondurable Manufacturing	3.54	6.24	4.67
Apparel	2.56	5.68	3.87
Wholesale Trade	3.70	5.93	4.67
Retail Trade	3.27	5.07	4.07
Weekly Compensation in Current Dollars			
Federal Government	4.74	7.62	5.94
State and Local Government	4.33	7.06	5.46

SOURCE: *Employment and Training Report of the President*, 1982, U.S. Government Printing Office, Washington, D.C., 1982.

Table 11.3: Spendable Weekly Earnings, Average Weekly Earnings, and Weekly Compensation (1967 Dollars)

Item	Rates of Growth per Year		
	1952–66	1966–76	1952–76
Average Spendable Weekly Earnings			
Total Private	1.61	0.06	0.97
Mining	1.91	1.46	1.73
Contract Construction	2.30	0.66	1.62
Manufacturing	1.83	0.34	1.21
Wholesale and Retail Trade	1.46	−0.18	0.78
Finance and Insurance	1.52	−0.17	0.82
Average Weekly Earnings			
Durable Manufacturing	1.97	0.51	1.54
Machinery	2.36	−0.028	1.37
Nondurable Manufacturing	2.11	0.63	1.49
Apparel	1.14	0.059	0.69
Wholesale Trade	2.33	0.31	1.49
Retail Trade	1.83	−0.54	0.85
Average Weekly Compensation			
Federal Government	3.15	2.00	2.67
State and Local Government	2.89	1.44	2.29

SOURCE: *Employment and Training Report of the President,* 1982, U.S. Government Printing Office, Washington, D.C., 1982.

price-deflated spendable weekly earnings increased at 2.30 percent per year. Since contract construction is an investment output and during 1952–66 financing for investment was readily available, there was a strong demand for construction labor.

In the 1966–76 period, among the private components only mining showed a significant increase in price-deflated weekly earnings. From 1966 to 1976 wholesale and retail trade showed a decline in price-deflated earnings per week. The period of financial turbulence and inflation has seen an end to the steady, across-the-board improvements in earnings that characterized the tranquil period.

During 1952–66 average weekly earnings in contract construction increased at a significantly faster rate than in consumer goods such as apparel. Unless labor productivity was increasing more rapidly in contract construction than in other industries, the differential wage movements meant that the price level of investment output was rising relative to the price level of consumer outputs. The differential rates of growth of wages, and therefore presumably prices, when compounded over a fourteen-year period implied a significant change in price ratios (3.47 percent per year for investment goods translates to 1.61, whereas 2.56 percent per year for consumption goods translates to 1.42); if productivity increases in investment-goods production and consumption-goods production were the same, then the price of investment goods rose some 13.50 percent relative to the price of consumption goods. This means that the flow of profits per unit of consumption output has to increase if the cost of investment output is to be validated.

Since 1966, average spendable earnings in contract construction have continued to increase at a rapid rate in nominal terms (6.26 percent per year); this translates, however, into a 0.66 percent rate of increase in price-deflated incomes. This rapid rate of rise in contract construction incomes has continued the increase in the price of capital assets relative to that of other outputs. In the era when financial instability has become an apparent characteristic of the economy, this relative rate of increase has been associated with episodes of severe decline in construction activity.

It is difficult to get data on the per capita compensation of government employees—whether they be state and local or federal. Using the national income accounts data on compensation of civilian employees and the *President's Employment and Training Report* data on government employment, annual and weekly compensation per employee can be derived. Also, with the aid of the CPI, these data can be transformed into price-level-deflated values, making it possible to derive price-adjusted growth rates of compensation per employee.

Over the twenty-four years from 1952 to 1976, the average weekly compensation of a civilian employee of the federal government increased by an annual rate of 5.94 percent, broken down into a 4.74 percent per year increase in the 1952–66 period and a 7.62 percent increase from 1966–76. When deflated by the CPI, compensation per federal government employee grew at a 3.30 percent rate in 1952–66, a 2.00 percent annual rate in 1966–76, and a 2.67 percent annual rate over the entire period.

In 1952–66 the rate of increase of price-level-deflated spendable weekly earnings of a worker in the private economy was 1.61 percent per year, half as large as the rate of increase of a federal employee. In the 1966–76 period the compensation of a federal civilian employee, after allowing for price level changes, increased at 2 percent per year; comparable spendable weekly earnings in the private economy for a worker with

Table 11.4:   Compensation of Federal Employees, 1952, 1966, and 1976

	1952	1966	1976
		(Billions of Dollars)	
Compensation of Employees			
Civilian-National Defense*	4951.00	8928.00	17562.00
Other Civilian	3163.00	7847.00	20750.00
Total Civilian Compensation	8154.00	16775.00	38312.00
Number of Civilian Employees†	2420.00	2564.00	2733.00
Annual Compensation/Employee	3369.00	65425.00	14018.30
Weekly Compensation/Employee	64.79	125.82	269.58
Weekly Compensation in 1967 $	83.28	129.44	158.11
		Growth Rate (% per Year)	
	1952–66	1966–76	1952–76
Total Compensation	5.15	8.26	6.47
Weekly Compensation/Employee	4.74	7.62	5.94
Weekly Compensation in 1967 $			
per employee	3.15	2.00	2.67

*Table 32, Federal Government Receipts and Expenditures, National Income Accounts.
†Table L1, Total Employment on Payrolls of Non-Agricultural Establishments, *Employment and Training Report of the President.*

three dependents increased at a 0.06 percent per year rate. Thus, the price-deflated earnings of a federal government employee increased more than thirty times faster than that of a worker in private employment. A similar, though a trifle more moderate, story is told of state and local compensation.

Throughout this period the rate of growth of compensation of federal, state, and local government employees has been substantially greater than that of spendable weekly earnings of workers in private employment. However, in the first age of tranquility the spendable weekly earnings of workers in private employment rose at a respectable 1.6 percent per year, whereas in the second age of turbulence the spendable weekly earnings in private employment virtually ceased to increase.

In a sense, government has put a triple whammy on the spendable, price level-deflated earnings of workers in private industry. Government compensation has increased faster than earnings in private business; transfer payments have increased relative to wages; and taxes, which need to rise as government spending increases, have tended to reduce workers' disposable real incomes. Whether because of taxes—such as rising Social Security levies—or inflation, the improvement in recent years in the lot of the poor, of the civil servant, and of the recipient of profits has been at the expense of the near poor, as the price-deflated take-home pay of hourly rated employees decreased.

TRADE UNIONS AND INFLATIONS

Excessive wage settlements in trade union contracts are often considered to be responsible for inflation. However, as inflations have occurred in economies with no effective trade unions and price stability has ruled in economies with comprehensive trade unions, the mere existence of strong trade unions does not necessarily imply that inflation will occur. Policies to constrain inflation have often taken the form of guidelines for trade union wage settlements. The pressure has taken the form of talk, wage and price controls, or an imprecise incomes policy.

For money wage settlements to lead to inflation, the employment of labor at higher money wages must be financed: money wage settlements lead to changes in the required financing. Whether the money wages can, in fact, be paid depends upon how funds to pay the wages are obtained.

Because money wages finance consumption spending, demand will rise with money wages if employment does not fall. Higher money wages raise both the supply and the demand curves for consumer goods. Since the demand for consumer goods is mainly financed by the wages from consumption, investment, and government employment, in order for the rise in money wages not to be accompanied by a fall in employment, the dollar value of wages from financed investment and financed government spending must increase. Wages in other than consumption-goods production need to rise if revenues from consumption-goods production are both to validate the higher wages and yield profits that support a higher supply price of investment.

If a rise in financed investment and government spending takes place when a close approximation of full employment rules, then a rise in profits in both investment and consumption production will occur. This will raise the employment that firms are willing to offer and will lead to a rise in money wages.

For inflation to persist, the dollar amounts of investment and government spending that are financed must increase. Such increased dollar amounts of financed investment and government spending are a necessary condition for the persistence of inflation, as is a high and rising demand for labor that leads to higher money wages. If increased financing of investment and government activity do not validate a rise in money wages, then inflation will be broken; workers will receive a lower consumption standard, and profits will not rise to validate asset prices.

For union settlements to lead to inflation, financed investment and government spending must increase. If government wages are indexed to private wages, if government purchase contracts are predominantly cost plus, and if transfer payments are indexed to the cost of living, then a rise in money wages will lead to a rise in government spending. As the federal government has not as yet had any difficulty in debt-financing its expenditures, an institutional arrangement that transforms money wage increases in private employment into inflation by way of induced increases in government spending is built into our economy.

The weak link in the financing of expenditures to validate negotiated money wage increases is investment: there is no built-in guarantee that financed investment will increase along with money wage increases. However, if the money value of financed investment lags behind the rise in money wages, the result will be unemployment, which in our economy now leads to a rise in government spending and a fall in its revenues. In such an economy a financed government deficit increases to offset all or part of the impact that the shortfall in financed investment has upon profits.

Trade unions seem to succeed in achieving significant increases in money wages when investment, government spending on goods and services, and transfer payments are increasing rapidly, thus raising the markup on unit labor costs. Trade unions are apparently successful in resisting declines in the purchasing power of money wages when the incomes available for spending on consumer goods from other than their production increases. What trade unions seem to do well is to *protect* their members from the effects of those policies and attributes of the system, such as increased investment and transfer payments, which tend to cut workers' price-deflated incomes. Consequently, the ability of investors and government to finance their activities determines how far an inflationary process will go.

As has been indicated, the turbulent years that have followed 1966 have seen a sharp rise in government spending. Transfer payments, compensation for federal employees, and the expenditures of state governments have increased more rapidly than GNP. But these rapidly growing portions of the economy do not directly finance higher wages in consumption goods production: they finance higher markups in the production of consumer goods. Similarly, the higher ratio of nonproduction workers in the total labor force does not directly affect the technologically determined costs; it affects the gross markup. The easy imputation from a change in money wages to prices will just not do: the changing markup is a critical part of the process.

Trade unions have not been successful in exploiting inflation to raise the price-deflated spendable income of production workers. It is clear that the classes of workers in private employment who are typically represented by unions did much better in terms of the rate of growth of their price-deflated spendable income in the era that saw money wages increase at a relatively moderate rate than in the turbulent inflationary era since 1966.

When organized workers have an opportunity to exploit some rapidly rising demand curve, large wage increases, which clearly depend upon the prior existence of rising demand, occur. An investment boom will lead to a rise in wages in construction, and a collapse of an investment boom will see an increase in the proportion of nonunion labor in construction. Medicare, Medicaid, and third-party (Blue Cross and Blue Shield) payment schemes have more to do with the rising cost of medical care than the trade union organization of hospitals, nursing homes, and doctors' offices. Over-the-road teamster wages rose rapidly when the interstate highway system dramatically increased the efficiency of trucking.

Although trade union wage bargains can exacerbate an inflationary thrust, the basic inflationary push comes from the excessive demands placed upon the economy from spending that is not derived from income earned in the production of consumer goods. Such an inflationary thrust would be blunted if workers in consumption-goods production passively accepted a reduction of their real wages when investment-goods workers, government employees, recipients of transfer payments, and profit earners who consume bid for increased shares of consumer goods.

The rate of increase of price-level-adjusted consumption expenditures per capita was 2.06 percent per year in 1952–66 and 2.47 percent per year in 1966–76. However, the rate of increase of average spendable weekly earnings in private employment of a standard production worker family was 1.61 percent per year in 1952–66 and 0.06 percent in 1966–76. Production workers' ability to buy consumption goods lagged behind that of the general population, especially in the 1966–76 period.

In 1952–66, when consumption spending grew at 2.06 percent per year, the spendable income of contract construction workers grew faster and mine workers grew about as fast (1.91 percent per year) as consumption spending. However, compensation for federal, state, and local government employment grew substantially more rapidly than the overall growth in consumption per capita.

In the 1966–76 period the only privately employed group of those listed whose spendable earnings increased more than price-deflated per capita consumption (2.47 percent) was mine workers; although the compensation of federal, state, and local government employees rose considerably, even their wages fell behind the rate of increase of overall consumption.

Since consumption per capita increased at an accelerated rate in 1966–76 even though the purchasing power of workers' income lagged far behind, consumption financed by other than price-adjusted wage incomes must have risen rapidly. Consumption financed by additions to the labor force as the large increase in labor force participation by women took place and by transfer payments is part of the explanation; another part is the greater use of profit income to finance consumption.

Money wage increases negotiated in collective bargaining can be realized only if the increase is financed. If there is no accompanying rise in available financing, gains in money wages will be accompanied by a decrease in employment and in profits relative to prices. And such a decrease in profit margins will adversely affect investment decisions. Indeed, without accommodating inputs to the inflationary process, money wage increases set up processes that weaken the ability of trade unions to keep the existing money wage gains and to negotiate further wage increases.

Negotiated money wage increases, however, can initiate an inflationary process if the policy environment sets some target unemployment rate or some target investment output. In these circumstances monetary and fiscal policies will be used to finance expenditures or to offer inducements to invest in an effort to achieve the targets. Only in the complex sense that the government will take expansionary fiscal and monetary policy actions if the system moves away from employment and output targets can autonomous money wage increases cause inflation. In a world in which the government is committed to building some targeted number of homes or achieving some unemployment rate, increases in money wages will trigger the increased financing of government and investment spending. Only if monetary and fiscal policy is set so as to maintain target employment levels or output can an autonomous rise in money wages lead to inflation.

Any attempt to deal with inflation by constraining wage bargains without simultaneously constraining those demands that increase the markup on unit labor costs can enjoy, at best, a transitory success. Inflation mainly results from feedbacks from the demands for various types of output that are placed upon the economy to demand for consumer goods rather than from the money wage policies of trade unions.

BIG GOVERNMENT AS A BLESSING AND AS A CURSE

Big Government is largely responsible for preventing the fragile and unstable financial system that has ruled since the mid-1960s from breaking down in a full-fledged financial crisis, debt deflation, and deep depression. Even so, the financial traumas since 1966 are associated with pauses and recessions of increasing severity. Bad as the recessions of 1974–75 and 1981–82 were, the fact that a big depression did not occur is a good thing. Thus, Big Government is a blessing when it prevents debt deflations and deep depressions.

Our combined government, state, local, and federal, as an employer and as a dispenser of transfer payments, is not only big, but has grown rapidly. Not only has the proportion of the labor force on government payrolls increased, but the compensation of government workers has risen faster than other employees. In addition, transfer-payment schemes have proliferated and have been effectively indexed. The reactions to the slowdown in 1966 and the recessions of 1970 and 1974–75 increased the size of government. (The defense expansion of 1981–82 increased government in more recent years.) When Big Government increases faster than the output of the economy inflation is induced; inflation induces inefficiency in investment decisions and is a cruel tax. Thus, Big Government is a curse when it leads to inflation.

The U.S. economy has avoided a deep depression since the mid-1930s because of the way Big Government sustains demand, sustains profits, and feeds secure assets into portfolios whenever income and employment fall. However, the very process by which Big Government prevents deep depressions leads to inflation, and feeding government liabilities into portfolios as the deficit is financed during recessions means that an ability to finance investment during a subsequent expansion is being stockpiled.

Financial instability is a deep-seated characteristic of a capitalist economy with a sophisticated financial system. But this does not mean that all capitalisms are equally unstable. A wide variety of capitalist economies has existed, and our fancies can construct an infinite number of possible capitalist economies.

If we are to do better, we have to attenuate if not eliminate the economy's thrust toward instability. This implies that the institutional framework within which our system functions and the policy operations have to be changed. There is no magic bullet: doing better will involve serious reforms that are best undertaken with an appreciation that *any* economy with private ownership of capital assets, private investment, and a complex financial system will be unstable. Indeed, one aspect of instability—inflation—results from the very steps taken to evade instability in the form of deep depression.

THE ABATEMENT OF INFLATION

Inflation of consumer prices occurs when wages in the production of consumer goods rise faster than the average productivity of labor in producing consumer goods, or when the components of the markup increase relative to the wage bill in consumer goods. Inflation will abate when money wage increases are moderated and when the components of the markup stop their relative rise.

The history of money wages demonstrates the efficacy of the inflation barrier, which constrains workers to accept lower real wages when the decline is mainly due to increases in the markup or declines in the average efficiency of labor. The inflation barrier is high when trade unions are weak and when unemployment is high: the higher recent unemployment, the higher the inflation barrier. In addition, high unemployment weakens trade union power. High unemployment thus has a compound effect on inflation—both directly and by way of its impact on union power.

The deficit on current trade and service account enters into the determination of the markup with a minus sign. One way to break an inflation is to flood the economy with consumer goods, and one way to accomplish this is to run a significant deficit on the international trade account.

Unemployment was very high in late 1982, federal government programs that financed increasing state and local expenditures were stabilized or diminished, while imports flooded the country in 1983 and 1984. In spite of a massive government deficit, the rate of inflation diminished. The Reagan "success" in easing inflation despite the enormous deficit and easing of the money supply was the result of breaking the wage reaction to the remaining inflation and running a large deficit on the international trade account.

The success of the Reagan program on the inflation front is not an anomaly from the perspective of our model of inflation.

POLICY

INTRODUCTION TO
POLICY

*If to do were as easy as to know what were good to do, chapels had
been churches, and poor men's cottages princes' palaces.*

— The Merchant of Venice

Shakespeare's Portia eloquently sums up the problem of economic policy: it is easy to list objectives, but much more difficult to deliver—to establish institutions and to start processes that will achieve those objectives. Few will argue that full employment, stable prices, and the elimination of poverty are desirable; the difficulty is finding a way to attain these and other equally admirable goals. The time when promises without effective programs will do is past: We must go beyond "what" to "how."

Even as I warn against the handwaving that passes for much of policy prescription I must warn the reader that I feel much more comfortable with my diagnosis of what ails our economy and analysis of the causes of our discontents than I do with the remedies I propose. We need to embark on a program of serious change even as we need to be aware that a once-and-for-all resolution of the flaws in capitalism cannot be achieved. Even if a program of reform is successful, the success will be transitory. Innovations, particularly in finance, assure that problems of instability will continue to crop up; the result will be equivalent but not identical bouts of instability to those that are so evident in history.

Political leaders and the economists who advise them are to blame for promising more than they or the economy can deliver. The established advisers have failed to make the political leadership and the public aware of the limitations that economic processes and the ability to administer impose

319

on what policy can achieve. Economists as advisers have failed to teach legislators and administrators that although government may propose, it is the economy that disposes. To be exact, our economic leadership does not seem to be aware that the *normal* functioning of our economy leads to financial trauma and crises, inflation, currency depreciations, unemployment, and poverty in the midst of what could be virtually universal affluence—in short, that financially complex capitalism is inherently flawed.

Economic advisers, whether liberal or conservative, believe in the fundamental "soundness" of the economy. Finding fault with one thing or another, they may advocate policies such as changing Federal Reserve operating techniques, tax reforms, national health insurance, and wars on poverty, but all in all they are satisfied with the basic institutions of modern capitalism. According to today's gospel what faults there are due to secondary, not to fundamental, characteristics.

That being the case, the economists of the policy-advising establishment differ about details: some propose to fine-tune the economy by fiscal tinkering, others want to achieve a noninflationary natural rate of employment through steady monetary growth. Neither, however, sees anything basically wrong with capitalism as such. The credit crunch of 1966, the liquidity squeeze of 1970, the banking crises of 1974–75, the inflationary spiral of 1979–80 and the distress, national and international, of 1981–82 are, in their view, aberrations, due to either "shocks" or "errors." Since nothing is basically wrong, they also hold that incisive corrective measures are not needed.

The truth of the matter is that something is fundamentally wrong with our economy. As we have shown, a capitalist economy is inherently flawed because its investment and financing processes introduce endogenous destabilizing forces. The markets of a capitalist economy are not well suited to accommodate specialized, long-lived, expensive capital assets. In fact, the underlying economic theory of the policy establishment does not allow for capital assets and financial relations such as exist. The activities of Wall Street and the inputs of bankers to production and investment are not integrated into, but are added onto, the basic allocation-oriented theory.

Economic policy discussions in recent years have centered on how much more (or less) of the one—fiscal policy—and how much less (or more) of the other—monetary policy—is necessary for economic stability and growth. If we are to do better in the future, we must launch a serious debate that looks beyond the level and the techniques of fiscal and monetary policy. Such a debate will acknowledge the instability of our economy and inquire whether this inherent instability is amplified or attenuated by our system of institutions and policy interventions.

As a first step, an agenda for public discussion must be prepared. The agenda is important because it establishes which alternatives are discussed and because the way in which the alternatives are presented is likely to influence decisions. In an address at the University of Essex in 1966 James Tobin, Nobel laureate in economics, aptly described the role of the adviser as censoring evidence and phrasing questions for his prince's attention. He pointed out that "the terms in which a problem is stated and in which the relevant information is organized can have a great influence on the solution."[1] Thus, simple-minded phrases are uttered by the powers that be about a trade-off between unemployment and inflation rates, without any awareness that the trade-off under discussion only existed for a brief period after World War II and that there is little, if any, evidence to support the idea that it still exists. Yet because this trade-off is built into the economic theory and the econometric models of the policy-advising establishment, the problems of policy are phrased in its terms. These models do not ask whether the trade-off reflects the character of the output produced by the increased employment: no distinction is drawn between a lower rate of unemployment achieved through the production of more consumer goods, which is deflationary, or through government transfer payments, defense spending or the production of more investment goods, which are inflationary.

To be precise, the most important concern in court politics is access to the mind of the prince. And if economics is too important to be left to the economists, it is certainly too important to be left to economist-courtiers. Economic issues must become a serious public matter and the subject of debate if new directions are to be undertaken. Meaningful reforms cannot be put over by an advisory and administrative elite that is itself the architect of the existing situation. Unless the public understands the reason for change they will not accept its cost; understanding is the foundation of legitimacy for reform.

THE IMPORTANCE OF THE AGENDA

Tobin's definition of the role of the house intellectual may be described as controlling the agenda. Princes and public alike depend on intellectuals to

---

1. James Tobin, "The Intellectual Revolution in United States Policy-Making," Noel Burton Lecture, University of Essex, 1966, p. 14.

formulate issues and define alternatives. In a democracy, the definition of the issues and even the order in which they are presented for consideration affects the outcome. For example, the thrust of the reforms of the budget process by Congress in the 1970s is an attempt to make the final budget the result of an overview of individual decisions rather than a ratification of an accidental sequence. Existing legislation—ranging from the agricultural programs through the various transfer-payment schemes to import quotas—is not the result of a design that reflects a consistent view of the economy but, rather, is a hodgepodge that reflects responses of the Congress, various administrations, and the public to problems as they were identified. Consequently, the existing economic structure is the result of sequential decisions that did not consider interactions among the programs and the institutions.

Today's economic crisis is as profound, though not as overtly critical, as that of the 1930s. The instability, inflation, and chronically high unemployment of the years since 1965 are not satisfactory, and the policy prescriptions that may have served well enough in the earlier postwar years can no longer achieve the desired results. Moreover, there is no consensus on what we ought to do. Conservatives call for the freeing of markets even as their corporate clients lobby for legislation that would institutionalize and legitimize their market power; businessmen and bankers recoil in horror at the prospect of easing entry into their various domains even as technological changes and institutional evolution make the traditional demarcations of types of business obsolete. In truth, corporate America pays lip service to free enterprise and extols the tenets of Adam Smith, while striving to sustain and legitimize the very thing that Smith abhorred—state-mandated market power.

Liberals, instead of articulating an incisive critique of our capitalism as such and pioneering innovative experimentation and change, are wedded to the past. They support minimum-wage increases without questioning whether these laws have served any real purpose since the Great Depression, when reflation was the policy objective. Liberals are unwilling to face up to the shortcomings of policies inherited from the past and are, fundamentally, timid about setting forth in new directions.

As a consequence, instead of analysis and ideas, we get slogans: free markets, economic growth, national planning, supply-side, industrial policy—imprecise phrases that face up to neither the what nor the how of policy objectives. The various programs for change are based on misconceptions of both the strengths and the weaknesses of market processes. One of the reasons for the intellectual poverty of policy proposals is that they continue to be based upon ideas drawn from neoclassical theory. Although economic theory is relevant to policy (without an understanding of how our economy works we cannot find cures), for an economic theory to be relevant what happens in the world must be a possible event in the theory. On that score alone, standard economic theory is a failure; the instability so evident in our system cannot happen if the core of standard theory is to be believed.

Today's economic policy is a patchwork. Every change designed to correct some shortcoming has side effects that adversely affect some other aspect of economic and social life. Every ad hoc intervention breeds further intervention. If we wish to improve upon what we now have, we must embark upon an age of institutional and structural reforms that will check the tendencies toward instability and inflation. Standard theory, however, offers us no guidance on that score; for the problems are outside the domain of relevance of the theory. A new era of reform cannot be simply a series of piecemeal changes. Rather, a thorough, integrated approach to our economic problems must be developed; policy must range over the entire economic landscape and fit the pieces together in a consistent, workable way: Piecemeal approaches and patchwork changes will only make a bad situation worse.

Poverty in the midst of plenty and joyless affluence are but symptoms of a profound disorder.[2] As we have pointed out, persistent financial and economic instability is normal in our capitalist economy. The commitment to growth through private investment—combined with government transfer payments and exploding defense spending—amplifies financial instability and chronic inflation. Indeed, our problems are in part the result of how we have chosen, inadvertently and in ignorance of the consequences, to run the economy. An alternative policy strategy is needed now. We have to go back to square one—1933—and build a structure of policy that is based upon a modem understanding of how our type of economy generates financial fragility, unemployment, and inflation.

THE APPROACH TO BE ADOPTED

The three policy slogans—the conservatives' call for free markets, the liberals' commitment to economic growth, and the pseudo-radicals' call for national planning and industrial policy—all have one thing in common: the

---

2. Tibor Scitovsky, *The Joyless Economy* (New York: Oxford University Press, 1976).

economic analysis that underlies their approach to policy is pre-Keynesian. Just as there never really was a Keynesian revolution in economic theory, there also never really was one in policy. Aside from Alvin Hansen's depression prescription, no one has actually thought through (much less implemented) the policy implications of Keynes. All that was assimilated from Keynes by the policy establishment and its clients was the analysis of an economy in deep depression and a policy tool of deficit financing. His deep critique of capitalism and his serious attempt to reformulate economic thought so that it could better deal with investment and financial relations were lost. Keynesian economics, even in the mind of the economics profession, but particularly in the view of politicians and the public, became a series of simple-minded guidelines to monetary and fiscal policy. What we need now is a policy strategy based upon an economic theory that recognizes that our economy is capitalist, has a sophisticated financial structure, and as a result is unstable because of processes internal to such an economy. In effect, we must base policy upon a theory that builds upon what was lost from Keynes's contribution as it was transformed into a part of orthodox theory.

The major points derived from the theoretical perspective that builds on Keynes are:

1. Whereas the market mechanism is an effective control device for a myriad of unimportant decisions, it fails important equity, efficiency, and stability tests.

2. A sophisticated, complex, and dynamic financial system such as ours endogenously generates serious destabilizing forces so that serious depressions are natural consequences of noninterventionist capitalism: finance cannot be left to free markets.

3. The decentralized market mechanism is particularly unstable and inefficient for an economy in which capital investment constitutes a significant portion of private national product, and investment goods are expensive to produce.

4. Under a capitalist form of organization, financial resources will not be risked on large-scale, long-lived capital assets without protection against market forces. As a result, legislated and institutionally legitimized monopolies and oligopolies are necessary if such industries are to be private. Capital-intensive monopolies and

oligopolies are best interpreted as special forms of tax farmers. Public control, if not out-and-out public ownership, of large-scale capital-intensive production units is essential.

5. Big Government capitalism is more stable than small government capitalism: this is shown by both the experience of the past century and by an economic theory that allows for financial institutions. This greater stability is because of the impact of government deficits as a contracyclical phenomenon in stabilizing profits. However, if Big Government is not to be conducive to inflation, the budget structure must be such that profits are constrained by surpluses when inflation rules.

6. Because the budget structure of Big Government must have the built-in capacity to generate surpluses when inflation appears, the tax revenues have to be a large proportion of GNP. Thus, the design of the tax system is vital, as taxes introduce allocational inefficiencies as well as inducing behavior designed to avoid or evade taxes.

In addition to these perspectives born of theory, a number of historical facts, institutional attributes, and policy thrusts must be integrated into any new foundation for economic policy.

1. The ideas underlying the institutional structure of our economy are pre-Keynesian. The institutional structure is largely the product of the Roosevelt era and reflects a bias—born of the Depression—favoring investment and capital intensity and against labor-force participation and deflation. Once Big Government succeeds in eliminating the threat of deep and prolonged depressions, however, this Rooseveltian institutional structure lends an inflationary bias to the economy.

2. The emphasis on investment and "economic growth" rather than on employment as a policy objective is a mistake. A full-employment economy is bound to expand, whereas an economy that aims at accelerating growth through devices that induce capital-intensive private investment not only may not grow, but may be increasingly inequitable in its income distribution, inefficient in its choices of techniques, and unstable in its overall performance.

3. It is difficult to decide whether the emphasis on capital-intensive production should be seen as a failure of theory or of policy. Certainly there is an unwarranted emphasis on investment as the source of all good things: employment, income, growth, price stability. But in truth, inept and inappropriate investment and investment financing deters full employment, consumption, economic growth, and price stability.

4. A too extensive and expensive system of transfer payments is socially destabilizing, tends to reduce real national income, and introduces an inflationary bias into the economy.

5. Our economy is characterized by the pervasive validation of private decisions by the public sector, even if such validation is detrimental to efficiency and equity. This reflects a natural fear of uncertainty. The lesson of Keynesian economics is that the overall cyclical uncertainty can be constrained by apt interventions, and a system of apt aggregate interventions makes it unnecessary and undesirable to intervene in the details.

6. Policy must always recognize that there are limitations to what can be administered competently. This limited competence to administer biases policy toward mechanisms that require the minimum of administration; in particular, mechanisms that use and rig markets are to be preferred to regulations and controls that affect the details of the economy.

It should be stressed that a program for full employment, price stability, and greater equity is not a simple one-shot affair. There is no magic economic bullet; no single program or particular reform will set things right forever. Standing by themselves, unaccompanied by the requisite companion measures, the individual parts of an integrated reform program might be futile. Any program that will make things better is bound to have a price; some units might be worse off, and there will be adjustment costs. But some units are already worse off, and there are adjustment costs from continuing on the present course. However, a program of reform that builds an economy oriented toward employment rather than toward growth should show benefits quickly. The primary aim is a humane economy as a first step toward a humane society.

CHAPTER 13

AN AGENDA FOR

REFORM

For a program of reform to be more than a reflection of prejudices it has to be based on a critique of the current system that identifies what is wrong and explains why what is wrong happens. Our identification of what is wrong is straightforward. Since the mid-1960s, the economy has been characterized by turbulence in the form of financial instability, inflation, and rising unemployment, along with a sharp slowdown in the pace at which living standards improve. This turbulence stands in sharp contrast to the tranquility and progress that ruled in the prior twenty years.

The conclusion of the analytical argument is that turbulence—especially financial instability—is normal in a capitalist economy; the tranquil era between 1946 and 1966 was an anomaly. Furthermore, the inherent instability of capitalism is due to the way profits depend upon investment, the validation of business debts depends upon profits, and investment depends upon the availability of external financing. But the availability of financing presupposes that prior debts and the prices that were paid for capital assets are being validated by profits. Capitalism is unstable because it is a financial and accumulating system with yesterdays, todays, and tomorrows.

The Reagan administration's economic program is based upon the belief that Big Government is the cause of inefficiency and inflation and that a simplistic pure price theory, which ignores the financing relations that are essential elements in the capitalist accumulation process, adequately represents the economy's behavior. But the existing institutional structure of product, labor, and financial markets, which were largely put in place during the first years of the Roosevelt administration, are not truly appropriate for a Big Government capitalism. These Roosevelt reforms preceded the appearance of Keynes's *General Theory* and reflect a price-level deflation due to cut-throat-competition theory of great depressions, rather than an explanation based upon Keynes's theory of aggregate demand or Kalecki's theory of profit determination: The Rooseveltian structure of reforms was pre-Keynesian.

The institutional evolution and legislative changes since the New Deal, including the input of the Reagan administration, have not changed the essential character of the institutional structure that was put in place in Franklin Roosevelt's first term. Because of the essential continuity of our economic structure since the 1930s, there never has been a Keynesian revolution in economic policy. The institutional structure has not been adapted to reflect the knowledge that the collapse of aggregate demand and profits, such as occasionally occurred and often threatened to occur in pre-1933 small government capitalism, is never a clear and present danger in a Big Government capitalism such as has ruled since World War II. Since 1967, the monetary and fiscal policy measures undertaken to sustain aggregate demand and profits have succeeded in substituting a stepwise accelerating, though cyclical, inflation and a cyclical trend of rising unemployment rates for a deep depression. The policy problem is to devise institutional structures and measures that attenuate the thrust to inflation, unemployment, and slower improvements in the standard of life without increasing the likelihood of a deep depression.

After World War II and until the mid-1960s, demand management conforming to rules derived from the standard Hicks-Hansen interpretation of Keynes was successful. The best that can be said about recent years is that demand management and lender-of-last-resort interventions have staved off a deep depression.

By the standard of not having a big depression, the performance of the American economy in the years since 1967 is superior to the performance over the epoch leading up to World War II, even though in terms of stability, unemployment, growth, and distribution of benefits, the years since 1967 are inferior to the 1946–66 epoch. The first two decades after World War II, which might be a practical test for the economy, were characterized by robust finance, responsible fiscal postures and a big, but not an overreaching, government.

My agenda for an integrated program of reform will be examined under four headings: Big Government (size, spending, and taxing), an employment strategy, financial reform, and market power. The details of the programs are, of course, negotiable; the hard contention is that one-dimensional or gimmicky programs, which are usually associated with slogans such as supply side, money matters, or industrial policy, will not do.

The agenda is an outgrowth of a theoretical perspective that recognizes the inherent and inescapable flaws of capitalism. However, even though all capitalisms are flawed, we can develop a capitalism in which the flaws are less evident than they have been since 1967.

A program of reform needs to come to grips with the strengths and limitations of market mechanisms. Decentralized markets are fine social devices for taking care of the particular outputs and prices of an economy, but they are imperfect devices for assuring stability and guaranteeing efficiency where large expensive capital assets are used in production. But most important, capitalist market processes that determine the prices of capital assets and the flow of investment introduce strong destabilizing forces into the system. Once we achieve an institutional structure in which upward explosions from full employment are constrained even as profits are stabilized, then the details of the economy can be left to market processes.

Because of limitations of the capacity of government to administer, decentralized markets are a preferred mechanism for coordination and control. Because what happens in markets is determined by profit opportunities, easily administered tax and subsidy measures can well be part of the arsenal of policy measures.

The proposition that capitalism is inherently flawed because it breeds inequality, inefficiency, and instability takes us quite far in setting out an ideological background for policy. However, inequality and inefficiency, though serious, have never been a barrier against the continued functioning of an economy. Instability and with it what Orwell called "the haunting terror of unemployment"[1] is the damning weakness of capitalism. Once the technical problem of eliminating the "terror of unemployment" is solved, that economic program is best which minimizes inequality. This means a preference for a low-investment, high-consumption, full-employment economy with a favorable disposition toward organizations that are small, thus minimizing bureaucracy. (Minimizing the profits that are distributed as bureaucrats' salaries will tend to constrain instability.)

Efficiency is an elusive goal. Economists jump to the conclusion that a simple-minded competitive exchange economy is efficient. The economists' peculiar notion of income, in which the costs of treating an environmentally caused disease is income but the value of a prevented disease is not, is a trivial illustration of the illusiveness of the concept of efficiency.

---

1. Orwell, George, "Looking Back on the Spanish War," *Homage to Catelonia* (New York: Penguin), p. 244.

On a deeper level, Jean and Peter Gray have pointed out that there are different types of efficiencies and a system that promotes allocational efficiency may be stability inefficient.[2]

Long before national income was devised as a measure of economic performance, Thomas Love Peacock in *Crotchet Castle* had the Rev. Dr. Folliott remark, "the nation is best off, in relation to other nations, which has the greatest quantity of the common necessities of life distributed among the greatest number of persons; which has the greatest numbers of honest hearts and stout arms united in a common interest."

BIG GOVERNMENT

Big Government is the most important reason why today's capitalism is better than the capitalism which gave us the Great Depression. With Big Government, a move toward a deep depression is accompanied by a large government deficit that sustains or increases business profits. With profits sustained, output and employment are sustained or increased. If its tax and spending schemes are properly designed, Big Government can also be a barrier to inflation. However, the proposition that Big Government is necessary does not imply that government need be as big as our present government, or that today's structure of government spending, taxes, and regulation is either necessary or desirable. Each structure of government has systemic effects, and the disturbing inflations of the 1970s and 1980s were largely due to the particular Big Government we had and still have.

How Big Should Big Government Be?

Before new institutions that promote employment and are effective barriers to inflation can be defined, we need to determine how big Big Government needs to be. Big Government must be big enough to ensure that swings in private investment lead to sufficient offsetting swings in the government's deficit so that profits are stabilized. This means that government must be of the same order of magnitude as or larger than investment.

2. Gray, Jean M. and H. Peter, "The Multinational Bank: A Financial MNC?" *Journal of Banking and Finance* 5 (Amsterdam: North Holland Publishing Co., 1981), pp. 33–63.

Private investment fell by significantly more than one-third between 1929 and 1930. The largest one-year declines in the era of Big Government occurred between 1974 and 1975, when private investment fell by 10.0 percent, and between 1981 and 1982, when it fell by 14 percent. In both 1929 and 1930 the federal government ran a surplus of some $.90 billion (see Table 13.1). Thus, in 1930 the sum of private investment and the government deficit fell by $6.1 billion, or almost 40 percent of the $15.3 billion total of 1929. In 1974, the deficit was $11 billion and in 1975 it was $69 billion: this $58 billion increase in the deficit more than offset the $23 billion fall in private investment. In 1981 the federal government deficit was $64 billion and in 1982 it was $148 billion, an increase of $84 billion. This more than offset the $69 billion decrease in investment.

The difference between 1929–33 period and recent downturns is most striking in the behavior of corporate profits; in 1929 corporate profits were $10.1 billion; in 1930, $6.6 billion; and in 1933, –$1.7 billion. In 1974 corporate profits were $83.6 billion, but in 1975 they rose to $95.9 billion. Thus, in 1930 the impact of government was not able to sustain profits, whereas profits were actually increased in the 1974–75 recession. With profits sustained, the recession was quickly halted and reversed.

Table 13.2 shows the comparative size of gross private domestic investment and federal government outlays in various years. In 1929 federal government spending was 2.5 percent of GNP; in 1940, with the country arming for World War II, government spending was 10 percent of GNP. Since World War II, the ratio of federal government outlays to GNP has risen from about 14 percent in the early years to almost 25 percent in 1983. (It was 27 percent in the recession year 1981.)

It is clear that federal government outlays in the neighborhood of 2.5 percent of GNP are not capable of generating a deficit that can stabilize profits in an economy where full-employment investment is about 16 to

Table 13.1:   Private Investment and the Federal Deficit, 1929–30, 1933, 1974–75, and 1981–83

	1929	1930	1933	1974	1975	1981	1982	1983
Gross private investment	16.2	10.1	1.4	229	206	484	415	472
Government deficit	–.9	–.9	+1.3	+11	+69	+64	+148	179
Total	15.3	9.2	2.7	240	275	548	563	651

SOURCE: *Economic Report of the President*, February 1985, U.S. Government Printing Office, Washington, D.C., 1985, Tables B15 and B74.

Table 13.2: Gross Private Investment and Federal Government Outlays

Year	GNP	Gross Private Domestic I	Federal Government Outlays	Percent of GNP Private I	Percent of GNP Federal Government
1929	103.4	16.2	2.6	15.7	2.5
1933	55.8	1.4	4.0	2.5	7.2
1940	100.0	13.1	10.0	13.1	10.0
1950	286.2	53.8	40.8	18.8	14.3
1955	400.0	68.4	68.1	17.1	17.0
1960	506.5	75.9	93.1	15.0	18.4
1965	691.1	113.5	123.8	16.4	17.9
1970	992.7	144.2	204.2	14.5	20.6
1975	1549.2	206.1	356.6	13.3	23.0
1980	2631.7	401.9	602.1	15.7	22.9
1983	3304.8	471.6	819.7	14.3	24.8

SOURCE: *Economic Report of the President*, February 1985, U.S. Government Printing Office, Washington, D.C., 1985, Table B1.

17 percent of GNP. It also seems reasonable to infer that the expansion of government outlays, as presently structured, to above 20 percent of GNP and government deficits are responsible for at least part of the acceleration of inflation in the past decade.

In 1929, GNP was $103.4 billion and investment was $16.2 billion—15.7 percent of GNP. In 1933, GNP was $55.8 billion and investment was $1.4 billion—2.5 percent of GNP. If income and investment had both grown at 3 percent a year during that period, then GNP would have been $116.4 billion and investment $18.2 billion.

The 1929–33 experience indicates that the size of government must be large enough to offset the effect on profits of a drop of investment to about 10 percent of its full-employment level. This implies that government must be at least the same order of magnitude as investment. A government whose spending is at least 16 percent and perhaps as high as 20 percent of prosperity GNP is necessary to protect the economy against a catastrophic decline in investment and profits.

In 1983—a recovery year—GNP was $3.3 thousand billion and the unemployment rate over the year was 9.5 percent. If we take a historically achieved unemployment rate of 6 percent as our interim measure of full employment and use the conventional 3 percent increase in GNP for every one percent decline in the measured unemployment rate, we get a rough estimate of a full-employment GNP of *$3.6 thousand billion*. This means that a 16 percent government would be $576 billion, an 18 percent government would be $648 billion and a 20 percent government $720 billion. The 1983 government receipts were estimated as $643 billion and expenditures as $826.2; receipts in a recovery year were almost 18 percent and expenditures were 23 percent of the full-employment income. By the standard of having a government that can generate a deficit that stabilizes profits in an economy with investment that is 16 percent to 17 percent of GNP at full employment, the government expenditures may be too large.

However, with GNP below its full-employment level government expenditures should be above and receipts below their respective full-employment levels. The fiscal posture of 1983 generated a deficit that was $186 billion or about 5 percent of the full-employment income. Investment in 1983 was about $47 billion or 13.1 percent of the rough estimate of full-employment income. If we take 16–17 percent of GNP as the full-employment investment in a big government economy then the order of magnitude of the deficit is somewhat larger than what was needed to stabilize aggregate profits.

By the generous measure that government should be about 20 percent of GNP ($720 billion), in 1983 the tax system was not out of line. But the expenditure system was too big by almost $100 billion for a balanced budget if an approximation to full employment could be achieved.

The Scope of Government: What Should Big Government Do?

Given that the 1983 full-employment GNP was about 3.6 thousand billion and that the need for stabilization calls for a government that is 20 percent of this GNP—or a $720 billion government—it might appear that there are not enough serious programs to enable us to reach the necessary amount of government expenditures. Unfortunately, in a world of arms races and seemingly permanent brush wars, the military takes up so much of GNP that resource creation and humane and cultural uses of Big Government are severely restricted.

Although government is frequently disparaged as an inefficient bureaucratic maze serving the interests of officeholders and time-servers rather than of the public, in the not too distant past government was an effective—though often bureaucratic—provider of services to constituents.

Political and intellectual resources must be invested in the creation and maintenance of an effective government apparatus because Big Government is here to stay if we are to avoid great depressions.

Inherited programs took up some 22.4 percent of estimated full-employment GNP in 1983. In order to use Big Government effectively, we advocate an employment strategy that will take up some 1.25 percent of full-employment GNP and a children's allowance that will take up another 1.33 percent of GNP. This means that the inherited programs plus the employment strategy will take up something less than 25 percent of GNP. The children's allowance plus the employment programs should allow us to dispense with almost all of AFDC and a good deal of the unemployment insurance.

Since the taxation program should balance expenditures at the target unemployment rate, a tax program will have to be developed that would yield 20 percent of the same full-employment GNP. However, in a world with transfer payments, the base for taxable income could well include transfer-payment receipts. The children's allowance will disburse 1.33 percent of full employment GNP and the tax system may collect about as much as 25 percent of the disbursements.

The theoretical analysis emphasized the resource-creating aspects of the economic process. Even before *The General Theory*, Keynes among others was emphasizing the value of debt-financed public works to contain and offset unemployment. Inasmuch as public works typically left behind roads, schools, hospitals, and so on—what today is called the infrastructure—the earlier emphasis and the first interpretations of the *General Theory* led to an emphasis upon public employment that created mainly public capital assets. But in the postwar era the government was big because of transfer payments that aimed to provide "cradle to grave" security.

The overall policy perspective is to substitute resource-creating public spending for the multitude of transfer payments and entitlements that now make up a major part of nonmilitary spending (see Table 13.3). By maintaining Social Security and other programs at current levels, cutting interest payments substantially, and cutting the non–Old Age, Survivors, Disability, and Hospital Insurance (OASDHI) component of government, we can develop a program that is within 20 percent of the GNP guideline. If the people, Congress, and the administration want to add to the national defense program or the non-OASDHI component, then the full-employment tax receipts should be increased.

The major changes will be within non-Social Security spending. A children's allowance of 1.33 percent of GNP and a series of programs to

Table 13.3:   Budget Outlays as a Percent or Actual GNP and an Estimate of Full-employment GNP, Fiscal Year 1983

Item	% of Actual GNP	% of Full-employment GNP	
		Actual Budget	Target Budget
Total outlays	24.7	22.5	20.35
National defense	6.5	5.9	5.30
Net interest	2.8	2.5	1.75
Non-OASDHI*	8.4	7.6	7.00
Social Security	5.3	4.8	4.80
Medicare	1.6	1.5	1.50

*OASDHI = Old Age, Survivors, Disability and Health Insurance.
SOURCE: *Economic Report of the President*, February, 1984, U.S. Government Printing Office, Washington, D.C., 1984, Table 1.1, p. 29, plus computations.

assure that a minimal income from work is readily available, at an estimated cost of 1.17 percent of GNP, will be added to government. This will require a serious reconstruction of the non-Social Security, nonmilitary programs if the overall target of a government that is about 20 percent of GNP is to be achieved.

One objective of reconstructing the government transfer-payments system is to remove transfer payments as barriers to participation in the labor market, two of which are means-tested AFDC and the provisions in the Social Security laws that limit the income from work of Social Security recipients.

In 1983 there were 55 million children under 16 years of age in the United States; there were also 16 million aged 16–19. A children's allowance of $900 per year ($75 per month) per child that stops at the sixteenth birthday will cost $49.5 billion or approximately 1.33 percent of full-employment GNP. The youth employment and the conservation corps programs discussed below will provide the opportunity for income from work to youths over sixteen.

Income from the children's allowance as well as from the youth employment and conservation corps programs should become part of the family's taxable income base. Thus, both programs will be in part recaptured by adding to the tax base. A universal children's allowance will help to remove from poverty those who have jobs but are poor because of the size of their family.

The agenda must also address government spending on agriculture. Even in a full-employment economy farmers may well need protection against severe downside movement in the prices of their output. This protection, however, should not prevent a downward movement in the consumer prices of agriculture if, as was true over much of the past fifty years, productivity increases in agriculture remain greater than productivity increases in manufacturing.

The Significance of a Balanced Budget

An initial condition for any discussion of the budget is the outstanding government debt. At the end of fiscal 1983 the gross federal debt was $1,382 billion, but some $240 billion was held by public agencies and $155 billion was held by the Federal Reserve System. Thus, about $1,000 billion of debt was held by banks, insurance companies, foreign governments, and other "private" entities.

Debts embody payment commitments, promises to make payments. For these promises to have value any debtor *has to be able* to generate a positive cash flow in its favor. It achieves this by operating in the various markets where it buys and sells so as to achieve a cash flow net of operating costs that exceeds the commitments to pay on account of debt. "Has to be able" does not mean does. A unit may have negative cash flows for a considerable period and its liabilities would still be of value because it is accepted that the negative cash flows are transitory. The unit will have a positive cash flow in circumstances that it is reasonable to expect will occur. Thus, the United States could run a huge deficit in World War II and suffer no deterioration in the quality of its liabilities because the war was transitory, victory was anticipated, and the precedent was that in peacetime the outstanding United States government debt is reduced.

A government can run a deficit during a recession without suffering a deterioration of its creditworthiness if there is a tax and spending regime in place that would yield a favorable cash flow (a surplus) under reasonable and attainable circumstances.

There is nothing special about government debt, and a flight from government debt can occur. For a foreign-held debt such a flight will lead to a deterioration of the currency on the exchanges; for a domestic debt the flight can lead to inflation and a need to pay ever higher interest rates to have the debt held.

Incidently, if the central bank—the Federal Reserve—monetizes government debts in order to maintain its nominal price in the face of a deteriorating willingness to hold such debt, then there can be a run from the Federal Reserve as well as from commercial bank liabilities. Just as private business debts have to be validated by profits, as bank liabilities by receipts from assets, as a foreign debt by an export surplus, so government debt has to be validated by an excess of tax receipts over current expenditures. These validating cash flows need not be forthcoming at every moment of time; it is sufficient that reasonable circumstances exist in which a positive cash flow is generated.

Thus, for government debt to retain its acceptability, the tax and spending programs must be in surplus—not now but when the war ends or when the unemployment rate is 6 percent or whatever. Until the Reagan tax measures of 1981, the U.S. budget was always in potential if not in actual surplus.

The Reagan tax measures and arms program opened a structural deficit, which is expected to be a substantial fraction of GNP at least through fiscal 1989 (see Table 13.4). To portfolio managers and those involved in the position-making operations of banks, a projection that the deficit will be reduced to 3.6 percent of full-employment GNP in 1989 is a projection that a serious deficit will rule as far out into the future as one wants to contemplate. An implication of the Reagan budget policies is that there will either be a run from the dollar or a substantial debt repudiation through inflation. Either way, interest rates will rise to new highs as markets react and as the Federal Reserve either moves to protect the dollar or stop inflation.

Table 13.4: Expected Deficits as a Percentage of Expected GMP

	Fiscal Years	
Actual	1983	6.1
Projected	1984	5.3
	1985	5.3
	1986	5.1
	1987	4.8
	1988	4.1
	1989	3.6

SOURCE: *Economic Report of the President*, February 1984, U.S.
Government Printing Office, Washington, D.C., 1984, Table 1.1, p. 29.

To repeat, any organization with large debts outstanding cannot deviate by very much or for very long from at least the promise of a cash flow surplus without having the quality of the debt deteriorate. Any deviation from a government budget that is balanced or in surplus must be understood as transitory—the war will be over, the resource-development program will be finished, or income will be at the full-employment level.

A second reason for a government budget posture that yields a balanced budget or a surplus at some anticipated performance of the economy, even as it yields a deficit if performance falls short of the anticipated, is that a deficit adds to profits and a surplus decreases profits. Business profits are the key element in determining how well a capitalist economy works. Policy to control the aggregate performance of the economy needs a handle by which it can affect profits. One such handle is monetary policy, but as has been argued, monetary policy affects income and employment by first affecting asset values and the liquidity and solvency of firms, households, and financial institutions. Monetary policy to constrain undue expansion and inflation operates by way of disrupting financing markets and asset values. Monetary policy to induce expansion operates by interest rates and the availability of credit, which do not yield increased investment if current and anticipated profits are low. A Big Government where the budget moves to surplus with high income levels and inflation and to deficit with low investment and incomes is the primary effective stabilizer of the economy.

Given the current problems with the quality of the U.S. government debt, the objective should be to have the budget balanced and go into surplus at a readily attainable level of performance. Although the annual unemployment rate has fallen to as low as 3.4 percent in the years since 1960, the poor performance of the economy over the past decade indicates that a tax and spending program that would balance the budget when the unemployment rate as now measured is at 6 percent should be the current target.

Tax receipts, in a tax system that depends upon the personal income tax or a value-added tax, are closely related to nominal income. If there is no adjustment in the tax schedule and if there is no indexing of public spending, then any inflation spurt—even if it takes place when the economy is working below its targeted employment rate—will lead to a decrease in the deficit or a rise in the surplus; profits will be smaller than they otherwise would have been because of this reaction to inflation.

Perhaps the major opening for serious inflation occurs when expenditure and tax programs are indexed. Rather than try to fight inflation by monetary policy in an economy where the fiscal weapon is abandoned, the anti-inflation program should emphasize the constraint upon inflation imposed by nonindexed government tax and spending programs.

Nonindexing of government payments and taxing will impose a hardship upon government suppliers, receivers of transfer payments, government employees, and taxpayers. The impacts of inflation could be offset by appropriate tax and spending schedule changes when inflation is attenuated, but the principal that inflation yields a net revenue gain to government, so that profits and, therefore, investment are constrained must be sustained. Fiscal measures are more powerful economic control weapons than monetary manipulations.

The reason for an in principle balanced budget is that government needs an implicit surplus if its debt is to be valuable and a swing of the government budget from deficit to surplus is an especially powerful anti-inflationary device.

Taxation

Once government is big, its tax take must be big and the structure of taxes will have a significant effect on relative prices, supply conditions, and financing practices. Given today's military priorities and inherited commitments, spending by this Big Government will be dominated by transfer payments and military spending on goods and services. Of the spending by Big Government, the suggested employment program and unemployment insurance will be inversely related to private GNP. A major portion of the profit stabilizing deficits and the inflation-controlling surpluses has to come from variations in the tax take.

On the basis of our analysis, the standard classification of particular taxes as progressive or regressive has little merit. A sales tax is usually classified as regressive whereas a corporate income tax is considered to be progressive, but as our analysis of price determination showed, a corporate income tax will show up in product prices just as a sales tax. Similarly, the employers' contribution to Social Security is a labor cost that must be covered by price. Whereas market interactions determine which prices carry the burden of corporate income taxes and Social Security taxes, policy decisions determine the proximate prices affected by excise and sales taxes.

Since any tax system that collects 20 percent of GNP will have some rates that hurt, a Big Government economy has to deal with tax avoidance and evasion. Tax avoidance, which is legal, is a modification of behavior that leads to a decrease or an elimination of the taxed activity. Tax evasion, which is illegal, is the nonpayment of taxes even though the taxed activity is carried out. Tax policy needs to consider the behavior modification aspects of tax policy and use the expected tax avoidance reaction to foster policy goals.

Most assuredly, all taxes have price-level effects. Excise taxes, corporate income taxes, value-added taxes (VAT) (total or partial, such as the employer's Social Security tax) tend to raise prices. Only the personal income tax tends to decrease prices by cutting demand, and even this tax may have some price-raising effect by reducing effort. Any tax system that seeks to offset inflationary pressures will have a progressive personal income tax as its centerpiece. Because a progressive personal income tax can be designed so that its yield is responsive to changes in nominal income, this tax can be an important stabilizer of prices as well as profits.

From our theoretical analysis it is evident that policy should aim at achieving and sustaining a robust financial structure. A key element in the robustness is the quality of the best available short-term asset—short-term government debt. An in-place tax structure that yields a surplus when the economy either does well on the income and employment front or poorly on the inflation front is a necessary condition for maintaining the quality of government debt.

Furthermore, as a financial structure is robust when hedge financing predominates, equity, which leads to no legally required payments, is the preferred instrument for financing business. A corporate income tax, which allows interest to be deducted prior to the determination of taxable income, induces debt-financing and is therefore undesirable. A corporate income tax also allows nonproduction expenses such as advertising, marketing, and the pleasures of the executive suites to be charged against revenues in determining taxable income. As advertising and marketing are techniques for building market powers and as "executive style" is a breeder of inefficiency, the corporate income tax abets market power and inefficiency just as the corporate income tax abets the use of debt-financing. Elimination of the corporate income tax should be on the agenda.

The achievement of an approximation to full employment is a major policy goal. As employer contributions to Social Security are a VAT on labor's contribution to value added, tax avoidance leads business to substitute capital for labor in choosing production techniques. Inasmuch as capital-intensive techniques and the debt-financing by business to which it leads are destabilizing, the employer's contribution to Social Security is a doubly pernicious tax, reducing employment and fostering instability. A universal VAT is superior to our partial VAT.

In an economy in which capital-intensive production methods are used, particular prices are, to a degree, arbitrary. Risk-averse bankers require the protection of borrowers' market power before they finance capital-intensive production techniques. Therefore there are no serious price-efficiency arguments against the use of excise taxes to promote policy objectives. Substantial excise taxes designed to use the price system and tax-avoidance behavior to achieve social objectives could well be part of a tax program.

In 1983 the individual income tax, the individual contributions to Social Security, and the corporate income tax yielded 11.9 percent of the estimated full-employment GNP (see Table 13.5).

The corporate income tax and the employers' contributions to Social Security are, for the reasons stated, highly undesirable taxes. An income tax that integrates the corporate income tax and the employees' contributions to Social Security should replace the present hodgepodge of income-based taxes.

Eliminating the corporate income tax leaves us with the problem of the use of a corporation as a tax-avoidance device. This is a problem that can be handled in a variety of ways. The analytically neat way would treat a corporation as if it were a proprietorship or a partnership. This would require a full imputation of per-share income to the stockholders regardless of whether or not dividends were paid. Alternatively, and perhaps more simply, administratively the REIT provision—by which the corporate income tax remains on the books but corporations that pay out 85 percent or 90 percent of profits in dividends are tax exempt—could be generalized

Table 13.5: Federal Budget Receipts, Fiscal 1983

Tax	Amount (billions)	% of Receipts	% of Full-employment GNP
Individual income tax	$289	48.1	8.0
Corporation income tax	37	6.2	1.0
Social Security tax and contribution	209	34.8	5.8
Excise taxes	35	5.8	1.0
Estate and gift taxes	6	1.0	.2
Customs duties	9	1.5	.3
Federal Reserve contribution	14	2.3	.4
All others	1	–.2	—
Total	$601	99.9	16.7

SOURCE: *Economic Report of the President*, February 1984, U.S. Government Printing Office, Washington, D.C., 1984, Table B72, p. 305.

to all corporations. Either way, a unified income tax should be the major pillar of the tax system; it might be constructed so as to yield some 12.5 percent of full-employment GNP or more than 60 percent of the total collected in taxes.

As was mentioned earlier, we already have a VAT on the value added by those workers for whom corporations "contribute" to Social Security. This tax now yields some 2.9 percent of full-employment GNP; a comprehensive VAT to yield 3.0 percent or so of GNP seems a very modest revenue target.

Given that a penal tax on gasoline and/or oil is desirable to promote conservation and divert imports to non-oil-producing nations, $108 billion or 3 percent of GNP (15 percent of the tax take) could well be raised by oil-related and other excise taxes.

The tax reform agenda addresses adequacy and structure. The tax program must yield enough to maintain the quality of government debt and allow swings in receipts to stabilize profits and constrain inflation. Political evidence indicates that the individual income tax cannot carry the entire burden of financing Big Government, and a serious program of VATs and excise taxes is necessary.

This tax program is different in kind from the Reagan tax reform package of 1985 and the various suggestions for simplifying the income tax that surfaced in Congress in recent years. Our program starts with the propositions that a government that is about 20 percent of GNP is needed to stabilize the economy and that the budget needs to be balanced when the economy is at or close to full employment. This means that if we use 1983 as a base and 6 percent unemployment as full employment, the tax system needs to raise 20 percent more income from a base line income that is some 10 percent greater than what ruled in 1983.

Because the income tax is part of a stabilization program, revenues should be sensitive to changes in income and prices. This argues for having a progression of tax brackets and rates over incomes in the middle range. Thus there should be more tax brackets than the President's 0, 15, 25 and 35 percent rate schedule implies. Because two income based taxes, the Social Security and the corporate income taxes, are eliminated, the tax rates can be higher throughout the range than the President proposes, and substantially higher at very high incomes.

These suggestions for tax reform reflect the stability, employment, and price-level effects of various taxes. Equity issues, which are obviously important, are largely ignored. The basic point of taxation is simple; taxes have allocational and distributional as well as macroeconomic effects.

A government can get the overall budget to serve the needs of stability, but because each tax has supply and price effects and induces avoidance and evasion behavior, the details may lead to perverse political and fairness results. Because the VAT and a greater emphasis upon excise duties are part of a package that reduces both perverse employer contribution to Social Security and corporate income taxes, the program might well improve distributional and allocational efficiency.

AN EMPLOYMENT STRATEGY

Although stabilization policy operates upon profits, the humane objective of stabilization policy is to achieve a close approximation to full employment. The guarantee of particular jobs is not an aim of policy; just as with profits, the aggregate—not the particulars—is the objective.

The current strategy seeks to achieve full employment by way of subsidizing demand. The instruments are financing conditions, fiscal inducements to invest, government contracts, transfer payments, and taxes. This policy strategy now leads to chronic inflation and periodic investment booms that culminate in financial crises and serious instability. The policy problem is to develop a strategy for full employment that does not lead to instability, inflation, and unemployment.

The main instrument of such a policy is the creation of an infinitely elastic demand for labor at a floor or minimum wage that does not depend upon long- and short-run profit expectations of business. Since only government can divorce the offering of employment from the profitability of hiring workers, the infinitely elastic demand for labor must be created by government.

A government employment policy strategy should be designed to yield outputs that advance well-being, even though the outputs may not be readily marketable. Because the employment programs are to be permanent, operating at a base level during good times and expanding during recession, the tasks to be performed will require continuous review and development.

There are four labor-market aspects to an employment strategy:

1. The development of public, private, and in-between institutions that furnish jobs at a noninflationary base wage.

2. The modification of the structure of transfer payments.

3. The removal of barriers to labor force participation.

4. The introduction of measures that constrain money wages and labor costs.

The four aspects of the employment strategy are linked. If the massive transfer-payment apparatus is to be dismantled, then alternative sources of income must be guaranteed for the current and potential recipients of such payments. If barriers to labor-force participation are removed, then jobs have to be available for those who are now free to enter the labor market. Constraints upon money wages and labor costs are corollaries of the commitment to maintain full employment.

Before sketching a program of government employment schemes and ways to constrain money wages in a full-employment economy, the modification of the structure of transfer payments and the removal of the barriers to participation in the labor force must be examined.

Transfer Payments and Barriers to Labor-Market Participation

The United States has embarked on a course that will lead to a major modification of the Social Security system. The legislation that forbids the involuntary retirement of workers before the age of seventy implies that, in time, either the benefit will be a variable that depends upon the age of retirement or beneficiaries will draw income from Social Security even though they continue to work. A barrier to labor-market participation, the constraint upon wage income allowed to Social Security recipients, is now politically untenable. Moreover, because of compound interest and longer life expectancy, the retirement annuity income increases significantly even with short delays in the retirement age. Thus, flexibility in Social Security, if structured like a private annuity, will both induce labor-market participation and decrease the chronic pressures for inflationary increases.

The most significant status-tested transfer-payment scheme is AFDC. When AFDC was instituted in the 1930s the social norm was that women with children, especially young children, would not work. Legislation for the support of dependent children quite naturally reflected this norm, and eligibility was restricted to mothers who did not have adequate income. But today's labor-market participation rates have made the sociological assumptions of the 1930s obsolete.

AFDC, despite its importance, is a minor government program in support of children; the major program is the children's exemption in the income tax, which yields a return that increases with family income.

A universal children's allowance should be substituted for AFDC, and this income should be part of the family's taxable income. The level might well be at $75 per month or $900 per year. This will provide a net benefit for all parents and a substantial benefit to the working poor with large families. A universal children's allowance means that AFDC can be eliminated and with it the barrier to work. But for this approach to succeed, jobs must be available.

The Road to Participation: The New Deal's CCC, NYA, and WPA

For income from work to be available to all, the demand for labor must be infinitely elastic over a wide range of labor types and geographical regions. At the same time, this infinitely elastic demand must not unduly decrease the supply of labor to other occupations and employers, creating upward pressure on wages. Furthermore the employer, while willing to hire all who offer to work, is not committed to hiring any particular number of workers. This can be achieved only by government-funded employment at wage rates that do not place upward pressure on private wages.

As the program offers jobs to all, it effectively sets a minimum wage. Once the power of Big Government to stabilize the economy against severe downturns is established, minimum wage legislation is an anachronism. A world with measured unemployment and minimum wages is internally inconsistent; an effective minimum wage program must guarantee that jobs are available to all at the minimum wage.

An employment strategy must deal with youth and adult unemployment as well as the provision of jobs for older adults. The instruments of an employment strategy can be identified by labels drawn from the 1930s: The Civilian Conservation Corps (CCC), the National Youth Administration (NYA), and the Works Progress Administration (WPA). In the New Deal days these programs were viewed as transitory, but in the light of the inherent instability of capitalism and the chronic shortage of jobs, they will be conceived of here as permanent.

The CCC, the most popular job program of the Roosevelt administration, provided youths with an ordered and controlled living and work situation. They were not part of a training school; the learning that took place was by doing. A principal task in the 1930s was the maintenance and improvement of the national parks and forests. In the 1980s the CCC could take up where it left off forty years ago.

In the 1930s the CCC enrolled about 250,000 youths; today it might aim at a program of 1,000,000. The target group will be youths sixteen through twenty years of age. In essence, the program would be a means of transition from being in school to being at work.

The CCC should provide keep and a modest income. Some $8,000 a year could be budgeted per participant; some $3,000 in wages and $5,000 in keep and job support. This program will take some $8 billion or 0.22 percent of the 1983 full-employment GNP per year.

A million is some 5 percent of the roughly 20 million in the target (sixteen through twenty) age groups, a group with chronically high unemployment rates. The CCC of 1 million, or even one considerably smaller, will have a sizable impact on youth unemployment.

The problems of youth, especially of youth employment, so evident today existed during the Great Depression. The NYA was a response to these problems. Like its predecessor, a resurrected NYA should take a number of forms because of the varied problems of the young. The basic target population should be sixteen to twenty-two years of age, in and out of school, as well as those in school who are somewhat older.

The NYA should provide jobs which will enable the children's allowance to be dropped at the sixteenth birthday. It should provide work-study employment for high school, college, and university students. These jobs would simultaneously aid colleges and universities by paying for necessary work in and around the institutions. It should also provide jobs for out-of-school youth, as well as summer employment. The NYA out-of-school programs and summer employment might well provide training.

There are seven age cadres in the target population (the target population overlaps with that of the CCC) or some 24 million. The program should mainly pay for the labor costs of participants; the schools, colleges, and government units that use the labor will supply the material, supervision, and administration. At an average of $3,000 per recipient, a program level of 0.5 percent of full-employment GNP, $18 billion in 1983, will employ some 6 million or 25 percent of the target population. Because of the overlap in target groups, NYA and CCC together could affect almost 30 percent of the target population.

The NYA should be a major resource-creation effort by the government. Ever since the Kennedy administration various schemes have attempted to induce economic growth and full employment by inducing or subsidizing investments. But ever since inducing investment has been a major policy objective, the growth, employment, and stability characteristics of the economy have deteriorated.

The war on poverty was a poorly conceived attempt that in part focused on creating resources by training target populations. While the NYA will have income-maintenance aspects, its main purpose will be to support the development of human resources and the institutions that produce developed human resources.

The WPA will provide jobs in lieu of adult welfare and extended unemployment insurance. Welfare cannot be eliminated unless something is put in its place. Jobs can replace welfare, however, only by an open-ended employment scheme. Since a full-employment economy is an unknown exotic environment, there is no way of really knowing how many welfare recipients, presently measured unemployed, and those out of the labor force will sign up for WPA jobs. In addition, to facilitate the reform of Social Security by allowing a recipient to work, the WPA effort should provide full- and part-time jobs for older workers.

Any estimate of the size of a WPA that would employ all comers when the economy is functioning well, especially as WPA will replace the existing welfare programs and will be available to supplement Social Security, is an act of faith. If we exclude youth unemployment, which CCC and NYA will attack, assume that thirteen weeks of unemployment insurance will continue to be available, and use a private-employment target that yields a 6 percent unemployment rate, some 2 million on WPA at full employment seems an ample first estimate of its scope. If some $7,000 per year is set as the wage of a WPA worker and $3,000 is allowed for overhead and materials, a WPA program for two million workers will cost $20 billion, or .055 percent of GNP.

In principle WPA should not be means-tested. Furthermore, because it will provide supplementary income to older adults as well as income for women with childcare responsibilities, the WPA might well have a mandate to develop part-time work programs.

It is envisioned that WPA, NYA, and CCC when fully developed will, together with normal government activity and private employment, provide income through jobs for all who are willing and able to work. These permanent programs will provide outputs—public services, environmental improvements, etc. that a transfer-payment government does not yield, as well as the creation and improvement of human resources. In our urban centers, where there are concentrations of unemployed and welfare recipients, the improvement of the public environment should be marked. WPA, CCC, and NYA will succeed precisely because they are job programs that perform useful tasks and yield visible outputs.

Money Wages

The standard analysis of the relation between money wage rate changes, price-level changes, and unemployment is based upon an assumption that a decrease in unemployment is derived from an increase in demand for goods and services. This implies that increases in employment will follow upward pressures on prices.

In the current policy strategy, an increase in unemployment leads to increases in government inducements to private investment and transfer payments, a decrease in tax rates, and an easing of financial-market conditions. The impacts of current policy strategy follow a path from a rise in aggregate demand to a rise in particular demands to a rise in employment; this path is conducive to price and wage increases.

Once the shift to an employment program has been assimilated, cyclical variations in employment will be replaced by variations in the proportion of workers on WPA. When demand for labor by private employers increases, the proportion of workers on WPA will decrease. With WPA, a fall in aggregate demand will not be turned around by increasing inducements to invest, increasing the money supply, or lowering tax rates. Because labor demand and wage income at a low hourly scale are central in this policy, its inflationary potential will be less than that of current policy.

The employment strategy will lead to tight labor markets, but as WPA wages are to be significantly lower than in private employment, the supply of labor to private employers will be infinitely elastic as long as WPA employment is positive. Under these circumstances, market and institutional factors are not likely to give rise to chronic and even accelerating pressure on wages.

Under current policy, aggregate demand is sustained by increasing the inducements to invest and transfer payments. Policy endeavors to maintain the demand for labor that produces investment output. This sectoral emphasis leads to an accretion of market power by the producers of investment of goods and their workers (construction and machinery workers), which leads to higher wages and thus higher markups in consumer-goods production. Chronic rising wages in investment-goods production, which is the result of the current policy strategy, first brings about a rise in markups and then a rise in money wages in consumption-goods production.

The employment approach has a lower inflationary potential than the present course. In a WPA, CCC, NYA strategy the pressures on money wages through induced investment demand and easier financing terms will be minimized. The base WPA wage should be rarely changed. If unemployment increases because wages in private employment are pushed up by trade union pressure, then the supply of workers to WPA will increase and the budget deficit will rise. If the wage in the WPA employment program stands fast, however, the money wage increases in private employment are likely to be undone by market competition; the differential between private and WPA wages will tend to be market-determined.

Of course, a policy that the WPA wage should be some ratio to the average wage could make an employment strategy a handmaiden of inflation. If the policy aim is wage stability and gradually falling prices that reflect productivity increases, the WPA wage, as well as wages in normal government employment and in military contracts, must not rise in response to mild and transitory inflationary pressures that reflect normal cycles in private investment and employment.

FINANCIAL REFORM

The history of capitalism is punctuated by deep depressions that are associated with financial panics and crashes in which financial relations are ruptured and institutions destroyed. Each big depression reformed the institutional structure, often through legislation. The history of money, banking, and financial legislation can be interpreted as a search for a structure that would eliminate instability. Experience shows that this search failed and theory indicates that the search for a permanent solution is fruitless.

In a Big Government capitalist economy with an activist central bank, debt deflations and deep depressions can be contained. Furthermore, central bank administrative actions and legislation can attempt to control and guide the evolution of the financial structure in order to constrain cyclical instability. In our economy the financial structure can be said to begin with the financing of investment and positions in the stock of privately owned capital assets. As, by and large, business corporations control capital assets and order investment output, the financial powers and practices of corporations are the starting points for policies to manage or contain instability.

The Federal Reserve was organized to control instability. Inasmuch as the Federal Reserve system now intervenes whenever a serious debt deflation threatens, the Federal Reserve must broaden its scope and take initiatives to prevent the development of practices conducive to financial instability. The Federal Reserve has to be concerned with the effect upon stability of the changing structure of financial relations. This definition of responsibility stands in sharp contrast to the hands-off policy with respect to financial usages and institutions that the Federal Reserve has typically followed. The Federal Reserve needs to guide the evolution of financial institutions by favoring stability enhancing and discouraging instability-augmenting institutions and practices.

Financial reform can be effective only as part of a general system of reform. As long as the main proximate objective of policy is to encourage investment, institutions, and ways of doing business that facilitate investment financing and capital-asset ownership will be fostered. But inappropriate financing of investment and capital-asset ownership are the major destabilizing influences in a capitalist economy. Thus, the substitution of employment for investment as the proximate objective of economic policy is a precondition for financial reforms that aim at decreasing instability.

The policy problem is to design a system of financial institutions that dampens instability. While banks are the central financial institutions of a capitalist economy, banking is a business encased in myth: it is an economic mystery wrapped in an enigma. Bankers are fiduciaries who advise and act in the interest of clients, even as their own income depends upon the services they sell to these same clients. Lines were drawn among commercial, investment, and savings banks aimed at moderating the conflict between the fiduciary and private-profit aspects of banking. Recent experience shows that the institutional lines cannot be sustained when there are large profit opportunities from breaching the lines.

Ordinary Corporations as Financial Institutions

Because corporations own most of the economy's capital assets, they collect most of the gross capital income, which is then apportioned by law and the liability structure to taxes, debt servicing (principal and interest), and gross equity income. Equity income may or may not be retained by corporations. Corporations are financial institutions that have special powers enabling them to collect equity funds from a large number of units and to go into debt. Corporations, by limiting the liability of stockholders, make the divorce between the ownership and management of business possible.

Since corporations can go into debt in their own name and not as agents of their owners, corporations facilitate investment and the use of large-scale capital assets. As Keynes pointed out, "The Stock Exchange revalues many investments every day and the revaluations give a frequent opportunity to the individual (but not to the community as a whole) to revise his commitments. It is as though a farmer ... would decide to remove his capital between 10 and 11 in the morning and reconsider whether he should return it later in the week."[3] Once corporations dominate in

---

3. Keynes, John Maynard, *The General Theory of Employment Interest and Money*, chapter 17.

owning capital assets and stock exchanges exist, the holding period of investors can conform to their changing needs and preferences even though the corporation's commitment to the ownership of capital assets can be for their expected productive life.

If capital assets are cheap, so that those needed for a business or trade can be easily acquired, then simple proprietorships or partnerships will do. Once capital assets become expensive and the expected profitable life exceeds the life expectancy of a mature individual, only corporations with their perpetual life can have holding periods that match the useful life of capital assets.

There are two classes of capital assets. One is like agricultural or urban land—the assets can be used for a wide variety of products, and there are many who are capable of profitably using the assets. The assets have a price or value independent of the particular owner or user. Moreover, because they generate cash in an impersonal way, these assets are suitable for mortgage financing, that is, for financing tied to the asset rather than to an owner. Assets that flow through the production processes and the channels of commerce (inventories) are also suitable for to-the-asset financing, as the funds to meet the debt will be obtained when the inventories are sold, i.e., are almost in sight when the financing takes place.

For both long-life general-purpose assets and short-life commercial assets that are fit for to-the-asset financing, the payment commitments on the debts used can be closely related to the cash flows that these assets are expected to yield. The financial flow relations are analogous to those that characterize hedge financing.

The other class of capital assets consists of plants and equipment with no significant value outside of particular uses. As they can generate cash flows only if they are used in a small set of production processes, they have no or little value except to firms that use these processes. These capital assets are not suitable for to-the-asset financing. The debts used to finance such special purpose capital assets must be of the organization that owns and operates the capital assets. If the period over which the asset is expected to yield cash exceeds the life expectancy of a representative proprietorship or partnership, then the ownership of such capital assets cannot be hedge-financed by a proprietorship or a partnership. If such capital assets are to be used, either the principal's personal funds must finance ownership or the financing must be speculative. Hedge financing is possible only if the time to maturity of liabilities can be of approximately the same duration as the period over which the asset is expected to yield cash.

The corporation is a social instrument that is best suited to hold and operate expensive special-purpose capital assets whose expected life as an earner of quasi-rents is long. Often corporate debts are not tied to the profits that any specific capital asset generates: they are mainly tied to the earnings of the organization and therefore are like a to-the-person loan. Given that the use of capital assets with overlapping life expectancies is required, a corporation operating special-purpose capital assets must have an infinite life.

If corporations did not exist, debt-financing of long-life special-purpose capital assets would have had to be speculative: the term of the debt would be shorter than the expected rent-generating life of the asset. By issuing long term debts corporations can achieve a hedge-financing liability structure—this can help to stabilize the financial structure.

But the corporate form or organization facilitates the divorce of financing from the ownership and acquisition of particular assets. If short-term debts are less expensive, corporations that borrow on the basis of their overall profitability are able to economize by using more short-term debt than is needed to finance their short-term assets. While corporations can be said to have begun as a vehicle for hedge financing of expensive, special purpose, and long-lived capital assets, the ability of corporations to issue debts that are not tied to specific assets means that corporations can borrow short to hold long assets. Consequently, the corporation, initially a device for extending hedge financing to long-lasting capital assets, can be a vehicle for speculative finance—and because it facilitates both capital-intensive modes of production and speculative financing, a destabilizing influence.

Thus, there is an inherent constitutional weakness in the financial structure. One part of the weakness is technologically based: The use of expensive capital assets with long lives is best financed by instruments that are amortized over a long term. The second part is preference-determined: asset holders want to control their holding period. The corporation is a device for handling the financing problems due to technology. But because corporations have a perpetual life, the preference problem leads to the need for a market in which individual holdings can be transferred. Accordingly, a stock and bond market is a necessary adjunct to the corporate form of organizing business. But such a market opens the door to the speculative financing of perpetual liabilities (equities) by the short-term debt of stock owners.

The corporate form eliminates the constitutional weakness due to the incongruence of the life expectancy of adults and of plant and equipment. The corporation cannot, however, eliminate the constitutional weakness arising from the preference of wealth-owning households for assets with a potential for short holding periods. Furthermore, this constitutional weakness is strong whenever the demand for financing is high and rising rapidly because short term financing markets are better able to respond by devising new instruments and new institutions; rising interest rates yield losses to holders of long-term financial instruments, which closes down the long-term market. As a result of these constitutional flaws, speculative finance and the growth of market institutions that facilitate the rolling over and refinancing of positions are destabilizing developments during prosperous times.

The cash flows that validate business debts and determine the market value of liabilities are the difference between corporate total revenues and the cost of labor and purchased materials. Many corporations are tax farmers, in the sense that their selling prices are determined by the cash flows needed to validate debt (just as taxes are set by the need for revenue). The determination of prices by the need for cash flows requires that market constraints should be slack; monopoly or near monopoly market positions are often a prerequisite for borrowing. As has been shown, Big Government prevents a downside collapse of the mass of profits that are available, and market power, often because of regulation, leads to protection of unit markups for particular users of capital.

Thus, if the expected cash flows of a firm with market power are insufficient to validate debt and serve as a basis for financing expansion, the firm will raise markups and prices. Because prices especially of regulated firms are usually lower than the unconstrained profit-maximizing monopoly prices, a rise in prices will lead to an increase in total profits. However, there is a possibility that the price will go above the monopoly price, so that net revenues do not rise or even fall. When this happens for a giant firm, government intervenes by means of subsidies, special tax credits, overt endorsements of debts, and steps to increase the flow of aggregate profits. The primacy of profits and debt validation as policy goals is evident in the behavior of government in recent periods of crisis.

Because the investment decisions of many organizations are validated by revenues resulting from private taxes, these investment decisions are like public decisions. Each brain scanner purchased by hospitals, for example, shows up in Blue Cross and Blue Shield rates, which are a cost of labor to employers that must be covered in product prices. In essence, we have a tax supported medical system in which taxpayers have no voice in determining the supply price of the service. The United States has a type of contingency socialism, in which the liabilities of particular organizations are protected either by overt government intervention or by the grant of monopoly price setting powers.

Financial reform needs to confront the public nature of much that is private. Big or giant organizations carry an implied public guarantee (i.e., contingent liability) on their debts. This introduces a financing bias favoring giant corporations and giant banks, for the implicit public liability leads to preferred market treatment. Government intervention to validate the cash flow commitments takes place even if investments are inept. One way the government intervenes is by generating a massive deficit. But these massive deficits are a basis for later inflation even as threats of private default are a basis for unemployment.

Because a large government implies that a profit-sustaining deficit will take place whenever income and employment falls, there is no need for policy to foster market power that protects profits by sustaining prices in recessions. In a world with Big Government, individual bankruptcies can be tolerated because they cannot lead to wholesale defaults. Thus, bankruptcy, which transforms a nonsustainable speculative or Ponzi financing structure into a sustainable hedge structure, should be made easy and cheap. Once bankruptcy is simplified, the inflation-constraining forces of competition are free to operate. If an economy is to be open to bankruptcy, no organization can be so large that its bankruptcy is politically unacceptable.

Furthermore, to decrease the instability-enhancing power of corporations, the bias favoring debt-financing due to high-rate corporate income taxes must be removed; *the corporation income tax should be eliminated.* In addition, short-term corporate debt should be to an asset, not to the corporation. Bank lending to corporations by way of documented loan and open-market lending to corporations by means of documented acceptances—where there is proof that a short-term flow through asset is being financed—must be encouraged. Such instruments should be given a special place in the process by which the Federal Reserve determines the cash base of banks and acts as a lender of last resort; that is, the Federal Reserve must stand ready to participate, through the discount window, in such financing.

Banks and Banking

Banks are the central financial organization of a capitalist economy. Once the assets and liabilities of banks are set, the economy's financing framework is largely determined. As bankers pursue profits they change the composition of their assets and liabilities; in particular, during good times the interactions between bankers and their borrowing customers increase the weight of assets reflecting speculative and Ponzi finance in the balance sheet of banks. As a result, the financial system evolves from an initial robustness toward fragility, and continuous control and periodic reform of the banking system are needed to prevent the development of a financially unstable economy that cannot readily be contained.

There is a correlation between the size of a bank and the size of business it can serve. A decentralized banking system with many small and independent banks is conducive to an industrial structure made up of mainly small and medium-size firms. Similarly, a highly concentrated banking system made up of large banks with branches throughout the nation is conducive to industrial concentration.

A bank with a lending line limit of several million dollars cannot handle the short-term financing needs of a giant corporation. Such a corporation naturally gravitates to the largest banks. Furthermore, the bank financing needed by a corporation in the billion-dollar class cannot be handled by any single bank; giant and even moderate size firms have multiple bank connections and lines of credit. No matter where a very large firm has its headquarters, it will have financing relations with the giant money-center banks.

Over the past decades, although the geographical autonomy of banking has been eroded, the United States has not traveled far along the road that leads to a banking system dominated by a small number of giant banks. Even though the system remains decentralized, the banking laws and their administration should be structured to foster and encourage the growth and prosperity of independent, smaller banks. This is not the direction the current changes in bank regulation and bank legislation are taking.

As pointed out in chapter ten, when banks finance a business, they become a partner in the business, for the repayment of the loan depends upon the success of what the borrower undertakes. Furthermore, banks and their business partners generally do repeated deals: they have a continuing relation.

As a result, bankers, motivated by the partnership in which the borrowing customer's prosperity determines the banker's profit, are sources of continuing advice and guidance to businessmen. To serve these customers fully, a banker should offer a wide array of financing options, both as a lender and as a placement agent. Restrictions on banks acting as dealers, underwriters, and financial advisers are unwarranted legacies of the 1930s.

To properly use the energies of the smaller banks for economic development, they should be allowed to function as investment and merchant bankers as well as commercial bankers; they should be allowed to underwrite and place equity and bond issues of smaller businesses.

Since specialized organizations already handle the investment and merchant banking needs of large firms, there may be merit in not allowing giant commercial banks to act in this capacity. Wall Street is not the entire economy. For many businesses the major locally available sophisticated financial adviser and guide—as well as the only practicable underwriter for equity issues or debt placements—is a commercial bank. If economic policy aims to support competitive markets, then commercial banks of modest size should be free to be underwriters, place debts with third parties, give financial advice for a fee, and collect fees for arranging mergers, divesitures, and takeovers.

The Federal Reserve tries to control the aggregate ability of banks to finance or to create deposits by regulating the reserves available to banks. If banks and financial markets were simply deposit-creating automatons and only affected economic activity by way of the excess or deficit of cash in portfolios, then the attempt to control the economy by controlling bank reserves might have some merit. In fact, banks are complex profit-seeking organizations that have a multitude of actual and potential types of liabilities and that innovate in response to profit opportunities.

In order to contain the destabilizing effect of banking, it is necessary to regulate the amount and the rate of increase of bank assets. The major control device is the permitted capital-asset ratio and the rate of growth of bank capital. As things now stand, the adequacy of bank capital is a concern of bank examination and supervision, not of monetary policy. In order to constrain the disequilibrating potential, to protect against debt deflation, and to remove the bias due to the higher asset-equity ratios allowed to giant banks, the Federal Reserve should be authorized to set an asset-equity ratio for all banks—that is, all institutions with deposits subject to transfer by check or withdrawal on demand. A 5 percent asset-equity ratio seems reasonable, especially if capital absorption by covert bank liabilities is taken into account. The Federal Reserve should have a right to vary the ratio if aggregate bank capital is compromised. A capital-adequacy condition should not be administered as a straightjacket, and a penalty constraint upon dividends should be assessed for significant shortfalls of capital.

The ability of the smaller banks to lend and invest will be increased by such a uniform capital-asset ratio. The problem of these smaller banks will still be to find assets and to place liabilities. More favorable financing conditions for smaller enterprises will result from the higher allowable asset capital ratio of the smaller banks, for they will be able to earn the market determined rate of return with a lower markup on a larger asset base. After reform, the market determined markup on money costs at the small banks might well fall even as the markup of the big banks rise. An evenhanded asset-equity ratio among banks will go some way toward equalizing the financing conditions of large and small businesses.

At present a well-managed, reasonably profitable bank can retain earnings so that its capital grows at a rate that exceeds the sustainable noninflationary growth of the economy. In order to have an internal rate of growth of bank equity consistent with stable prices, the pay-out ratio for bank earnings will have to rise.

Control over the capital-asset ratio and the pay-out ratio for banks are powerful weapons for guiding the development of banking. Once set, the uniform capital-asset ratio should not be changed routinely, but the authorities regulating banking should be granted the power to vary the pay-out ratio if the growth of bank equity is too fast or too slow.

Ease of entry or free entry into markets should also be a policy objective. Banking reforms that remove barriers against flexible financing options from smaller banks should also ease entry into markets by smaller business. The regulatory climate should move to ease entry into banking.

Banking is not so profitable that free entry would lead to an explosion of bank capital. The control of the rate of growth of banking by means of limiting retained earnings is more likely to lead to a noninflationary increase of available finance than the proven futile effort to govern the expansion of bank assets by regulating bank reserves.

Banks provide a large portion of the in-being and stand-by credit used by business and nonbank financial institutions. If banks concentrate on to-the-asset financing, then the short-term debts of business will lead to payment commitments that are consistent with business cash receipts. The bank debts of firms would be part of a hedge-financing relation.

The idea that banks should be constrained to to-the-asset financing is a tenent of the real bills doctrine. This doctrine holds that if banks only financed goods in the process of production, then the right amount of money would be created; this right amount of money would lead to stable prices. It has long been known that restricting assets of banks to real bills could not prevent an inflationary growth of the money supply.

The idea is not so much to assure that a noninflationary quantity of money exists, as to assure the stability of the financial system. This implies that profit opportunities of banks must be biased by the regulatory authorities to favor hedge financing, and the to-the-asset financing of inventories is a form of hedge financing.

The Federal Reserve Act initially provided that only bank loans reflecting short-term to-the-asset financing were eligible for rediscounting.

In the early years of the Federal Reserve, rediscounting was a major source of bank reserves. After the crash of 1929, the dominance of rediscounting as the source of bank reserves gave way to the use of open-market operations in Treasury securities.

When the Federal Reserve acquires assets as a result of financing some activity, then the banking system acquires reserves or the public acquires currency. If the Federal Reserve mainly acquires Treasury debt, as it does when open-market operations are the source of bank reserves, it abets the financing of government activities. But when the Federal Reserve acquires private business debts through the discount window, it is mainly cofinancing business. In addition, if the Federal Reserve supplies reserves through the discounting of to-the-asset short-term business debt, the Federal Reserve is participating in and encouraging hedge financing.

Thus, bank reserves against overt liabilities should be retained much as at present, even though their main function has changed; they are valuable not as a means of affecting economic activity but because the process of creating reserves throughout the discount window makes the Federal Reserve a participant in the financing of particular activities by particular instruments. Inasmuch as this cofinancing increases specific supplies of credit and makes these supplies more assured, participation by the Federal Reserve will guide business and bank financing practices.

There are pervasive influences that reflect fundamental characteristics of a capitalist economy that lead to instability. Biasing banks in favor of shortterm to-the-asset financing will attenuate this thrust. Other financial institutions—sales finance companies, life insurance companies, even ordinary business corporations—should also have direct or indirect access to the discount window by discounting eligible paper. The eligibility requirement for discounting can be used to assure that to-the-asset financing flourishes.

Central Banking

The evolution of financial practices must be guided to reduce the likelihood that fragile situations conducive to financial instability will develop. Central banks are the institutions that are responsible for containing and offsetting financial instability and, by extension, they have a responsibility to prevent it.

Central banks affect the normal functioning of the financial structure because they intervene in financial markets. Restricting the central bank to the regulation of member banks and to the control of the money supply is wrong. Regulating commercial banks or money may have been a good enough definition of central bank responsibility when other financial institutions were less important, but such restricted responsibility is no longer appropriate.

A central bank, as the lender of last resort, must assure that the supply of funds in key position-making markets is not disrupted by a run, and it must clearly define the financial markets it will protect. The lender-of-last-resort intervention is a delicate operation that allows particular units and branches of industry to fail even as it assures that the total available financing does not collapse.

Central banking increases in importance when the financial structure is such that business liabilities need to be refinanced. In particular, central banking exists because Ponzi and speculative financing exist. As long as commercial banks do the financing, refinancing, and contingency financing of non-bank speculative financing organizations, the central bank need deal directly only with them. But the central bank, even if it deals only with commercial banks, needs to recognize its responsibility for the normal behavior of all of finance.

During the great contraction of 1929–33, the Federal Reserve System did not prevent the breakdown of the financial system. As a result, a number of specialized partial central banks were created, making the actual United States central banks a decentralized operation, with the Federal Reserve as the preeminent body. A minor, but not insignificant, structural reform would have the specialized institutions—FDIC, the Comptroller of the Currency, and the specialist insurance and supervisory agencies for thrift institutions—become departments within the Federal Reserve.

In a modem capitalist economy with a complex financial structure, innovations result from profit opportunities. Central banking is a learning game in which the central bank is always trying to affect the performance of a changing system. Central banking can be successful only if central bankers know how the institutional structure behaves and correctly assess how changes affect the system. Central banks have to steer the evolution of the financial structure.

The central bank controls its own portfolio, except where the law lays down provisions, as with a gold standard, that all of some asset offered or demanded must be bought or sold. The central bank affects how business is financed by its power to define the assets it will protect and by selecting the assets it will use to furnish reserves to the banking system. The assets it acquires in creating reserves finance some activity which then receives favorable terms. As long as banks need central bank deposits as reserves and as long as the central bank has a monopoly of currency issue, the central bank can affect bank portfolios.

If finance is robust, speculative and Ponzi finance characterize a small portion of the financing postures of business and businesses hold substantial stocks of money and other liquid assets. Robust finance means that bank assets will be heavily weighted by government debt and private debts that reflect hedge financing. In these circumstances, it is all right for the central bank to operate mainly in Treasury debt.

In a robust financial structure, open-market operations can constrain the financing available without inducing significant present-value reversals. When investment in process is largely financed by investor's own rather than borrowed funds, the cash needed to fulfill payment commitments does not increase substantially when interest rates rise. In addition, long-term financing terms and asset values will not react strongly to transitory changes in short-term interest rates. Thus, variations in financing terms by banks will have an effect on the level of activity, but not on the viability of financial relations. Central bank efforts to restrict bank lending by decreasing bank reserves will not lead to a decline in financing available from banks; banks will simply substitute business debt for government debt in their portfolios. The effect will be on interest rates on Treasury debt.

But a robust financial environment is a transitory state, for it means that credit can expand more rapidly than the credit base during periods of expansion and can contract less rapidly when the base contracts. The cumulative effect of such bank credit changes leads to a fragile financial system. In the shift to fragility, the use of Treasury debt by banks as the position-making instrument decreases.

If Treasury debt is not used as the position-making instrument, even as the operations of the central bank are mainly in Treasury debt, no direct business contact exists between commercial banks and the central bank. If a banking system is fragile, constraint of bank reserves is almost fully reflected in the rate of growth of bank loans; there is no Treasury debt safety valve or shock absorber. Thus, a given central bank action has a larger effect on available financing and interest rates in a fragile than in a robust financial structure.

In a fragile financial environment, central banks cannot blindly follow rules and apply the techniques that were successful when the financial system was more robust. When Treasury securities are of small importance in bank portfolios and are not the position-making instrument, open-market operations are an inept way to guide the financial system. Variations in bank reserves must be related to the assets owned by banks; the discount window is the appropriate instrument for controlling reserves. The need for banks to cofinance their assets by borrowing from the central bank is a central bank technique that can influence banks' asset preferences and thus affect the way business is financed.

If business and banking practices can lead to a fragile financing structure, the central bank has a responsibility to operate to induce banks to hedge finance business. The authorities must look through the veil of the bank's balance sheet to the balance sheets of the organizations that the banks finance.

The first question a banker asks a potential borrower is, "How are you going to repay me?" The same principle should guide the management of the central bank. The access of banks to central bank cofinancing should be through business assets that reflect hedge financing.

The Federal Reserve should stop relying upon open-market operations to determine reserves of the banking system. As an alternative to open-market operations, the Federal Reserve can furnish bank reserves by discounting bank assets. In the discount technique, bank reserves are furnished when the central bank buys or lends on specified, eligible types of paper that are a result of financing business. The Bank of England money-market relations prior to World War I can serve as a model for an apt relation between the Federal Reserve, commercial banks, and money-market institutions.[4] In this model, the reserve base of banks (as well as the currency supply) would be largely the result of the Federal Reserve's discounting bank loans (or open-market paper) that arise in the financing of short-term business activity. The preferred or eligible paper for Federal Reserve discounting would be to-the-asset paper that reflects commercial or manufacturing inventories. Thus, once the financial system is fragile, the classical British discount market structure is appropriate for central bank control over the short-run supply of credit.

If bank reserves are largely the result of discounting short-term paper tied to the ownership of business inventories, then as loans fall due and are repaid bank reserve balances fall. To bring reserves to target levels, banks would have to discount paper and there would be a continuing business relation between banks and the Federal Reserve. Thus, a *major* necessary reform is for the Federal Reserve to shift from the open-market technique to discounting. The discount window method for creating the reserve base

---

4. R. S. Sayers, *Bank of England Operations (1890–1914)* (London: P. S. King & Sons, 1936).

induces favorable terms for the hedge financing of short-term positions and blunts the tendency toward fragile financing structures.

In the discount-window technique, the Federal Reserve uses paper that arises as business is financed to create reserves. The Federal Reserve both creates a market for this paper by its purchases and assures that it will have a protected status in financial markets. Such paper will therefore be in a preferred risk class. The guidance of the structure of financing relations will run from the Federal Reserve portfolio to a favored interest rate in the market for the eligible paper.

In this system, a portion of the reserve base is extinguished each day and the market needs to discount at the Federal Reserve in order to replenish reserves. In a complex financial structure, each bank will have a variety of ways to make position. A net deficiency of reserves, however, will lead to some bank borrowing at the discount window. Each bank should have a line of credit at the discount window and be able to borrow up to its line at a preferred rate; borrowings above the line of credit will be at a penal rate. The bank's line of credit at the preferred rate might very well equal its capital and surplus account, thereby inducing banks that have high asset-capital ratios to retain earnings.

The interest rate for rediscounting set by the Federal Reserve becomes the critical rate in determining financing terms. In particular, bank and money market rates for financing by means of ineligible paper will be at a premium over the rate on eligible paper. Thus, the interest rates on speculative and Ponzi financing will be higher than on hedge financing. Although the supply of reserves would be infinitely elastic to all who hold eligible paper, the interest rate would be fixed by the Federal Reserve according to its presumed impact on the economy.

The Federal Reserve would have two controls over bank financing. One would be the capital requirement, the second the reserve requirement. The capital requirement is a longer-run constraint, with a penalty on dividends and perhaps on the discount rate for falling below target, whereas the reserve requirement is a shorter-term control.

In the present system it is difficult to discover or invent a serious reason for the existence of twelve Federal Reserve Banks. The New York Federal Reserve Bank is the agency for Federal Reserve Operations and therefore is the only one that has a reason for being. If the Federal Reserve shifts to a discounting technique, then the highly decentralized banking system will require regional money markets. The regional reserve banks would then have a lender's relation with individual banks and with the district's money market; the district setup is compatible with a discount-window operating technique.

The discounting technique sets up financing relations between the central bank, commercial banks, and various money-market institutions. Bankers well recognize that a lender has the right to look over the shoulders of borrowers in order to be assured of their continued probity and creditworthiness. The Federal Reserve, as the potential and actual lender to commercial banks, would have the right to look over the shoulder and comment on the adequacy of a bank's practices. Too great a growth of ineligible paper would mean a review of the availability of credit for a bank. Bank examination would then be a natural outgrowth of the banking relation between banks and the Federal Reserve.

The volume of bank holdings of eligible paper may decrease because of a decline in the borrowing needs of business, as happened in the great contraction of 1929–33. A similar contraction cannot take place in a world with Big Government and the large deficits that occur in a downturn. The deficit means that financial markets have to absorb Treasury securities—as private debt decreases banks can keep fully invested by acquiring Treasury debt. Once banks acquire Treasury debt the Treasury-bill market is an effective position-making market. When banks are acquiring Treasury debt and the Federal Reserve wishes reserves to grow rapidly, it can augment the reserve base by purchasing Treasury bills from the open market.

Thus, the mechanism by which the Federal Reserve generates the reserve base must adjust when the instruments used by the banking system change. The discount window–discount market technique of reserve creation is appropriate for a system in which financial crises can occur because of the development of liability structures heavily weighted with speculative finance. Encouraging paper tied to the assets that flow through the production process is a way of favoring hedge finance, although in a capitalist world a thrust to speculative financing will always take place during tranquil times.

Because a thoroughgoing debt deflation leading to a deep depression cannot occur as long as the government is big, the significance of the Federal Reserve's lender-of-last-resort function changes. After a financial trauma, the Federal Reserve needs to facilitate deficit-financing by making bank reserves available outside the normal discounting channel.

Because Big Government sustains profits, the Federal Reserve can stand back and allow firms and financial institutions to go bankrupt before it steps in and refinances. Federal Reserve intervention should operate under the principle that organizations that are fully viable at normal incomes with a restructured debt and normal financing terms, but that are not solvent or liquid with crisis financing terms and recession incomes, are eligible for concessionary refinancing. The longer the Federal Reserve delays its intervention, the larger the decline in income and employment following a crisis. On the other hand, the quicker the intervention, the sharper the subsequent rise in prices and the more fragile the financial structure with which the next expansion begins.

Whenever the Federal Reserve steps in and refinances some positions, it is protecting organizations that engaged in a particular type of financing, and is expected to do so again. But it is an untoward expansion of speculative and Ponzi finance that causes the fragility that leads to a crisis-prone system. The central bank virtually assures that there will be another crisis in the near future unless, of course, it outlaws the fragility inducing financial practices. Clearly, central bank lender-of-last-resort interventions must lead to legislated or administered changes that favor hedge financing.

The Federal Reserve can deliberately trigger a financial crisis by adopting a sufficiently restrictive posture with respect to bank reserves. Such a monetary policy introduces uncertainty into portfolios, even as Big Government and lender-of-last-resort interventions reduce uncertainty. If Federal Reserve policy instruments are used to force crunches and squeezes, then the future growth of portfolios that lead to fragile financial structures is constrained.[5]

Federal Reserve policy therefore needs to continuously "lean against" the use of speculative and Ponzi finance. But Ponzi finance is a usual way of debt-financing investment in process in a capitalist society. Consequently, capitalism without financial practices that lead to instability may be less innovative and expansionary; lessening the possibility of disaster might very well take part of the spark of creativity out of the capitalist system.

The Federal Reserve position favoring hedge financing does not mean that Ponzi and speculative financing will not take place. The need to structure deals means that bank loan officers and loan committees will always face situations when the activity they are financing is really a Ponzi deal—in that next-stage borrowings are expected to provide the funds to meet the interest and principle.

If the central bank is leaning against speculative and Ponzi finance, and commercial banks are authorized to engage in underwriting, then bank

---

5. Hyman P. Minsky, "The New Uses of Monetary Powers," *Nebraska Journal of Economics and Business* 8, no. 2 (Spring 1969); reprinted in Hyman P. Minsky, *Can "IT" Happen Again? Essays on Instability & Finance* (Armonk, N.Y.: M. E. Sharpe & Co., 1982), pp. 179–91.

loan officers can arrange for the funding of bank loans into either intermediate- or long-term bonds or equities. A financial structure in which commercial banks have access as middlemen to life insurance companies, pension funds, other money managers, and private persons for the placement of the debts and equities of their customers is conducive to hedge financing.

The sustaining of hedge financing by business is a major, proximate policy objective of the Federal Reserve. The more the Federal Reserve can tilt banking toward financing trade and production inventories with short time spans, the more stable the financial system and the smaller the special refinancing needed to prevent a full-blown crisis. A financial structure that is supportive of stability must start with the techniques available to corporations to finance capital-asset ownership, continue with the biasing of banks toward to-the-asset financing, and finally change the perceptions, objectives, and instruments of the Federal Reserve.

INDUSTRIAL POLICY: ALTERNATIVES TO DOMINANCE BY GIANT CORPORATIONS

The institutionalized and bureaucratic nonspecialized corporations that now dominate business are young. Corporations, as we know them, did not exist in 1776, or even 1876. They became the dominant form of business organization because they can issue long-term and equity shares that are not tied to the fortunes of specific persons or assets. Because of this, the financing costs of long-lived, specialized, and expensive capital assets for corporations are lower than for proprietorships or partnerships. Corporations thus foster the dominance of capital-intensive productions techniques and tilt the economy toward the use of labor-saving techniques.

The result of the dominance of capital-intensive production techniques can be a chronic labor surplus. It is now necessary to invent and promote enterprises that put idle and potentially productive labor to work. Policies are needed to enable labor-intensive and capital-intensive modes of production to coexist.

The role of the corporate form of organization is a proper concern of policy, but policymakers should distinguish between bureaucratic and institutionalized corporations on the one hand and entrepreneurial corporations on the other. The first draws its strength from its financial position and market power. The management of a bureaucratic corporation is professional; its leading officers either progressed through the ranks or were hired from outside as executives and had little if anything to do with the founding and earlier growth of the corporation.

An entrepreneurial corporation, however, is largely the extension of the personality of a founder or a founding group. Its present leadership is mainly responsible for the organization's growth and development. Even though it may now be financially strong, its main strength does not rest upon its financial resources.

Competitive markets are devices to promote efficiency, and ease of entry is a mechanism that promotes competition and change. The market is an adequate regulator of products and processes except when market power or externalities exist; once they exist—whether caused by government or by market processes—regulation can be necessary to constrain the exercise of power.

Regulation and government intervention in markets are valid when they make markets behave as if they were competitive markets. Such intervention is necessary when market power exists or when other reasons lead to market failures. Interventions to constrain or channel market power are necessary. An industrial policy that takes the form of promoting competitive industry, facilitating financing and aiding and abetting the development of a labor force that is trained and productive, is highly desirable.[6]

Government and society are also suppliers of knowledge. The utilization of knowledge by competitive industries guarantees that such knowledge becomes the basis of widespread well-being, not the rent-producing assets of a few. In addition regulation and intervention are devices for assuring that cross subsidization takes place in the form of guaranteeing some minimum level of services to units that may not be able to cover the out-of-pocket, let alone the capital costs, of these services.

In a world where profits are cyclically unstable, market power can arise from the banker's requirement that unfavorable outcomes must be constrained before capital-intensive production techniques are financed. Once market power exists, however, it can and has been exploited to restrict output, to impede the entry of firms, and to sustain prices and profits. In these conditions, government intervention to set rules of fair competition or to

---

6. Henry C. Simons, "A Positive Program for Laissez-Faire"; reprinted in Henry Simons, *Economic Policy for a Free Society* (Chicago: University of Chicago Press, 1948).

create results in markets where power exists that mimic competitive solutions is indicated. At best, regulation to control and channel market power has enjoyed transitory success: all too often the regulated becomes the regulator.

In a small-government capitalism where aggregate profits are unstable, the requirement by bankers that the units being financed have market power is sensible. In Big Government capitalism, market power leads to markup increases and the dissipation of profits into business-style overhead costs. The prolix corporation with a huge overhead that is capable of losing a billion dollars a year or more when demand falls is the result of the allocation of profits that result from the exercise of market power to business-style overheads.

Once Big Government stabilizes aggregate profits, the banker's reason for market power loses its force. Obviously, with overall profits sustained it is possible for a particular corporation to make losses; presumably such losses are due to inept management decisions or impersonal and unforeseen developments that affect the markets for particular products. Special-purpose and long-lived capital assets will still be able to find financing even in the absence of market power if the prospects for validating cash flows pass a serious scrutiny Experience with Chrysler, Lockheed, and the various debacles in nuclear energy shows that market power is no substitute for bankers and investors doing their homework.

Anti-trust, as presently operated, is a failure; the legal approach to antitrust has meant that the issues of market power are not addressed. An industrial policy aimed at generating conditions conducive to competitive markets should investigate policies that set a size limit on assets or employees that any particular organization can deploy. The size limit may vary, depending upon the industry.

Much of the growth of corporations to gigantic size reflects financing and financial-market conditions. The proposal that central and commercial banks shift to to-the-asset financing and diminish the availability of short-term to-the-firm financing will remove some of the advantages of giant business. The proposal that smaller banks be allowed to act as investment bankers for their customers would also decrease some of the financing advantages of giant firms. In addition, allowing smaller banks to act as investment bankers would facilitate the entry of firms into various industries.

The changes in the corporate income tax and the shift in Federal Reserve operating techniques that were discussed earlier, along with the greater availability of investment banking facilities for smaller business, should facilitate the entry of new firms and the expansion of existing smaller firms.

With an effective minimum wage provided by the WPA device and stabilized aggregate profits, a generalized fall in wages and prices of the dimensions of the early 1930s cannot recur. Those devices in agriculture, labor, manufacturing, and trade that constrain downward price flexibility are therefore not relevant to a properly organized Big Government capitalism, because they tend to exacerbate inflationary pressures.

As is evident from the recent history of the railroads, some electric utilities, Lockheed, and Chrysler, the present fluctuations in interest rates, unemployment, and inflation lead to an erosion of the financial strength of many corporations. Since many corporations now carry heavy debt burdens, the loss of market-power protections resulting from tax and financing reforms will cause them financial difficulties. Furthermore, any positive limitation on size of assets managed will undoubtedly begin by making only several of the very largest firms candidates for devolution into several smaller, more manageable units.

The United States has a broad and deep capital market that can handle equity and debt issues of enormous size. This ability of the capital market to handle large issues means that socialization of industries that require financial restructuring can be considered a transitory step. When a Chrysler is bankrupt, the bankruptcy should be handled by a government refinancing corporation, which would take over the business and break it into parts that can survive in the market and parts that cannot generate profits. The first potentially or even presently viable part should be sold off in the capital market as a new and independent private entity. The second nonviable part may be viable as a high-risk possibility if enough new funds are forthcoming. If the refinancing corporation sees an ability to go private at the end of some period of reconstruction, then the funds to rebuild and restructure should be forthcoming. If not, the government refinancing corporation should proceed to liquidate the remnants.

There are two capital-intensive industries that private enterprise manages poorly: railroads and nuclear power generation. Both are industries combining capital intensity with enormous externalities. Although even the suggestion raises difficult political questions, public ownership should be tried; where these industries work well in other advanced economies they are almost always publicly owned. At this writing, there is no way the enormous funds needed to reconstruct these industries with relevant technology will be forthcoming except through some government-financing device; the simple straightforward way—and one with historic precedent to lessen the political problems that would be raised—is to set up a government agency like the Tennessee Valley Authority to manage these parts of the economy.

The railroads are not only capital-intensive, they are also large-scale employers. One of the recent lessons to be learned from the experiment with revenue sharing in various forms is that subsidies and free monies are quite often turned into higher pay and more elaborate bureaucracies for employees. A government employee–government industry wage policy is a necessary prelude to massive government investment in industries such as railroads and nuclear electricity generation. Although a generalized wages and incomes policy is not feasible because it cannot be administered, a government employee–government contract wage policy can be effective.

CONCLUSION

The policy failures since the mid-1960s are related to the banality of orthodox economic analysis. In turn, the banality of economic analysis is related to the transformation of Keynes's economics from a serious critique of capitalism to a series of trivial policy manipulations. The essential Keynesian result, that capitalism is flawed mainly because it handles capital poorly, nowhere enlightens current policy actions. Policy and mainstream economic thinking about our economy blithely ignore the need for and the effects of lender-of-last-resort interventions by the Federal Reserve.

Keynes recognized the flaws in capitalism because he, more than his predecessors, contemporaries, and successors, understood the financial and time-related aspects of a capitalism that uses capital. The Big Government socialization of profit maintenance and lender of last resort mix of policies that were legitimized by Keynes's analysis eliminated the possibility of a deep depression. As a result of Big Government, a regime in which free competitive markets are the instrument for constraining inflationary pressures on prices becomes palatable. The Big Government that is needed can (and does) provide floors to the economy that assure minimum levels of living and service to all, thereby making the argument that free markets will lead to a degradation of labor standards irrelevant. Once we recognize and accept the fact that a government that is big enough to constrain fluctuations in aggregate profits is a prerequisite for a successful capitalist economy, the economy can be restructured to remove barriers to competition and to simplify liability structures. Only an economics that is critical of capitalism can be a guide to successful policy for capitalism.

The policy suggestions that have been put forward here are best interpreted as an agenda for discussion rather than a nonnegotiable program. The analysis argues for a system of changes, not for isolated changes. There is no simple answer to the problems of our capitalism; there is no solution that can be transformed into a catchy phrase and carried on banners.

Every gain has a cost. But in an economy that lives in historic time, the gain may precede the cost. Between 1946 and 1966 we, along with other advanced capitalist economies, had the gain of a long period of improvement that left people as a whole substantially better off in 1966 than in 1946. In the years since 1966, the economy has been much more unstable and further gains have been small and insecure. Furthermore, on several occasions a deep depression threatened, which if realized, would have undone much of the good of 1946–66.

What is needed is a restructuring of the economy, reducing the inflationary impetus due to Big Government even as it retains the power of Big Government to prevent deep depressions. Such a restructuring will enjoy only transitory success. After an initial interval, the basic disequilibrating tendencies of capitalist finance will once again push the financial structure to the brink of fragility. When that occurs, a new era of reform will be needed. There is no possibility that we can ever set things right once and for all; instability, put to rest by one set of reforms will, after time, emerge in a new guise.

FINANCING STRUCTURES

HEDGE FINANCING

The cash flow, capital value, and balance-sheet characteristics of a unit that engages in hedge financing will be formalized in this section. In doing this, we define the variables that will also be used to characterize units that use speculative and Ponzi finance, and to examine the impact of financing characteristics upon system behavior.

CCs are the contractural cash payment commitments on debts. The Q_is and σ_{Qi}^2 are the quasi-rents and its variance that businessmen and their bankers expect. For the hedge financing of a position we have that

$$CC_i < \bar{Q}_i - \lambda\sigma_{Qi}^2 \text{ for all } i \tag{1}$$

where λ is sufficiently great so that the subjective probability assigned to $Q_i < CC_i$ is acceptably small.

Equation (1) can be rewritten as

$$CC_i = \tau(\bar{Q}_i - \lambda\sigma_{Qi}^2), \text{ for all } i, \tau < 1. \tag{2}$$

The margin of safety in the cash flows is measured by τ; the smaller τ, the greater the margin of safety.

If the cash-flow commitments and the quasi-rents that capital assets are presumably assured of earning $(\bar{Q}_i - \lambda\sigma_{Qi}^2)$ are capitalized at the same rate, K, then the capitalized value of the cash payment commitments is K(CC) and the capitalized value of the expected quasi-rents is

$$P_{k,i} = K(\bar{Q}_i - \lambda\sigma_{Qi}^2). \tag{3}$$

Inasmuch as $CC_i < (\overline{Q}_i - \lambda\sigma^2_{Qi})$ for all i, then $P_{k,i} > K(CC)$. There is a margin of safety in the market value of assets over the market value of the debts which can be rewritten as

$$P_k = \mu K(CC); \mu > 1. \tag{4}$$

The margin of safety in capital values is measured by μ; the greater μ, the greater the margin of safety.

To a debtor the cash payment commitments on debts are more certain than the cash flows from the capital assets. Furthermore, there is a penalty in not fulfilling debt commitments. The owners of debts also assume there is greater variability in the Q_i than they are willing to tolerate in the cash they receive; this is why they own debts rather than either capital assets or equity. As a result, the capitalization rate by both borrowers and lenders of the borrowers' cash commitments is likely to be greater than the capitalization rate on the cash flows from capital assets. As a result, the need for a margin of safety in the market value of assets over that of liabilities, that is, $\mu > 1$, implies that the $\overline{Q}_i > CC_i$ by some good margin. The expected quasi-rents need exceed the cash-payment commitments due to debts by a significant amount before a margin of safety in capital values exist. Thus, the requirement for a margin of safety in asset values over the value of debts means that the margin of safety in expected cash receipts over contractual payments needs to be large. One way of assuring this is by having a thick equity position.

A hedge-financing unit expects the cash flow from operations to generate sufficient cash to meet payment commitments on account of debts. However, accidents (and recessions) can happen, and the cash flows from operations may fall short of anticipations and of the amount required by commitments on debts. To protect against such possibilities, a unit will own money and marketable financial assets beyond what is needed for transactions. As Keynes noted, it is convenient (as an implicit insurance policy) to hold assets in the form in which debts are denominated. Thus, a balance sheet of a hedge investor will include $\eta K(CC)$ of money or of other liquid assets in addition to the $P_k K$ of capital assets; this money or liquid assets are not needed by the operations of the unit. The balance sheet of a hedge unit can be characterized by

$$P_k K + \eta K(CC) = K(CC) + Eq.; \eta \gtrless 1, \tag{5}$$

where Eq. is the equity and η, which will be called a liquid asset kicker, is the measure of the margin of safety in assets superfluous to operations.

There are three parameters that characterize the financial posture of a unit. These are the cash flow margin, τ; the capital value margin, μ; and the margin provided by the liquid asset kicker, η. For a hedge unit $\tau < 1$, $\mu > 1$, and $0 < \eta \underset{<}{\overset{>}{-}} 1$ for all periods. The smaller τ, the greater μ, and the larger η, the greater the margins of safety for a hedge unit.

Given that the realized quasi-rents, Q_{iR} exceed the payment commitments in each period $Q_{iR} > CC_i$ for all i, a net money flow, $Q_{iR} - CC_i$, will tend to accrue to a hedge-financing unit. Thus, if it wishes, a hedge financing unit can increase its cash holdings relative to payments; in each period operations will tend to increase η. Furthermore, if we assume that the income portion of Q_{iR} exceeds the income portion of CC_i, the equity of the organization will increase in each period; μ will tend to increase. Thus, unless the firm does something to modify its portfolio, $d\eta/dt$, $dEq./dt$, and $d\mu/dt$ will be greater than zero.

A firm can use the increase in equity, as well as the accrual of cash, to finance the acquisition of capital assets. There is an acquisition of capital assets in excess of the increment to equity that will leave the debt-equity ratio unchanged. Successful fulfillment of the expectations of a hedge-financing unit leads to an ability to debt finance capital-asset acquisition without any deterioration in the margins of safety.

It is also worth noting that in a world with equity markets, the book value of the equity shares increases as a hedge unit fulfills expectations. Owners of such shares might well receive income in the form of appreciation of share prices. If the economy operates so that the commitments and expectations involved in hedge financing are satisfied, the additional external financing of operations necessary to keep the debt-equity ratio at its previous level, or even to raise this ratio, should be forthcoming.

SPECULATIVE FINANCE

A unit engages in speculative finance when the cash payment commitment, CC_i, for some periods, typically near term, are greater than the expected $\bar{Q}_i$ for these periods. In particular, a unit speculates when CC_i exceeds an expected $\bar{Q}_i$ because the CC_i includes the repayment of principal. Such repayment of principal on debt in excess of the quasi-rents is usually associated with short-term debt. Thus, a speculative unit can be defined as one for which some near term i, $CC_i > \bar{Q}_i$, is small.

However, as later expected $\overline{Q}_s$ are greater than the payment commitments on currently outstanding debts for those dates, for a speculative unit the capitalized value of the Qs exceeds the capitalized value of the CCs, that is, $P_{ki} > K(CC_i)$. This is so because once the principal on early CCs is paid, no further payment commitments due to these debts enter into the capitalization of CCs. The expected gross earnings of the capital assets after the dates of the speculative debts yield a margin of safety in asset values. The margin of safety in asset values is what induces both the lender and the borrower to engage in speculative finance.

For speculative finance units, the difference between CC_i and $\overline{Q}_i$ for these early periods has to be met by refinancing. Thus, a prerequisite for speculative finance is for a market to exist in which both borrower and lender believe that the firm will readily raise $CC_i - Q_i$, of cash at the required dates. Furthermore, this financing is expected to be available on terms that do not adversely effect the likelihood that other outstanding financial commitments will be fulfilled.

If $CC_i > \overline{Q}_i$ for near term i's and $P_k > K(CC)$ at a ruling set of capitalization rates, then at another set of capitalization rates, associated with higher interest rates, $K(CC) > P_k$. Thus, for an organization engaged in speculative finance, solvency (the excess of P_k over $K(CC)$) depends upon the set of ruling interest rates falling within an appropriate range. The longer-term viability of a unit engaged in speculative finance depends upon the existence of a margin of safety in the value of capital assets over the value of debts. *By its very nature, speculative finance rests upon the presumption that interest rates will not move outside some acceptable range.* Rising interest rates decrease the margin of safety of a speculative firm simply because the expected Qs, which offset the early on cash-flow deficiency, occur later. If interest rates fluctuate widely, technical, and, hopefully, transitory insolvency is likely to occur for organizations that engage in speculative finance.

The need for a unit engaged in speculative finance to regularly raise $CC_i - Q_i$ of cash implies that the success of a speculator depends upon some set of financial markets functioning normally. Whereas a hedge-financing unit is dependent only upon the normal functioning of product and factor markets (or for a financial unit, upon the fulfillment of contracts), a speculative unit is dependent upon the normal functioning of product, factor, and money markets. A speculative financing unit is exposed in ways that a hedge unit is not.

Even though a speculative unit has some near period CCs that exceed the expected Qs, the income portion of the Qs exceeds the income or interest portion of the associated CCs. A speculative finance unit is in a position to decrease its short-term debt if business and financing conditions warrant; that is, it can increase its equity relative to liabilities.

A speculative unit will also carry a liquid-asset kicker $\eta K(CC)$ in order to protect the unit against transitory quasi-rent or money-market difficulties. We can expect η to be greater for a prudent speculative unit than for a hedge unit, if other things are equal.

For a speculative unit the cash flow relations are

$$CC_i > \overline{Q}_i + \lambda\sigma^2_{Qi} \text{ for some } i < t \text{ and}$$

$$CC_i \leq \overline{Q}_i - \lambda\sigma^2_{Qi} \text{ for } i \geq t, \tag{6}$$

so that

$$CC_i = \tau(\overline{Q}_i + \lambda\sigma^2_{Qi}); \tau > 1 \text{ for some } i < t$$

$$= \tau(\overline{Q}_i - \lambda\sigma^2_{Qi})\tau \leq 1 \text{ for } i \geq t. \tag{7}$$

For the near term i's, τ measures the exposure to risk. The greater τ the greater risk exposure.

Note that in computing the cash-flow relations for a speculative unit $\overline{Q}_i + \lambda\sigma^2_{Qi}$ was used to measure the cash receipts from operations for the near-term periods, whereas for a hedge-financing unit and for the later periods we used $\overline{Q}_i - \lambda\sigma^2_{Qi}$. Thus, there is an ambiguous class of units and dates for which $\overline{Q}_i + \lambda\sigma^2_{Qi} \geq CC_i \geq \overline{Q}_i - \lambda\sigma^2_{Qi}$. For these units on these dates payment commitments will or will not be met out of cash flows depending upon the quasi-rents actually earned. Such borderline firms and these dates are best considered to be marginally speculative in character, or as units in transition between being hedge and being speculative.

Both the CC and the Q_R, the realized quasi-rents, can be separated into an income and a principal component. If we think of a quasi-rent earned by a capital asset as if it were the payment on a fully amortized mortgage, then the appropriate capital consumption relation will detail the shifting proportions, over the lifetime of the capital asset, of interest and recapture of investment. For an amortized contract, the payment commitments are separated into interest and principal repayment by the annuity formula. For a capital asset the shifting proportions reflect the capital consumption relations in accounting and tax law conventions. Let us call CC_y and Q_y the income portions of the payment commitments and the quasi-rent. Then for a speculative unit,

$$Q_y > CC_y; \tag{8}$$

the income portion of the cash flows exceeds the interest portion of the debt. If the CC includes the conventional payment of dividends, then the income statement of the organization will show a positive retained earnings; if dividends are not included in CC_y, a policy choice may lead to $CC_y > Q_y$. There are ample examples of management that pay dividends out of cash flow, even if such dividends imply a decrease in the future earning capacity of the organization and increase the speculative nature of the unit's financial posture. At times this type of dividend policy reflects unwarranted optimistic expectations; at other times it reflects an attempt to sustain or increase the market value of equity shares.

With $Q_y > CC_y$, even though $CC > Q_R$ the debt, $K(CC_j)$, $j < t$, entered into to refinance maturing debt, may be smaller than the maturing debt. Thus, for a speculative unit we have that $\frac{dk(CC)}{dt} < 0$ if management so desires; there is some room for debt-financed capital-asset acquisition if the expectations with respect to quasi-rents of speculative-financing units are fulfilled, without any increase in the ratio of debts to equity in the balance sheet.

For a speculative unit the present value of the quasi-rents exceeds the present value of the payment commitments.

$$P_k > K(CC); \; P_k = \mu K(CC), \; \mu > 1. \tag{9}$$

Because this capitalized value includes periods, i small, where $Q_i < CC_i$ and periods, i large, where $Q_i > CC_i$, $\mu > 1$ will be true for some set of discount rates and $\mu < 1$ will be true for others. Given that the i's for which $Q_i > CC_i$ typically come later than the i's for which $Q_i < CC_i$, equal arithmetic increases in both long- and short-term rates will tend to lower the present value of those items for which $Q_i > CC_i$ by a greater ratio than it lowers the present value of near-term returns in which $CC_i > Q_i$. Thus, equation (5) has to be rewritten so that the dependence of the inequality upon r's is recognized. We have

$$P_k > K(CC), \; \hat{r} > \bar{r} \tag{10}$$

where $\bar{r}$ is a combination of long and short rates for which $P_k = K(CC)$. Thus, for speculative finance to be sustained, the existence of an upper limit to interest rates ($\hat{r}$) is necessary. *This has obvious policy implications: the larger the weight of speculative finance, the greater the importance of preventing the emergence of very high interest rates.*

Speculative-financing units and their bankers fully expect cash payments on debts to exceed cash receipts from operations in some periods. We expect that speculative-financing units will keep a cash kicker that is related to the CCs it expects to pay in the near future. The balance sheet will read:

$$P_k + \eta \sum_{i=1}^{n}(CC_i) = K(CC) + Eq., \eta < 1. \qquad (11)$$

Once again we have parameters that measure the cash flow, portfolio, and cash margins. The initial difference between hedge and speculative finance conditions is that near τ's are >1 even though later τ's are <1, a secondary characteristic is in the size composition, and importance of $\eta \Sigma(CC)$. A third difference is that whereas for a hedge unit $P_k > K(CC)$ for all capitalization rates, for a speculative unit there exist some rates for which $K(CC) > P_k$.

PONZI FINANCE

The label *Ponzi finance* is evocative of fraud; the reference is usually to a scheme that fulfills promises of extravagant returns to investors who enter the scheme early by using the principal of funds committed by those who enter the scheme at a later date. However, Ponzi finance, simply defined as the payment of cash to debt holders with funds raised by either additional debt or decreasing cash kickers, is not an unusual event—and it is not necessarily fraudulent. A firm in a highly seasonal industry that pays equal quarterly dividends through the year, even though in some quarters it does not earn enough to meet its dividends, is engaging in an uninteresting type of Ponzi finance. Although such harmless examples exist, an increase in advertent or inadvertent Ponzi finance schemes is a symptom of a thrust toward a fragile financial structure for an economy.

In terms of the symbols we have used, a Ponzi finance unit can be characterized by:

$$CC_i > Q_i + \lambda \sigma_Q^2, \text{ for all i except } i = n (?) \qquad (12)$$

There is a question mark with respect to the i's that the inequality ranges over because in all but the most obviously fraudulent Ponzi schemes there exists some pie in the sky event that leads to $Q_n > CC_n$ by a sufficient margin to offset past $\Sigma CC_i > Q_i$. That is, at some interest rates and if some favorable event occurs, the capital value of a Ponzi financing scheme will be positive. Ponzi schemes are often, but not always, quests for an El Dorado: Micawber's belief that something will turn up might characterize a Ponzi-financing promoter, who, in his own mind, is not committing a fraud.

A difference between a Ponzi and a speculative-finance scheme is in the income versus principal components of CC and Q. For a Ponzi scheme, with y referring to the income component,

$$CC_y > Q_y$$

whereas for a speculative financing setup

$$Q_y \geq CC_y.$$

With speculative finance, net worth and liquidity can increase even as debt is refinanced, whereas for a Ponzi unit net worth and liquidity necessarily decrease.

A further characterization of a Ponzi scheme is the

$$P_k > K(CC_i); \quad (?) \tag{13}$$

the positive net worth is questionable. As time progresses the K(CC) will grow so that initially $P_k > K(CC_i)$ and eventually $K(CC_i) > P_k$. Because Ponzi schemes are so dependent upon the continued sale of debt, Ponzi financing units should carry large cash kickers. The cash kickers will quickly disappear if difficulty in selling liabilities occurs: liquidity can evaporate rapidly whenever continuous short-term financing is needed.

Legitimate Ponzi-type finance occurs when units are engaged in investment programs that are large relative to the scope of their other operations, and when income is not in cash but in the form of accruals. The take-out financing of an investment project as it becomes a capital asset transforms a Ponzi-financing project into a hedge-financing arrangement.

The investment program type of Ponzi finance could be included under the rubric of payouts on the basis of accruals. A REIT that financed construction by taking deeply discounted paper from the builder receives an accounting income, but no cash, as the asset appreciated. Given the dividend-payment requirement upon REITs, a REIT with accrued income has to sell debt or decrease its cash to fulfill its obligation to pay cash dividends.

The line between Ponzi and speculative finance depends upon the income component of the cash flows and whether a positive present value exists. A speculativefinancing unit that needs to turn debt over may be confronted by markedly higher interest rates upon refinancing than anticipated; such interest rate escalations can make $Q_{Ry} < CC_y$ even though Q_{Ry} has not fallen below expectations. Floating interest rates that can increase CC_y on a large outstanding debt can transfer a $CC_y < Q_{Ry}$ into a $CC_y > Q_{Ry}$.

Ponzi finance involves a continuous erosion of equity $\left(\dfrac{dEq}{dt} < 0\right)$. When Ponzi finance reflects the financing of a large-scale investment project, the course of equity over time can be very substantially affected by delays in the construction program. Financing practices that can be interpreted as Ponzi equivalent are most generally engaged in during an investment boom, especially when labor and material shortages raise costs and delay completion. Such delays and cost increases combined with high and rising interest rates can lead to a rapid erosion of equity. Ponzi finance is an element in the financial structure that is most exposed to asset revaluation. The viability of the unit depends upon a big event occurring or favorable take-out financing. Indeed, the emergence of a skeptical attitude toward the big event materializing leads to funds not being available to keep the project afloat. *An increase in the ratio of Ponzi, finance, so that it is no longer a rare event, is an indicator that the fragility of the financial structure is in a danger zone for a debt-deflation.*

CONSUMER PRICES AND
REAL WAGES

The price level of consumption goods for the skeletal specification of the economy is

$$P_C = \frac{W_C}{A_C}\left(1 + \mu\frac{N_I}{N_C}\right) \tag{1}$$

where μ is the ratio of wages in investment goods production to wages in consumption goods production $\frac{W_I}{W_C}$, We therefore have that

$$\frac{W_C}{P_C} = \frac{A_C}{1 + \mu\dfrac{N_I}{N_C}} \tag{2}$$

the purchasing power of the wages depends directly upon the average productivity of labor and inversely upon the ratio of employment in investment-goods production to employment in consumption-goods production. Inasmuch as $A_C = \dfrac{Q_C}{N_C}$, the above reduces to

$$\frac{W_C}{P_C} = \frac{Q_C}{N_C + \mu N_I}; \tag{3}$$

the purchasing power of wages is directly related to the output of consumer goods and indirectly related to employment and the relative wages in investment and consumption goods. Increased employment in investment-goods industries and an increase in relative wages in investment-goods production will lower the purchasing power of wages in consumption-goods industries.

If investment increases the average productivity of workers in consumption goods industries, then Q_c will increase, which tends to raise $\dfrac{W_C}{P_C}$. In a regime with constant money wages, if investment increases productivity in consumer-goods production, prices will tend to fall. The, normal functioning of a technologically progressive economy leads to downward pressure on prices.

The skeletal model also yields that

$$P_C - \frac{W_C N_C}{Q_C} = \frac{W_I N_I}{Q_C}; \qquad (4)$$

the average profit margin in consumer-goods production is the wage bills in investment goods divided by the output of consumer goods. As the output of consumer goods rises, the profit margin per unit of output will tend to decrease even as labor costs per unit of output fall. The price of output, P_C, will tend to fall faster than unit labor costs. If the increase in productivity results from an increase in capital assets, then profit per physical unit of capital assets declines. Either gross profits or the capitalization rates of profits need increase for capital-asset prices not to fall. Gross profits can rise if investment increases, which means that either money wages or employment in the production of investment goods expands.

If there is slack in the economy, investment-goods production can increase. If there is no slack, the nominal value of the capital stock can be maintained by increasing money wages in investment goods or by shifting workers from consumption-goods to investment-goods production. Inflating out downward pressure on prices due to productivity increases by rising wages, so that prices—including the normal profits supply price of investment goods—do not fall, helps sustain the viability of debt financing. The greater the extent of external financing of investment and positions in capital assets, the more important are rising wages that offset the tendency for prices and profit margins to fall due to increased output. As external financing increases when the complexity and expense of capital assets increase, a capitalist economy that uses capital-intensive modes of production and whose authorities are afraid of a deep depression will have an inflationary bias.

An expansion of investment tends to lower the purchasing power of wages in consumption-goods production. If money wages in investment goods rise relative to money wages in consumption goods, then $\dfrac{W_I}{W_I} > \dfrac{P_C}{P_C} > \dfrac{W_C}{W_C}$ may be true; that is, the purchasing power of wages in investment goods increases even as the purchasing power of wages in consumption goods decreases.

If increased labor productivity is not offset by an increase in the production of investment goods or of wages in investment goods output, then profits per unit of output decrease. Gross profit flows may be too small to sustain the market value of the capital stock.

If we examine more complex relations that allow for government, consumption out of profits and savings out of wages, we get*

$$P_C = \frac{W_C}{A_C}\left(1 + \frac{W_I N_I}{W_C N_C} + \frac{Df}{W_C N_C} + \frac{T_\Pi - \Pi_G}{W_C N_C} + \frac{c\overset{*}{\Pi}}{W_C N_C} - \frac{s\overset{*}{W}}{W_C N_C}\right) \quad (5)$$

or

$$\frac{W_C}{P_C} = \frac{A_C}{1 + \dfrac{W_I N_I}{W_C N_C} + \dfrac{Df}{W_C N_C} + \dfrac{T_\Pi - \Pi_G}{W_C N_C} + \dfrac{c\overset{*}{\Pi}}{W_C N_C} - \dfrac{s\overset{*}{W}}{W_C N_C}} \quad (6)$$

The purchasing power of money wages is positively related to the average productivity of labor and inversely related to the size of the demands for consumption goods that are financed by other than the income derived from the production of consumer goods. Inasmuch as $A_C = Q_C N_C$, the equation could be written as

$$\frac{W_C}{P_C} = \frac{Q_C}{N_C\left(1 + \dfrac{W_I N_I}{W_C N_C} + \dfrac{Df}{W_C N_C} + \dfrac{T_\Pi - \Pi_G}{W_C N_C} + \dfrac{c\overset{*}{\Pi}}{W_C N_C} - \dfrac{s\overset{*}{W}}{W_C N_C}\right)} \quad (7)$$

An increase in the output of consumer goods without a proportionate increase in employment in consumer goods production will tend to increase the purchasing power of money wages. Furthermore, if the wage

---

* In these equations, we have Df = the government deficit, T_Π = the taxes on profits, Π_G = profits from producing output for the government, $c\overset{*}{\Pi}$ = consumption out of after-tax profits and $s\overset{*}{W}$ = savings out of after-tax wages. These relations can be further expanded and elaborated.

bill in consumer goods production increases because N_C and Q_C increase in (approximately) the same proportion, then the price-deflated wage will tend to increase. Symmetrically, if any of the numerators of these ratio (except $s\overset{*}{W}$) falls, the price-deflated wage will rise. Note that a rise in the deficit lowers and a decline raises the price deflated wages of consumer goods workers.

INDEX